THE GREAT BOOK OF
WASHINGTON D.C. SPORTS LISTS

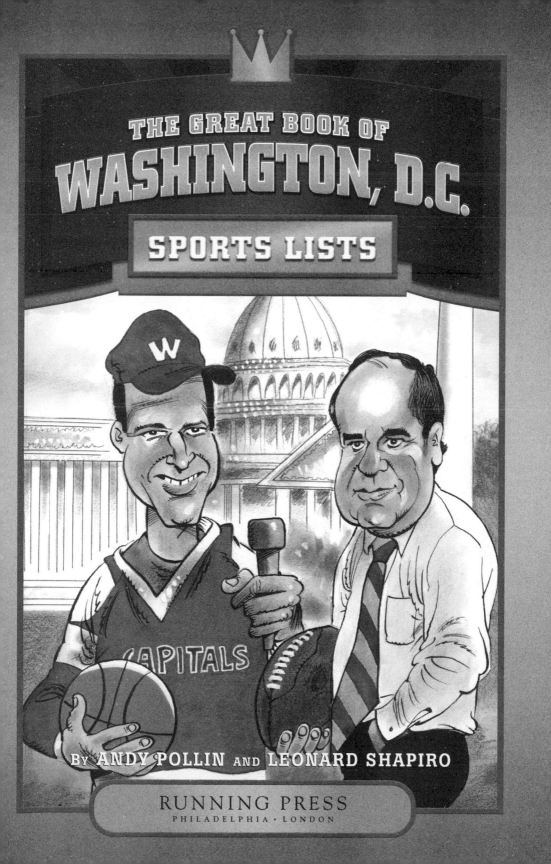

THE GREAT BOOK OF WASHINGTON, D.C.

SPORTS LISTS

By ANDY POLLIN and LEONARD SHAPIRO

RUNNING PRESS
PHILADELPHIA · LONDON

© 2008 by Leonard Shapiro and Andy Pollin

All rights reserved under the Pan-American
and International Copyright Conventions

Printed in the United States

*This book may not be reproduced in whole or in part, in any form or by any
means, electronic or mechanical, including photocopying, recording, or by
any information storage and retrieval system now known or hereafter
invented, without written permission from the publisher.*

9 8 7 6 5 4 3 2 1

Digit on the right indicates the number of this printing

Library of Congress Control Number: 2008926942

ISBN 978-0-7624-3356-8

Cover and Interior Designed by Matthew Goodman
Edited by Greg Jones

Running Press Book Publishers
2300 Chestnut Street
Philadelphia, PA 19103-4371

Visit us on the web!
www.runningpress.com

CONTENTS

Dedication

To Joseph and Julia Shapiro, mom and dad, forever No. 1 in my heart and mind, for everything.

—Leonard Shapiro

Dedicated to my mother who shared the same first name as legendary columnist Shirley Povich, although she was never listed in "Who's Who Among American Women" as he was. Shirley Pollin preferred a night at the opera over a day at the game, but always encouraged my love of sports and the endless discussion of it. If every friend she left behind buys this book, it's bound to be a bestseller.

—Andy Pollin

Acknowledgments

So many lists, so many people to say heartfelt thanks for your help, your advice, your creativity and even your criticism.

Many of our pals in the media get a co-byline and our deepest gratitude: (in no particular order) Andy Beyer, Charles Brotman, Tom Boswell, Liz Clarke, Ken Denlinger, John Feinstein, Bill Gildea, Steve Goff, Jim Hage, Frank Herzog, Johnny Holliday, Chris Knocke, Tony Kornheiser, Jimmy Roberts, Angus Phillips, George Solomon, Dan Steinberg, Scott Van Pelt, Ed Werder, Tony Perkins, Kevin Blackistone, Dave Feldman, Phil Hochberg, Al Koken, Mike Kelly, Christine Brennan, Scott Linn, Carol Maloney, Chuck Sapienza, Steve Buckhantz, Tim Kurkjian, Erik Rydholm, Matt Kelliher, Bonnie Berko, Al Galdi, Thom Loverro, and Ernie Baur.

We also called on many athletes, coaches and sports administrators who generously took the time to offer advice, or make their own lists: Herman Boone, Matt Day, Vaughn Gatling, Darrell Green, Lenny Hale, Calvin Hill, Sam Huff, Tom McMillen, Brian Mitchell, John Thompson, Ryan Kuehl, and Doc Walker. Not to mention politicos Bob Ehrlich and Lee Cowen.

We also owe a tribute to the sources we used for inspiration and fact-checking, including *The Redskins Encyclopedia* by Michael Richman, *Washington's Expansion Senators* by James R. Hartley, and *The Redskins A to Z* by Rich Tandler.

Many thanks to Greg Jones of Running Press Book Publishers, who approved the project, then edited the book with great care, even as he recovered from a Joe Theismann-like and very painful broken leg suffered in a men's league ice hockey game, with Lawrence Taylor nowhere to be seen.

Introduction

Washington—first in war, first in peace and last in the Capital Division.

If you're old enough to remember the Capital Division, you know just how old and corny that joke is. That was the late 1960s when the Redskins were terrible, the Senators were looking for a way out of town, and the NBA and NHL were years away from putting teams in D.C. This is not your father's sports town any more.

The Great Book of Washington D.C. Sports Lists compiles the great and not-so-great moments and events that have turned Washington in to a fully loaded sports city with beautiful new places for the teams to play (FedEx Field definitely not included). You'll learn things like how a local college basketball coach kept his job after a 1-27 season while a Redskin coach was fired halfway through his first season with a 3-3-1 record. You'll read about triumphs in Super Bowls, NBA Finals and NCAA championship games, and tragedies like the deaths of Len Bias, Glenn Brenner and Sean Taylor.

As you peruse these lists, we hope you'll nod your head more often than you shake it from side to side. But in a town where Democrats face off against Republicans on a daily basis, you have to expect disagreement. If you can't remember Sonny versus Billy, ask your Dad. Better yet, read about it here. And if you think we omitted anything on these lists, or you don't like the order of some items, feel free to fix them. Hey, it's a paperback. Write in your own corrections, and maybe we'll just do it again.

Many of the lists come from our heads (with some cross-checking on Google, media guides and a few books), but we've also relied on some experts. Who better to rank Brian Mitchell's kick returns for touchdowns than B-Mitch himself? You think there's someone better than former Maryland basketball All-American and U.S. Congressman Tom McMillen to judge the best basketball players in Congress? How about Hall of Fame Redskins linebacker Sam Huff's choices for top Redskins linebackers? And the favorite "Mister Tony" moments from "Mister Tony" himself, Tony Kornheiser—and many, many more.

Man can't live on sports lists alone, so we've thrown in a few about movies, TV and, of course, food. You've probably engaged in some of your best sports debates with the juice of charred meat dripping down your chin, so we'll also tell you where you can get the best burger in D.C.

So learn, agree, disagree and keep this book handy the next time somebody says, "Oh yeah? Name them." We've even got John Feinstein. His sports books are always fixtures on the bestseller list, clearly not the only reason we asked him to contribute a list, but his presence in these pages sure can't hurt.

—Andy Pollin and Len Shapiro

In nearly 40 years of writing about sports for *The Washington Post*, I've seen more than my fair share of Super Bowls, Olympics, and Final Fours. But one of the great joys of the job has always involved going to far less glamorous venues—a high school gym, an inner-city football field—to witness the start of something big, getting one of the first looks at a promising young athlete, a budding broadcaster, or a rookie taking the initial baby steps down the road to far greater glory. I've had the privilege of seeing several of those memorable journeys, some of them beginning right here in the Nation's Capital. My all-time favorite was particularly up close, and very personal.

10. Cornelius Green. As the *Post's* high school football writer in the early 1970s, I was assigned to cover a game at Dunbar High School in the District, where a flashy young quarterback was starting to make a name for himself. When I first saw Cornelius Green play as a junior, he was all over the rocky, dusty, mostly dirt Dunbar field, running, throwing, returning, and playing defense. In my story the next day, I called Green the "flamboyant Flim-Flam man." He must have liked it. The following week, he wrote the word "Flamboyant" with black Magic Marker on a piece of tape and stuck it on the front of his helmet, just above his eyes. Flamboyant eventually was shortened to "Flam," a nickname he carried all the way to Ohio State, where he became the school's first black starting quarterback and MVP of the 1974 Rose Bowl.

9. Bernard and Albert King. Researching a book on college basketball recruiting in 1973, I tagged along for a week on a recruiting trip with then LSU basketball coach Dale Brown. One day, we went to a public housing project in a tough section of Brooklyn, NY, to visit a promising young prospect named Bernard King. There wasn't much furniture in the apartment, but the living room was cluttered with countless trophies and plaques of all sizes. Bernard listened to Brown's recruiting pitch with some interest, and before we left, he told the coach about another promising player in the family. "If you think I'm good, you ought to see my 14-year-old brother play," Bernard said that day. He was talking about Albert King, already a playground legend himself. Bernard wound up at Tennessee, and then went on to a distinguished NBA career, including a league scoring title and a stop in Washington. Albert was one of Lefty Driesell's prize recruits at Maryland, considered the best high school player in the country the same year Magic Johnson came out. He played nine years for four NBA teams and also ended his pro career in Washington.

8. Ken Beatrice. In 1977, WMAL Radio invited a number of local sports celebrities and members of the media to a reception at the old Duke Zeibert's Restaurant on L Street, Northwest. They were launching a show that night, several hours of a relatively new format called "sports talk." The host was Boston native Ken Beatrice, and he quickly became a Washington institution, a man equally adept at describing the attributes of an obscure college linebacker as he was in pushing the curly fries at Arby's, one of his longtime sponsors, even if he admitted he was not allowed to eat them, or even sip the Jamoca shakes. His catch phrase to fans holding on the line to speak with him on the air was "Yaw Next," and he always reminded listeners, "I have neither the sauces or the resauces" to scout high school athletes. He had enough sources and resources (real or imagined, as some suspected) to last on the air for 23 years before retiring in 2000.

7. John Ed Bradley. I was working as an assignment editor when *Post* sports editor George Solomon came by my desk one day in 1982 and asked me to read an unsolicited manuscript he'd just received in the mail from a young writer living in Opalousis, Louisiana. It was a first-person account about what it was like to go back home to the real world after playing big-time college football at the state university for four years. John Ed had been a starting center for the LSU Tigers, a hometown high school and college hero who had his picture posted in the Opalousis barber shop. An injury prevented him from playing pro ball, so the son of a football coach and a high school English teacher decided he wanted to pursue writing as a career. Good choice. That first piece blew me away, and soon we had him writing other stories. He eventually joined the staff and stayed for four memorable years before moving on to New York to work at *Sports Illustrated* and produce some fabulous fiction. The man could write, and right from the start.

6. John Thompson. The first time I met Big John was in a dingy little gym at the now defunct St. Anthony's High School in Northeast Washington. His office was the size of a broom closet, but his ambition to succeed as a basketball coach knew no bounds. He had already started to assemble one of the strongest teams in the city, and he told me that day over the course of a rambling two-hour interview about how he had discovered his star player, a 6-foot-8 center named Donald Washington. A few years earlier, Thompson had been driving around the city, stopping at playgrounds where he knew some of his players would be running in pick-up games. At one court, he noticed a tall kid playing in a pair of dungaree overalls. Thompson got out of the car, introduced himself to the 6-4 eighth grader and gave him a few pointers. Eventually, Washington took the entrance exam at St. Anthony's and passed. By his senior year, when he actually lived in the Thompsons' home, he had become one of the most highly recruited players in the country, eventually signing to play at North Carolina.

5. Patrick Ewing. On October 15, 1981, I got a call from Thompson, asking if I wouldn't mind giving his new prize recruit, Patrick Ewing, a tour of *The Washington Post*. He wanted Ewing to see the inside of a newspaper and talk to a reporter about what he might expect from the media trying to cover him over the next four years at Georgetown. We met across the street from the newspaper office at the Madison Hotel, where Ewing devoured several cheeseburgers and drank a gallon of orange juice (I kept track, because I insisted on paying) before we took the tour of the newsroom and composing room. Young Patrick was pleasant enough, but didn't say much over the next two hours. His coach did most of the talking, which was pretty much the same pattern over Ewing's four stunning seasons at Georgetown. He led the Hoyas to two Final Fours and a National Title, but hardly ever said much to the media on the rare occasions he was made available.

4. Mark Murphy. When he showed up in Carlisle, PA, in 1977 for his first training camp with the Washington Redskins, undrafted free agent Mark Murphy blended right in with a typically thin rookie crop, save for one feature—his huge feet. A 6-foot-4 safety from Colgate, Murphy wore size-15 limousines for those puppies, though it hardly slowed him down on the practice field. Knowing he had gone to Colgate, I wondered one day if he'd ever run in to my younger brother David, who graduated in the same Colgate class and played varsity soccer himself. Yes, Murphy said, he knew of him. Over the next few weeks, I began to pay more attention to Murphy, who clearly was making an impression on the coaching staff with his willingness to make big hits and his long, rangy stride that put him in the right place at the right time far more often than most rookies in camp. I wrote about him a few times, once right before the final cut, which he eventually survived to make the team. He backed up veteran Jake Scott that year and mostly played special teams, but Murphy eventually earned a starting job, played in a couple of Pro Bowls, and also went back to school earning an MBA and a law degree while still an active player. He eventually worked for the NFL player's union, became athletic director at Colgate and Northwestern, and now can truly big-foot it as the team president of the Green Bay Packers.

3. Tiger Woods. Now that Tiger has become a semi-native son, what with his own signature golf tournament played every year at Congressional in the Washington suburbs, we'll include him on this list. I first saw him play in the 1995 Masters, where he made the cut and finished 41st as low amateur in the field at age 19. But I also was there the day he won his first event on the PGA Tour two years later. He was only 21, but hit some stunning shots down the stretch to win the old Las Vegas Invitational at the end of the 1996 season, prevailing in a playoff against Davis Love III. My most indelible memory that afternoon came from the victory ceremony, where a kid who had just finished his sophomore year of college posed for pictures holding his winner's check surrounded by several rather scantily clad showgirls imported from the Vegas strip. Young Tiger seemed far more interested in the cleavage all around him than he was with the trophy, and quite frankly, he was not alone.

2. Adrian Dantley. It was the O'Connell Christmas Tournament in December, 1970, an annual event for another powerful DeMatha basketball team. The Stags became even more powerful the night I happened to show up to cover one of the opening tournament games. That evening, a somewhat pudgy freshman came off the bench in the second quarter, and by the end of the game, a kid his classmates called "Baby Fats" had double digit points and rebounds and head coach Morgan Wootten had himself a budding superstar. Young Adrian commuted to the Hyattsville school from Southwest Washington, where he lived with his single mother and his aunt. By the time Dantley was a senior, he had shattered all the school records and was named a first-team high-school All-American. His senior year at DeMatha, he also allowed myself and fellow *Post* writer Ken Denlinger to chronicle his season for a series on college recruiting that appeared in the paper, and later was expanded into a book, *Athletes for Sale*. Dantley had a brilliant career at Notre Dame, where he was named national player of the year in 1976, and spent 15 years in the NBA, where he won two scoring titles and averaged 24 points a game. He'd come a long way from O'Connell High.

1. Taylor Shapiro. My son became a household name mostly in his own household when he gave up a promising high school soccer career to become a trusty placekicker at the Woodberry Forrest School in Orange, VA. It began when Taylor noticed that far more people were watching the Woodberry varsity than attended his freshman soccer games. That spring, he said he wanted to see if his strong right leg might also translate into kicking a football. I went to the Modell's sporting goods store in Manassas and bought a Jan Stenerud signature ball, complete with tee and kicking instructions. Over his spring break, we went over to a local junior high to give it a try. Taylor's first few kicks were low bouncers or ugly line drives, until he went back to Stenerud's instructions after about ten misses. Pardon the expression, but something clearly had kicked in, because suddenly the ball began to rise end over end and actually go through the uprights at least half the time, with several more close misses. That summer before his sophomore year, I shagged and he kicked, gaining enough confidence to try out for football. He made the varsity that year, kicked field goals, extra points, and kickoffs for three straight years, and made Saturdays in the fall the most pure joy I've ever experienced at any athletic event I've ever attended, bar none. What a kick, Taylor, and many thanks for so many special memories.

Why We Loved RFK Stadium

A state-of-the-art, multi-purpose venue that held 55,000 fans for football, RFK opened as D.C. Stadium in 1961. Eight years later, it was renamed for Robert F. Kennedy, the former attorney general in his brother John F. Kennedy's cabinet and a senator in New York who was assassinated in Los Angeles during his own campaign for the presidency in 1968. The building was home to the Redskins, old Washington Senators, new Washington Nationals, four different soccer franchises and the Washington Federals of the U.S. Football League, as well as the site for concerts, religious revivals and tractor pulls.

10. The soccer crowds were always spectacular, a fabulous ethnic mix from a wide variety of countries, most of them from Central or South America.

9. The press box was open—no windows—mostly because Shirley Povich, the late, great and widely respected *Washington Post* columnist, insisted on being able to hear the football crowd, even on the coldest days of the fall and early winter.

8. In the final years of the Washington Senators, team owner Robert Short actually brought in an omelet man for the pre-game Sunday brunch before ball games.

7. The public address announcer for many years was Phil Hochberg, a longtime Washington communications attorney. He handled those chores for the Redskins and the old Senators with a basic nuts-and-bolts, information-only approach.

6. Bobby Mitchell finally integrated the RFK end zone in 1963, and became the first African-American player in team history, one of the all-time most popular Washington Redskins.

5. The intimacy of the venue was never duplicated at FedEx Field. With only 55,000 seats for football, fans were right on top of the action, even in the upper deck, and because only 14,000 season-ticket holders controlled those seats, everyone seemed to know the people in the next seats, the rows in front and behind, and a family atmosphere pervaded the venue.

4. Seats in the upper decks of the outfield were painted to show where Washington Senators slugger Frank Howard's towering, tape-measure home runs landed.

3. The decibel level, particularly for Dallas Cowboys games, was ear-shattering, and the stadium literally shook after a big play, never more so than when Redskins safety Ken Houston tackled Cowboy running back Walt Garrison at the goal line to save a key victory in 1973.

2. When Jack Kent Cooke owned the Redskins, the owner's box was a Who's Who of Washington's power elite, including presidents, members of Congress, media pundits, big-time athletes and sparkly Hollywood types.

1. The whole package provided the greatest home-field advantage for any team in the NFL, at least according to virtually any opposing coach or player who ever had to compete there.

10. The hard wooden seats were designed for skinny people, and leg room was adequate only for children under 10 and circus midgets.

9. It's the infamous venue where Redskins quarterback Joe Theismann suffered one of the ugliest injuries in the history of professional football when a Lawrence Taylor tackle broke his leg in two in 1985.

8. The very same open press box Shirley Povich adored was hated by most visiting scribes used to writing in air conditioned comfort in the heat of summer baseball or composing their stories while toasty and warm behind glass windows on frosty fall football days and nights.

7. Nothing worse than getting a couple of freebie tickets from a so-called friend, only to find yourself sitting behind a pillar with an obstructed view of the field.

6. There were lines at the ticket windows manned by some of the slowest and rudest clerks in all of sports. There were lines at the concession stands that took two or three innings or half a football quarter just to get a warm beer or a soggy pretzel. There were lines in the stinky bathrooms that forced you to miss even more action, holding your nose all the way.

5. Metro hardly ever got it right. There were never enough trains coming or going, especially after night games, leading to massive crushes on the escalators, on platforms and in train cars. And heaven help you if you didn't have the exact change for a fare card to get through the turnstiles.

4. Many players quickly discovered escape routes from the home team locker rooms, meaning that they could shower, dress and slip out a side door and never have to be interviewed by the media throng after a game. Several reporters eventually discovered Sonny Jurgensen's path to freedom and simply met him at his car parked underneath the stands.

3. The concession stands served by far the worst hot dog in press room history— boiled little hunks of greenish mystery meat that not even a generous supply of mustard could help make go down without gagging

2. The visiting locker room was about the size of Jack Kent Cooke's master bedroom closet at his Middleburg estate, making it virtually impossible for opposing players to shower or dress in any comfort, especially when the media horde descended en masse into a room that quickly became a sweltering post-shower sauna.

1. The elevators from the press and owner's boxes also were under-sized, and frequently became stuck between levels, not a pretty picture when assistant coaches were trying to get down to the locker room at halftime and after the final gun. The auxiliary press box also was at the very top of the stadium, a climb up steep steps to Mount Everest for the worst view in the building, and an equally offensive halftime hot dog.

Washington has been a Redskins kind of town since the team moved here from Boston in the 1930s, and over the years they've provided countless memorable games. Then again, so have many other Washington teams, college and pro, so we'll offer our own list of the very best of the best, and the downer of all downers when the Washington Senators left town in 1971.

10. Capitals and the Cup. On June 4, 1998, Joe Juneau's overtime goal earned the Washington Capitals a 3-2 victory in Game Six of their Stanley Cup semifinal series against the Buffalo Sabres. The win clinched the franchise's first and only appearance in the Finals. Their joy was short-lived; Detroit dominated the Finals and won the Cup with a four-game sweep.

9. Patriot Days. George Mason became the first 11th seed in 20 years to advance to the NCAA Final Four with a stunning 86-84 upset victory over No. 1 seed Connecticut on March 26, 2006. It was the Patriots' first appearance in the Final Four and came on a night when they rallied from an early 12-point deficit to prevail in overtime in the greatest victory in school history.

8. Happy New Year. On December 31, 1972, the Redskins overwhelmed the Dallas Cowboys, 26-3, in the NFC Championship game at RFK Stadium to advance to the first Super Bowl in franchise history. Fans rushed the field, and George Allen was carried off on the shoulders of his players. The sell-out crowd floated home that night, but two weeks later reality, in the form of the undefeated Miami Dolphins, set in: Miami 14, Washington 7 in Super Bowl VII.

7. Nats No More. On September 30, 1971, the Washington Senators played their final game before the franchise was moved to Arlington, Texas. The Nats were leading the N.Y. Yankees in the bottom of the ninth, but fans angered by the impending move stormed the field and order could not be restored. The Yankees were awarded a 9-0 victory on a forfeit.

6. Greatest Game. The fourth-ranked Maryland basketball team lost in overtime to David Thompson's North Carolina State team, 103-100, in the championship game of the ACC Tournament in Greensboro, N.C. The March 1974 contest is considered one of the greatest games in college basketball history and also kept the Terps from going to the NCAA Tournament, which only included conference champions that season. Because of that game—and the injustice of the great Maryland team missing the dance—the next year the tournament was expanded from 25 teams to 32.

5. Upset Special. On April 1, 1985, Villanova posted one of the most stunning upsets in college basketball history, beating a heavily favored Georgetown team led by center Patrick Ewing, 66-64, in the championship game of the NCAA Tournament at Rupp Arena in Lexington, KY. Villanova, an eighth seed, remains the lowest seeded team ever to win the title. Some people in the area still don't believe it happened.

4. The Hug. The nation's two most celebrated centers—Georgetown's Patrick Ewing and Houston's Hakeem Olajuwon—faced off in the NCAA championship game in 1984, and the Hoyas prevailed, 84-75, for the only National Title in John Thompson's storied 27-year tenure. In the final seconds, Thompson enveloped guard Fred Brown in a lingering bear hug. Brown had thrown the errant pass in the final seconds that led to the Hoyas' loss to North Carolina in the title game two years earlier. The hug was both a celebration and an act of atonement.

3. Turtle Power. Maryland's basketball team, led by guards Juan Dixon and Steve Blake, wooshed through the 2002 NCAA basketball tournament and posted a 64-52 victory over Indiana to win its first national championship. Head coach Gary Williams, who had played point guard for the Terrapins in the 1960s, became the first coach to lead his alma mater to the title since Norm Sloan's N.C. State team won in 1974.

2. The Fat Lady Sings. On June 7, 1978, the Washington Bullets won the only NBA title in franchise history, beating the Seattle SuperSonics on the road, 105-99, in the seventh game of the championship series on a team led by Hall of Famers Wes Unseld and Elvin Hayes. Ironically, the two men despised each other off the court, but put their differences aside to help secure the title. First-year head coach Dick Motta had said earlier in the playoffs that "The opera ain't over 'til the fat lady sings," and it became the team's mantra until the title was secured.

1. Super Bowl Skins. How do you pick the best of the Redskins three Super Bowl triumphs? Well, let's just lump them all together instead, starting with the first on January 30, 1983 and the 27-17 victory over the Miami Dolphins in SB XVII, secured by John Riggins' late touchdown run. "Ron (Reagan) may be president," Riggins said afterward, "but for tonight, I'm the king." On January 31, 1988, the Redskins broke twenty Super Bowl records with a 42-10 triumph over the Denver Broncos as Doug Williams threw for 380 yards and four touchdowns and was named MVP of SB XXII as the first black quarterback to win a Super Bowl. On January 26, 1992, the Redskins stuffed the Buffalo Bills, 37-24, and quarterback Mark Rypien was named the game MVP in SB XXVI as Joe Gibbs became the first head coach to win three Super Bowls with three different quarterbacks. Hail to the Redskins!—times three.

Obviously losing a playoff game or the Super Bowl provides the biggest long-term hurt, but in the moment here's 10 times we've keeled over in pain since the AFL-NFL merger in 1970.

10. December 15, 1996, Cardinals 27 – Redskins 26. With a chance to go 9-6, set up what would be a playoff-clinching win over Dallas in the final game at RFK Stadium the following week, and avenge a gut-puncher from Arizona a month earlier, the Skins blew it. Up 26-24, they allowed Kent Graham to go four-for-six on a drive that ate up the last seven minutes of the game. The drive was kept alive at one point by a Romeo Bandison facemask penalty on a fourth down pass that fell incomplete. Kevin Butler kicked a 28-yard field goal for the game winner as the final gun sounded on the game and the Redskins' playoff hopes.

9. November 10, 1996, Cardinals 37 – Redskins 34 OT. Up 27-13 in the third quarter, the Redskins seemed on their way to a 7-2 record, a more than comfortable cushion to start the second half of the season. But nooooooo! Boomer Esiason, on his way to a 531 yard passing day, rallied the Cards for a pair of scores to send the game to overtime. Still the Redskins appeared to have it won when Scott Blanton kicked a 38-yard field goal in overtime. But a holding penalty on Scott Galbraith pushed Blanton five yards back and he missed the retry. A short time later, Kevin Butler blew a 37-yard attempt, but the Skins were called for offsides. With only 33 seconds left in overtime, Butler kicked the game winner and the Redskins kicked themselves.

8. November 13, 2005, Buccaneers 36 – Redskins 35. With a big day from Clinton Portis—144 yards and a touchdown to put the Redskins up 35-28 with just over six minutes left—this had the look of a win and a 6-3 record. But Chris Simms threw a 30-yard touchdown pass to Edell Shepherd with less than a minute left. Still, even with the extra point, the game appeared headed to overtime. But the Skins were called offsides trying to block the kick, and Bucs coach John Gruden used the shorter distance to the end zone to trot out Mike Alstott for a two-point try. The referee said he got in, coach Joe Gibbs insisted he didn't, but inside of two minutes he couldn't challenge.

7. December 2, 2007, Bills 17 – Redskins 16. In what would turn out to be the last regular-season loss of Joe Gibbs's coaching career, he pulled what may have been his biggest blunder. In the final seconds of the game, he used not one, but two timeouts to try to ice Bills' kicker Ryan Lindell on a 51-yard field goal attempt. Back-to-back timeouts are a rules violation and it cost the Redskins 15 yards for unsportsmanlike conduct. Lindell's kick was good from 36 yards for the win. A day later the team flew to Miami for the funeral of teammate Sean Taylor.

6. January 15, 1999, Buccaneers 14 – Redskins 13. After Brian Mitchell returned the second-half kickoff 100 yards for a touchdown and Brett Conway kicked a 48-yard field goal, the Skins led 13-0 late in the third quarter and appeared headed to the NFC Championship game in St. Louis. But driving to try to go up 20-0, Brad Johnson was picked off by John Lynch at the 27. The Bucs then drove 73 yards in six plays to cut it to 13-7 and went ahead on a one yard touchdown pass from Shaun King to John Davis. Still there was one last chance to win with just over a minute left on a 52-yard attempt from Conway, but the snap from Dan Turk rolled along the ground and the kick was never attempted. Turk spent the night walking through Tampa and never got on the team plane home. He died of cancer a short time later.

5. November 16, 1975, Cardinals 20 – Redskins 17 OT. In the last 30 seconds of regulation, the Skins appeared to have held on for a narrow win at Busch Stadium in St. Louis. Jim Hart's fourth-down end-zone pass to Mel Gray was knocked away by Pat Fischer. But the referees huddled for three minutes and somehow managed to come up with the conclusion that Gray had both feet down with possession of the ball. Jim Bakken's extra point tied it at 17. After the Cards won the overtime toss, Bakken kicked the game winner from 37 yards out.

4. January 14, 1973, Dolphins 14 – Redskins 7. With just over two minutes left in Super Bowl VII, Miami was about to put the perfect 14-0 ending on a perfect 17-0 season. But Bill Brundige blocked Garo Yepremian's 42-yard field goal attempt, Yepremian attempted to throw the blocked kick, and Mike Bass scooped it up and returned it for a touchdown. That and a defensive stand that gave the Redskins the ball back with 1:14 left had you believing they would pull out a miracle. Not quite. Billy Kilmer was swallowed up by Miami's "No Name" defense and the perfect season was clinched. Still you were left with the feeling that a healthy Sonny Jurgensen (out with a torn Achilles, he was banished to the press box by George Allen) the Redskins might have scored more than 14 and won.

3. January 22, 1984, Raiders 38 – Redskins 9. After a record-setting season of 561 points and an incredible plus-43 turnover ratio, a win in Super Bowl XVIII would have made it two straight championships and a place among the greatest teams of all time. It wasn't to be. Down 14-3 with the ball at their own 12 with just 12 seconds left in the first half, it looked like a good time for Joe Theismann to take a knee and regroup at halftime. Joe Gibbs decided to gamble. He lost. Theismann's "Rocket Screen" was picked off by Jack Squirek and returned for a 21-3 lead. The Skins never recovered.

2. November 28, 1974, Cowboys 24 – Redskins 23. On this famed Thanksgiving Day, it appeared to be time to carve the turkey with the Skins up 16-3 in the third quarter and Roger Staubach out of the game with a concussion. Not so fast. In to spend his 15 minutes of fame came the rookie from Abilene Christian, Clint Longley. The "Mad Bomber" reared back and fired two touchdown bombs, including a 50-yarder to Drew Pearson with 28 seconds left for an appetite-killing Cowboy victory.

1. December 16, 1979, Cowboys 35 – Redskins 34. A day that started with the Redskins in a three-way tie for the NFC East lead with Dallas and Philadelphia, and which included a 13-point lead in the fourth quarter, ended with the Skins out of the playoffs. A 66-yard touchdown run by John Riggins put the Redskins up 34-21 with 6:34 to play. Cue the comeback kid. In his last career regular-season game, Roger Staubach had one more drop of magic left. He threw a 26-yard scoring pass to Ron Springs to cut it to six with 2:20 left, and drove the dagger into the Skins' hearts with a seven-yard scoring pass to Tony Hill with less than a minute left. One final indignity: after getting the ball to the Dallas 42, Joe Theismann couldn't get the officials' attention to call time-out, and the clock ran out. To this day, Mark Moseley claims he would have made the 59-yarder.

When you've been around for 75 years, you're bound to have a few of these. We found more than enough of them to come up with a top 10 list, but here's the best of the worst.

10. October 30, 2005, Giants 36 – Redskins 0. A classic let-down effort. A week before, the Redskins had rolled over San Francisco 52-17. This time it was the Skins' turn to get rolled. The Giants out-rushed the Redskins 262-38, and it actually seemed worse than that. Tiki Barber ran for 206 yards on only 24 carries. It was the only time that Joe Gibbs was ever shut out in a regular-season game.

9. October 14, 1951, Browns 45 – Redskins 0. The Skins served this one up on a silver platter with three interceptions and three fumbles. But what makes this one significant is, even though the season was only three games old, owner George Preston Marshall fired coach Herman Ball after the game. Dick Todd took over and won five of the last nine games, earning the Skins…nothing.

8. October 28, 2007, Patriots 52 – Redskins 7. Yes it was against the best offensive team of all time, but this was a game that had columnists urging Hall of Fame coach Joe Gibbs to get out. The Pats did punt twice, but were pretty much unstoppable every other time they got their mitts on the ball. Tom Brady threw for 306 yards and three touchdowns playing just over three quarters. The Redskins did avoid a shutout, but it was in garbage time against New England backups.

7. October 10, 1993, Giants 41 – Redskins 7. This was the Redskins worst home loss in 45 years and an early indication that coach Richie Petitbon was going to be one-and-done as a head coach. The Giants ran for 199 yards and made it a laugher by halftime when running back Dave Meggett threw a 42-yard option pass to Mike Sherrard for a touchdown. Darrell Green, then in his 11th year, said, "It was the most disappointing and embarrassing game I can remember since I've been a Redskin."

6. October 18, 1998, Vikings 41 – Redskins 7. Green, at this point in his 16th year, found a game that ranked as a new low. He called this one "rock bottom," and was even seen crying on the bench. Even coach Norv Turner called the offense "totally inept." Vikings rookie sensation Randy Moss failed to get in the end zone, but it seemed that just about everybody else wearing purple did.

5. November 5, 1961, Giants 53 – Redskins 0. This was the last season owner George Preston Marshall had his all-white roster, which he maintained in order to keep television ratings up in southern states. You reap what you sow, and the all-white Skins were whitewashed at Yankee Stadium. Y.A. Tittle threw three touchdown passes, while Norm Snead was sacked twice in the end zone as the Giants built a 25-0 halftime lead. For the game, the Redskins managed only 82 yards of total offense. It was, in no uncertain terms, a whitewashing.

4. September 24, 2001, Packers 37 – Redskins 0. This turned out to be Jeff George's last stand. After being yanked in the 30-3 season-opening loss at San Diego for not following the playbook, George was told by Marty Schottenheimer to do it by the book. The Skins held the ball for less than 23 minutes, George threw for only 102 yards and two days later was shown the door. The Redskins managed only eight first downs for the game.

3. December 14, 2003, Cowboys 27 – Redskins 0. The final score doesn't do justice to what a butt-kicking this was. Tim Hasselbeck managed a Blutarski-like quarterback rating of 0.0. He completed only six passes for 56 yards and was intercepted four times. It was a rainy, cold day which no doubt had coach Steve Spurrier dreaming of getting back on the golf course in Florida. Two weeks later that's where he was when he phoned in his resignation.

2. November 7, 1954, Browns 62 – Redskins 3. The Browns under Paul Brown were the class of the league in those days with quarterback Otto Graham. Incredibly this rout was accomplished with Graham sitting out part of this one with an arm injury. George Hatterman (George Hatterman!) threw three touchdown passes. The Browns rolled up more than 500 yards of offense and held the Redskins under 100.

1. December 8, 1940, Bears 73 – Redskins 0. Number-one all-time ass-whooping for any NFL game. And this one happened to be for the championship. It got so out of hand that the referees asked the Bears to stop kicking extra points in the fourth quarter, but not to have mercy on the hapless Skins. In those days, there was no net raised behind the goal posts, and fans who caught kicks were allowed to keep them. They were running out of footballs! Nobody could see this coming. Three weeks earlier, the Redskins had beaten the Bears, 7-3.

The best sports nicknames come from fans, teammates, and the media, and here we offer a cornucopia of some of our all-time favorites.

Redskins

The Red Roach—Sonny Jurgensen

No. 9—Sonny Jurgensen

Riggo—John Riggins

The Diesel—John Riggins

Whiskey—Billy Kilmer

Furnace Face—Billy Kilmer

Slingin' Sammy—Sammy Baugh

The Squire—Jack Kent Cooke

Bullet Bill—Bill Dudley

The Dancing Bear—Ron McDole

The Peach from Long Beach—Jerry Smith

EBW—Edward Bennett Williams

Tank—Harold McLinton

Curly—Earl Lambeau

Turk—Albert Glen Edwards

Stinky—Mark Schlereth

Joey T—Joe Theismann

Sweetpea—Roy Jefferson

Mad Dog—Mike Curtis

Bullets/Wizards

Agent Zero—Gilbert Arenas

Earl the Pearl—Earl Monroe

E—Elvin Hayes

Spoon—Nick Witherspoon

Truck—Leonard Robinson

The Rave—Dave Stallworth

Bobby D—Bob Dandridge

Rags—Mike Riordan

Little Drummer Boy—Kevin Porter

Hot Plate—John Williams

Muggsy—Tyrone Bogues

Googs—Tom Gugliotta

Senators

Big Train—Walter Johnson

Hondo—Frank Howard

Goose—Leon Allen Goslin

Killer—Harmon Killebrew

Zorro—Zoilo Versalles

Teddy Ballgame—Ted Williams

Squirrel—Roy Sievers

Super Jew—Mike Epstein

Capitals

Bugsy—Brian Watson

Garts—Mike Gartner

Olie the Goalie—Olie Kolzig

Zeds—Richard Zednik

Yogs—Jaromir Jagr

Chief—Craig Berube

Gates—Gaetan Duchesne

Loffer—Craig Laughlin

Others

Red—Arnold Auerbach, George Washington

Bay Bay—John Duren, Georgetown

Big Sky—Craig Shelton, Georgetown

Sleepy—Eric Floyd, Georgetown

Lefty—Charles Driesell, Maryland

Buck—Charles Williams, Maryland

Baby Fats—Adrian Dantley, DeMatha

Flamboyant—Cornelius Green, Dunbar, Ohio State

Superman—Eugene Simms, Cardozo, Illinois

Junior—John Feinstein, author

The Bird of Prey—David Falk, player agent

The Night Owl—Marion Barry, ex-mayor

It's called a uniform, as in uni (one) form. The idea is for all the players to dress exactly the same so they look like a team. Occasionally, an individual will offer a variation to the uniform and it catches on. Michael Jordan's long shorts with the Bulls may be the best example of that (unfortunately, by the time he got here he was long in the shorts AND long in the tooth). Here are 10 from the area that gave the local uniform a slightly different look.

10. The Hair Shirt. Well, it actually wasn't a hair shirt, but the shirt was opened up to reveal way too much hair. Sportscaster Mike Wolfe, who TV trivia buffs will remember as being between Warner Wolf (no relation) and Glenn Brenner at Channel 9 from 1976 to '77, liked to wear his shirts unbuttoned to almost his navel. He accessorized the look with a gold chain and medallion. Very 70s. Neither the look nor Wolfe lasted. Brenner took his place after less than a year on the job.

9. Black High-Topped Cleats. Tony McGee was a pass-rushing specialist with the Redskins from 1982-84 as he finished up a career that began in 1970. Maybe he got the idea trying to chase Johnny Unitas, but McGee was wearing the same footwear as the great Colts quarterback when he came to the Redskins. The rest of the team wore white shoes. Ironically, McGee now works as the uniform cop at Redskin home games, issuing fines to players who don't strictly conform to the NFL's uniform code. If he was playing now in those high-topped black shoes, he'd have to fine himself.

8. The Sweatsuit. What else would you call what Maryland basketball coach Gary Williams is wearing late in the second half of a big ACC game? By that time, Gary is usually drenched in sweat. It's great for the dry-cleaning industry and Duke students who hold up signs that read, "Sweat Gary, Sweat."

7. White Knee Socks. Many NBA players wore them in the 70s, probably just to cut down on the exposed skin between the shoes and those old short shorts. But we have to credit Walt Williams for bringing back the look at Maryland from 1989-93. "The Wizard" inspired D.C. native Lawrence Moten to bring the same look to Syracuse where he set the all-time Big East scoring record.

6. Wrist Bands on a Kicker. His Redskin teammates used to give him grief about how much time he spent in front of a mirror before a game, but Mark Moseley wanted to make sure he looked good. He primped his perm (very popular in the early 80s) even though he had to put a helmet on it on the field. They never did figure out how wearing wristbands helped his kicking, but nobody complained in 1982 when he made 23 straight and was named the NFL's MVP.

5. The Visor. It may have made sense to Steve Spurrier when he wore it on the sidelines in Gainesville in September, but in Chicago in December it really wasn't the right look. Spurrier not only liked to wear the visor when he coached at the University of Florida, he liked to throw it when his quarterback screwed up. With the Redskins in 2002 and 2003, the quarterback was only part of the problem and, after a while, Spurrier didn't even bother to throw it.

27

4. The Burgundy Baseball Hat with the Gold R. George Allen made this sideline look popular in the 70s. He also used the underside of the brim to wipe his thumb after he'd nervously lick it. One of the great photos from the 1972 NFC title game win over Dallas shows a fan grabbing that hat off Allen's head as he celebrated the victory. Joe Gibbs also wore the burgundy hat during both of his coaching runs. In the second one, he started out wearing a black baseball hat until he was convinced by fans to go back to his old look. The look returned, but the glory never did.

3. The White Towel on the Shoulder. It was probably more for function over form when John Thompson first draped one on his shoulder while coaching at Georgetown in the 70s, but it became a trademark. Thompson used his to wipe the sweat off his face; the opponents were tempted to waive theirs when some of his great Hoya teams took the court.

2. Uniform Number Zero. The Redskins had a running back named Johnny Olsewski who wore number 0 from 1958-60, but it was most likely because his named started with an O. Wizards guard Gilbert Arenas started wearing his at the University of Arizona when doubters told him he would get zero playing time. In fact Arenas became a star at Arizona and seems to have made the number popular everywhere.

1. The T-Shirt under the Basketball Uniform. Local hoop historians may want to debate this one, but we remember American University guard Butch Slappy wearing one in 1977. In those days, the AU home games were played in Fort Myer Arena, which was usually kept at a temperature suitable for storing meat. However, the credit for this fashion statement goes to Patrick Ewing, who put one on while suffering from a cold during his freshman year. He liked it enough to keep the look for four years. Also give Nike some credit for never passing up a marketing opportunity. The T-shirt Ewing originally wore in games had a picture of a Nike shoe on the sleeve. The next year the NCAA ruled that the T-shirt had to be the same color as the uniform and without any logos.

It's hard to critical of something that's God–given (or for example in Lefty Driesell's case, taken away), but how hair (or lack of it) is handled is the basis for judgement here.

Best

5. Mike Jarvis. Of course the former George Washington basketball coach is bald. We know that. But at a time (the mid-90s) when most follically challenged African American men were shaving their heads (see Wilbon circa 1993) to make you guess, "is he or isn't he?," Jarvis kept it full on the sides with a full beard. It gave him a look much like Uncle Phil on *The Fresh Prince of Bel Air*. We credit Jarvis for proudly displaying all the hair that he *could* grow.

4. Sonny Jurgensen. The only thing more beautiful than Sonny's red hair in the 60s was the tight spiral he threw on the football field. More than 40 years after he came to D.C. from Philadelphia, Sonny still has zip on his throws and a tinge of red remains. The top of the head of few men his age looks that good.

3. Wes Unseld. It's thinned a bit and is mostly gray, but Wes still has the afro that he came to Washington with, along with his Bullets teammates, in 1973. With the amazing ability to be one of the best rebounders in the game at 6-foot-7, he may have felt that the hair made him appear just (pun intended) a hair taller. When you're giving up more than five inches to guys like Chamberlain and Thurmond, you need every edge you can get.

2. Steve Buckhantz. Although he doesn't appear on camera as much these days doing Wizards games on TV, "Buck" is willing to credit at least a small part of his long run on Channel 5 in the 80s and 90s to his blond hair. A life-long bachelor, he has the time and money to get to the stylist often enough so it never appears as if he's had a haircut.

1. Bambale "Boom" Osby. He's certainly not the first to take to the basketball court with a huge 'fro, but nobody was ever more beloved for it. During his two years of playing at Maryland, he sometimes showed up in cornrows, but more often than not the hair was "out." At home games during the 2006-07 and 2007-08 seasons, groups of four fans would show up wearing huge wigs and spelling out "BOOM" on T-shirts.

Worst

5. Red Auerbach. Another bald guy who couldn't do much about it and didn't try. But with a nickname of "Red," you always had to ask yourself two questions about his hair. When was it red? And when did he have it? No wonder Bob Cousy always called him by his real name, Arnold.

4. Willard Scott. We're straying from sports here, but you never knew with the legendary weatherman. He sometimes wore his toupee and sometimes he didn't. It was very confusing. Then to top it off (no pun intended this time) he was the original Ronald McDonald, wearing yet another wig.

3. Jim O'Brien. One of Lefty's first recruits at Maryland, he's legendary for his heroics in a 31-30 overtime win over South Carolina in 1971 when the Gamecocks were ranked number two in the country. Even in college, O'Brien was losing his bright-red hair. He didn't, however, do himself any favors by letting what remained of his curly locks grow. It gave him a look that led to the unavoidable nickname, "Bozo."

2. George Michael. When he was the king of rock and roll radio in the 60s and early 70s in Philadelphia and New York, the hair was long. And by the time he landed on Channel 4 doing the nightly sports in 1980, there was still plenty of it. But over the years, while "King George's" star never receded, his hairline did. By the end of the 90s, his head was kind of like the façade at Yankee Stadium. There was a bit up front, but nothing behind it in the back.

1. Tony Kornheiser. While hitting for the cycle in newspaper, radio, and television, Tony has always made fun of his baldness. He even named a book collection of his columns, *Bald As I Wanna Be*. But Tony has refused to call it a day up top. Even with just a tiny bit left, he combs over what he's got. Just a few strands remain. Wilbon calls it, "the seatbelt." Ironically the more hair he loses, the more successful he becomes on television. *Pardon the Interruption* is a hit show on ESPN and he's becoming a mainstay on *Monday Night Football*.

My Top 10 Red Heads :: Dave Feldman

Note: In a town where TV sportscaster stability is no longer a trademark, Dave Feldman, who arrived in D.C. in 2001, is the dean of the local sports heads. Channel 5 plucked him from ESPN despite the red hair, which may have doomed former channel 9 Sports Director Ken Broo (actually in his case it was more than just the hair). Growing up in Palo Alto, California, Feldman played high school basketball with Stanford football coach Jim Harbaugh. "Feldy" likes to say that they once combined for 47 points in a game (Harbaugh had 40). You can see why he chose a career in TV rather than athletics, or for that matter, standup comedy. Anyway, here are the redhead's top 10 redheads.

10. Bill Walton. Not just a redhead, but a famous Dead Head. Wasn't a bad shot-blocker either.

9. Angie Everhart. No stranger to brief nudity in Treat Williams movies. Nice.

8. Isla Fisher. Great in *Wedding Crashers*. Married to Sacha Baron Cohen (*Borat*).

7. Dennis Johnson. Loved his tight red afro. I believe it was his natural color.

6. Lucille Ball. Great battles with Fred Mertz. Amazing that she became known as a redhead on black-and-white TV.

5. Debra Messing. Love her despite cheating on Ben Stiller in *Along Came Polly*.

4. Sandy Feldman. My mom. (Editor's note: let's hope she doesn't get her hands on this book. Mom rates only number 4?)

3. Ron Howard. Most of the great red hair is gone, but Opie can still bring it.

2. Rod Laver. A gentleman, an Aussie, and the only tennis player to win the Grand Slam twice.

1. Red Auerbach. Like Lucille Ball, he became famous when TV was still in black and white. Was the greatest basketball coach of all time.

George Allen started it all back in the 1970s when the Redskins' quirky Hall of Fame head coach realized the Cowboys were usually the team to beat in the NFC East. He demonized them any chance he got, and his players drank the Kool-Aid as well. When he walked around his backyard the week of a Dallas game and spotted an ugly weed, he'd tell his kids, "If I get this darned thing out in one piece, we'll beat the Cowboys on Sunday." He once publicly accused the Cowboys of cheap-shot crack-back blocks, and even insinuated that iconic Hall of Fame quarterback Roger Staubach threw out of the shotgun because he couldn't read defenses. He flat-out hated the Pokes, and his players and many of their fans were with him all the way.

10. Tex Schramm. The late team president and general manager was one of NFL Commissioner Pete Rozelle's closest advisers, and George Allen always thought the two of them were conspiring to screw the Redskins somehow, some way. Schramm also spent pre-game warm-ups inspecting the right shoe of kicker Mark Moseley, convinced that he had lead in the toe for added distance, further infuriating the Redskins and their fans.

9. Charles Haley. Easily one of the surliest players in the history of the league, the James Madison product hardly got along with anyone, particularly the media he cursed when they got anywhere near his locker nearly every day. Even some of his teammates were convinced the powerful defensive end also had a screw or three loose inside his helmet.

8. Clint Longley. The Mad Bomber rookie quarterback came off the bench in a famous Thanksgiving Day game in 1974 and threw two fourth-quarter touchdowns, including a 50-yarder to Drew Pearson in the final seconds, to help beat the Redskins 24-23 and keep them from clinching a playoff spot. Longley also sucker-punched beloved teammate Roger Staubach two years later, earning him a ticket to football oblivion not long thereafter.

7. Texas Stadium. When they first opened the place in 1971 it had obscenely opulent Texas-sized luxury suites and always seemed a tad too ostentatious a setting for a football game. They also built it with a silly hole in the roof, prompting linebacker D.D. Lewis to once say it was there "so God can watch his favorite team." Oh please.

6. Duane Thomas. The running back from West Texas State helped lead the Cowboys to a Super Bowl title in 1971, but was not much of a teammate, declining to talk to the media, his fellow players, coaches, and the front office for long stretches of time. He was signed by the Redskins in 1973 and played sparingly for two seasons. Even George Allen, who loved having the occasional renegade semi-psycho on his side, had no idea how to handle Thomas, and cut him before the 1975 season after he became far too much of a dreaded distraction.

5. Jerry Jones. The oil and gas mogul/wildcatter turned football owner and so-called general manager thinks he's a master of the football universe, even if it's been a dozen years since the Pokes have been to the Super Bowl on his watch. He bought the team in 1989 and clumsily fired Tom Landry almost immediately. When his teams won three Super Bowls, mostly because of head coach Jimmy Johnson's good work, Jones took lots of credit, once saying that "any one of 500 coaches could have won those Super Bowls" given the talent he had helped assemble. Then he fired Johnson. He also "mentored" Redskins owner Dan Snyder when he bought into the league in 1999. Need to know any more?

4. The Cheerleaders. The Cowboys' bimbo brigade helped spawn several generations of scantily-clad, blow-dried, mascara-to-the-max, air-headed foofs now prancing on sidelines around most of the National Football League. Every year there seems to be more cleavage and less spandex, which actually can be a good thing, but if the girls think we're watching because we admire their slick choreography, they're even dumber than they look.

3. Terrell Owens. After once infuriating Texas Stadium fans by stomping on their star logo at midfield as a member of the San Francisco 49ers, the Cowboys and their fans now embrace him as their big-play receiver, despite his longtime prima donna act and propensity to drop balls in critical situations. Great talent, yes, but a bright and shining poster boy for the me-first athlete of the 21st century.

2. Michael Irvin. All you have to know is that a guy who dabbled in coke, booze, and hookers, flirting with jail and suspensions many times as an active player, got into the Pro Football Hall of Fame a year ahead of our own Art Monk, who had more catches, touchdowns, and yards, not to mention so much more class and grace.

1. "America's Team." Says who?

Note: Calvin Hill played running back for the Dallas Cowboys from 1968 to 1975, when George Allen signed him as a free agent to play for the Redskins. Hill was in Dallas at the dawn of the Redskins-Cowboys rivalry, and still has vivid memories of a few men in burgundy and gold who always rubbed the Pokes the wrong way. Here are his top five, along with the reason he and his teammates didn't care much for them.

5. Sam Wyche. He was their No. 3 quarterback and never got onto the field. But Sam liked to yap a lot. In that NFC Championship game in 1972 (a stirring 26-3 Washington victory) he was on the sidelines yelling stuff like "Die you Cowboy dogs." It was out of line, especially from a guy who didn't even play, never had to man up.

4. Charley Taylor. Charley was a good guy, but they always used him on a crack-back block that was just deadly. One year, he used it on our great linebacker, Chuck Howley, and pretty much ended his career. Charley was only doing what the coaches wanted him to, but he was a big, strong guy and that made it even more dangerous. We got back at them, because we had our own receiver, Lance Alworth, crack back on Jack Pardee the next time we played. That block was legal back then, but you're not allowed to do it any more, and I think the stuff we did to each other was a big reason why.

3. Verlon Biggs. Without a doubt, far and away the absolute dirtiest player I ever saw. He played defensive end for the Redskins, and our nickname for him in Dallas was just "Dirty Biggs." He'd poke you in the eye, step on your hand, kick you in the crotch. It didn't matter, he was just pure dirty, and we hated him. No wonder he became a professional wrestler after he stopped playing. Probably a villain.

2. Diron Talbert. He was a big old defensive tackle whose brother had played for the Cowboys and was not really treated right when Dallas let him go. Diron definitely held a grudge. I considered him the Tokyo Rose of the Redskins. He always put out messages about Roger Staubach, which we all knew were put in his head by George Allen. He'd say the Cowboys use the shotgun because Roger couldn't read defenses, stuff like that. He just kept the chatter going any time we played, and he did it to get Roger's mind away from the game. It never worked, because Roger was smarter than that.

1. George Allen. I played for him when I came to the Redskins in 1975, and I respected him. He always knew the road to the Super Bowl had to go through Dallas, so he did everything he could to get the Redskins players to hate us. We definitely didn't trust him. Before a lot of Redskins-Cowboys games, we'd go practice at the stadium so he couldn't spy on us. Our old practice field in Dallas had a hotel at one end, and we'd buy up all the rooms on the top floor so he couldn't send somebody to watch our practices. His ethics were questionable to say the least. Tom Landry always used to tell us that George called him every week during the season when he was coaching the Rams, but he didn't call him any more now that he's in Washington. George tried to demonize us. We knew it, so we never took him that seriously.

The Top 10 Reasons the Cowboys Hate the Redskins
:: Ed Werder

Note: Ed Werder has been following the fortunes, and occasional misfortunes, of the Dallas Cowboys for twenty years, first as the Cowboys' beat reporter for the *Fort Worth Star Telegram* and then *The Dallas Morning News*. Since 1998, he's been the Dallas-based correspondent for ESPN, a constant presence on *SportsCenter* and various NFL pre-game and highlight shows. Of course, when he covers Skins vs. Pokes, he remains totally objective, as usual.

10. Cowboys fans remain insulted that George Allen's legendary hatred for Dallas rendered him unable to use the Texas city's name even when referring to one of his own players, defensive end Dallas Hickman, who never heard the head coach utter his first name. "George Allen never used to say 'the Dallas Cowboys,'" recalls John Wilbur, a Redskins guard of that time. "It was always 'the goddamned Dallas Cowboys.'"

9. The only man Roger Staubach ever admitted to hating was Diron Talbert, who tricked the Cowboys Hall of Famer into appearing to demonstrate poor sportsmanship. Once, Staubach extended his hand to Talbert at a midfield meeting of team captains for the pre-game coin flip and Talbert refused to shake. According to Staubach, before the teams met the next time, Talbert "goes and tells the press, 'Hey watch the coin toss. Staubach won't shake my hand.' The press is looking at this, so they write this big article that Staubach is a sore loser: He won't shake Diron Talbert's hand."

8. The Redskins' fierce pride never allowed the Cowboys to beat them more than 10 consecutive times.

7. LaVar Arrington ran Troy Aikman off the field and all the way up into a broadcast booth when he chased the quarterback down before he could scramble to the sideline at Texas Stadium in 2000. Arrington delivered a blow that caused Aikman's helmet to bounce twice off the artificial turf, prematurely ending the Hall of Famer's career with another in an endless series of concussions.

6. Current Redskins owner Daniel Snyder purchased a Texas institution—the Six Flags Over Texas amusement park—and has turned it into a shameful something that one Redskins employee now jokingly calls "Two Flags."

5. Proving his Christian sensibilities apparently find the big-haired, boob-job Dallas crowds somewhat offensive, Hall of Fame Redskins coach Joe Gibbs—who beat the Cowboys in his final regular-season victory before heading off to his second retirement—called Cowboys fans the ugliest people on Earth. This from a man who coached a group of overweight behemoths known as The Hogs.

4. When George Allen compiled a list of pro football's 25 greatest games, he chose six of Washington's victories over Dallas.

3. Roger Staubach, a former Navy officer, polished civil leader, and model of proper behavior, contradicted that image and forever tainted his reputation when he became so incensed during a game that he punched cornerback Pat Fischer and was penalized for unsportsmanlike conduct. As a result, Staubach doesn't even have a statue next to Tom Landry's at Texas Stadium.

2. Before playing a late December game for the 1979 NFC East title, Cowboys defensive end Harvey Martin received a funeral wreath from the Redskins with a card that read: "Sympathy for an Impending Loss." After Roger Staubach inspired a 35-34 Cowboys victory that eliminated the Redskins from the playoffs, Martin opened the door to the Redskins locker room and flung it inside, yelling, "Take this back to Washington with you."

1. Jimmy Johnson would never have uttered his famous "How 'bout Them Cowboys?" line and Jerry Jones would not have sold enough $8 beers to build a new $1 billion stadium had former Redskins owner George Preston Marshall succeeded in preventing the Cowboys from being born. In 1960 when the franchise was formed, it was approved as a member of the National Football League over the initial objections of Marshall, who relented only when outwitted by prospective Cowboys owner Clint Murchison. Before the voting, Murchison met bandleader Barnee Breeskin, who had composed the music and owned the copyright to Washington's fight song, "Hail to the Redskins." Desperate for money following a divorce, Breeskin sold the rights to the song to Murchison for $5,000. Murchison used the purchase to leverage Marshall for his consent to allow the Cowboys into the league by informing him that Marshall would never hear the Redskins fight song at another game unless he supported the Cowboys.

A Fish Out of Water—the 10 Toughest Things about Covering the Cowboys as a Redskins Fan
:: Kevin Blackistone

Note: Growing up in Prince Georges County, Kevin was among the fortunate to spend fall Sundays at RFK Stadium hating the Dallas Cowboys with season tickets that had been in his family forever. After graduating from Good Counsel High School in 1977, he headed to Northwestern where he watched bad football and learned great journalistic skills. As fate would have it after graduation, opportunity knocked at the *Dallas Morning News*. He would spend 20 years there, working his way up to sports columnist. But when the paper offered buyouts in 2006, he jumped and headed home. You see him now as a contributor on ESPN's *Around the Horn* and read his columns on AOL Sports. Here is Kevin's list of the toughest things he had to endure during those two decades in Big D.

10. Hearing, reading, seeing anything proclaiming the Cowboys "America's Team."

9. Watching Jack Kent Cooke sign Norv Turner from the Cowboys to coach the Redskins, knowing full well that Turner had as much to do with the Cowboys early 90s success as any guy in Texas with a 10-gallon hat.

8. Hearing Michael Irvin's name called for the Pro Football Hall of Fame while Art Monk—with as many Super Bowl rings, four more seasons, almost 200 more catches, nearly 1,000 more yards, and zero run-ins with the law—would have to wait some more.

7. Learning that Redskins fan and NBA player Darrell Armstrong, during a stint with the Mavericks in 2005, had his freedom of speech rights trampled up after the Mavericks fined him $1,000 for taking the microphone before a basketball game at their American Airlines Center and announcing, in the wake of the Redskins 35-7 stomping of the Cowboys, "How 'bout those Redskins!"

6. Trying not to run whenever I saw a car adorned with that hideous Cowboys blue star, which, of course, made any car look like a police cruiser.

5. Watching a Potomac, MD, native—and, obviously Skins fan, Paul Palmer—run for more than 100 yards for a winless Cowboys team at RFK Stadium and lead it to a 13-3 upset over our hometown team. It was Jimmy Johnson's first season (1989) in Dallas, his only win in his rookie NFL coaching season, and the launching of his unfortunately fabulous run in Dallas, which included two Super Bowl wins.

4. Having to sit in the most antiseptic sports stadium, Texas Stadium, in all of professional football while the most sedate (or was it comatose?) fans in the NFL reacted like zombies to elevator music pumped out of loud speakers whenever the Cowboys did something as mundane as make a first down.

3. Constantly having to remind Dallas fans that each time the teams met in the play-offs—the NFC Championship, no less—it was their team that went home for the season with a loss.

2. Hearing the cacophony of laughter in 2000 when Dan Snyder handed over $56 million to Deion Sanders to play for his newly purchased Redskins after Sanders was cut by Dallas because he was too expensive, too often injured, too old at 32, and too much of a shadow of his former All-Pro self.

1. Watching Jimmy Johnson break into a grin in 1991 in the bowels of RFK Stadium after I told him Joe Gibbs said Johnson out-coached him—throwing onsides kicks and all sorts of trickeration—to ruin what was starting to look like an undefeated season for Gibbs's team.

The Top 11 "Cowskin" Stories

So intense was the Redskin-Cowboy rivalry in the 1970s, that players who came to Washington from Dallas were treated like Egyptians joining the Israeli Army. That changed greatly in the 90s when free agency allowed players to move freely from team to team. However, Darrell Green recalls that Norv Turner didn't exactly endear himself to the Redskin veterans when he took over as head coach in 1994 and brought some of his former players with him from Dallas. Here are the top 11 who came here from there with varied success.

11. Tony Banks QB (Cowboys and Redskins 2001). Banks is just one of the many odd stories from the 2001 season. He signed as a free agent in Dallas before the season with the promise of being able to compete for the job Troy Aikman had just vacated by retiring. Surprisingly, Banks was cut in training camp by the Cowboys. With Jeff George out with a sore arm, the Redskins picked him up to be their backup. But when George was released after losing the second game of the season 37-0 at Green Bay, Banks became the starter. Admitting he barely knew the playbook and had only one audible to work with, he somehow led the Redskins to wins in eight of their last 11 games. He turned an 0-5 start into an 8-8 finish. He was released when new coach Steve Spurrier arrived and immediately signed ex-Gators Shane Matthews and Danny Wuerfful.

10. Ray Shoenke OL (Cowboys 1963-64, Redskins 1966-75). Shoenke was an 11th-round draft pick out of nearby SMU in 1963 and was a backup on an emerging young team. Released in 1965, he caught on with the Redskins in '66 and managed to stick around for 10 years by being able to play every position on the offensive line. He was smart about making political contacts (including the Kennedys) while playing in Washington and forged a successful career in business and politics after leaving football.

9. John Wilbur G (Cowboys 1966-69, Redskins 1971-74). After playing at Stanford, where he was a free thinker, Wilbur never embraced Tom Landry's mechanical ways in Dallas. He was happy to land back in California with the Rams in 1970 and even happier to follow George Allen to Washington the following year. Wilbur was part of Allen's 1971 draft-day haul of his ex-players including Maxie Baughn and Diron Talbert for draft picks. He was a starter on the 1972 Super Bowl team.

8. Eddie Murray K (Cowboys 1993, Redskins 1995, Cowboys 1999, Redskins 2000). For a guy who spent the first 12 years of his career in one place, Detroit, Murray sure did a lot of bouncing around at the end of his career. Even though the Redskins had drafted Chip Lomiller in the second round of the 1988 draft, coach Norv Turner cut him loose early in training camp in 1995. Murray had been solid on the Cowboys '93 Super Bowl team, and even at age 39, Turner thought he could do the job. Younger kickers followed the next few years before the kicking crisis of 2000—Brett Conway was released after getting hurt and replacements Kris Heppner and Michael Husted failed. Although he was 44 by this time, Murray was called to the rescue again. This time Norv drowned. After holder Tommy Barnhardt called a timeout in the final seconds to tell Turner that the 44-year-old kicker couldn't kick a 49-yarder, Turner told him to kick it anyway. The kick was short, the Skins lost to the Giants 9-7, and Turner was fired. Serves him right for trusting an old Cowboy.

7. Scott Galbraith TE (Cowboys 1993-94, Redskins 1995-96, Cowboys 1997). Galbraith was a great locker room talker, but not so great as a tight end. And certainly not so great at blocking on field goal attempts. He's best remembered for the '96 game against Arizona at RFK Stadium. The Redskins appeared to win a wild over-time game on a field goal from Scott Blanton, but Galbraith was called for holding and the Redskins went on to lose 37-34. Once a Cowboy, always a Cowboy. Of course he went back to Dallas after being cut.

6. John Gesek C (Cowboys 1990-93, Redskins 1994-95). An over-the-hill veteran that Turner had to have when he came to Washington. This was one of those unwelcomed players Darrell Green talked about. He looked great snapping the ball to Troy Aikman, but not so great snapping to Heath Shuler and Gus Frerotte. After two injury-filled seasons Gesek was done.

5. Jean Fugett TE (Cowboys 1972-75, Redskins 1976-79). Drafted out of Amherst in the 13th round by Dallas, he was an emerging talent when the NFL some-how let free agency slip into the game in 1976. George Allen was one of only a few to take advantage of it, landing John Riggins, whose contract had run out in New York and Fugett, who doubled his salary by leaving the Cowboys. But in those days he paid for it. The old Redskin veterans hated Dallas. Longtime equipment manager Jay Brunetti tells a story of Diron Talbert grabbing an injured knee and yelling in pain, "Why couldn't this have happened to Fugett?" Talbert and teammates didn't seem to mind him so much when he made the Pro Bowl in 1977.

4. Brig Owens S (Cowboys 1965, Redskins 1966-77). Dallas was smart to draft the former University of Cincinnati quarterback in the seventh round of the '65 draft. They were very foolish to let him get away to their division rival a year later. Owens became a 12-year starter in the secondary and was one of the classiest play-ers ever to wear a Redskins uniform.

3. Duane Thomas RB (Cowboys 1970-71, Redskins 1973-74). Few play-ers in NFL history have let more talent go to waste than Thomas. Unhappy with his contract, he decided to stop talking to the media in Dallas and then extended the silence to his teammates and coaches. But when it came time to play, he performed. Thomas had 95 yards in the Super Bowl VI blowout of Miami. But after he called coach Tom Landry, "The Plastic Man," Dallas tried to trade him to San Diego. The Chargers sent him back when he refused to take a physical. George Allen decided to overlook the odd behavior a season later, but Thomas never returned to the level he'd reached in Dallas. After a brief jump to the World Football League, he was out of the game for good before his 28th birthday.

2. Calvin Hill RB (Cowboys 1969-74, Redskins 1976-77). Hill was one of the top running backs in football in the early 70s, making the Pro Bowl four times and running for over a thousand yards twice. But the Yale-educated star wanted to get paid for his talent and jumped to the upstart WFL. After the league folded, George Allen was only too happy to scoop him up, even though he already had Larry Brown, Mike Thomas, Moses Denson and John Riggins on the roster. Like Duane Thomas before him, Hill never reached that Dallas level in Washington. He ran for only 558 yards and one touchdown in two seasons. But he was such a positive locker room influence that Cleveland kept him on the roster for four seasons after that. Now he likes to tell people he's more famous for being Grant Hill's father.

1. Deion Sanders CB (Cowboys 1995-99, Redskins 2000). There is no bigger symbol of the out-of-control spending that went on before the 2000 season than Deion Sanders. From the time he showed up for his introductory news conference in a burgundy and gold suit until the day he announced he wasn't coming back for a second year, Deion was all sizzle and no steak. Despite being past his prime-time, Dan Snyder had to have the formerly great cornerback who was at one time the most dangerous punt returner in the game. He gave him an enormous bonus and said everything would be fine as long as Deion played more than one year. He didn't. After one year as a decent corner, but a lousy returner, Deion sent word that he had no intention of playing for new coach Marty Schottenheimer. His quote was, "I don't trust Marty as far as I can throw him." Deion retired, costing the Redskins $8 million in dead money the following year. Amazingly he sat out three full seasons, but returned to play two more for the Ravens in 2004 and '05.

Note: A college buddy remembers Al sitting in the laundry room while a student at American University, trying to pick up the radio reception of his beloved hometown St. Louis Blues games. In his senior year, the Caps entered the NHL as an expansion team and Al was finally able to show his pals the game he loved. That game now helps pay the bills. For more than 25 years, Al has been involved in TV coverage of Caps games. Doing sideline and some play-by-play work, Al can be seen on some away and most home games on Comcast Sportsnet. He's also one of the co-hosts of the *John Thompson Show* on Sportstalk 980. Here are his picks for top Caps trades.

10. Kris Beech, Ross Lupaschuk, Michel Sivek and future considerations to Pittsburgh for Jaromir Jagr and Frantisek Kucera, July 11, 2001. I know, I know, Jagr was a huge disappointment. But by numbers, it was actually an amazing steal by general manager George McPhee. Jagr was a diva, but a producer. In 190 games, he posted 98 goals and 118 assists. That's 190 more points than Beech produced in Pittsburgh.

9. Pat Ribble and a second-round pick in 1982 to Calgary for Bobby Gould and Randy Holt, November 25, 1981. Gould is best remembered as the guy who registered the one-punch knockout of Mario Lemieux, but he also scored 18 or more goals five times. He played more than 600 games as a Capital and had a nice two-year run as an enforcer, racking up an amazing 525 penalty minutes in just 123 games.

8. Brian Engblom and Ken Houston to Los Angeles for Larry Murphy, October 18, 1983. A Hall of Famer, Murphy never became a fan favorite in D.C., especially to a group that would chant, "whoop, whoop, whoop," every time he touched the puck. They were idiots. Murphy was one of the game's best offensive defensemen. He had two 20-plus goal seasons and 344 points in 453 games as a Cap. Dale Hunter's breakaway goal against Ron Hextall and the Flyers in game seven of the 1988 playoffs is considered the greatest goal in Capitals history. Hunter was sprung on a brilliant pass by Murphy.

7. Claudio Scremin to Minnesota for Don Beaupre, November 11, 1988. The classic prospect-for-veteran-nearing-the-end-of-the-line deal. As it turned out, Beaupre thrived under goaltender coach Warren Strelow, who had the same job with the 1980 U.S. Olympic "Miracle on Ice" team. Beaupre played five seasons as the number one goalie and is second in team history with 128 wins. Scremin played 17 games in the NHL, none with Minnesota.

6 and 5. (6) Sergei Gonchar to Boston for Shaone Morrison and first- and second-round picks in 2004, March 3, 2004. (5) Robert Lang to Detroit for Tomas Fleischman, a first-round pick in 2004, and a fourth-round pick in 2006, February 27, 2004. These deals need to be viewed in tandem. With a lockout looming, George McPhee had been instructed by owner Ted Leonsis to blow up the team and rebuild at the end of the dismal 2003-2004 season. Morrison became a top 4 defenseman and Fleischman is a contributing forward. But the picks really tip the scales. The Detroit deal produced Mike Green, who led all NHL defensemen in goals scored in 2008 and the Boston deal brought in another rising defenseman in Jeff Shultz. As for the traded vets, Gonchar left Boston at the end of the season and Lang played only one more year in Detroit.

4. Clint Malarchuk, Grant Ledyard and a sixth-round pick in 1991 to Buffalo for Calle Johansson and a second-round pick in 1989, March 7, 1989.
A deadline deal for an immediate playoff run turned out to be a tremendous long-term investment. Johansson went on to log 983 games in a Caps uniform, racking up 474 points as the most consistent puck-moving defensemen in club history. Two weeks after the deal, Malarchuk suffered one of the most gruesome injuries in sports history when he spouted blood from his juglar vein after an on-ice collision. Fortunately he survived and continued his career.

3. Gaetan Duchesne, Alan Haworth and a number-one pick in 1987 to Quebec for Dale Hunter and Clint Malarchuk, June 13, 1987.
Tired of seeing his skill players intimidated by the physical Philadelphia Flyers, general manager David Poile got immediate return on this deal. Just 26 seconds into the '87 opener in Philadelphia, Hunter went toe to toe with renowned Flyer tough guy Craig Berube and the Caps never had to look over their shoulder again. Hunter and Kelly Miller are the only Caps to appear in 100 playoff games and Hunter's 72 points (including 25 goals) in those games is the current gold standard. He's one of only three Caps to have his number (32) retired.

2. Bobby Carpenter and a second-round pick in 1988 to the New York Rangers for Kelly Miller, Mike Ridley and Bob Crawford, January 1, 1987.
Coach Bryan Murray got so fed up with former 50-goal scorer Carpenter that he not only benched him, he essentially dismissed him from the team early in the 1986-87 season. It took weeks and weeks for Poile to clean up the mess, but he finally got Ranger GM Phil Esposito to bite on New Year's Day, 1987. Miller would go on to play 940 games in D.C., and Ridley 588. After only 28 games in New York, an exasperated "Espo" dealt Carpenter to Los Angeles.

1. Ryan Walter and Rick Green to Montreal for Rod Langway, Doug Jarvis, Brian Engblom and Craig Laughlin, September 9, 1982.
Poile's first trade remains the best in franchise history. Owner Abe Pollin gulped when Poile told him he was trading his beloved Captain Walter. But Langway changed the fortunes of the team, while Jarvis, Engblom and Laughlin proved to be versatile players. Plus "The Locker" is one of the great voices of local TV sports. Langway's number (5) was the second one that the team retired.

Note: Longtime *Washington Post* columnist William Gildea has been a regular in the press box at Capitals games since the franchise began play at the old Capital Centre in 1975, when the first team went 8-67-5, with 21 points and won only one game on the road. Here are his top 10 Caps.

10. Yvon Labre. Considered the "original" Capital. Drafted by Pittsburgh, he was selected by Washington in the 1974 NHL expansion draft. He scored the Capitals' first home goal, but he was primarily a defensive defenseman. An extremely popular player, he was named captain from 1976 to 1978 and was the first Capital to have his sweater retired. He was the only Washington player to wear No. 7. After his playing days, he remained with the team, best known for his work in the community.

9. Kelly Miller. There are several players who played for the Capitals who were much better scorers. But Miller rates a place in the Capitals' "top 10" because he, as much as anyone, represents the quintessential team player that epitomized the Washington franchise for decades. Miller, whose brothers Kevin and Kip also played for the Capitals, came to Washington in a trade with the New York Rangers involving former first-round pick Bobby Carpenter. Miller was a Capital from 1986-87 through 1998-99. A left winger mostly, he was an excellent passer and playmaker, a tough checker, and a solid face-off man.

8. Scott Stevens. One of the top defensemen ever in the NHL, he played more seasons with the New Jersey Devils than the Capitals. But while with Washington through most of the 1980s, he was a stellar part of the team's defense-first approach. He went on to become captain of the Devils and a Hall of Famer in 2007.

7. Calle Johansson. The Capitals have had higher profile players but virtually no one who was so consistent for such a long time. A defense-minded defenseman, Johansson played for the team from 1988-89 until 2002-03. He was a quiet leader off the ice and a quiet leader on the ice, one who was penciled into the lineup by coaches almost automatically and delivered by breaking up countless plays by the opposition.

6. Mike Gartner. A first-round, fourth-overall pick by Washington in the 1979 entry draft, he played on the team until traded to Minnesota in March, 1989. He played with five NHL teams and scored more than 700 goals overall, making the Hall of Fame in 2001. He was a swift forward who never missed a game in eight of his 19 seasons. When he left the Capitals, he was the team's leader in career goals, assists, and points.

5. Dale Hunter. A tenacious center iceman who starred for the Capitals from 1987-88 to 1998-99. He was obtained from Quebec and is the only player in NHL history to score two overtime winners in ultimate games of a Stanley Cup playoff series. His value as a face-off man would be hard to overestimate. He is the second most penalized player in league history and once was suspended for 21 games for hitting the New York Islanders' Pierre Turgeon from behind. His No. 32 was retired by the Capitals in 2000.

4. Peter Bondra. He played longer with the Capitals than Gartner, but was a similar scoring machine. He holds team records in goals, points, power-play goals, game-winning goals, short-handed goals, and hat tricks. He was drafted by Washington and joined the team in 1990-91, and remained a lightning-fast presence on the wing until traded in 2004.

3. Olie Kolzig. "Olie the Goalie" and the Capitals are practically synonymous. He was drafted by the team in 1989 and played briefly in 1989-90. After thorough seasoning in the minor leagues, he was brought up in 1995-96 and went on to become a game-in, game-out presence for the Capitals and one of the NHL's top goaltenders. He won the 2000 Vezina Trophy as the league's best goalie, and has played more games in the NHL than any active goaltender except Martin Brodeur.

2. Alex Ovechkin. If he is able to play his entire career without being slowed by serious injury, Ovechkin will go down as the greatest Capital, a superstar in the NHL, and a certain Hall of Famer. In his first few seasons, he has established himself as one of the new "faces" of the league. A fast skater and hard shooter from the wing, he goes to the net fearlessly and draws multi-player coverage. He is also big and strong and has developed into a force defensively. Selflessly, he will give up the puck for an assist any time the opportunity presents itself. By the time he is finished, he should rank with the legendary offensive players of the game.

1. Rod Langway. In terms of hockey, he was Washington's "Secretary of Defense." A stay-at-home defenseman, Langway won back-to-back Norris Trophies as the NHL's top defender in 1983 and 1984. A member of a Stanley Cup championship team in Montreal, he came to Washington in a blockbuster trade in 1982-83 and led the Capitals to 11 straight postseason appearances. He was unquestionably the team leader, and particularly visible on the ice because of his height and the fact that he was one of the last players not to wear a helmet. His No. 5 was retired in 1997 and he earned the NHL's Hall of Fame in 1999.

Note: Thom Loverro is a longtime columnist for the *Washington Times* who special- izes in baseball and boxing. He previously worked for the *Baltimore Sun* and if you don't blink, you can see him in episodes of HBO's *The Wire*. Here are Loverro's top 10 boxers from the Washington D.C. area.

10. Johnny Gant (45-15-3, 26 KOs). Gant was born in Baltimore on New Year's Day in 1949, but fought many times in the Washington area. He made his debut in the District in August 1968 when he stopped Hurricane Hart in four rounds. Gant fought Sugar Ray Leonard in January 1979 at the Capital Centre in Landover, losing in eight rounds.

9. Holly Mims (64-27-6, 13 KOs). Mims was born in Washington in 1927 and although he never was a world champion, fought all the top middleweights of the 1950s and 60s—among them, Sugar Ray Robinson, Emile Griffith, and Dick Tiger. Mims lost a 10-round decision to Joey Giardello at the Capitol Arena in 1959. He also had a 1-1 record against Jimmy Ellis when he was a middleweight. Ellis later won the heavy- weight title. Mims died of kidney failure in 1970.

8. Keith Holmes (40-5, 25 KOs). Born in Washington in 1969, Holmes was a tall, lefthanded middleweight who became a two-time World Boxing Council champion. He won his first title by stopping Quincy Taylor in nine rounds in Las Vegas in 1996. But Holmes lost the belt to Hacine Cherifi in a decision in France in 1998. A year later he regained the title by stopping Cherifi in seven rounds before hometown fans at the MCI Center (now Verizon Center).

7. Maurice Blocker (36-4, 20 KOs). Blocker was born and raised in Washington and became a two-time welterweight champion. He defeated Marlon Starling to win the WBC title in 1990, but lost it in a legendary fight against his good friend and fellow Washington fighter Simon Brown. In 1991 he captured the IBF title by beating Glenwood Brown, and defended it once. Blocker lost the title in 1993, when he was knocked out in two rounds by Felix Trinidad. He retired in 1995.

6. William Joppy (39-5-1, 30 KOs). Born in Silver Spring, Maryland, on September 11, 1970, Joppy made his pro debut in February 1993, winning a four- round decision over Duane Tennet. Three years later he pulled a huge upset in Japan where he beat WBA middleweight champion Shinji Takehara in nine rounds. A year later Joppy lost the title to Julio Cesar Green, but then beat Green to win it back five months later. Joppy has fought 16 times in the Washington area.

5. Sharmba Mitchell (56-6, 30 KOs). Born August 17, 1970, in Takoma Park, Maryland, Mitchell made his pro debut just after turning 18 by knocking out Eddie Colon in three rounds. He became a fixture on the Washington boxing scene for the next 20 years, competing against the best lightweights and junior welterweights of his time. In 1998 Mitchell won the WBA title by dominating champion Khalid Rahilou in 12 rounds in Paris. He successfully defended his title four times. Mitchell's nickname is "Little Big Man," and he is the cousin of NBA star Steve Francis.

4. Simon Brown (47-12, 34 KOs). Born in Jamaica on August 15, 1963, Brown made his home in Washington and was considered one of the best welterweight fighters of the late 1980s and early 90s. He would capture the IBF welterweight championship by stopping Tyrone Trice in 14 rounds in 1988. Brown successfully defended his title nine times before losing to James "Buddy" McGirt in 1991. In 1993 he won the junior middleweight title by beating heavily favored champion Terry Norris. Brown lost to Norris in a rematch the following year and retired from boxing in 2000.

3. Mark Johnson (44-5, 28 KOs). Born in Washington on August 13, 1971, Johnson became the first black fighter to win the World Flyweight championship when he defeated Francisco Tejedor in 1996. Johnson was considered one of the best pound-for-pound fighters of his era and successfully defended his title 13 times before losing to Rafael Marquez in a split decision in 2001. He later won the WBO Super Flyweight championship in 2003.

2. Bob Foster (56-8-1, 46 KOs). Foster was born in Albuquerque, New Mexico in 1938, but made his home in Washington. His pro debut was in D.C., a second-round knockout of Duke Williams. Foster won the light heavyweight title by knocking out Dick Tiger in the fourth round at Madison Square Garden in 1969. Foster remained light heavyweight champ until 1974. While champion, he tried twice to move up the heavyweight division, losing both times to Joe Frazier and Muhammad Ali.

1. Sugar Ray Leonard (36-3-1, 25 KOs). Born in Palmer Park, Maryland, on May 17, 1956, Leonard was one of the most talented and charismatic fighters of his time and went on to become a world champion in five different weight classes. He won a gold medal at the 1976 Olympics and won the WBC welterweight title three years later by stopping champion Wilfredo Benitez. Sugar Ray had two legendary bouts with Roberto Duran, losing the first in a close decision and forcing Duran to quit ("No Mas") in the second. In his brutal battle with welterweight champion Thomas Hearns, Leonard was behind on all three scorecards before stopping Hearns in the 14th round. Leonard came out of one his several retirements to win a disputed decision over Marvin Hagler in 1987. Leonard's final fight was a five-round loss to Hector Camacho in 1997.

Note: Longtime *Washington Post* writer and columnist William Gildea has been to many of the major championship fights of the last four decades, and covered all of Sugar Ray Leonard's title bouts, retirements, and then more title bouts. We asked him to pick his all-time list of local boxers.

10. Darryl Tyson. Several Washington-area fighters would qualify for a place in this top 10, but the nod goes to Tyson because of the championships he achieved and the consistently high level of opponents he fought. The 5-foot-7 Tyson worked both as a lightweight and a light welterweight, and achieved significantly in both divisions. During his career, he held the WBC Continental Americas lightweight and the NABF lightweight titles, and the USBA and NABF light welterweight titles. He won 24 of his first 25 fights, but is remembered as much for taking on, though unsuccessfully, the likes of Zab Judah and Oscar De La Hoya.

9. Sharmba Mitchell. Nicknamed "Little Big Man," Mitchell won his first 31 fights, many by knockout. He became the WBA junior welterweight champion in 1998 by outpointing Khalid Rahilou in France. He kept the title until 2000, making four successful defenses. At his best, Mitchell, a 5-foot-7 southpaw, was an excellent boxer as well as a big puncher.

8. Maurice Blocker. He won the WBC welterweight title from Marlon Starling in 1990. In his next bout, Blocker lost the title when he was stopped by his friend Simon Brown. In 1991, Blocker beat Glenwood Brown to win the vacant IBF welterweight title. Blocker defended it once before moving up in weight class to challenge for the WBC light middleweight title, only to be stopped by Terry Norris.

7. Georgie Abrams. A middleweight contender in the 1940s, Abrams was a boxer-puncher who fought top talent but couldn't quite win a title. In defeat, he went the distance against Tony Zale, Marcel Cerdan, and Sugar Ray Robinson. Robinson once said that Abrams gave him his hardest fight—a supreme compliment given Robinson's top-notch opponents. For most of his career, Abrams was managed by Chris Dundee, older brother of Angelo Dundee.

6. Holly Mims. An underrated middleweight even in his prime—the 1950s and 1960s—Mims was highly respected by opponents. Mims was a tough customer who fought the best, often on short notice. He twice beat the welterweight Johnny Bratton, but lost to Dick Tiger, Joey Giardello, and Sugar Ray Robinson. A stylist, Mims compiled a record of 64-27-6 and was often ranked among the top 10 middleweights.

5. Simon Brown. Avoided by many early in his career, the Jamaican-born Brown was a dangerous puncher who knocked out Tyrone Trice to win the vacant IBF welterweight championship in 1988. Brown successfully defended the title nine times, including a unification battle in which he knocked out Maurice Blocker. Brown lost his next fight to Buddy McGirt, but came back in 1993 to score a stunning fourth-round knockout of Terry Norris to win the WBC's light middleweight title.

4. Riddick Bowe. He won the heavyweight championship in 1992 by beating Evander Holyfield over 12 rounds, and used his superior height and weight to win two of three from Holyfield in a significant boxing trilogy. He knocked out Holyfield in their third fight. Bowe would have had a much longer and more distinguished career had he been able to maintain focus on the sport and keep in better shape. He simply discarded the WBC heavyweight belt that he had won. And his career faltered after he took great punishment in two bouts with Andrew Golota, both of which were awarded to Bowe when Golota was disqualified for repeated low blows.

3. Mark Johnson. He would have attained greater recognition had he fought in a heavier weight class. As it was, Johnson, nicknamed "Too Sharp," was the first African American boxer to win a flyweight championship. He won the IBF flyweight title in May, 1996, and defended it 13 times over the next three years. A southpaw, he stood 5-foot-3 but delivered a big punch. He scored the majority of his victories by knockout.

2. Bob Foster. A Hall of Famer who was born in Albuquerque, NM, and retired there, Foster fought many of his fights out of Washington. Foster was one of the best light heavyweights of all time. He was tall at 6-foot-3, with an ample reach and an excellent knockout punch with either hand. Forty-six of his 56 victories came by knockout. He KO'd Dick Tiger in the fourth round to win the title in 1968 and successfully defended it 14 times before retiring (for the first time) in 1974. He could not match up with the great heavyweights, however. He was knocked out by both Joe Frazier and Muhammad Ali, with the world heavyweight title at stake in the Frazier bout and the NABF title on the line against Ali.

1. Sugar Ray Leonard. One of the greatest welterweights ever. The 1976 Olympic light welterweight gold medalist was born in Wilmington, SC, and grew up in Palmer Park, MD. Speed was his forte. His hand speed ranks with the best of all time; he was fast on his feet and a great defender who constantly presented angles and head movement, making him difficult to hit. A charismatic figure who held titles in five weight classes, Leonard was an outstanding closer and compiled a 5-1 record in what might be considered his most important fights: against Wilfred Benitez, Roberto Duran after losing a 15-round decision to Duran, junior middleweight champion Ayub Kalule, Thomas Hearns in their first meeting, and Marvin Hagler. Leonard's 1987 split decision over Hagler, one of the greatest middleweights, remains one of boxing's artistic beauties and classic upsets. Leonard was "Fighter of the Decade" for the 1980s, and is enshrined in the International Boxing Hall of Fame.

Note: Doc Walker played the last six years of his nine-year NFL career with the Redskins, starting at tight end on the Super Bowl XVII and Super Bowl XVIII teams. While still an active player, he did radio and television work and made a smooth transition to broadcasting after retiring in 1985. Doc is a top football analyst and has done hundreds of college and pro games on local, regional, and national television and radio. He also hosts the *Doc Walker Show* daily on Sportstalk 980. Here are 10 guys he shared the locker room with during the Redskins' glory years whom he'll never forget. He can't bring himself to put this list in any order, so we'll go alphabetically.

Jeff Bostic, Center (1980-93). "Bosco" was a ringleader and a prankster, but a real pro. Of the original Hogs, he was the last one still on the field at the end of the 1993 season. He played hard off the field, but worked hard on it.

Pete Cronan, Linebacker (1981-85). A man's man. They called him "Cronan the Barbarian" for his recklessness on special teams. He was also great for getting everybody in the mood to play a game. That's not an easy thing to do. Consider all the energy he had to expend and still have enough left to do his own job on the field.

Dexter Manley, Defensive End (1981-89). That Dexter is a character is no secret to anybody, but you may not know about a Friday game that Jeff Bostic and I used to play. "Bosco," who also has done radio and TV work during and after his playing days, was the co-host of my make-believe TV show. We would award a most valuable Redskin trophy (usually a six pack of soda) and Dexter would almost always win. And he took it seriously. We would say, "Is it true no man can block you?" And Dexter would say, "No man can block me." Every once in a while we'd give it to somebody else and Dexter would insult the winner. It was a scream.

Mark Moseley, Kicker (1974-86). Nobody took more crap and saved our butts more often. Moseley had a cosmetic rack in his locker, which we messed with constantly. We threw him in the water, duct taped him, and generally drove him nuts. While he may have been irritated, he never got mad. And when it came time to deliver the game-winning kick, he always came through.

Mark Murphy, Safety (1977-84). "Murph" was a great leader on the field and has gone on to great things off it. He's now the president of the Green Bay Packers. He is very smart, and I was smart enough to do what he did. I called him "Lobster" because every morning his skin would turn red while he sat in the hot tub for 20 to 30 minutes to get his muscles ready for the day. I started doing the same thing and it really helped. No surprise Murphy was our union leader and helped keep the team together during the 1982 strike, the year we won our first Super Bowl.

Mike Nelms, Kick Returner (1980-84). The best locker room prankster in the world. His number one move was putting Vaseline in your pants pockets while you were in the shower. He also invented the cold shot to the back. He would wait until you closed your eyes to shampoo your hair in the shower and then blast you in the back with a bucket of ice water. It felt like a thousand needles hitting you at once. Also, pity the guy (often George Starke) who went in the bathroom stall with a newspaper under his arm. That guy would always get hit with a bucket of cold water. More importantly, Nelms was a great player. He made the Pro Bowl my first three years with the Redskins. Nelms would have been a great safety, but they considered him too valuable as a return man.

John Riggins, Running Back (1976-85). "Riggo" was the star of the team, but was down with everybody. No matter how silly the prank, JR was in. And when we all went down to Dallas for the game that decided the NFC East title in 1983 wearing Army fatigues, you knew it was on when Riggo showed up wearing his.

Dan Riley, Strength Coach (1982-99). "D-Boy" had as much to do with our success as anybody who put on a uniform. He had the ability to get you through the drudgery of weight training at your best level. He'd crank up the music, talk trash, appear in costume, whatever it took to motivate. Riley could work with a group and still give you the one-on-one attention necessary. He is truly a unique individual and the best at what he does.

George Starke, Offensive Tackle (1973-84). Starke had already been in Washington for close to a decade by the time I got here. He was single and was the only Redskin who lived in the city. Starke knew his way around and was always happy to give the newcomers a D.C. initiation. He kept you safe and out of trouble and you became a "made guy" once you'd been in the hot tub that sat behind his house.

Joe Washington, Running Back (1981-84). This was a man who had star quality, but is also a quality person. He should have won the Heisman at Oklahoma, but the Sooners were on probation when he played there in the mid 70s. Little Joe (his father was a legendary high school coach in Port Arthur, Texas, and was called "Big Joe") was always humming, and we hummed along with him. But his oddest quirk was the uniform: it had to be exactly right. So he had one for pre game, one for the first half, and one for the second half. Equipment manager Jay Brunetti had to haul all that gear for every road game. The only time I saw Joe get mad was when Jay forgot to bring a belt for one of the three uniforms to a game in San Diego.

Sports and sports figures certainly have had their share of controversies. But they also show us, at times, the best of humanity. Here are ten of the top class acts, and actions, we've witnessed.

10. Art Monk. Though he was unfairly snubbed by Pro Football Hall of Fame selectors throughout the decade (finally elected in 2008), the leading receiver in Redskins history has never once uttered a bitter word of criticism about the process, or the selectors, even if they ought to be slammed, and ashamed.

9. Tom Kite. In the third round of the 1993 Kemper Open, Tom Kite happened to be paired with eventual champion Grant Waite, who was about to incur a two-shot penalty at the fourth hole for taking part of his stance in an area that was marked ground under repair. Kite stopped Waite from swinging, telling him, "we don't need any penalties, that's for sure." The next day, Waite won the tournament, finishing a shot ahead of the honorable runner-up, Tom Kite.

8. Jack Kent Cooke. Though the late Redskins owner could be a bullying ogre and a businessman who took no prisoners, he built his team a new stadium in the Maryland suburbs, the largest in the NFL, using his own money to foot the entire bill. It was named Jack Kent Cooke Stadium, also known as The Big Jack, but now is called FedEx Field.

7. Abe Pollin. At a time when gun violence was at an all-time high in the District of Columbia and many other cities around the country, the owner of Washington's NBA franchise decided to change the name of his team from Bullets to Wizards. It happened in 1997, the same year the team moved into a new downtown arena built by Pollin, then known as the Verizon Center, a venue that helped revitalize the surrounding neighborhood.

6. Manute Bol. The 7-foot-7 former NBA center was among the tallest men ever to play professional basketball, but he also had a higher calling—spending virtually every penny he ever earned to save lives and draw attention to his native Sudan, a country racked by a genocidal civil war.

5. Daniel Snyder. The Redskins owner had fired Marty Schottenheimer after the 2001 season, but when Schottenheimer's son Brian was diagnosed with thyroid cancer in 2003, Snyder, himself a survivor of the same form of cancer, immediately contacted the physicians who had treated him at the Mayo Clinic and made certain that they also would treat Brian Schottenheimer.

4. Joe Gibbs. The day before the funeral of murdered star safety Sean Taylor, Gibbs made one of the worst mistakes of his coaching career, calling back-to-back timeouts trying to ice a kicker, only to be told the second timeout was against the rules. Buffalo had been facing a 51-yard attempt that became a game-winning 36-yard chip shot, but Gibbs never hesitated in pointing the finger of blame at himself, taking full responsibility for not knowing the rule. His team then rallied around him down the stretch, winning four straight games to make the playoffs after a 5-7 start.

3. Fred Funk. The longtime PGA Tour professional and former University of Maryland golf coach has devoted himself in recent years to raising funds for the medical care and education of J.T. Townsend, a former Jacksonville high school football player who became a paraplegic after a catastrophic injury during a game in 2004. In addition to donating his own money to help build the youngster and his family a new home, Funk hosts an annual charity tournament to benefit the athlete.

2. Tiger Woods. The No. 1 golfer in the world has dedicated his signature golf tournament in Washington—the AT&T National hosted by Tiger Woods—to honoring America's military men and women. The son of a former Green Beret officer, Woods allows all military personnel free entrance to his tournament, and also donates a part of the tournament profits to various charitable causes specializing in helping wounded veterans.

1. John Thompson. On January 14, 1989, Georgetown basketball coach John Thompson walked off the court just before the tip-off of his team's game against Boston College to protest the recently passed NCAA Proposition 42 that set up minimum standards for athletes to be eligible for competition. Thompson felt Proposition 42 discriminated against black college athletes. The protest lasted for two games and touched off a national discussion on the issue, eventually leading the NCAA to modify the rule at its annual convention a year later.

Some of the how-low-can-you-go moments in recent history.

10. "Thompson the Nigger Flop Must Go." That was the ugly message on a bedsheet banner hung briefly from a window at McDonough Gymnasium on the Georgetown campus midway through the 1974 basketball season. The Hoyas had lost six of their previous seven games in John Thompson's third season as head coach, and there was grumbling on and off campus that perhaps he wasn't the right man for the job. The bedsheet was displayed during "The National Anthem" before a game against Dickinson College and was almost immediately pulled down, and the university rallied around Thompson and his players in what many believe was a turning point in the program.

9. The Bolivian Firecracker. That was the nickname some members of the media bestowed upon Marlena Cooke, the fourth wife of Redskins team owner Jack Kent Cooke. Though she once had served 3 months in a federal prison for conspiring to import cocaine into the country, they were married in 1990 but hardly lived happily ever after. In 1993, Marlena was stopped by police in Georgetown when a young man, definitely not Mr. Cooke, was sprawled on the hood of her Jaguar. They were still man and wife when Cooke died in April, 1997, though they usually lived in separate dwellings. Nevertheless, "The Firecracker" eventually settled with Cooke's estate for $20 million before being deported and now lives in a Rome villa.

8. Jaromir Jagr. The Capitals obtained the perennial all-star from the Pittsburgh Penguins in 2001 and gave him a seven-year, $77 million guaranteed extension on his contract. In return, they got a sullen, sulking, slumping, and often-injured player who showed very occasional flashes of brilliance, but mostly seemed disinterested during 2 seasons in town. After alienating most of his teammates, his coaches, and upper management, he was finally traded to the N.Y. Rangers in January, 2004, with the Capitals forced to pay about $4 million a year over the next four years to fulfill the guarantee in his contract. Upon leaving Washington, his game improved dramatically, as he scored 123 points the following season for the Rangers.

7. Training-Camp Punchout. In August of 1997, Redskins wide receiver Michael Westbrook decked his teammate, running back Stephen Davis, as both watched a training camp practice from the sidelines. Television cameras recorded the brutal incident, and weeks later it was learned that Davis apparently had called Westbrook a pejorative synonym for homosexual. Still, the team fined Westbrook $50,000 and he was ordered to apologize to Davis and his teammates in one of the uglier incidents in team history.

6. Kermit Washington. The finest basketball player in American University history, Washington is far better known as the man who threw "The Punch." On December 9, 1977, Washington and several of his Los Angeles Lakers teammates were involved in an on-court brawl with the Houston Rockets. Houston forward Rudy Tomjanovich was running toward the fray when Washington wheeled and hit him, knocking him unconscious in a pool of blood, fracturing his face and ending his season. Washington, a player with a mostly mild-mannered reputation, was suspended for 26 games, but the stigma of one of the ugliest incidents in NBA history stayed with him for years. He retired after ten seasons in the NBA in 1983 and in recent years, has drawn much praise for his charitable work in Africa.

5. Jack Pardee and Ken Houston. In 1980, Jack Pardee was completing his third and final season as head coach of the Washington Redskins and Ken Houston was in his last year as a Hall of Fame safety, a man George Allen once described as the greatest strong safety ever to play the game. Houston had announced he would be retiring at the end of a season that also saw him break his arm. He was healthy enough to play in the Redskins last home game against the Giants on December 13, but much to the chagrin of the home crowd at RFK Stadium, Pardee never put him in the game, saying afterward he'd simply forgotten and didn't realize Houston had never gone onto the field. Redskins fans were outraged, and within weeks, Pardee was fired at the end of a 6-10 season, replaced by Joe Gibbs. The Houston debacle had been one final nail in his head coaching coffin.

4. PGA Tour Abandons Washington. Almost. Though the Washington area had played host to a highly successful event since 1980, the tour left the Nation's Capital off the 2007 season schedule when it reorganized its tournament lineup to accommodate a shorter season. Booz-Allen, a McLean, Virginia-based consulting firm and tournament title sponsor for three years, had been pressing the tour for a better date on the calendar, but company officials were stunned the day Tour commissioner Tim Finchem announced the new schedule and said Washington's event would be moved to its fall schedule. Booz-Allen then decided not to return as a title sponsor, and Washington was out, though not for long. In January, 2007, the International tournament in Colorado folded, and the tour announced several weeks later that Tiger Woods would be hosting a new event in Washington, sponsored by AT&T.

3. Norv and The Danny. The Redskins had just lost a critical late-season game to the N.Y. Giants in 2000, their fourth defeat in five games, when team owner Dan Snyder told head coach Norv Turner he wanted to meet with him after the game. Turner waited at the stadium for two hours, but Snyder never showed up, so he finally left the building. The next day, Snyder fired Turner even though the owner was constantly meddling with the club, even insisting on signing quarterback Jeff George, who became a divisive force in the locker room. The Redskins still had a chance to make the playoffs when Snyder fired Turner, replacing him with interim Terry Robiskie when defensive coordinator Ray Rhodes refused the job. But the Redskins lost two of their last three games to finish 8-8 and out of the postseason.

2. George Allen Goes West. Late in the 1977 season, Redskins coach George Allen announced that, for the first time anyone could remember, he was going to miss a Saturday walk-through practice to watch a college game at the University of Richmond, where his son Bruce was the starting punter. But Allen never went south. Instead he headed to Dulles Airport for a quick trip to Los Angeles, where he secretly negotiated with then Rams owner Carroll Rosenbloom about returning to coach the Rams for the 1978 season. Allen had also been negotiating with the Redskins on a new deal, but eventually was fired by team president Edward Bennett Williams. Unbeknownst to Williams, however, Allen had already agreed to coach the Rams. During the Rams' training camp before the 1978 season, Allen managed to alienate a number of veteran players as well as several team executives, including Rosenbloom's son Steve, and was fired before he ever coached a regular season game. Allen never again coached in the NFL.

1. Baseball Leaves the Nation's Capital. Three years after he outbid Bob Hope to purchase the Washington Senators for $9.4 million, Minneapolis trucking magnate Robert Short announced late in the 1971 season he was moving the team to Arlington, Texas because of poor attendance. Of course, he had helped decimate the team with a disastrous trade in 1970 to acquire pitcher Denny McLain from the Detroit Tigers, who then lost a league high 22 games. The final game at RFK Stadium nearly turned into a riot as fans stormed onto the field in the ninth inning with their team leading the N.Y. Yankees, 7-5, forcing umpires to forfeit the contest, giving the Yanks a 9-0 victory. It turned out that Short had negotiated a sweetheart deal for himself in Texas that included a guaranteed $7.5 million radio/TV rights package. Short's treachery turned him into the most reviled sports figure in Washington history and led to 33 years of no baseball in the Nation's Capital until the Montreal Expos became the Washington Nationals in 2005.

He was only 34-years-old with no sports experience when he took over as owner of the Redskins in 1999. But that didn't stop him from believing he had things figured out. No owner in NFL history has spent more and won less than the boy wonder, whose first decade of ownership has been marked by impatience and poor decisions. Snyder's Skins had only three winning records in his first nine seasons with only two playoff victories during those years. Here are the top 10 moves that came back to bite him.

10. Berating Norv. This occurred after Snyder's sixth game as owner of the Redskins. They had lost 38-20 at Dallas, which ended a four game winning streak, but was the second loss of the season to the Cowboys. Details of exactly what was said between Snyder and coach Norv Turner, are known only by the two men involved. But we do know that the media was kept waiting for Norv for half an hour after the game ended, and that Turner showed up in the locker room to talk to the players with reddened eyes. Brian Mitchell (the kick returner on that team) says that it appeared Norv had been crying and that team's confidence in their coach dropped considerably after that.

9. Firing Frank Herzog. During their glory years, the Redskins had one of the most popular radio teams in the NFL. Hall of Famers Sonny Jurgensen and Sam Huff teamed with local TV sports anchor Frank Herzog to become three of the main identities of the organization. All you had to say was, "Sonny, Sam, and Frank," and everybody knew exactly what you were talking about. One of the great things about them was they were free to speak their minds; they weren't paid by the Redskins. Herzog, in fact, in his role as a reporter with Channel 9 in 1981, asked 0-5 coach Joe Gibbs if he feared for his job. But that kind of candor apparently wasn't appreciated by Snyder.

Herzog was fired after his 25th season as the play-by-play voice of the Skins and replaced by team employee Larry Michael. Besides weak play-by-play skills, Michael is a company man, and you never hear anybody say, "Sonny, Sam, and Larry."

8. Firing Norv Turner in 2000. You could certainly make the case that Norv should have been fired before Snyder even took over the team. However, Danny boy did bring him back after the Redskins won the NFC East title in '99, expecting even better things the following season after spending wildly on free agents. A 9-7 home loss to the Giants was the Redskins' fourth loss in five games, but they were still in the playoff hunt at 7-6. Snyder thought he could salvage the season by firing the head coach. Great move. The Skins lost their next two by scores of 32-13 and 24-3 at Dallas and Pittsburgh. They finished the season 8-8 and out of the playoffs.

7. Firing Marty Schottenheimer. Maybe this was a bad marriage from the start, but Snyder insisted Marty was his man. Schottenheimer told Snyder the only way he'd become head coach of the team was with complete control, which he received. The start was terrible, with the Redskins beginning the year (2001) 0-5. But they won their next five and were amazingly still in the playoff hunt in mid-December. The 8-8 finish should have been a sign that the team had turned the corner and were poised to be very good in 2002. Maybe so, but Snyder had decided he didn't like being left out of the day to day operations of his team and told Marty he was taking back some of the control he'd handed him. Marty balked and was shown the door. The Skins wouldn't play a playoff game for four more years.

6. Signing Jeff George. One of the first things Snyder asked when he took over the Redskins, was could he rescind the trade that had brought in Brad Johnson from Minnesota? Good thing he couldn't, because Johnson threw for four thousand yards and 24 touchdowns that season as the Redskins won the NFC East. That apparently wasn't good enough for Snyder. He absolutely had to have the man with the million-dollar arm and ten-cent head. Snyder signed the free agent George for more money than he was paying his Pro Bowl quarterback. The friction caused by the George signing proved to be another factor in the terrible 2000 season.

5. Signing Deion Sanders. Another shiny object of Snyder's affection. Dallas knew Deion was done when they decided not to re-sign him after the 1999 season. But Danny had to have him. Deion wasn't terrible as a cornerback, but was ineffective as a returner. Still, that wasn't the worst of it. When asked about the big contract Deion received, the answer from player personnel director Vinny Cerrato was, "We're fine as long as Deion doesn't retire." Deion retired. After one season on the job, he said he couldn't play for new coach Marty Schottenheimer because, "I can't trust him as far as I can throw him." It cost the Redskins $8 million in dead cap money.

4. Head Coach Pepper Rogers? This was denied by Snyder in a 2004 radio interview on Sportstalk 980, but sources insist it actually happened. Rogers had been a successful head coach in college and the United States Football League, but was in his 70s by the time he hooked up with Snyder as part of the Federal Express sponsorship on the stadium. Snyder apparently liked what he was hearing from the feisty Pepper, and according to reports, offered him the job as head coach when he fired Norv Turner with three games to go in the 2000 season. The idea was reportedly floated by several assistant coaches, who told Snyder the team would never play for Pepper; it would be considered a joke. Instead, Snyder made Terry Robiske the interim coach. At the news conference to announce the move, Pepper told the media, "Football is a game of fight." Thanks.

3. Issuing Bobby Mitchell's Number to a Back-up Tight End. Mitchell was

entering his 40th season in the Redskins organization when he was summarily slapped in the face. Before Steve Spurrier's first season as head coach in 2002, some of the new players who came in picked jersey numbers that had been unofficially retired. Spurrier said he didn't see what the big deal was when Shane Matthews took Sonny Jurgensen's number 9 and Danny Wuerffel grabbed Joe Theismann's number 7. But Redskin fans did see the big deal and Spurrier finally had those players take other numbers. Yet, nobody corrected the injustice when the number 49 Mitchell wore during his Hall of Fame career went to backup tight end Leonard Stephens. Mitchell kept his mouth shut during the season, but resigned at the end of the year, citing the number fiasco as a major factor in wanting to separate himself from the organization.

2. Danny World. There's nothing like the combination of greed and stupidity. Snyder

came up with the idea of charging fans to watch training camp practices at Redskins Park in 2000. He figured the dollars he'd bring in would offset the competitive disadvantage such a move would bring. The admission charge allowed scouts from other teams to buy tickets and watch; something that's not allowed when fans are admitted for free. Safety Mark Carrier later said it set the team back because they weren't able to practice on the field what they'd been learning in the classroom. The Skins finished 8-8 and the idea was scrapped after a year.

1. Hiring Steve Spurrier with Himself as General Manager. With the prop-

er structure, Spurrier might have been successful as a head coach in the NFL. He had done great things in college, including winning a National Championship and even winning at Duke. But Spurrier proved to be ill-suited for the pro game, and with Snyder calling the shots on players, drowned. After seasons of 7-9 and 5-11, Spurrier phoned in his resignation from the golf course.

Hopes were high when Steve Spurrier became the Redskins' 25th head coach in 2002. His pass-oriented offense had produced a National Championship at the University of Florida and it was hoped he'd bring some excitement to a team coming off a pair of .500 seasons. While Spurrier proved to be a failure on the field (12-20 in two seasons), he was incredibly honest and a real hoot as a quote-giver. Here are his top 10.

10. "He looked great in Osaka." All the games Spurrier coached in college counted. He didn't grasp the concept that the outcome of preseason games didn't matter. The first one he had as coach of the Redskins was the American Bowl in Osaka, Japan, against the 49ers. Spurrier put his former Florida Heisman Trophy winner Danny Wuerffel in during the second half and watched him light up the scoreboard in a 38-7 win. Never mind it was against third and fourth stringers who would soon be driving beer trucks. So when Wuerffel struggled during the regular season, the "Ol' Ball Coach" issued this one to defend his insistence on playing Wuerffel.

9. "Which field would you like to practice on?" Spurrier's question to defensive coordinator Marvin Lewis. At Florida, where he had about a hundred players on the roster, the offense and defense practiced on separate fields. Lewis politely told him that NFL rosters had only 53 players and there weren't enough bodies to hold separate practices. The offense needed to work against the defense.

8. "Patrick will be ready to play this time next year." Figuring he was all set at quarterback with his former Gators Wuerffel and Shane Matthews, he told Sportstalk 980 that he really felt no need to play rookie first-round pick Patrick Ramsey in 2002. That idea lasted exactly three weeks. After watching his team lose 37-7 to Philadelphia and 20-10 at San Francisco, Ramsey was bumped up to backup for week four at Tennessee. Ramsey replaced an injured Wuerffel in the first quarter and led the Skins to a 31-14 win. He started the next two.

7. "They were cheap and available." Why he signed former Florida receivers Chris Doering and Jacques Green before his first season.

6. "Hindsight is always 50-50." Why he wouldn't second guess himself for a decision made during the game.

5. "Rob Johnson? He doesn't even know which way to turn his head." The answer to what Sportstalk 980 host Steve Czaban thought was a mundane question in 2003 on how ready backup quarterback Rob Johnson was to play, given that starter Patrick Ramsey was taking a beating in Spurrier's pass-happy offense. Two days later, sure enough, Johnson was released and Tim Hasselbeck was signed.

4. "We should win our division; there're only three other teams in it." Spurrier was full of bravado at his introductory news conference. As it turned out, the Redskins finished third in the division both of his seasons, winning only one game each year against division opponents.

3. "He's not in jail, is he?" This was in response to the question of why he would sign Darrell Russell midway through the 2003 season. Russell was coming off an 18-month suspension for substance abuse and prosecutors had recently dropped criminal charges against him; they couldn't prove that Russell had videotaped a woman being raped by two of his friends. Russell was released at the end of the season and died a few years later in a car accident.

2. "What do I have to give for optimism for next year? I can't think of anything right now." A response to a question by Sportstalk 980 host Andy Pollin, as Spurrier prepared for the final game of the 2003 season, as to what Spurrier could give the fans to be optimistic about for the 2004 season. Two days later, with three years left on a five-year contract, Spurrier phoned in his resignation from the golf course.

1. "Well we wound up 5-11, not the best, but not the worst either." Spurrier's opening remark in what turned out to be his last news conference as coach of the Redskins. It began at noon a day after the 2003 season ended and was over by 12:05. Thanks for the memories, Ball Coach.

10. "What I want is everything. I want the talent, a kid who can run and leap and shoot, but I want him to have enough intelligence, discipline, character or whatever so that he'll walk when I tell him to, run when I want him to, pass if that's what I want. Without talent, all the character in the world won't do it, but talent alone isn't enough." —Georgetown basketball coach John Thompson on what qualities he looked for in recruiting a player for his team.

9. "No Mas." —Roberto Duran to referee Octavio Meyran in the eighth round of his controversial welterweight title fight against D.C. boxer Sugar Ray Leonard at the New Orleans SuperDome on November 25, 1980. "No more" was the translation, and with Duran wanting to quit 17 seconds into the round, the fight was stopped and Leonard was declared the winner by a technical knockout in the second of three fights between the two men.

8. "I gave him an unlimited budget, and he exceeded it." —Edward Bennett Williams, the late Redskins team president, on George Allen's extravagant spending.

7. "Let's go to the videotape." —Pioneering Washington sportscaster Warner Wolf, one of the first to make extensive use of taped highlights in his nightly sports segment on Washington's CBS affiliate, WTOP Channel 9.

6. "I'm bored, I'm broke, and I'm back." —Hall of Fame running back John Riggins, when he ended a season-long holdout and reported to the Redskins training camp in 1981.

5. "Losing is like death." —George Allen, usually any time the Redskins lost.

4. "Come on Sandy baby, loosen up. You're too uptight." —A teeny-bit-tipsy John Riggins to Supreme Court Justice Sandra Day O'Connor, sitting at his table during a Washington Press Club dinner in 1985.

3. "He said, 'He's gone.'" —Redskins owner Daniel Snyder recalling what Sean Taylor's agent, Drew Rosenhaus, told him in an early morning telephone call informing him that the Pro Bowl Washington safety had died at the age of 24 a few hours earlier after being shot in a botched burglary attempt at his home on December 3, 2007.

2. "The future is now." —George Allen's mantra when he took over as head coach of the Washington Redskins in 1971 and immediately began trading draft choices for veteran players, the better to win immediately rather than build for the long term.

1. "Bitch set me up." —Washington Mayor Marion Barry to FBI agents and D.C. police who arrested him on drug charges during a sting operation at Washington's Vista Hotel on January 18, 1990. Barry's former girlfriend, Hazel "Rasheeda" Moore— the so-called bitch he was talking about—was in the room with him. At the time, Barry was in the final stages of completing a deal with Redskins owner Jack Kent Cooke to build a new stadium in the District of Columbia. Barry was forced to resign soon after his arrest and Cooke could not come to a similar deal with his successor, Sharon Pratt Dixon. He eventually decided to build his own stadium in Landover, MD.

Note: Growing up in Bethesda during the Redskins' glory years in the 1980s, Ryan Kuehl, like most area football-playing kids, dreamed of playing for the burgundy and gold. This kid made his dream come true. After graduating from Whitman High School and the University of Virginia, Kuehl caught on with the Redskins as a free agent in 1996 as an undersized defensive tackle. Smart as he is tough, after a couple of years as a Redskin Kuehl realized he wouldn't be in the league long trying to get by 340-pound offensive linemen and learned the skill of long-snapping. It's earned him employment with the Cleveland Browns and New York Giants for more than a decade. At press time, Kuehl hadn't quite achieved the ultimate thrill of playing in a Super Bowl, but he did earn a ring as a member of the Giants on injured reserve in 2007. Here are the reasons that made playing for the Redskins so special for a hometown boy.

13. First game. My first regular-season action in Buffalo against the Bills in 1996 is something I will never forget. We got run all over, but for the few plays I was in, I made a tackle and stopped the ball when it came to my side.

12. First RFK Stadium game. It was a preseason game against the Bengals in '96. Growing up here in the 80s, that place was the Vatican to me. I watched so many players come out of that mysterious dugout, and now I got to do it . . . unbelievable! My tired legs felt like jelly from training camp, but I was energized.

11. Solo tackle for a loss on Barry Sanders. It was the fifth game ever played at Jack Kent Cooke Stadium (now FedEx Field). I am pretty sure I tripped and fell, and he just ran in to me. But a TFL is a TFL.

10. Practicing against big Tre Johnson. It was no fun at all, but he and I actually got along real well. He was some kind of beast (about 340 pounds), but he always was respectful and worked hard. I always had a ton of respect for how he went about things, and still do. Plus, I never wanted to piss him off!

9. Starting at Dallas on Thanksgiving in 1997. A career highlight. Not sure of my stats, but I played pretty damn well against Nate Newton! I know I got Emmitt Smith for a loss and got to Aikman. I really need to check up on those stats and see if I did what I think I did.

8. My first start. We were playing at Chicago in the middle of the '97 season. I played alongside Marc Boutte and we stuffed up the Bears' running game pretty much all day. I think I puked three times before the first play, but it was worth it! We won the game and that meant I got another start.

7. Sonny, Sam, and Frank. Hearing a tape of the legendary radio team talking about my play was really cool. For a young guy growing up in this town, those guys were my connection to the Skins. Of course, it was not as cool when I played like dog crap.

6. Introduction by JKC Stadium announcer Phil Hochberg. I was good friends with Phil's son growing up and was in his house all the time. What a thrill it was to run out of the tunnel in your hometown with your friends and family watching and be introduced as a starter. I wish more kids got to live out that type of dream. No matter how long I played, nobody would ever be able to take that away from me.

5. Working with trainer Bubba Tyer and strength coach Dan Riley. Man, those guys were great people. I remember one day when I was on the bike and Bubba walked by, put his hand on my shoulder and said, "I like your style young man. You are going to be in this league for awhile." What a thing to say to a young guy trying to forge an identity within the NFL and the Redskins. I never forgot that, and 12 years later, I think he was right. Those guys were what the Redskins were all about in the 1980s and 90s.

4. Darrell Green. I grew up rooting for him. He is such a class act and so respected, it was just a great thrill to get to play with him for a few years. The best football player and person this town has ever seen.

3. Tony Kornheiser column mention. Tony wished me a happy new year in the *Washington Post* in December of 1997. He always liked how I managed to acquire a deli sandwich in my locker after games, but before the media came in. One of the clubhouse guys would always put a sandwich, chips, and a few Bud Lights in there for postgame nourishment and hydration. When Tony would come up and ask questions, I was always munching away while talking. I guess he thought that was unique. I always thought it was unique to get to talk to him, so maybe we were even.

2. Skipping the line at Third Edition in Georgetown. The coolest part of all. There was no finer establishment for a young, single professional to be in than Third's on a Friday or Saturday night. Throw the "local kid plays for the Redskins" angle in to the mix and you take it to another stratosphere! For the sake of marriages across this town of ours, I will not divulge any of the details, but I have not forgotten ANYTHING!!

1. Family. Making your parents proud and representing my family name as best I could was my whole focus and goal while playing in D.C. So many people supported me over the years, I just wanted to make everyone proud of being associated with me. That was the best motivation I could have ever imagined.

Note: John Ricca (son of former Redskins defensive tackle Jim Ricca) was a two-way star at Georgetown Prep, where he led his team to undefeated seasons as a junior and senior. He went on to become an All-American defensive end at Duke. Drafted by the New York Jets in 1974, Ricca played professionally in the NFL, WFL, and CFL. He then spent 15 years as head coach at St. John's High School in D.C. and four more at St. John's Prospect Hall in Frederick, Maryland. He currently coaches at Catholic University. Here are his top picks based on a lifetime of playing and coaching football in the area.

Top 10 Private School Players

10 a. Mike Kruczek QB (St. Johns '71, Boston College, Steelers, Redskins). Was an All-American at BC and played on three Super Bowl championship teams in Pittsburgh.

10 b. Jay Williams DT (St. Johns '90, Wake Forrest, Rams, Panthers, Dolphins). Was a four-year starter at Wake and played 12 years in the NFL.

10 c. Tyoka Jackson DL (McNamara '89, Penn State, Bucs, Rams, Lions). Best defensive lineman I ever coached against. Played 15 years in the NFL.

9. Marcus Mason RB (Georgetown Prep '05, Youngstown State, Redskins). All-time leading rusher in Maryland history.

8. Joe Howard-Johnson WR (Carroll '85, Notre Dame, Vikings, Redskins). Tremendous all-around player. Also played basketball at Notre Dame.

7. Marvin Graves (Carroll '89, Syracuse, CFL). Best high school quarterback I ever saw.

6. Terence Wilkins WR (O'Connell '94, Virginia, Colts, Rams). Did everything for O'Connell and enjoyed a long NFL career as a return man.

5. Jamal Williams LB (Carroll '94, Oklahoma State, Chargers). Played linebacker at 280 pounds in high school! All-Pro with San Diego.

4. Brian Westbrook RB (DeMatha '98, Villanova, Eagles). Hurt his senior year in high school. Dominated in college and became an All-Pro in Philadelphia.

3. Lawrence Moten WR (Carroll '90, Syracuse, Grizzlies, Wizards). The best player I ever coached against. Is the leading scorer in Big East history.

2. Eric Metcalf RB (O'Connell '85, Texas, Browns, Falcons, Chargers, Cardinals, Redskins, Packers). Maybe the most dominant Catholic league player ever. World class track athlete.

1. Jonathon Ogden (St. Albans '92, UCLA, Ravens). Future Hall of Famer. May be the best ever. Also a college track star.

Top 10 Public School Players

10 a. Eric Seivers TE (Washington-Lee '79, Maryland, Chargers, Rams, Patriots). Had a long NFL career.

10 b. Josh Cribbs RB (Dunbar '01, Kent St., Browns). All-Pro return man.

10 c. Ebenezer Ekuban DE (Bladensburg '95, North Carolina, Cowboys, Broncos). Has enjoyed a long NFL career.

10 d. Mark Robinson S (Kennedy '80, Penn State, Chiefs, Bucs). Hard-hitting safety who had a good NFL career.

10 e. Jerry Porter WR (Coolidge '96, West Virginia, Raiders, Jaguars). Was a quarterback in high school who became a great wide receiver.

9. LaMont Jordan RB (Oxon Hill '97, Maryland, Jets, Raiders). Dominant runner who holds the University of Maryland all-time rushing record. Has become a good NFL running back.

8. Derrick Williams WR (Eleanor Roosevelt '05, Penn State). Was the number-one prospect in the nation who has had a great career at Penn State. Will be in the NFL.

7. Bob Windsor TE (Blair '63, Montgomery College, Kentucky, 49ers, Patriots). Was the first Montgomery College player to make it to the NFL.

6. Richie Anderson RB (Sherwood '89, Penn State, Jets, Cowboys). The best all-around back I ever saw in high school.

5. Shawn Springs CB (Springbook '93, Ohio State, Seahawks, Redskins). Number-two pick of the 1997 NFL draft. Has enjoyed a strong career.

4. Julian Peterson DE (Crossland '96, Michigan State, 49ers, Seahawks). Has become an All-Pro in Seattle.

3. Vernon Davis TE (Dunbar '02, Maryland, 49ers). Freakish physical specimen. Should be a star in the NFL.

t-1. Shawne Merriman DE (Douglass '02, Maryland, Chargers). All-Pro. May be the best pass rusher in the NFL.

t-1. Mike Curtis LB (Richard Montgomery '61, Duke, Colts, Seahawks, Redskins). All-Pro in Baltimore. Started on their 1970 Super Bowl team.

Hit Their Peak in High School

10. Ahmad Brooks (Hylton '02)

9. Tyrone Jackson (DeMatha '87)

8. Derrick Fenner (Oxon Hill '86)

7. Andre Jones (DeMatha '88)

6. Billy Maloney (Georgetown Prep '72)

5. Terry Caulley (Patuxent '02)

4. Ricky Summerour (Richard Montgomery '71)

3. Marc Bason (Gaithersburg '90)

t-1. Clement Stokes (Carroll '94)

t-1. Chris Kelley (Seneca Valley '00)

Note: Herman Boone coached the 1971 T.C. Williams High School team that won the Virginia state football championship, going 13-0 and outscoring opponents by a 338-38 margin, with nine shutouts. The Alexandria team and its coach were immortalized in the wildly successful motion picture, *Remember the Titans*, starring Denzel Washington, although Disney took a number of big-time liberties with the storyline. "They got a lot of it right," Boone said. "But it's Hollywood, and the way it was explained to me, it happens all the time." Now retired, splitting time between homes in Washington and South Florida and playing a lot of golf in both locales, Boone offered a number of truth/fiction examples, the most important, he emphasized, that he was definitely much better looking than Denzel Washington.

10. Alexandria in 1971 was hardly the small, sleepy "Mississippi Burning" racially explosive town depicted in the film. "There were racial divisions," Boone said, "but not as much as they showed."

9. T.C. Williams had actually been racially integrated in 1965, when the school first opened its doors, not before the start of the 1971 season when Alexandria closed several other smaller high schools and consolidated the students under one roof. There also were no racial protests in front of the school on the first day of class in 1971.

8. That was not a brick thrown through the front window of Boone's home. It was a commode, and the real-life Boone never went looking for his rifle, because he didn't own a gun.

7. The opponent in the state championship game was not Arlington's Washington and Lee High School and its legendary coach, Ed Henry. The Titans that year actually faced W&L in the eighth week of the regular season and prevailed, 34-0. In the state title game, they beat Andrew Lewis High of Salem, coached by Eddie Joyce, in a 27-0 blowout.

6. Bill Yoast, Boone's assistant and former head coach at Hammond, one of the schools consolidated into T.C. Williams, was not denied entry into the Virginia High School Hall of Fame because of his association with Boone and the Titans. At the time, there was no Virginia High School Hall of Fame.

5. The Titans did not sing and dance in their pre-game warm-ups. Mostly, they did jumping jacks and stretching exercises.

4. The bigoted movie character, Ray Budds, who was kicked off the team by team captain Gerry Bertier in a dramatic locker room confrontation, never existed, and the incident never happened.

3. Boone did not wake his team up at 3 a.m. during training camp for an inspirational run through the cemetery at the Gettysburg battlefield, though the team did attend its summer training camp at Gettysburg College. Boone did take the players on a regular daylight battlefield tour, with a guide, not the coach, doing most of the talking.

2. Bill Yoast's cute-as-a-button movie daughter, Sheryl, was not quite the football fanatic in real life. She occasionally attended practices and came to the games, but did not help her father break down film or draw up plays. In real life, she also lived with her mother and three sisters, not with Yoast, portrayed as a single father in the film, and she never went to Boone's house to play with his daughter. They were not friends.

1. Star player and high school All-American linebacker Gerry Bertier was involved in a car accident after the state championship game had been played. He actually lost control of his mother's new Corvaire while driving home from the football team banquet and was paralyzed for the rest of his life. In the movie, Bertier's accident occurred the week before the state title game and he was hospitalized, a win-one-for-the-Gipper inspiration to his teammates. Not true. He played in the state title game. Ten years later, he was killed in another accident by a drunk driver. At the time, he was a passionate advocate for the disabled and a past gold medalist in the national Wheelchair Olympics, coached by his friend, Bill Yoast.

The Top 10 University of Maryland Football Players Since 1972

Why '72? That was the year Jerry Claiborne took over as head coach and the program finally became respectable. Yes, we realize Jim Tatum had great teams in the late 40s and early 50s, winning Maryland's only National Title in 1953. But let's understand something. That "National Title" was voted on *before* Maryland lost to Oklahoma 7-0 in the Orange Bowl. And in the 16 years in between the time Tatum left and Claiborne arrived, Maryland had only two winning seasons. So with all due respect to the pre-'72 stars like Dick Modzelewski, Jack Scarbath and Bob Pellegrini, here are our selections for the top 10 players of the "modern Maryland football" era.

10. Steve Atkins RB (75, 76, 77, 78). Atkins had his best numbers as a senior, running for more than 1,200 yards, including a 98-yard touchdown run against Clemson. He was named honorable mention All-American that year. But his sophomore year is one of those "what might have been" stories. In an odd year where Penn State wasn't on the schedule, the Terps were rolling through an undefeated season when Atkins hurt his knee midway through the season. They still finished the regular season unbeaten, but lost to Houston in the Cotton Bowl 30-21. With a healthy Atkins, Maryland may have been able to keep the ball out of the wishbone hands of Houston and finished its only unbeaten season. A National Title wasn't possible. Tony Dorsett and Pitt took care of that by winning the Sugar Bowl.

9. Lamont Jordan RB (97, 98, 99, 00). Jordan holds most of the Maryland rushing records including attempts (807), yards (4,147) and 100-yard games (18). His problem was timing. Jordan came along during the four-year Ron Vanderlinden era and played in only 15 wins over his entire career. He had high hopes of making a bowl game as a junior, but after a 5-2 start, Maryland lost its last four including the homecoming game to Duke (Duke!) to finish 5-6.

8. D'Qwell Jackson LB (02, 03, 04, 05). Yes Shawne "Lights Out" Merriman was from the same era, but Jackson was slightly more distinguished as a college player. He made several All-American teams as a senior and was named the team's MVP as a junior and a senior.

7. Chuck Faucette LB (83, 84, 85, 86). One of the most emotional players ever to play at Maryland. After the famous game at the Orange Bowl in 1984, when the Terps came from being down 31-0 to Miami in the first half to win 42-40, Faucette literally passed out. He was an honorable mention All-American his last three years at Maryland and was named the team's MVP as a senior.

6. J.D. Maarleveld OT (82, 83, 84, 85). One of only five players at Maryland since '72 to be named consensus first-team All-American in 1985. That was after overcoming Hodgkins disease. He won the Brian Piccolo Award for that in 1984. Maarleveld was a huge security blanket for three quarterbacks who went on to play in the NFL—Boomer Esiason, Frank Reich and Stan Gelbaugh. And when *Sport* magazine made Maryland the 1985 preseason pick for the national title, Maarleveld was featured on the cover.

5. Vernon Davis TE (03, 04, 05). After being named first-team All-American as a junior it only made sense for Davis to turn pro. He was the sixth pick of the draft by the 49ers. In his last year, Davis caught 51 passes for 871 yards and six touchdowns. He was a finalist for the John Mackey award as the top tight end in the country.

4. Boomer Esiason QB (80, 81, 82, 83). Has become even more accomplished as a broadcaster than he was as a football player. And that's saying quite a bit. The lefty quarterbacked coach Bobby Ross' first two Maryland teams to a pair of 8-4 finishes in '82 and '83. As a senior he led the Terps to a 6-0 ACC record, including a 28-26 upset of North Carolina, which was ranked third in the country at the time. After being drafted in the second round of the '84 draft by Cincinnati, Boomer went on to play 14 years in the NFL. His most recent contribution to the program was getting athletic director Debbie Yow to finally wise up and hire Ralph Friedgen as head coach in 2000.

3. Joe Campbell DE (73, 74, 75, 76). Was a consensus first-team All-American as a senior and was the leader of a defense that pitched shutouts in its last three games on their way to an 11-0 regular season. Campbell was the seventh pick of the 1977 draft and won a Super Bowl with the Oakland Raiders.

2. E.J. Henderson LB (99, 00, 01, 02). Is the best linebacker in the history of the school and is one of the best linebackers in the history of the ACC, which is saying something when you consider North Carolina produced Lawrence Taylor. He is Maryland's only two-time consensus first-team All-American and was ACC player of the year as a junior. Henderson was the defensive leader of two of the best teams in Maryland history in '01 and '02. They combined to go 21-3 with a 30-3 Peach Bowl win over Tennessee and an appearance against Florida in the BCS Orange Bowl.

1. Randy White DE (72, 73, 74). One of the best defensive linemen in the history of college football. As a senior he rang up all the awards: Outland, Lombardi, ACC Player of the Year, unanimous first-team All-American. He is in both the College and Pro Football Halls of Fame. White was so quick off the line that he often met the running back as he was taking the handoff from the quarterback. Believe it or not, White was recruited out of Delaware to play fullback. He was one of the first Maryland players to discover the value of the weight room and became known for bench-pressing 500 pounds when weightlifting was still considered an option for football players.

Note: Jimmy Roberts is a 1979 graduate of the University of Maryland as well as an alumnus of Bentley's, a popular campus watering hole that once employed him. He got plenty of up close and personal looks at Maryland football players when they bellied up to the bar before leaving College Park for far more gainful employment. That would include 12 years as an ESPN journalist before joining NBC Sports in 2000 as an award-winning studio host, reporter, and essayist.

10. Gary Williams. I know, I know. He's a basketball guy. But if he's got any eligibility left, he'd make a great strong safety.

9. Mike Sochko. How could we possibly be so bad against Penn State? Isn't 1-35-1 a misprint in the media guide? Sadly, no. We almost beat them one year in the late 1970s, but Sochko missed the kick.

8. Ed Modzelewski. An All-American fullback on the 1952 team, I remember seeing him pictured in one of those silly "stop action" poses in a frame in the Cole Field House hallway. I had to ask how to pronounce his name, but it was the first time I had a sense that we had a long-standing and proud football tradition.

7. Randy White. Everybody's All-American defensive lineman and a Hall of Famer for the Dallas Cowboys. Forget about the fact that he may well have been one of the best to ever play the game. When I got to school, the urban legend was that he had once ripped a urinal out of the wall at "Town Hall." Now that's a football player!

6. Ralph Friedgen. Da Coach, a very big man on campus who finally brought some respectability back to the program. He actually came home to his alma mater when he had a lot of other choices. How could you not love that?

5. Mark Manges. My freshman year, he quarterbacked the team to the Cotton Bowl (back when the Cotton Bowl actually mattered) and a shot at a top ranking. I thought this was the way it was supposed to be every year.

4. Boomer Esiason. Isn't he on everybody's list? An All-American quarterback who loved to yak; a journalist's delight who now gets paid to talk by CBS.

3. Tim Brant. Terp for life, talented broadcaster, and an outstanding linebacker back in the 1970s. Great guy, good friend. Someone told me he named his oldest child Testudo.

2. Charlie Wysocki. A great running back; 28 years after his last carry, he's still Maryland's second-leading rusher. He was electric, but a tragic figure too, a manic-depressive whose life story after football was terribly sad. Got to know him when I did a feature on him for ESPN in 1990.

1. Peter Zachary. A defensive back from 1973-1975, "Zach" was the older brother of one of my closest friends. Watching him play and rooting for him gave me my first real connection to Terps football, and I've been a huge fan ever since.

Although Maryland has competed in basketball for nearly a century, it wasn't until Lefty Driesell arrived in 1969 that the "Terps" became a national power. As you can see from this top–10 list, most of the top players made their mark in the last 40 years.

10. Walt Williams, 1988–92. The "Wizard" did more than any other player to save the program after the firing of Bob Wade and the probation that followed. Knowing that he wouldn't have a chance to be on television or participate in postseason play, Williams stuck around, passing up the chance to transfer or go to the NBA. As the only real scorer left, Williams averaged 18.7 and 26.8 points a game his last two years and was named All-American as a senior. He was the seventh pick of the '92 draft and had a long pro career.

9. Juan Dixon, 1998–02. A great player on the court and a great story off it. Both of his parents died of AIDS from intravenous drug use, but he overcame the odds. Coach Gary Williams was criticized for signing the skinny guard out of Baltimore, but after a redshirt season, Dixon went on to become the star of Maryland's only NCAA championship team. He's the only player in NCAA history with 2,000 points, 300 steals and 200 three-pointers.

8. Gene Shue, 1951–54. Best known as a coach with the Bullets and 76ers, he could also play. Averaging 22 points a game as a junior and senior, Shue was an All-American both years and was the third pick of the NBA draft by the Philadelphia Warriors.

7. Albert King, 1977–81. Was one of Lefty's greatest recruiting scores. He was considered the number-one high school player in the country, averaging 38 points and 22 rebounds a game, when Lefty brought him down from Brooklyn. King averaged more than 17 points a game during his four years in College Park. Although he may have made a mistake staying for his senior year (his scoring and rebounding numbers dropped by four points and one rebound a game) he still was an All-American and the 10th pick of the NBA draft by New Jersey.

6. Buck Williams, 1978–81. Despite being only 6-foot-7, he was one of the great rebounders in NCAA history. Averaged 11 rebounds over his three years to go with a scoring average of 13.6. Despite teaming with King for three years, Maryland failed to win an ACC championship or get to the Final Four, but they made up one of the most feared duos in school history.

5. Joe Smith, 1993–95. The greatest surprise in school history. Was not highly recruited coming out of Norfolk, Virginia, but proved to be an instant star. Smith averaged 19 points and 11 rebounds as a freshman and was Player of the Year as a sophomore. Got Maryland to two Sweet 16s and was the number-one pick of the NBA draft.

4. Len Elmore, 1971–74. Helped to put Maryland on the basketball map when he signed out of Power Memorial High School, Kareem Abdul-Jabbar's alma mater, in 1970. At 6-foot-9 he was an incredible rebounder and was named All-American as a senior. After playing 10 years in the pros, Elmore became the first former pro basketball player to graduate from Harvard Law School.

3. Tom McMillen, 1971–74. Decades before LeBron James, McMillen became the first high school player to appear on the cover of *Sports Illustrated*. McMillen originally committed to North Carolina, but Lefty swooped in and sweet-talked his mother into getting him to go to Maryland. McMillen was a three-time All-American and a three-time Academic All-American. After a year of study at Oxford as part of his Rhodes Scholarship, McMillen played 11 years in the NBA and was elected to the U.S. Congress in 1986.

2. John Lucas, 1972–76. Was part of the first freshman class allowed to play varsity and was the starting point guard from day one. Lucas was a three-time All-American in basketball and an All-American in tennis. Became the number-one pick of the NBA draft, but had a career checkered by drug problems. Managed to overcome his addiction and has coached in the NBA while helping others with addiction problems.

1. Len Bias, 1982–86. The most tragic sports figure in the history of the D.C. area. It's staggering to think how great he would have been in the NBA if he didn't die of a cocaine overdose hours after being drafted number two by the Boston Celtics. Digger Phelps' description of Bias as "Jordan with size" is haunting. Bias was an All-American as a junior when he averaged 19 points a game, but was unstoppable as a senior when he averaged 23 points a game. If you're too young to have seen Bias play, watch his game at North Carolina in 1986 when it runs on ESPN Classic.

Note: ESPN's Scott Van Pelt, a 6-foot-6 force when he played at Sherwood High School in Montgomery County, once tried to walk on to the Maryland basketball team, but Lefty Driesell wasn't all that impressed. Van Pelt hit it big anyway, earning his stripes at the Golf Channel starting in 1994 until ESPN recruited him for the anchor desk and other top assignments for *SportsCenter*. Only Maryland fans really get his signature on-air line—"Let's Go to Bentley's!!"—after he reports Terrapin football and basketball victories. Van Pelt spent an evening or three himself at the College Park bar as an undergrad, and look what it did for him.

10. Bambale "Boom" Osby. I just want to hug the guy. There's something impossible NOT to love about him.

9. Keith Gatlin. Full disclosure: he's a friend then and now. The alley oops to Lenny Bias, the inbounds pass off Kenny Smith, AND . . . he couldn't check me.

8. Adrian Branch. The J to beat Virginia . . . the knee pads . . . the lefty stroke. How many times did we say, "No, no, good shot, Adrian?"

7. Brad Davis. "From Monaca, Pennsylvania." I still have a sweatband he gave me. Like Mo Howard, he made a lasting impression on a young Terp fan.

6. Albert King. I was at his first game; I think it was against Navy. You always had a sense that he was THE guy. So many memories. I still have the *Sports Illustrated* covers.

5. Walt Williams. How do you thank the guy who stayed after the Len Bias tragedy when anyone else would have bailed? He kept the program alive.

4. Mo Howard. He took me shooting hoops in the North gym as a kid. The kind-hearted Philly kid was a gem.

3. Buck Williams. The student section used to have a chant about something opponents shouldn't do with Buck, as in "Don't (expletive deleted) with Buck." It rhymed, and they were right.

2. The Entire 2002 Title Team. Heart, soul, our one and only NCAA basketball championship. Thank you, fellas, thank you.

1. The late, great Leonard Bias. Period. End of discussion.

Gary Williams' Greatest Giant Killings

Six times since becoming basketball coach at Maryland in 1989, Gary Williams has walked off the court with an upset of the top-ranked team in the country. Here's how we rank them.

1. January 19, 2008, Maryland 82 – North Carolina 80. Not only was this one on the road at the Dean Dome, but it came during what was looking like a lost season. Maryland had suffered embarrassing early-season losses at home to mid-majors Ohio and American. To hand the top-ranked Tar Heels their first loss of the season on their own home court was a stunner. Senior James Gist turned in one of the best performances of his career with 22 points and 13 rebounds, and Bambale "Boom" Osby—with one of the great afros in hoop history—scored the game-winner on a falling-down layup with 21 seconds left.

2. January 14, 1998, Maryland 89 – North Carolina 83, OT. After the final buzzer at Cole Field House, Terrell Stokes ran over to the ESPN broadcast table and screamed into Dick Vitale's microphone, "We shocked the world babeee, we shocked the world!" Just 11 days earlier, the Terps had lost at home to third-ranked Duke 104-72, dropping them out of the rankings. North Carolina with Antawn Jamison and Jerry Stackhouse looked like a team capable of winning it all, but the unheralded Laron Profit (19 pts) and Mike Mardesich (12 pts, 9 reb) were able to send the Heels back to Chapel Hill at 17-1.

3. February 17, 2002, Maryland 87 – Duke 72. Maryland had the number three ranking at the time, so beating a team ranked only two spots higher on their home court may not seem like such a big deal, but this one slayed many demons. A year earlier on Super Bowl Sunday eve, Maryland was up 10 with less than a minute left at Cole Field House and somehow managed to lose in overtime in what became known as, "Gone in 54 Seconds." In the Final Four, Maryland was up 22 on Duke in the first half and lost by 11. And a month before this one, Duke blew them out in Durham by 21. The signature play of the game was Steve Blake picking Jayson Williams' pocket and scoring on a layup just before halftime as Williams glanced over at Duke coach Mike Krzyzewski.

4. February 7, 1995, Maryland 86 – North Carolina 73. Maryland was ranked eighth for this one at Cole Field House. Joe Smith, on his way to being player of the year and the number-one pick of the NBA draft, had 14 points and 16 rebounds. Guards Duane Simpkins and Johnny Rhodes, from Gary's first big recruiting class of '92, finished with 21 points apiece. Only a day earlier Carolina had regained the number one ranking. Rasheed Wallace called it, "a bad omen." We guess it was; the Heels lost to Arkansas in the Final Four.

5. January 18, 2003, Maryland 87 – Duke 72. The Blue Devils became the last team in the country to lose, falling to 12-1. It was the first big win at the brand new Comcast Center and put to rest fears of losing a great home court advantage with the exit from Cole. Drew Nicholas had 24 and Ryan Randle finished with 15 points and 17 rebounds.

6. December 10, 2003, Maryland 69 – Florida 68, OT. Not only was this Gary's 300th win as coach at Maryland, it seemed to put the stamp of approval on his post-National Championship recruiting class. Three members of it came up huge. Nik Caner-Medley had 22 points and 13 rebounds, John Gilchrist had 18 points, and Travis Garrison hit the game-winner in overtime. That trio would help lead Maryland to the ACC Tournament championship later that season. It turned about to be the class's last hurrah.

When it comes to college basketball, one superstar can change the fortunes of the entire program. Georgetown's three trips to the National Title game with Patrick Ewing is the best example of that. Ironically, Maryland's National Title in 2002 was accomplished with a group of lightly recruited players. Here are 10 (or maybe a few more) who came to College Park with high hopes that were never fulfilled.

14. Terence Morris (1997-2001). Morris was a starter on Maryland's first Final Four team, but never lived up to the promise he showed when he teamed up with Steve Francis as a sophomore to average 15 points and 7 rebounds a game on a team that was ranked number 5 in the country.

13. Exree Hipp (1992-96). Along with Johnny Rhodes and Duane Simkins, he was part of Gary Williams' big post-probation recruiting class. Listed at 6-foot-8, 183 pounds, Hipp looked like a pipe cleaner, but was effective as sophomore and junior averaging 13 points a game. However, before his senior year, then-Washington Bullet Chris Webber talked him into gaining weight to improve his NBA chances. Hipp showed up for his senior year more than 40 pounds over his freshman weight and averaged less than seven points a game on a Terp team that went out in the first round of the NCAA tournament.

12. Danny Miller (1999-2001). One of the few McDonald's All-Americans ever signed by Gary Williams. As a junior, Miller lost his starting job to Byron Mouton and transferred to Notre Dame for his senior year. Watching his former teammates cut down the championship nets as he red-shirted in South Bend couldn't have been an enjoyable experience.

11. Jap Trimble (1970-74). Came out of Power Memorial High School along with teammate Len Elmore as part of the freshman class that Lefty Driesell proclaimed would make Maryland, "The UCLA of the east." Trimble teamed with Elmore and Tom McMillen on an awesome freshman team, but a knee injury limited Trimble to only 53 varsity games over his career.

10. Tom Roy (1971-75). Is considered to be one of the best high school players in the history of Connecticut. Roy may have had the talent to play major minutes, but couldn't get many with McMillen, Elmore and Owen Brown in the starting lineup. Roy was, though, a major contributor on the three-guard (John Lucas, Mo Howard and Brad Davis) 1975 team that made it to the Elite Eight.

9. Brian Magid (1975-77). Was an incredible shooter on the Blair High School team that won the 1975 Maryland state championship. Proved not to be quick enough to play in the ACC and wound up finishing his career at George Washington.

8. Reggie Jackson (1979-82). Not only had a Hall of Fame name (no, we're not talking about Mr. October here), he was the Philadelphia high school player of the year. Jackson was a part-time starter, but finished his career averaging only 3.9 points a game.

7. James "Turkey" Tilman (1975-77). Lefty went local for one of the top D.C. inner-city stars and came up with a turkey. Tilman's disappointing career came to an end after only 41 games when Lefty put him back late in a blowout game and he refused to go in.

6. Jo Jo Hunter (1976-78). Pretty much another Tilman, just a year later. Had talked about being one of the early high schoolers to go directly to the NBA, but decided to tear up college basketball. Hunter never clicked with Lefty and wound up leaving after two years for Colorado.

The post-National Title recruiting class of 2002:

5. John Gilchrist. As a sophomore, had one of the great weeks in Maryland basketball history in leading the Terps to the ACC tournament championship. Considered going to the NBA, but reluctantly came back for his junior year. Gilchrist never had his head back in the game and left early only to be undrafted.

4. Travis Garrison. Was a rare McDonald's All-American who stayed home after a great high school career at DeMatha.

3. Nik Caner-Medley. Was considered to be the best high school player in the history of Maine. Had some moments, but proved that Maine is not a basketball talent pipeline.

2. Chris McCray. Somehow managed to become academically ineligible midway through his senior year. Without him, the much-hyped class finished their careers in back-to-back NIT's. The final game was a loss to Manhattan in a game that started at 11 a.m. in front of a few thousand sleepy fans at Comcast Center.

1. Moses Malone. Lefty pulled off his most impressive recruiting victory landing Moses out of Petersburg, Virginia in 1974. Moses had honed his game playing pickup at the local jail and was a man among boys. With starting guards John Lucas and Mo Howard returning from a team that had been ranked 5th in the country, Moses figured to make Maryland an instant contender for the National Title. It never happened. Moses attended one class and left. He became the first high schooler to go directly to the pros when he signed a contract with the ABA's Utah Stars.

My Top 10 Favorite All-Time University of Maryland Athletes :: Governor Robert L. Ehrlich Jr.

Note: Robert Ehrlich was Governor of Maryland from 2003 to 2007. After an All-American high school football career at the Gilman School in Baltimore, Ehrlich went on to co-captain the football team at Princeton. While attending Wake Forrest Law School, he worked as a graduate football assistant. He often attends University of Maryland football and basketball games and is a favorite golf partner of Tony Kornheiser. Here are his Terrapin favorites.

10. Keith Booth, basketball, 1993-97. He made it okay for Baltimore kids to attend College Park again.

9. Boomer Esiason, football, 1980-83. One reason Maryland can claim the title of "Quarterback U."

8. John Lucas, basketball and tennis, 1972-76. He took the University of Maryland by storm as a two-sport athlete (Lucas was an All-American in both sports).

7. Jack Scarbath, football, 1950-53. National Champs! Enough said (Scarbath was the quarterback of the 1953 National Championship team).

6. Len Bias, basketball, 1982-86. His record speaks for itself. We can only dream of what could have been. . . .

5. Gene Shue, basketball, 1951-54. Terp All-American, NBA All Star, NBA coach of the year (Shue coached the Baltimore Bullets and Philadelphia 76ers to the NBA finals).

4. Tom McMillan/Len Elmore, basketball, 1971-74. Great players in a glory era, they were great students as well. Unable to select one without the other.

3. Darryl Hill, football, Navy 1962, Maryland 1963-64. Football is tough enough without having to endure racial slurs (Hill was the first black football player at Navy and the first black athlete in the history of the Atlantic Coast Conference).

2. Randy White, football, 1971-73. Revolutionized the college game with weight training.

1. Gary Williams, basketball, player 1965-67, head coach 1989-present. Homegrown, he turned the basketball program around from its darkest hour.

Ten Reasons to Love Baltimore

Charm City is only 40 miles down the road from the Nation's Capital, but it might as well be on another planet. They loved their Colts, and now their Ravens, as much as we adore the Redskins. Now that Washington has a baseball team and a gorgeous new stadium, *our* Orioles have become *their* Orioles, just as it should be, but the city still has plenty to offer, and it's only an easy hour away down Interstate-95.

10. *Diner.* Baltimore native Barry Levinson's directorial debut became an instant movie classic as old high school pals reunite at the Fells Point Diner before one of their own gets married. Loved the Colts quiz the prospective bride had to pass for the wedding to go on. And Daniel Stern, a graduate of Montgomery-Blair High School, had his first big movie role as "Shrevie" Shreiber, the groom who administered the test to his betrothed—a young, pretty, and sports-obtuse Ellen Barkin.

9. Hon. As in the generic nickname "honey," which gets you sued for sexual discrimination in every other big city in America, but is considered the local term of endearment used by every waitress in town, some even sporting bee-hive hair-dos.

8. Artie Donovan. He was known as "Fatso" when he played defensive tackle for the old Colts of the 1950s and became a cult figure off countless appearances over the years on the *David Letterman Show* as a wise-cracking charmer with his unique Baltimore-by-way-of-the-Bronx fractured syntax.

7. Camden Yards. When "Orioles Park at Camden Yards" opened in 1992, it ushered in a new era of downtown, big-city ball yards. With the city's skyline visible over the outfield walls, it remains a retro gem, with easy access in and out, no matter how big the crowds. We also love the new pro football stadium right next door and its team named for a poem.

6. The Wire. Another in a long line of classic HBO original drama series, this direct descendant of HBO's *Homicide: Life on the Streets* (also set in Baltimore) touches all the right bases—the inner city, the gangs, the cops, the courts, the newspaper guys, and the mayor's office. Must-see TV, even for Washingtonians.

5. Harborplace and the Inner Harbor. This mega-commercial, retail, office and residential redevelopment project conceived by Columbia's Rouse Company in the 1970s revitalized downtown and pumped billions into the local economy. If you can't find a decent crabcake in this part of town, you're not even trying.

4. Babe Ruth. He was born here in 1895 and lived at 216 Emory Street, where the Babe Ruth Birthplace Museum now welcomes more than 60,000 visitors a year to a facility that honors his memory and offers lessons on Baltimore's rich baseball history.

3. The Earl of Baltimore. That would be Earl Weaver, the fiery Orioles manager who loved to stir the pot, kick dirt on umpires' spikes, and lead the cheers for all those three-run homers he loved to see on a team we all grew to love back when they were winning American League pennants and World Series titles with the likes of Brooks Robinson, Frank Robinson, Boog Powell, Jim Palmer, and so many more.

2. Johnny U. He was pigeon-toed and wore ugly black high-top cleats. But hardly anyone ever threw a football downfield with more poise or precision than No. 19, the Hall of Fame Colts signal-caller, the man with the golden arm, and arguably the greatest quarterback in NFL history—at least if you come from Baltimore.

1. Cal Ripken Jr. The most durable baseball player in Major League history, we Washingtonians adopted him as one of our own, marveling at his longevity and his considerable skills. How could you not shed a tear or three that night of September 6, 1995, when he broke Lou Gehrig's 56-year-old Iron Man record by playing in his 2,131st straight game. Cal did a joyous victory lap around the ball park that memorable evening, high-fiving one and all, a shining moment we'll never forget.

Sure they're our neighbors, but that doesn't mean we have to be neighborly toward them. Here are our top ten reasons why any self-respecting Washingtonian would hate that little city to the east.

10. Carroll Rosenbloom. He grew up in Baltimore but always had eyes for Hollywood, a goal he achieved when he made a deal in 1972 with Robert Irsay to swap NFL franchises. Irsay had purchased the Los Angeles Rams for $19 million, then traded his club to Rosenbloom, who owned the Rams until his death by drowning in 1979. Irsay then took over the Colts, and five years later slithered out of town with the team like the snake he was. We'll get to him down below.

9. Memorial Stadium. We loved the old ball park at 33rd Street just a few blocks from the Johns Hopkins campus, but we absolutely hated the city officials who allowed the place to be demolished in 2001. Parts of the building were used to build a crab-friendly reef in the Chesapeake Bay, and the site now includes the city's biggest YMCA and a couple of apartment buildings. For shame.

8. Orioles Park at Camden Yards. As much as we loved the coolest baseball stadium in the country, we Washingtonians hated the fact that it belonged to Baltimore, not us. Same for the football stadium on the other side of the parking lot. We've got FedEx Field. No fair.

7. Ray Lewis. Many believe the Ravens' veteran linebacker got away with murder in Atlanta after the Super Bowl in January, 2000. He and two members of his posse were indicted for murder in the stabbing death of two men, but Lewis plea-bargained into a misdemeanor count of obstruction of justice in exchange for testifying against his two pals, who later were acquitted. Lewis was sentenced to a year of probation and fined $250,000 by the league, but Atlanta authorities still believe he and his friends were very much involved and should have gone to jail.

6. Pimlico Race Course. It's the site of the Preakness, the second leg of horse racing's Triple Crown, but limited parking, nightmarish traffic, and out-of-control drinking among thousands partying all day in the infield detract from what should be one of racing's greatest spectacles.

5. The Block. One of Baltimore's longtime institutions, a long stretch of East Baltimore Street, once was filled with saloons, tattoo parlors and strip joints, but has been shrunken nearly out of existence in recent years, thanks to reform-minded politicians who rubbed out one of the city's more unique (pardon the phrase) assets. Pollack Johnny's sausage emporium right in the middle of it all was a great attraction, until it closed in the mid-1980s. Heavens to Blaze Starr, what were they thinking?

4. The Orioles. Now that we have a team to call our very own, and Cal, Brooks, and Frank Robby are retired and Hall of Famers, we couldn't care less about those dirty Birds these days.

3. The Colts. When they were the *Baltimore* Colts, they regularly drilled the Redskins in one of the more lopsided rivalries in sports, particularly in the 1960s. They had all the stars—Johnny U., Lenny Moore, John Mackey, and Raymond Berry—and won championships. We had Norm Snead, Dick James, Joe Rutgens, and Walter Rock, and won bupkus, losing nine straight from 1960 to 1969.

2. Robert Irsay. As much as we disliked the Colts, we had even more contempt for the team's last owner, plumbing contractor Robert Irsay, who used to show up drunk on the sidelines during games and tell his coaches what plays to run. On the night of March 28, 1984, he sent the Mayflower moving vans over to the team's training facility in the dead of a snowy winter night. They cleaned the joint out and moved lock, stock, and jock straps all the way to Indianapolis, taking the Colts' horsehoe logo and the team colors with them and breaking Baltimore's heart until the Ravens showed up a dozen years later.

1. Peter Angelos. A man who made millions winning class-action suits for asbestos victims, he's run the Orioles like a mom and pop operation since he bought the team in 1993. Even worse, for many years he led the charge in keeping major league baseball out of Washington, arguing that a team in the Nation's Capital would cut into his attendance. Wrong, asbestos breath, total mismanagement and fielding mediocre baseball teams took care of that, and also led *Sports Illustrated* to recently declare him as the worst owner in sports. We'd have accepted a bottom-feeding tie with Dan Snyder, but that's for another list.

Note: Lee Cowen is a lobbyist with extensive experience on Capitol Hill. He was majority counsel for the House Budget Committee and was a senior staff member of the House Education and Labor Committee. He was also an advisor to Robert Ehrlich in his successful 2002 campaign for governor of Maryland. Lee currently is senior vice president of Dutko Worldwide and, full disclosure, is Andy Pollin's brother-in-law. Here are his top 10 who have served in Congress based on their athletic accomplishments.

10. Representative Heath Shuler (D-NC). Okay, okay, remember this is a list of top 10 congressional athletes, so the pool of eligible members is not that deep. Come on, he was the runner up for the Heisman Trophy and a first-round pick of the Redskins coming out of Tennessee. Redskin fans know the rest. Poor play and injuries led to a very short and disappointing NFL career. In fact, in a 2004 ESPN ranking of the biggest sports flops of the past 25 years, Shuler was listed at number 17.

9. Representative Wilmer David "Vinegar Bend" Mizell (R-NC). Mizell makes the list almost solely on his nickname, which actually comes from a town in Alabama where he played baseball as a kid instead of some kind of wicked curve ball. Mizell was a pitcher in the big leagues from 1952 to 1962, serving in the Army from 1953 to '54. He was a regular participant in the annual congressional baseball game.

8. Representative J.C. Watts (R-OK). Watts was a star quarterback at the University of Oklahoma, earning MVP honors in the 1980 and '81 Orange Bowls. He went on to play six years in the CFL and was selected as the 1981 Grey Cup MVP even though his team lost.

7. Representative Tom McMillen (D-MD). A former Terp who played for Lefty Driesell, McMillen played for four different teams in the NBA between 1975 and '86, finishing his professional career with the Washington Bullets. He was a member of the 1972 U.S. Olympic basketball team that lost the controversial gold medal game to the Soviets; and he is believed to be the tallest person (6-foot-11) ever to serve in Congress.

6. Representative Jack Kemp (R-NY). A former presidential candidate and V.P. nominee, Kemp played quarterback in the pros for 13 years, mostly in the American Football League. He is the all-time AFL leader in pass attempts, completions and yardage. Kemp played in five of the 10 AFL championship games, winning two. He was the league's MVP in 1965 and a seven-time AFL All Star.

5. Representative Jim Ryun (R-KS). Ryun was a three-time Olympian, winning the silver medal in 1968 in track and field. In 1966, at the age of 19, Ryun set the world records in the mile and half-mile and was named *Sports Illustrated's* Sportsman of the Year.

4. Senator Bill Bradley (D-NJ). Bradley won an Olympic gold medal in basketball in 1964. A year later, he almost single-handedly led Ivy League Princeton to a third place finish in the NCAA tournament. He won two NBA championships with the New York Knicks and was elected to the Hall of Fame in his first year of eligibility.

3. Senator Jim Bunning (R-KY). Bunning pitched in the bigs for 17 years, with seven All Star Game appearances and election to the Hall of Fame. He is one of only five pitchers to throw a no-hitter in both leagues; the second one was a perfect game for the Phillies in 1964.

2. Representative Steve Largent (R-OK). Largent played for the Seattle Seahawks for 13 years and retired with NFL records for most catches, most yards, most touchdowns, and consecutive games with a reception. He is a member of Pro Football's Hall of Fame.

1. Representative Bob Mathias (R-CA). Mathias won the Olympic decathalon in 1948 (at age 17) and again in 1952. He also played football for Stanford and pulled a Rose Bowl double in 1952. He played for Stanford there and won his second decathalon in the famed stadium. Mathias was drafted by the Redskins, but never played in the NFL. He did, however, play himself in the 1954 movie, *The Bob Mathias Story*. He was the Michael Jordan or Tiger Woods of his era.

Honorable Mention: Representative Bob Ehrlich (R-MD). Also Governor of Maryland, Ehrlich was captain of the Princeton football team and a good friend of mine, so I know if I didn't mention him he'd be very upset!

Meaningless Observation: All the former athletes went on to serve in Congress as Republicans, except for the basketball players, Bradley and McMillen, who were Democrats. Oh wait! I almost forgot about Heath Shuler. He is currently serving as a Democrat. Of course, I'm sure there are plenty of Redskin fans who would like to forget about Shuler.

One Final Note: Cowen is both a Republican and a Miami Dolphin fan, so you can understand why frustration may lead him to want to rub it on the Redskins.

Many American presidents have honed their competitive spirits in a different sort of non-political arena, including one who actually turned down a chance to play in the NFL. Many played sports in high school and college, and several stayed fit and active playing games all their lives. Here are the top ten athletes to reside in the White House in recent memory.

10. Richard Nixon. He had a golf swing like a rusty gate, though he may have been the best bowling president of all time, for what that's worth. He also was a member of the Whittier College football team, but hardly ever played.

9. Harry Truman. As a farm boy from Missouri, there wasn't much time for organized sports growing up. In the White House, he was known as a serial walker, a man who used to leave Secret Service agents, members of his staff, and reporters in his wake when he went out for his daily walks. A power walker in every sense of the expression, and a skilled poker player, as well.

8. Theodore Roosevelt. Teddy fancied himself an outdoors type who loved to hunt and fish, and also dabbled in boxing and jujitsu. He rowed at Harvard and was runner-up in the university's boxing championship as an undergraduate. He also was quite the horseman, often leading his Rough Riders into battle mounted on his horse.

7. Bill Clinton. A self-described junk-food junkie, Clinton tried to control his weight by running, often in short shorts that revealed some serious thunder thighs. He also loved to play golf, and was known to take a mulligan or three and occasionally fudge a bit on his official scores. Then again, he was a decent enough player who occasionally broke 90. Well sort of, give or take a few gimmes.

6. George Walker Bush. He was good enough to play freshman baseball at Yale but dropped the sport as an upperclassman, preferring the rough and tumble of rugby instead. As president, he was a runner when he first got to the White House, but sore knees eventually forced him to switch to mountain biking.

5. John Kennedy. He played tennis, golf, football and baseball at Choate in high school and was on the Harvard football team until a back injury ended his career. Back problems plagued him for the rest of his life, but he still was considered a fine golfer and was an enthusiastic participant in family touch-football games.

4. Ronald Reagan. He was an all-around athlete in high school and once bragged that he'd saved 77 lives working as a lifeguard over summer vacations in rural Illinois. He played college football at Eureka, re-created Chicago Cubs baseball games for a Des Moines radio station and starred as George Gipp, the famous Notre Dame football star, in the movies.

3. Dwight Eisenhower. He played baseball and football in high school and was a promising running back for the Army football team until a knee injury ended his playing career. Mostly though, he was a passionate golfer most of his life, even installing a putting green at the White House. He was a member of Augusta National, and generally shot in the 90s.

2. George H.W. Bush. The 42nd president played baseball and soccer at Andover and was a fine left-handed first baseman who captained a Yale baseball team that played in the first College World Series. Bush also was a passionate golfer who occasionally could shoot in the 80s, though he was better known for almost always completing 18 holes under three hours.

1. Gerald Ford. It was duck and cover for spectators following his golfing exploits after he left office in 1976, but Gerry Ford is easily the greatest jock president by virtue of his college football career. Ford was a three-year letterman at center and linebacker for Michigan and helped win national championships in 1932 and 1933. He was Michigan's MVP in his senior year and was offered contracts to play for both the Detroit Lions and Green Bay Packers. He turned them both down to go to Yale Law School, where he also helped coach the football and boxing teams.

Note: Members of the House and Senate have been playing full-court, pick-up basketball in the basement of the Rayburn Building on Capitol Hill for years, usually convening three or four times a week at 4 p.m. for ninety minutes of hoops in between votes on the floor. The cast of characters often changes from year to year, if only because many of the players lose elections every now and then. We asked Tom Downey, a former House member from Long Island, and Tom McMillen, who once represented a House district in the Maryland suburbs for six years, for a nonpartisan scouting report on players past and present in the so-called "Members Basketball Association (MBA)."

10. Senator Al Gore, Democrat, Tennessee. The former senator and vice president was a regular in the game for many years. Downey convinced him to come down for a game one day in 1994, and Gore promptly ruptured his Achilles tendon. "He's never forgiven me," Downey said. Tipper, too, no doubt.

9. Senator Bill Bradley, Democrat, New Jersey. Bradley, an NBA Hall of Famer, normally would be ranked as the best all-time player in the game, but he only showed up a few times during his tenure on the Hill. "I think he played once because he thought it might help him pass a tax reform bill," Downey said. "He also threw passes none of us could fathom."

8. Senator John Ensign, Republican, Nevada. The only Pentecostal member of the Senate, he's got a good all-around game, with a decent shot and a deft touch in his passing game.

7. Rep. Ed Markey, Democrat, Massachusetts. The dean of the Massachusetts House delegation, he's been in Congress since 1976 but still plays regularly. He's considered a lethal shooter from the perimeter.

6. Senator Mike Oxley, Republican, Ohio. He's been the unofficial commissioner of the MBA in recent years, but the position became vacant when he announced in 2005 that he would be retiring from the Senate in 2007. Also considered a terrific outside shooter.

5. Rep. Tom Downey, Democrat, New York. Elected to Congress at the age of 25, Downey had a great advantage on the court when he first arrived in the MBA—young legs. "I was a pretty good shooter," he said. "You had to be or you'd never touch the ball in a game where a shot usually goes up after a maximum of two passes."

4. Senator William Cohen, Democrat, Maine. He first came to Washington serving in the House in 1972 and was Secretary of Defense from 1997-2001. He played high school basketball and also starred on the Bowdoin College basketball team. He was best known in the Rayburn gym for a wicked two-handed set shot.

3. Rep. Marty Russo, Democrat, Illinois. A product of rough and tumble Chicago politics, Russo, who is no longer in Congress, had a reputation as a good all-around athlete. A highlight of his Congressional hoops career was catching a length-of-court no-look pass from interloper Magic Johnson, who came down to play one day. The lowlight—decking a player on the George Washington University WOMEN'S basketball team in an exhibition game.

2. Rep. David Bonior, Democrat, Michigan. A fine all-around high school athlete in his native Detroit, the former Democratic whip also excelled on the court as a tough rebounder, decent passer, and shooter who liked to mix it up inside, just the way an arm-twisting whip might be expected to play.

1. Rep. Tom McMillen, Democrat, Maryland. At 6-foot-11, he was the tallest player, and arguably the best player, in the history of the MBA. Of course he was an All-American star at Maryland, played on the 1972 U.S. Olympic basketball team, and had a solid, 12-year NBA career before running for Congress in 1986 and serving three terms.

There are countless political power couples all over town, but the local sports community has had more than its fair share over the years, as well.

10. James Carville and Mary Matalin. Okay, okay, this is more politics than sports, but Democrat super-flak James often seems to spend more time in the fall on radio and television talking NFL point spreads and SEC football than most local sports talk show hosts. Miss Mary, his sharp-tongued Republican counterpart, would be wise to keep her eye on the family checkbook if James is backing all those predictions with a few bucks headed toward his neighborhood bookie.

9. George Preston Marshall and Corinne Griffin. He moved the Redskins from Boston to Washington and kicked off a love affair with his football team that's lasted more than 70 years. She left a Hollywood career as an actress to marry the big lug, then wrote the lyrics for "Hail to the Redskins," assuring her own place in Washington sports lore.

8. Joe Theismann and Cathy Lee Crosby. The Redskins quarterback split up with his first wife for a long fling with the Hollywood hostess and so-called actress in the mid-1980s, but it ended badly for both of them, culminating with Joey T. suing for half her assets in 1992 and Cathy Lee immediately declaring bankruptcy. Still, it was fun while it lasted, including the announcement at a Super Bowl in 1987 that they were engaged. Never happened.

7. Jeff and Denise Austin. The brother of tennis star Tracy Austin, Jeff was a decent enough tennis player himself who gave up the pro game to become a highly successful Washington-based sports agent. His wife Denise, a former gymnast who's always looked lovely in leotards, has been the longtime reigning Queen of the Workout Video and a frequent television presence, with complicated lines that mostly include "four more . . . now three . . . and two. . . ."

6. John Thompson and Mary Fenlon. They met when he was coaching basketball at St. Anthony's High and she was teaching at the tiny Northeast Washington Catholic school. A former nun, "Miss Fenlon" jumped to Georgetown when Thompson became head coach and served as his chief academic counselor, sounding board and overall conscience of the program until they both retired after 27 years. Despite whispers to the contrary, they were simply colleagues and great friends. End of story.

5. George Michael and Pat Lackman. Now hear this. George did most of the sports talking on the air at Channel 4 for all those years, but many of the words he uttered actually were composed by Ms. Lackman, his brilliant chief writer, not to mention his wife, a class act and the main behind-the-scenes brains of the Michael Machine.

4. Calvin and Janet Hill. This was a match made originally in the Ivy League, where Calvin starred in football for Yale and Janet was an academic superstar at Wellesley, where she was also a suitemate of Hillary Clinton. Calvin now works for his first NFL employers, the Dallas Cowboys, in player education and job counseling, and Janet is a high-profile consultant on Capitol Hill. They live in Great Falls and are also the properly proud parents of NBA superstar Grant, a graduate of South Lakes High in Reston and Duke.

3. Robert and Sheila Johnson. Before their highly publicized marital break-up in the late-1990s, together they launched the Black Entertainment Network, often airing the lowest common denominator of programming, as in vile Gangsta Rap and low-rent situation comedies that eventually translated into Very Big Money when the network was sold to Viacom for $3 billion in 1999. They split their fortune when they split the dishes, and both are now heavily involved in the sports world, he as owner of the NBA franchise in Charlotte, she as owner of the Washington Mystics in the WNBA and minority partner in the Wizards and Capitals.

2. Daniel and Tanya Snyder. They met when his friends set him up on a blind date in 1993, he the budding mogul and she the former model and fashion designer from Atlanta. They married in 1994, five years before The Danny bought the Washington Redskins. The *Post* has called Tanya "The Babe in the Box" and together they've become one of the more highly visible power couples in the Nation's Capital, as well as big-time charitable givers to a wide variety of good causes. Now, if he could just figure out how to run a football team.

1. Abe and Irene Pollin. They're the chairmen and owners of the Washington Bullets and Capitals, and by far the most powerful of all Washington sports power couples. They've always considered themselves true partners in life, and everything else. We normally don't quote media guides, but a recent Wizards publication really did say it best. "What distinguishes Abe and Irene Pollin from their peers is a commitment to social responsibility. They share a passionate need to give back to the community and have made helping people a way of life. Their philanthropic and humanitarian endeavors know no bias or boundaries, which is evident by the numerous public service and community organizations to which they selflessly devote enormous time and energy." Good for them. Better for all of us, and many thanks, as well.

Take one from Column A and another from Column B and occasionally you get a combination that can't be beat, especially in the wide world of Washington sports.

10. Russ Grimm and Joe Jacoby. The two perennial Pro Bowlers manned the left side of the Redskins storied offensive line in the 1980s—Grimm at guard, Jacoby at tackle—and helped running back John Riggins plough his way into the Hall of Fame. One of these days, the best two Hogs should get there, too.

9. John Thompson and Tom Hoover. They were the twin towers of one of the greatest high school basketball powers in Washington history when they played at Carroll High School in the 1950s on a team that also included the future president of Notre Dame (Monk Malloy) and mayor of Boston (Ray Flynn), as well as another high school All-American, George Leftwich, who became a highly successful Washington high school coach himself.

8. Steve Blake and Juan Dixon. Blake ran the point and Dixon was the shooter and clutch big-play maker. In a dream backcourt, together they helped lead Maryland to the national basketball championship in 2002.

7. Mo Howard and John Lucas. Another pair of slick Maryland guards, they were part of one of the greatest recruiting classes in the school's basketball history in the early 1970s. They played on a team with another potent inside duo in forward Tom McMillen and center Len Elmore. Their freshman team was so good, they beat the varsity, much to Lefty Driesell's delight.

6. Patrick Ewing and Michael Graham. The Hoyas were missing a premier power forward to take some of the burden off All-American center Patrick Ewing in order to become a Final Four team. When John Thompson recruited bad-boy Michael Graham from Washington's Interhigh League, he took a lot of heat, but it paid off with a national title. Ewing eventually graduated and became a perennial NBA All Star; Graham dropped out of school the next year and hasn't been heard from on a big-time basketball court since.

5. Joe Theismann and Art Monk. The Redskins quarterback aimed early and often at his favorite wide receiver, and the two formed one of the more lethal pitcher-catcher combinations in the NFL in the early 1980s, culminating with a Super Bowl title in 1982, even though Monk missed the game with a broken leg.

4. Sonny Jurgensen and Charley Taylor. The man with the golden arm had plenty of choices to aim his laser throws, but Jurgensen hooked up most often with wide receiver Taylor on some of the more breathtaking passing plays in team history, a main reason both men are in the Hall of Fame.

3. Joe Gibbs and Bobby Beathard. The Redskins Hall of Fame coach was hired by Beathard, the team's general manager, in 1981. For the next ten years, Beathard supplied the talent and Gibbs coached them up to three victories in four Super Bowls.

2. Wes Unseld and Elvin Hayes. Two more Hall of Famers played together for the Washington Bullets in the 1970s, leading to the only NBA title in franchise history in 1978. Off the court, they plain didn't like each other, but put them on a hardwood floor and they made sweet hoops music.

1. Sonny Jurgensen and Sam Huff. For more than 25 years, they've agreed to usually disagree as the dearly beloved analysts for Redskins radio broadcasts. Jurgensen handles the offense, Huff does defense and even though their act at times gets a tad hokey and they tend to more than occasionally root root root for the home team, they seem to get more popular with every passing season.

Felix and Oscar made sweet music in the movies, but the Washington sports scene has had its own share of real-life, odd-couple entanglements over the years.

10. George Allen and Edward Bennett Williams. Washington's ultimate power lawyer, Williams was a hard-core, left-leaning Democrat with great respect for free speech and freedom of the press. He hired a right-wing California Republican who invited Richard Nixon out to his practices and even let him draw up plays, and closed most of his practices to the media. It clicked for a couple of years and a Super Bowl appearance in 1972, but the two began a hate-hate relationship not long after that ended with Williams firing Allen after the 1977 season.

9. Gary Williams and Debbie Yow. Williams, the Maryland basketball coach, has never made much of a secret about his disdain for Yow, the school's athletic director, who did not hire him and wouldn't dare fire the only Maryland coach ever to win a national basketball championship. They co-exist, but it's hardly peaceful.

8. Joe Gibbs and Richie Petitbon. Gibbs was a bible-thumping, praise-the-lord offensive genius who had the good sense to hire Petitbon to run his defense when he took over as the Redskins head coach in 1981. Petitbon, a swashbuckling native of New Orleans who liked his bourbon, his ponies and his blitzing schemes, was the perfect fit for that time, even if they almost always went their very separate ways after leaving Redskins Park.

7. Muggsy Bogues and Manute Bol. In 1987, the Washington Bullets used the 12th overall pick in the first round of the NBA draft to select Muggsy Bogues of Wake Forest, at 5-foot-3 the shortest player in NBA history. Three years earlier, they had selected Manute Bol with a second-round pick, making him at the time the tallest player in league history. They were on the same team for one season before both were traded, a tragedy for photographers all around the league. Bogues led the team with 404 assists that year and Bol led the club with 208 blocked shots.

6. Daniel Snyder and Steve Spurrier. The Redskins' owner somehow convinced Spurrier to leave the University of Florida for his first NFL head coaching job, a match made in Hades. Spurrier was a free-spirited offensive whiz but not much on the details, more than occasionally forgetting the names of his players. Snyder, a Type A master of his universe, never was able to get a handle on his scratch-golfer head coach, who actually called the owner from a golf course to announce that he wouldn't be coming back for a third season.

5. Tony Kornheiser and Mike Wilbon. A nice Jewish boy from Long Island with a rapier wit and a tendency to kvetch and kvel teamed up with a lovely African-American guy from Chicago with a brilliant writing touch and a Walter Payton-like sweetness personality to host *Pardon the Interruption*, one of the most popular shows in ESPN history. Their point/counterpoint on-air approach doesn't need much scripting and was honed for years way off-camera in the sports department of the *Washington Post*, where both were award-winning columnists. They're also best friends who agree to disagree, and look how that's worked out for them.

4. Glenn Brenner and Gordon Peterson. Brenner was the wise-cracking former minor league baseball pitcher who became one of the most popular sportscasters in Washington history at Channel 9. Peterson was a hard-core, all-news reporter and anchor who loved to banter with Brenner before and after every sports report. Together, they made on-air magic for 16 years until Brenner's tragic death from a brain tumor in 1992.

3. Sonny Jurgensen and Sam Huff. They both joined the Redskins in 1964 and have been associated with the team almost ever since, including most of the last quarter century as the Frick and Frack analyst opposites on radio broadcasts of the games.

Jurgensen, a *bon vivant* known to slip out of his training camp dormitory to make last call at the local pub, is a Hall of Fame quarterback some believe may be the greatest pure passer in the history of the league. Huff, a coal miner's son from West Virginia, was a rough and tumble middle linebacker and also is enshrined in Canton, ensuring that they'll be joined at the hip in perpetuity.

2. Wes Unseld and Elvin Hayes. Unseld was the longtime team captain of the Washington Bullets, a burly under sized center who more than held his own in the paint. Hayes arrived in a trade with San Diego in 1972 and became the NBA's consummate power forward, teaming with Unseld to lead the Bullets to a world championship in 1978. Both are in the Hall of Fame, and truth be told, never really got along that well. Call it another hate-hate relationship off the court with sweet music between the lines.

1. John Thompson and Mary Fenlon. The longtime Georgetown basketball coach met the former nun when both were working at now-defunct St. Anthony's High School in the 1960s, he as a coach, she as a teacher. Thompson hired her as his academic coordinator and to handle a wide variety of other administrative duties when he took the Georgetown job in 1972. She traveled with the team, sat on the bench and was a constant presence in Thompson's life on and off the court, though both have always insisted it was strictly Hoya basketball that brought them together, and nothing else.

Some strange stuff involving local teams and players has occurred over the years. Here are ten weird Washington tales.

10. Mark Moseley. The greatest kicker in Redskins history actually knocked around the NFL for several years before George Allen signed him as a free agent in 1974. Moseley became available courtesy of then Houston Oilers head coach Bill Peterson, who waived him in the preseason that year just as the team was boarding a bus. Peterson told him in the parking lot he'd dreamt earlier in the week that he'd cut Moseley, and was merely following through. Moseley was picked off the waiver wire and went on to become the NFL's most valuable player in 1982 when he made 20 of 21 field goal attempts and set a league record with 23 straight kicks (three coming in 1981).

9. Charles Johnson. When the Washington Bullets first signed the 6-foot guard who recently had been waived by the Golden State Warriors in January, 1978, he made one of the grand entrances in NBA history, arriving for his first game at the old Capital Centre in a helicopter that landed in an outer arena parking lot. The Bullets desperately needed him that day because they had only seven healthy players and Johnson initially came to town on a 10-day contract. He stayed for two memorable seasons and hit one of the greatest shots in team history, a half-court bomb to end the third quarter of his team's Game 7 victory over Seattle in the NBA finals. CJ, who died after a long bout with cancer in 2006, scored 80 points in the Bullets' last four games of that series.

8. Tommy McVie. The Washington Capitals' colorful head coach in 1975-76 was a player-coach for the Johnstown Jets in the Eastern League in 1972-73, and he's always said the movie *Slapshot*, starring Paul Newman, was more of his own biography than it was Hollywood fiction. Newman's character had been a winger in a higher league, just as McVie had been. He was a player-coach, just as McVie was in Johnstown, and Newman's movie wife left him during the season, just as McVie's had done in real life. "I came home from a road trip one day and we got back around 7 in the morning," McVie once recalled. "There was nothing there for my family, so I come home and they are all dressed in their Sunday clothes. My wife had our three little boys all lined up, and she said, 'All four of us love ya, dear, but we're outta' here.' A cab pulled up, they went to the airport and flew back to Oregon. At the end of the movie, Newman gets a job in a higher league, just like I did after Johnstown, so because of the similarities, I'm really watching my life when I watch the film."

7. Tommy McVean. The Redskins equipment manager during the George Allen years, McVean also was something of a hustler, always trying to make a buck on the side. Not long after wildly popular quarterback Sonny Jurgensen retired with a push from Allen during the 1974 season, McVean invested in several dozen jerseys with Jurgensen's No. 9 on the back. After a rainy-day practice, McVean laid out the jerseys in a practice field end zone and asked the players to clean their cleats on them. He then sold them to the public for $100 each, advertising the item as "the jersey Sonny Jurgensen wore in his last game."

6. Murray The K. The famous New York disc jockey was also known in the 1960s as "The Fifth Beatle" because he helped promote the band in its early U.S. appearances. Murray Kaufman was hired by the old Washington Darts soccer team to spin records for an entire game during the 1971 season in hopes that his presence might boost attendance at its Catholic University stadium. It seemed like a fine idea, but on the day he was scheduled to appear, wind and rain prevented him from setting up his equipment, and the promotion fizzled, never to be attempted again.

5. Bobby Wadkins. The veteran professional golfer from Richmond came to the par-five sixth hole in the final round of the 1994 Kemper Open holding a one-shot lead at the TPC at Avenel. When he walked off the green, he had taken a triple bogey with a lost ball after hitting his second shot into a tree. The ball caromed into a patch of deep grass and thick rough, and more than 50 spectators tried to help him find it. At least a half-dozen golf balls were located, none of them belonging to Wadkins, and after the mandatory five minutes allowed, he had to give up the hunt. He went on to tie for second place, losing the tournament by three shots, the closest he ever came to winning a regular PGA Tour event before joining the Champions Tour in 2002.

4. Davis Love III. In 1995, he was leading the Kemper Open five holes into Saturday's third round when he struck a wayward tee shot down the left side of the very same sixth hole at Avenel that cost Wadkins the tournament the year before. The ball struck a spectator, 50-year-old Sandy Zober of Bethesda, knocking her unconscious and sending her to the hospital, where she was listed that night in critical condition. Love was so unnerved, he bogeyed two of his next five holes and soon faded out of contention. Zober was released from the hospital several days later, and said she felt badly that Love didn't go on to win the tournament.

3. Andre the Giant. The 7-foot-4 professional wrestler was the star attraction at a raucous press conference called by the Washington Redskins in 1975 to announce the team was interested in giving the 400-pounder a tryout. He was introduced that day at the old Touchdown Club in downtown Washington by Tim Temerario, a 5-foot-4 aide to George Allen, the Redskins eccentric head coach. Allen was intrigued by the idea of getting Andre on the field, at least until Temerario told him that he already was pulling down $400,000 a year on the wrestling circuit and would have had to take a major pay cut to play pro football.

2. Billy Malinchak. A wide receiver and special teams ace for the Redskins in the 1970s, Malinchak had a great gift for blocking punts and placements before he retired from football after the 1974 season and secured a trading seat on the N.Y. commodities market. In 1976, the Redskins were facing four crucial games down the stretch in their drive to make the playoffs when Allen called Malinchak and begged him to come back for the final weeks of the season. Four weeks later, Malinchak blocked a punt in the Redskins 27-14 victory over the Dallas Cowboys, a huge play in a win that clinched a postseason berth. After the season, he retired one more time, and Allen never called again.

1. Mike Bass. His 49-yard touchdown return of a blocked 42-yard field goal attempt by Miami kicker Garo Yepremian came in the final minutes of Super Bowl VII in 1972 and has been called by many the strangest play in Super Bowl history. Yepremian's low kick was blocked by Redskins defensive tackle Bill Brundige. Yepremian picked up the loose ball and frantically tried to throw it to Larry Csonka, who was on the field as a blocker. Instead, the ball flew straight up in the air and Bass picked it off and scored untouched, cutting Miami's lead to 14-7 with 2:07 remaining. The Redskins got the ball back with 1:14 left on the clock, but could not score again, allowing the Dolphins to complete a 17-0 season.

All right, stop laughing. Go ahead and use the line from *Airplane* ("Here's some light reading, a pamphlet on the greatest Jewish athletes. . ."). Granted, Washington has done much better with Jewish owners like Abe Pollin (Bullets/Wizards and Caps), Jerry Wolman (Philadelphia Eagles), Ed Snider (Philadelphia 76ers and Flyers) and Dan Snyder (Redskins) than Jewish athletes. But this list wasn't as hard to put together as you might think. Don't be a noodnick.

10. Paul Goldstein (tennis). Although he's never won a tournament as a pro, Goldstein has managed to hang in there for more than a decade, earning close to $2 million dollars playing tennis. He was a four-time All-Met at Sidwell Friends and four-time All-American at Stanford. He's also one of the few to compete on the pro circuit with a college degree. Goldstein turned pro in 1998.

9. Brian Magid (basketball). May be one of the best shooters in the history of Maryland high school basketball. Magid was All-Met at Blair, graduating in 1975. He played two years at the University of Maryland before transferring to George Washington. He led the Colonials in scoring at 15.6 points a game as a senior and was a 92 percent free-throw shooter. Magid really would have benefited from the three-point line, which didn't come in to existence until after he graduated.

8. Joe Jacobi (kayak). A very famous sports name in D.C. (although the former Redskin spells his last name with a "y"). Jacobi teamed with Scott Strausbaugh to win the first-ever gold medal for the United States in the whitewater canoe slalom at the 1992 Olympics in Barcelona. Jacobi has competed and coached in the sport for many years.

7. Ron Watts (basketball). Was a star at Wilson High School before becoming a two-time All-ACC player at Wake Forrest. After graduating in 1965, Watts was drafted by the Celtics and played parts of two seasons in Boston. Injuries ended his career after only 28 games, but he became famous in the 70s by mocking his pro playing days. Watts made a television commercial for Bell Telephone with Bill Russell. In it, Watts tells the all-time great that he, not Russell, was the *real* star of the Celtics.

6. Phil Perlo (football). Was one of the greatest D.C. high school athletes of the early 1950s, making All-High in three sports. He captained Roosevelt to the city championship and went on to star at linebacker at the University of Maryland. Perlo is believed to be the only Jewish Washingtonian to play pro football, appearing in seven games for the Houston Oilers in 1960, before a neck injury ended his career.

5. Bernie Wolfe (hockey). Wolfe played goalie on some really bad Caps teams over four seasons between 1975 and '79. His career record was 20-61-21 with one shutout. But come on, it's not like we had a huge selection of Jewish hockey players. Wolfe stayed in the area after his retirement and, oy vey, thank God, his career as a financial planner has been much more successful than his days between the pipes.

4. Harold Solomon (tennis). Raised in Silver Spring, Solomon played tennis at Rice University after graduating from Springbrook in 1970. At 5-foot-6, 130 pounds, he wasn't going to overpower anybody, but he got to everything and was awfully tough to beat on clay. He made it to the French Open final in 1976 and made the U.S. Open semifinals in '76 and '77 and won 22 singles titles over his career. Solomon was ranked in the top 10 in the world for most of the second half of the 70s and teamed with Eddie Dibbs on the number-four doubles team in the world in 1976. They were called, "The Bagel Twins."

3. Mike Epstein (baseball). Traded from the Orioles to the Senators in 1967 for Pete Richert, Epstein teamed with Frank Howard to become an impressive one-two power punch. After hitting 30 home runs in 1969, Epstein (in a less politically correct time) became known as "Super Jew." He hit 20 more homers in 1970, but when he slumped in 1971, a fan at RFK was heard yelling, "Hey Epstein you haven't had a hit since your Bar Mitzvah." The Senators traded him to Oakland, where he was the A's starting first baseman on their 1972 World Series championship team.

2. Jeff Halpern (hockey). Raised in Potomac, Halpern isn't just the first Jew from the area to make it to the NHL, he's believed to be the first player, period. Halpern spent a year at Churchill before finishing high school at a private school in New England. He was a good-but-not-great player at Princeton and signed with the Caps as a free agent in 1999. Surprisingly he made the team as a rookie and was a solid forward for six seasons, totaling 19 goals and 46 points in the 2003-04 season. Caps fans (particularly the Jewish ones) nearly plotzed when Halpern signed with Dallas as a free agent before the 2006 season. He was traded to Tampa Bay in 2008.

1. Buddy Myer (baseball). Born Charles Solomon Myer in 1904, he was a mainstay in the Senators infield in the 1930s. Except for most of the 1927 season and all of the '28 season when he played for the Red Sox, Myer was with the Senators from 1925 to 1941. Playing mostly second base, Myer was a .303 lifetime hitter and led the American League in batting with a .349 average in 1935. He was an All-Star in 1935 and '36 and if he didn't play on mostly bad teams, might have gotten consideration for the Hall of Fame. Myer spent most of his life outside baseball in Mississippi and died there in 1974.

Honorable Mensch: Red Auerbach. Arguably the greatest basketball coach and one of the greatest coaches who ever lived, he played at George Washington in the late 30s and kept his main residence in D.C. for the rest of his life. Eras are difficult to compare and record keeping wasn't the greatest when Red played, but he did score 334 points in 56 games over a three-year period between 1937 and 1940. George Washington named him to their All-Century basketball team and named the court at the Smith Center in his honor.

Note: If Galdi's pro wrestling knowledge was his only calling card, you'd worry. No one should know this much about this. But Galdi is a well-adjusted, hard worker who grew up in the 80s and 90s when the WWF was king and got swept up in the passion. He currently provides morning sports updates on the nationally syndicated *First Team on Fox* hosted by Steve Czaban and performs various on-air duties on Sportstalk 980. The promotions referred to on this list are the National Wrestling Alliance (NWA), World Championship Wrestling (WCW, which is what the Atlanta-based portion of the NWA eventually became after Ted Turner bought it in 1988) and the Vince McMahon Jr.-owned World Wrestling Federation (WWF, which became World Wrestling Entertainment—WWE—in 2002).

5. NWA Capitol Combat, May 19, 1990, D.C. Armory

What made the show good: Any show headlined by a cage match involving the legendary Ric Flair versus Lex Luger can't be bad. It also featured some of the era's best tag teams—Midnight Express versus Brian Pillman and Tom Zenk, Steiner Brothers versus Doom and Rock 'n' Roll Express versus the Fabulous Freebirds.

What made the show memorable: Robocop saving the promotion's top fan favorite, Sting, from an attack by the Four Horsemen. This was one of those "so bad it's good" moments. The NWA treated Robocop as an actual person and had three of its top heels (Arn and Ole Anderson and Sid Vicious) back down from "him" in a moment as goofy as it was implausible, even by pro wrestling standards.

4. WWE SummerSlam, August 21, 2005, MCI Center

What made the show good: The Rey Mysterio–Eddie Guerrero ladder match didn't quite live up to expectations, but it took on historical significance after Guerrero's death less than three months later. The quality of the John Cena–Chris Jerico WWE championship match surprised many. The main event, a Hulk Hogan versus Shawn Michaels dream match, was another case of Michaels getting a decent match out of an athletically limited opponent.

What made the show memorable: The politics. Hogan's WWE contract reportedly included a "creative control" clause, meaning he didn't have to do things he didn't want to (i.e. lose). Michaels is notorious for avoiding "jobs" (pinfall losses), but his political skills were no match for Hogan's, and Hogan, then 52, pinned Michaels, then 40. The next night on WWE RAW, Michaels gave a sarcastic, unconventional, and in many ways unprofessional interview. He poked fun at Hogan's age, essentially saying he was "made" to lose the previous evening. Of course he was made to lose, but you're not supposed to say that on the company's flagship television show.

3. WCW Starrcade, December 28, 1997, MCI Center

What made the show good: A mega-event atmosphere, as this pay-per-view was as well-built as any in WCW history. While most of the matches were disappointing, they featured many performers from what was perhaps the most star-laden roster ever in pro wrestling; Hulk Hogan, Randy Savage, Sting, Goldberg, Curt Henning, Diamond Dallas Page, Chris Benoit, Eddie Guerrero, and Lex Luger.

What made the show memorable: It marked the pinnacle of WCW. It was the culmination of a year-plus long buildup of a Sting versus Hulk Hogan match. But the Starrcade 1997 was also the beginning of the end for the WCW. The finish of the main event was supposed to involve a fast three-count by heel referee Nick Patrick on Sting to set up newcomer Bret Hart saving the day. But Patrick inexplicably delivered a normal count, making Sting appear as if he had legitimately lost and Hart look foolish for saving a match that didn't need saving. Insiders have always questioned how Patrick, a respected veteran, could botch something so simple. Some believe Hogan instructed Patrick to purposely screw up his count in order to help preserve Hogan as one of the company's top acts. Whatever the case, the finish of this match, and about a hundred other mistakes, had WCW out of business by late March 2001.

2. WWF Survivor Series, November 19, 1995, USAir Arena

What made the show good: This was your classic sleeper show where expectations were low and satisfaction was high. The main event where Bret Hart ended the 51-week WWF title reign of Diesel (Kevin Nash), was perhaps the best match of Nash's career and another example of why Hart is among the best in-ring performers ever. The undercard was highlighted by four four-on-four elimination matches, three of which were good. And the event included the surprise return of "Mr. Perfect" Curt Henning as a color commentator.

What made the show memorable: Two moments in the main event, both of which pointed toward the more risque direction the WWF would take in the coming years (and the incredible financial success that would come with that change in philosophy). First was Hart flying through a table at ringside late in the match. This kind of violence was rarely seen until the late 90s. The second was Diesel clearly mouthing "mother f— —r" after he lost. Both spots represented Vince McMahon taking his product from G-rated to PG-13, and even R.

1. WWF Backlash, April 30, 2000, MCI Center

What made the show good: One good to great match after another. Rock versus Triple H in the main event; Chris Benoit versus Chris Jericho; Eddie Guerrero versus the underrated Essa Rios; Dean Malenko versus Scotty Too Hotty; Edge and Christian versus X-Pac and Road Dogg. Even matches that figured to be mediocre (Dudley Boyz versus Test, and Albert and Big Show versus Kurt Angle) were fun.

What made the show memorable: In what was the WWF's best year from a creative standpoint, this was the best pay-per-view event. Not only was the in-ring action very good, so was the crowd. The pop for the return of "Stone Cold" Steve Austin was one of the loudest I've ever heard. This event was what Starrcade '97 should have been for WCW. And perhaps not coincidentally, it is the WWE that is still in business.

When Joe Gibbs had his hands on the controls the second time around (2004-07), he dealt away many of his draft picks for veterans and restricted free agents. He lost more games than he won (31-36). The first time around with Bobby Bethard actually using the draft picks, things went much better. The foundation of the Camelot years was built with the first draft Bethard picked for Gibbs. The NFL network recently ranked the Redskins' 1981 draft as the seventh-best of all time. Here is that draft, with the number of Super Bowl championships each player won while playing for Gibbs.

Round 1, Mark May (2). Was expected to be their left tackle of the future. It turned out he was better suited for guard. He stayed there for ten years and became a mainstay on the legendary "Hogs."

Round 2, Joe Washington (1). Yes he was a five-year veteran by the time he got here, but the pick was all it took to pry him loose from the Baltimore Colts. Washington actually started ahead of John Riggins, leading the team in rushing with 916 yards in '81.

Round 3, Russ Grimm (3). Became an instant starter and made the Pro Bowl four times. Grimm was named to the NFL's 75th Anniversary Team of the 80s. He has been a finalist for the Hall of Fame several times.

Round 4, Tom Flick (0). This may have been a swing and a miss, but Joe Theismann had hit his 30s by the this time. They were looking to develop a quarterback. Flick wasn't it.

Round 5, Dexter Manley (2). The Redskins all-time career leader in sacks with 97.5. He remains one of the great characters in the history of the franchise.

Round 6, Larry Kubin (1). A Penn State linebacker who they thought might turn out to be better. Kubin wound up as a special teams contributor for three years.

Round 7. Pick traded to the Rams.

Round 8, Charlie Brown (1). A run that was short, but sweet. Brown played in two Pro Bowls and had spectacular leaping ability. An excellent complimentary receiver to Art Monk.

Round 9, Darryl Grant (2). Taken out of Rice as an offensive lineman, he was converted to defensive tackle. Grant helped Dave Butz stuff the run and made one of the greatest plays in Skins' history when he intercepted a tipped pass and took it in to the end zone to clinch and NFC title game win over Dallas in 1983.

Round 10, Phil Kessel and Alan Kennedy. Kessel never played in the NFL, but Kennedy played in San Francisco and won a ring there.

Round 11, Jerry Hill. Hey, it's the 11th round!

Round 12, Clint Didier (2). Played at Portland State and probably wasn't on anybody's radar. Didier was discovered when Neil Lomax (who went in the first round to the St. Louis Cardinals) needed somebody to throw to in pre-draft workouts. Didier caught one of Doug Williams' record-setting four touchdown passes in the second quarter of Super Bowl XXII.

After the draft was over:

Free agent, Joe Jacoby (3). At 6-foot-7, 300 lbs, believe it or not "Jake" was considered too big to play offensive line in the NFL at the time. After first thinking he was a defensive lineman, Gibbs soon realized Jacoby was a better fit at left tackle than first-rounder Mark May. He went on to make four Pro Bowls and hopefully will someday get his rightful place in the Hall of Fame.

That's a total of 17 Super Bowl rings from one draft!

Worst Redskins First-Round Draft Picks

When it comes to the NFL draft, it's possible that no team in history has done less with more than the Redskins. Between 1969 and 1993, the Redskins used their own first-rounder only three times and had two hits, Art Monk (1980) and Darrell Green (1983), and one miss, Bobby Wilson (1991). True, some of those picks were spent wisely to trade for veterans, but draft day hasn't brought much excitement around here over the years. No wonder Mel Kiper Jr. chooses to live in Baltimore. Here are the worst first-round choices.

12. Norm Snead (1961). After a 1-9-2 finish in 1960, the Redskins wound up with the second and third picks of the draft. Snead went number two out of Wake Forrest, and tackle Joe Rutgens, who had a solid career, was taken with the third pick. However, they passed on future Hall of Famers Mike Ditka, Jimmie Johnson, Herb Adderley and Bob Lilly. This would have ranked higher, but the Skins were smart enough to deal Snead for Sonny Jurgensen before the 1964 season.

11. Jim "Yazoo" Smith (1968). Had a good rookie year at safety, but suffered a neck injury in the last game of the season and never played again.

10. Jack Scarbath (1953). Picking second, they may have gotten carried away with a hometown boy. Scarbath had led Maryland to the national title, but he lasted only two years with the Skins.

9. Michael Westbrook (1995). He looked the part and talked the part—calling himself "Michael Jordan with a football"—the day he was made the fourth pick of the draft. Injuries and attitude limited him to one good year, 1999, when he had 65 catches.

8. Don Allard (1959). The quarterback was the fourth pick out of Boston College. He never made it in the NFL, playing a total of only 5 games with the New York Titans and Boston Patriots of the AFL in 1960 and '61.

7. Richie Lucas (1960). The Redskins didn't learn easily in those days. Again they took an eastern quarterback (Penn State) with the fourth pick. Lucas took the better money to play with the Buffalo Bills of the upstart AFL and was out of football in two years.

6. Ray McDonald (1967). A panic buy. Needing a running back in the first common NFL-AFL draft, they took the Idaho (Idaho?) star with the 13th pick, passing up future Hall of Famers Alan Page (15) and Gene Upshaw (17). After two lackluster seasons, new coach Vince Lombardi cut McDonald on the spot in training camp when he showed up late for a meeting.

5. Charlie Gogolak (1966). It marked the first time a kicker had ever been taken in the first round. He lasted three years.

4. Heath Shuler (1994). Only two years after he was named the MVP of Super Bowl XXVI, they were through with Mark Rypien and just had to have a quarterback with the third pick. Shuler had been a star at Tennessee, but now remains in the discussion for biggest draft bust of all time. He was out of the game within five years and is now—what else?—a Congressman.

3. Desmond Howard (1992). It seemed to be an embarrassment of riches coming off a Super Bowl season. Even though they had the posse—Art Monk, Ricky Sanders and Gary Clark—still performing at a high level, two first rounders were dealt to move up to the fourth pick. Gibbs said, "This is the only player we have ever scouted with no weaknesses." There was one: he couldn't get off the line of scrimmage. Jacksonville mercifully claimed him in the '95 expansion draft. And don't say, "Super Bowl MVP." That was as a kick returner.

2. Andre Johnson (1996). They had to have this offensive tackle from Penn State so they sent their second and third rounders to Dallas for the last pick of the first round. Johnson was so bad he never got on the field for a regular-season snap.

1. Cal Rossi (1946 and 1947). You can't get any dumber than the moves on this guy. Rossi was a star back at UCLA. Without doing much research, Rossi went ninth to Washington in '46. It turned out he had another year of eligibility. No problem. In '47, they used the THIRD pick of the draft to take Rossi. He said, "Thanks a lot, but I've decided not to play pro football." Two years, two blown picks. Thanks for playing.

The last pick of the NFL draft is still referred to as "Mr. Irrelevant." However, with only seven rounds nowadays, going last doesn't mean what it used to. At one time the draft was 30 rounds, and as recently as 1992 it was 12 rounds. In fact the last true "Mr. Irrelevant" may have been Matt Elliot, who made the Redskins as the 336th and last player picked in the 12-round 1992 draft. Here are the top eight Skins drafted in round 10 or higher.

8. Joe Tereshinski (11th round 1946). Was a solid tight end for eight years on some mediocre teams.

7. Raleigh McKenzie (11th round 1985). Had a terrific 10-year career in Washington, playing on two Super Bowl champions. A smart player who could play anywhere on the offensive line.

6. Monte Coleman (11th round 1979). Was a safety coming out of Arkansas State and became a big-time contributor at what became known as "nickel linebacker" for 16 years.

5. George Starke (11th round 1971). Played football and basketball at Columbia. Starke became a starter in 1973 and was the elder statesman at right tackle when "piglets" Joe Jacoby, Russ Grimm, Jeff Bostic, and Mark May joined him on the offensive line in 1981. Starke dubbed himself the "Head Hog" and played four more years.

4. Mark Schlereth (10th round 1989). Certainly the most successful broadcaster taken by the Redskins in the late rounds (Mark May was a first rounder). Schlereth took May's spot at guard and made the Pro Bowl as the Redskins won Super Bowl XXVI. They would later regret letting him get away, as the man who goes by the misnomer "Stink" would help Denver win two more Super Bowls.

3. Gene Brito (17th round 1951). Taken out of Loyola of California, Brito became a real star in Washington in the 50s, making the Pro Bowl five out of six years between 1953 and 1958.

2. Eddie LeBaron (10th round 1950). Small in stature, LeBaron gave the Redskins some very solid post-Sammy Baugh years. He made the Pro Bowl three times in the 50s and helped keep the Redskins somewhat respectable.

1. Chris Hanburger (18th round 1965). Thought to be too small to play linebacker in the NFL, Hanburger not only lasted 14 years, he made the Pro Bowl nine times. How this man doesn't get Hall of Fame consideration remains a mystery.

The Catcher and the One They Couldn't Catch:
Art Monk and Darrell Green's 11 Seasons Together

They each put up incredible numbers, while combining to play 36 years in the NFL. Monk was the first receiver to catch more than 100 passes in a season and was, for a period of time, the leading pass catcher in history. Green, who was still running a 4.4 40 after the age of 40, played an unprecedented 20 years at cornerback, all for the Redskins. Although the quiet Monk and the chatty Green are opposite personalities, they are two of the most beloved Washington athletes of all time. Fittingly they were elected to the Pro Football Hall of Fame on the same day. Here is how we rank their 11 seasons as teammates.

11. 1993. This was the only year together under a coach other than Joe Gibbs. (Richie Petitbon's one year was a 4-12 disaster.) Green was solid for a defense that was old and beat up, intercepting four passes. Monk had 41 catches and was still productive, but wound up leaving for the Jets at the end of the season in a bitter salary dispute. It was a shame to see him break Steve Largent's record of 177 straight games with at least one catch while wearing a green uniform.

10. 1988. The post-Super Bowl hangover seemed to get the best of everybody as the Skins finished 7-9. Green intercepted only one pass and Monk put up solid numbers: 72 catches, 946 yards, 5 TD.

9. 1992. Gibbs' last year in his first go-round. Super Bowl MVP quarterback Mark Rypien had held out in training camp and turned in a lousy year. He struggled to get the ball to Monk, who managed to catch only 46 balls for 644 yards and 3 TD. Green broke his arm early in the season and played in only eight games. He did however intercept a pass for the 10th straight season and the Redskins made the playoffs at 9-7, winning a wild-card game at Minnesota.

8. 1985. It will always be remembered as the year Joe Theismann broke his leg. However, it didn't seem to affect Monk. He was selected to his second Pro Bowl, catching 91 passes for 1,226 yards and 2 TD. Green had two interceptions, but failed to make his second Pro Bowl. The Skins wound up 10-6, but missed the playoffs.

7. 1989. Another 10-6 season without postseason play thanks once again to the stinkin' Cowboys who won their only game of the season, 13-3, at RFK Stadium on November 5th. Monk had a big year with 86 catches for 1,186 yards and 8 TD. Green continued to lock up the other team's best receiver while picking off two passes.

6. 1990. You never would have guessed it at the time, but Green, now 30-years old and in his eighth season, would go on to play another dozen years after this one. He had a terrific season with four interceptions, a touchdown, and selection to his fourth Pro Bowl. Monk, now in his 11th year, was as solid as ever with 68 catches for 770 yards and 5 TD. He also, for one of the few times in his career, spoke up at a meeting and inspired the team to avenge the famed "body bag" game earlier that season. They went back to Philadelphia and won their wild-card playoff game before losing to eventual champion San Francisco in the second round.

5. 1983. In a regular season featuring huge team numbers—561 points and plus-43 on turnovers—the dynamic duo put up relatively small individual numbers. Monk caught only 47 passes for 746 yards and 5 TD. Green, in his rookie year, intercepted two passes. His most famous play was running down Tony Dorsett from behind in his first game, a Monday-night home loss to Dallas. Neither made the Pro Bowl and what should have been a dream season, crashed with a 38-9 Super Bowl loss to the Raiders. Still, it was a Super Bowl season.

4. 1986. The Giants were just too good that year, beating the Skins three times, including a wind-blown 17-0 whitewash at the Meadowlands in the NFC title game. But Monk and Green were at the top of their games. Monk was picked for his third straight Pro Bowl with 73 catches for 1,068 yards and 4 TD. Green joined him in Hawaii with five interceptions.

3. 1984. Trying to get to a third-straight Super Bowl, the Redskins were stunned at RFK by the Bears in the divisional playoff round. Numbers-wise though, this was the best combined season for the two. Monk became the first receiver to catch 100 balls with 106 for 1,372 yards and 7 TD. Green intercepted five passes and returned one for a score. Each made the Pro Bowl for the first time.

2. 1987. Monk's second strike season and Green's first. Fifteen games were played, but three were with scabs. Monk caught only 38 passes, but six went for touchdowns. Green went to his third Pro Bowl with three interceptions. What puts this season so high on the list is the way it ended. Green made two enormous plays in the playoffs. He returned a punt 52 yards at Chicago while clutching torn rib cartilage and then preserved the NFC Championship the following week by knocking a pass away from Minnesota's Darrin Nelson at the goal line in the final minute. The 42-10 blowout of Denver was Green's first Super Bowl victory and the first Monk was a part of. He missed the victory over Miami with a broken foot in '83 and, finally, in his eighth year in the league, Art Monk walked off the field a champion.

1. 1991. The last hurrah and the year it all went right. With the exception of a Thanksgiving weekend loss to Dallas (stinkin' Cowboys!) and a meaningless end-of-season loss at Philadelphia, it was nearly a perfect season. Monk had his last big year with 71 catches for 1,049 yards and 8 TD. Green picked off five passes and went to the Pro Bowl for the fifth time. The Skins won their third Super Bowl by blasting Buffalo 37-24. Ah, the good old days.

The Five Best Redskins Linebackers Since I Retired :: Sam Huff

Note: Sam Huff came to the Washington Redskins in a controversial trade with the N.Y. Giants in 1964. He played five seasons in Washington, including a year as a player coach under Vince Lombardi in 1969, and for most of the last five decades, he's been one of the main voices on the team's radio broadcasts, teaming with his best friend, Sonny Jurgensen. Huff, a middle linebacker, was voted into the Pro Football Hall of Fame in 1982.

5. London Fletcher. He plays middle linebacker the way it's supposed to be played; a rough, tough guy who loves to hit. When the Redskins got him before the 2007 season, it really solidified their defense with a guy who became a team leader the day he walked in the door.

4. Harold McLinton. We used to call him "Tank" because that's what he looked like. I helped coach him when he first came into the league, and he once hit a guy so hard in St. Louis, they called unnecessary roughness on him, even though it was a clean play. Bill Austin, our head coach that year (1970), started chewing him out for taking a penalty and I went over to Austin and started chewing his ass out. "Don't you ever tell one of my linebackers not to hit hard," I told him. That's what we do.

3. Wilber Marshall. He had been a great player on that Chicago Bears team in 1985, and we were lucky to get him. He loved to hit and he was pretty good in pass coverage, too, a real warrior who gave you everything he had and made a lot of big plays the first time around with Joe Gibbs.

2. LeVar Arrington. He may have been the most talented linebacker who ever played here. He had everything: size, speed, and a real knack for the football. Unfortunately, out on the field, he did not have a mean streak, and I don't think you can play the position unless you do. He also got screwed up by his coaches. Seemed like he had a different one every year, and that didn't help him. I really liked the guy. He could have been one of the best there ever was.

1. Chris Hanburger. Why isn't this guy in the Hall of Fame? I played with him and I coached with him, and he's one of the best linebackers I've ever seen. He could blitz, he could cover, and he could hit. He was one of the great high tacklers. Maybe a little undersized, but he made up for it with his speed and his understanding of the game.

10. The Orioles Anthem. It's a carry-over from the non-Nationals days, when Washingtonians had to migrate over to Baltimore to get their baseball fix. At Camden Yards, the crowds bellow OHHHHHHH!!!! when the National Anthem begins with "Oh say can you see " They do it again near the big finish of "oh say does that star spangled banner still wave." You still hear it all the time at Washington sports events, but OHHHHHHH, please, this is an outside-the-beltway tradition we could all do without inside the beltway.

9. Woodberry Forest vs. Episcopal. The two Virginia prep schools, Episcopal in Alexandria and Woodberry Forest in Orange, have been playing football home and away every year since 1901. It's the nation's longest high school rivalry south of the Mason-Dixon Line. No wonder it's simply called "The Game" and tweed-jacketed, buttoned-down crowds of 15,000 are not unusual at either site.

8. Victory Song. At the University of Maryland, it's played and/or sung after every Turtle touchdown, and head coach Ralph Friedgen, an alum, heads to the student section after Maryland home victories (and sometimes away) to sing the school's spirited fight song. Maryland's students also like to berate opposing players by screaming "Hey, You Suck!" at football and basketball games.

7. Jack the Bulldog. Georgetown's longtime mascot has been around since 1979, but a dog has been a school symbol ever since the 1920s, when a feisty little terrier named Stubby, who actually accompanied his owner to the trenches of France in World War I, came back to bark about it. The pooch became a fixture at football games when his owner returned from the war and enrolled in the Georgetown Law School.

6. Sparklies in the Box. When Jack Kent Cooke owned the Redskins, binoculars in the RFK Stadium stands often were focused on his box above the 50-yard line where all manner of A-List guests—the occasional president, big-time politicians, media pundits and a Hollywood type or two—often watched the games. Dan Snyder's game-day posse is a tad less glittery, though Tom Cruise has been known to show every once in a long while.

5. The Army-Navy Game. Neither team has competed for a national title in ages and the game is always played at a neutral site, usually in Philadelphia. Still, the football game remains a very big deal in the Washington area, particularly at the Pentagon where the services collide in the corridors every day. After the final gun, both teams walk across the field and meet at the 50-yard line to shake hands. Then these future officers and gentlemen soldiers and sailors go en masse to sing the Army alma mater to the Corps of Cadets, then over to the Navy side to sing the Navy Blue and Gold anthem to the Brigade of Midshipmen. In this game, everyone really is playing for the same side.

4. The Diesel. During the Redskin's first Super Bowl season in 1982, every time John Riggins carried the football, the airhorn of a diesel truck blasted in the background of game radio broadcasts. The same joyful foghorn could also be heard at RFK Stadium, signaling the sound of a big rig known as Riggo rolling toward the end zone.

3. Congressional Baseball Game. It's been Republicans vs. Democrats playing real hardball almost every year since 1909 with a game at the long-gone American Park in Northwest Washington. Republican Congressman John Tener, a former major league pitcher and later president of the National League, organized the first game, and *Roll Call*, which bills itself as the newspaper of Capitol Hill, has sponsored it since 1962.

2. "Hail to the Redskins." The second but arguably the best professional football team fight song was composed by society musician Barnee Breeskin with lyrics by George Preston Marshall's wife Corinne in 1938, and has been a fixture at Redskins home games ever since. So, too, is the Redskins Marching Band, still performing in full Native American regalia, no matter how politically incorrect. And the Hogettes? Just a bunch of fatso piggy boys in drag. Another 25 years and maybe we'll call it a tradition. And by the way, the first pro football fight song was the eminently forgettable "Go, You Packers, Go" in 1931.

1. "Play Ball!" on Opening Day. Benjamin Harrison was the first president to attend a major league baseball game in 1892 at Wasington's old Swampdoodle Grounds. But on April 14, 1910, William Howard Taft became the first president to throw out the first ball on Opening Day to kick off the Washington Senators' new season, and the great Walter Johnson caught his pitch. The tradition has endured ever since, though several presidents had to travel to Baltimore to do the honors when the Nation's Capital had no team between 1971 and 2004.

10. Cole Field House. Once the home court of the University of Maryland basketball team, it was the site of the historic 1966 Final Four when Texas Western, with five black starters, won the NCAA basketball championship. It also hosted the 1970 Final Four, when UCLA won its fourth of seven straight NCAA titles. Old Cole, seating 14,500, was replaced by the far more modern Comcast Center in 2002. The big barn is still standing, filled with memories, but definitely not Division I basketball.

9. Fort Dupont Golf Course. For many years, this was the hidden gem of District public golf courses, a rolling, wooded layout in Southeast Washington with one hole ending in an elevated green that seemed so close to the Capitol building, you could reach out and touch the dome. The woods also provided plenty of cover for petty thievery of golf balls, and the place finally closed down in 1970 after three off-duty cops were robbed on a green just before they were putting out.

8. Broadview Farm. Until lush and lovely Great Meadow came along in 1985, the annual Virginia Gold Cup steeplechase races had been held at Broadview Farm, just outside Warrenton, VA, since 1924. Developers bought the property, and the old race course now houses a subdivision.

7. Old Redskins Park. George Allen came to Washington in 1971 and immediately convinced team ownership to build a state-of-the-art training facility not far from Centerville, VA. It was located in an industrial park and surrounded by woods, but 20 years later, the main building was considered too small and the locker room and office space totally inadequate. The Redskins abandoned the place in 1992 for a new Redskins Park about four miles up the road in Ashburn, and the D.C. United soccer team trained there for several years until the land and building were sold to a church in 2001 by the estate of former Redskins owner Jack Kent Cooke.

6. Uline Arena. Built in 1941 by Mike Uline to house his hockey team, the Washington Lions, in the Eastern League, the building still stands at Third and M Northeast, not far from Union Station. Renamed the Washington Coliseum in 1959, it had 7,000 seats and was the site of the first Beatles concert in the U.S. in 1964. From 1994 to 2003, the building was used as a trash-disposal transfer center by Waste Management, the garbage company, and it's now an indoor parking lot.

5. Fort Myer Gym. George Washington and American Universities both played their home basketball games at "The Fort" for many years. It was a tiny bandbox of a gym with cramped locker rooms, about 3,000 seats and, often in the dead of winter, very little heat. Both schools now play in thoroughly modern campus facilities, and "The Fort" is mostly used for Army competitions.

4. McDonough Gymnasium. Once the home of Georgetown basketball starting in 1951, the multi-purpose, 2,500-seat arena has been rarely used by the Hoyas since the team began playing regularly in the old Capital Centre in 1981 and then the Verizon Center downtown. Former NFL Commissioner Paul Tagliabue, a Hoyas' star in the 1950s, threw plenty of elbows back then—great preparation for his future work. And John Thompson Jr. had his basketball office—with a deflated basketball on his desk to reminds his players there was life after hoops—on the second floor for years. It's now mainly used for intramural and recreational sports.

3. Griffith Stadium. The old Washington Senators called the ball park at Georgia Avenue and W St. Northwest, their home field from 1911 to 1960, and the Redskins played there for 24 years until both teams moved to D.C. Stadium (now RFK) in 1961. The stadium where the great Walter Johnson usually mowed down the opposition with a warp-speed fastball was leveled in 1965 to make way for the Howard University Hospital.

2. Capital Centre. Abe Pollin's state-of-the-art arena built right off the Washington Beltway opened in 1973 and was home to the Washington Bullets/Wizards, Capitals and Georgetown Hoyas, as well as serving as the venue for a wide variety of events (wrestling, boxing, horse shows, concerts, religious revivals) until Pollin's new down-town palace, now known as the Verizon Center, opened in 1997. The building was imploded in 2002 to make way for a new town-center-style shopping mall.

1. RFK Stadium. It's still standing, but for how long? In its prime, 55,000-seat RFK was the definition of home field advantage in the NFL. With the stands right on top of the action and noise trapped by the intimacy of it all, the decibel level was ear-splitting and intimidating to countless opponents from the day it opened as D.C. Stadium in 1961 until the last Redskins home game December 22, 1996, a 37-10 victory over the Dallas Cowboys, before the team moved to FedEx Field in the Maryland suburbs at the start of the 1997 season. The Washington Nationals played there for three seasons until moving into their own ball park in the spring of 2008. D.C. United still calls the place home and the stadium is still used for a wide array of events, from tractor pulls to rock concerts.

Ten Local Chains We Miss Shopping At

Call it the "McDonaldsization" of America if you will, but it seems that no matter where you go these days, the stores all seem to have the same names. It wasn't always that way, but in the last 20 years, most chains that got their start in D.C. have either been swallowed up by national chains or have gone out of business completely. Here are 10 we will always remember as being our own that no longer exist.

10. Garfinkel's. True, most guys didn't spend much time there unless they were waiting for their wife to try on a dress, while scoping out other women in the store. Still it was a bit sad when Julius Garfinkel and Company went out of business in 1989. The building that housed the original store at 14th and F still stands, but few remember the days you could go in and buy fancy clothes there.

9. Hecht's. When the last one changed its name to Macy's in 2006, it truly marked the end of the local department store. The Hecht Company had been a solid competitor for home needs, including clothing. It was fun to take the 20-percent-off coupons and match them up with the marked down shirts to see if it was possible they would actually have to pay you to walk out with a Hathaway or an Arrow. The May company had actually owned the chain for more than 20 years before Macy's took over.

8. Woodies. It may have sounded like a sports bar or a hot rod shop to out-of-towners, but it was only local slang for the very classy Woodward and Lothrup, a Washington institution for more than 100 years. It was one of Washington's first department stores and the original location stayed put at 11th and F until its sad closing in 1995.

7. Irving's Sporting Goods. We're not sure if there actually was an Irving, but it was a funny name for the place you bought your first baseball glove and bottle of needsfoot oil. The most popular location was at Colesville and Georgia Avenues in Silver Spring. Like many businesses in the early 90s, it couldn't compete with the larger national chains. It was finally done in by Sports Authority.

6. Raleigh's. Here's how you know this was a longtime operation. Its actual name was Raleigh Haberdasher, but became Raleigh's when everybody except your grandfather stopped using the word, "haberdasher." The salesmen had all been there forever and kept records of your measurements (even as you grew over the years) and what was in your closet. By the early 90s that kind of personal service had gone out of style and Raleigh's sold its last suit in 1993.

5. Hechinger's. Another nickname. Few knew that the real name of the home improvement store was Hechinger. John Hechinger was a pioneer in the do-it-yourself business when he opened his first store in 1911. For the next 80 years or so, it was the place to go when you needed everything from a socket wrench to new plants for the garden. Once again though, they couldn't survive the big national chains. Hechinger didn't quite make it out of the 20th century thanks to Home Depot and Lowe's. It liquidated its assets in 1999.

4. Dart Drug. Credit Herbert Haft with a great post-World War II idea: discount drugs. Herbie's first corner drug store opened in 1955 and eventually the chain grew to 100 stores. It lasted until 1984 when the chain was sold to Fantle's. It folded up in 1990.

3. Trak Auto. Another good idea from Haft: discount auto parts. This chain eventually grew to 55 stores before it was sold to Advance Auto Parts in 2002.

2. Crown Books. You could probably make a TV mini-series out of this one. Such drama. Crown was actually started by Haft's son Robert who used to do his own radio ads that opened with a high-pitched nasally Robert saying, "Books cost too much, that's why I started Crown books." The discount books concept worked. Starting with one store in 1977, by 1993 he'd built the third largest book chain in America behind Barnes & Noble and Borders. Unfortunately the chain crashed when Haft's parents, Herbert and Gloria, went through a bitter divorce. Robert sided with mom and all hell broke loose. Herb fired Robert, who then sued, and by the time the dust settled Crown Books was forced to liquidate in 2001.

1. Peoples Drug Stores: Opened in 1904, this was the place to go at midnight when the baby had a cough. You didn't say, "I'm going to the drug store." You said, "I'm going to Peoples." Generations of Washingtonians crammed the store after the first day of school to buy supplies for the year. More importantly, if you looked in either the outfield or the end zone at RFK Stadium for more than 30 years, you saw that half-oval Peoples sign. A wonderful image. Just months short of the 90th anniversary of the chain in 1994, the last Peoples sign was ripped down and replaced by the letters CVS. Ugh!

Before the private high schools really got serious about recruiting, you could find talent in the suburbs. Often they were kids rich enough to have hoops attached to their garage (yes you have to have a garage in order to attach a hoop to it), where they spent hours honing their shots. Had there been a three-point line in the 1970s, these guys would have really posted some eye-popping numbers. But from the days of the short shorts hiked up on their pasty-white legs, here are the top 10 white guys who lit it up from the outside in Montgomery County gyms in the 70s.

10. Steve Graham, B-CC, All-Met 1970. Teamed up with his younger brother, Spencer, to form one of the top teams in the area. Steve got some looks from Division I schools, but had his best days as a high schooler.

9. Spencer Graham, B-CC, All-Met 1971. A better player than his older brother who got some real serious looks from the top Division I schools. Lefty Driesell caused quite a stir when he showed up with his assistant George Raveling at one of Spencer's games during his senior year. Spencer led his team in some legendary games against Springbrook. One of the games was so packed that they put the overflow crowd in the cafeteria and showed it on closed-circuit TV. No mean feat in 1971. Like his older brother, he never developed as a college player.

8. Herb Krusen, Northwood, All-Met 1976. Managed to make All-Met in one of the great years for guards in the Washington area. Included in the class was Jo Jo Hunter who went to Maryland and John Duren who went to Georgetown and later played in the NBA. Krusen was the county's second-best player that year behind Mike Owens, who went on to win an NIT title with a freshman named Ralph Sampson at Virginia in 1980.

7. Stu Klitenic, Northwood, All-Met 1973. Good enough to become a four-year scholarship player at South Carolina. Now works as a sportscaster in Atlanta.

6. Craig Davis, Peary, All-Met 1974. Despite being only 5-foot-10, Davis could light it up, once scoring 42 points in a game (again that's without a three-point line). Although he was mostly a backup at North Carolina State, Davis was recruited to replace graduating point guard Monte Towe from State's 1974 national championship team. Davis was actually coach Norm Sloan's second choice for that spot. His first choice decided to go to Notre Dame and play football. You may have heard of him: Joe Montana.

5. Craig Esherick, Springbrook, All-Met 1974. Best known as the longtime assistant to John Thompson and later head coach at Georgetown. Esherick was actually the third-best shooter at Springbrook in the 70s, but has the best collegiate singular moment. In his senior year at Georgetown, February 22, 1978, with Georgetown down two to cross-town rival, George Washington, Esherick swished a 35 footer at the regulation buzzer (again no three-point line) to send the game into overtime. Georgetown won 78-77. Asked about the shot after the game, Esherick said, "Every time I shoot it, I expect it to go in." Montgomery County pride, baby.

4. Steve Nuce, Northwood, All-Met 1970. Nuce had the best team college success of this group. He played on the famed 1974 National Championship team at NC State that knocked off seven-time defending champion UCLA in the Final Four. Nuce gave that team some solid minutes off the bench and made Montgomery County kids believe they too could reach the highest heights of the game.

3. Brian Magid, Blair, All-Met 1975. Led Blair to the 1975 Maryland State championship and decided to stay home and play college basketball for Lefty Driesell amid quite a bit of hype. Every time he entered a game in his freshman and sophmore years, the fans at Cole Field House would yell, "Shoot!!!" Several times he did so to either win it or send the game into overtime, but Magid just didn't have the quickness to get major minutes in the ACC. He transferred to George Washington and led the team in scoring as a senior at 15.6 points a game.

2. Ed Peterson, Springbrook, All-Met 1969 and '70. Is considered to be the godfather of Montgomery County shooters. Many of the guys on the list say they learned how to shoot from Ed. Held the school's scoring record for more than 30 years before Folarin Campbell, who played on a Final Four team at George Mason, broke it. Peterson played at South Carolina for a couple of years, but didn't keep up academically and dropped out.

1. Buzzy Braman, Springbrook, All-Met 1972 and '73. How can you not make the man who billed himself as "The Shot Doctor" number one on the list? Braman went on to play at East Carolina for a couple of years. His greater fame came later on when he talked his way into a job with the Philadelphia 76ers as a shooting coach. Braman told Sixers owner Harold Katz that he could teach him to make 10-straight free throws. Katz knocked them down and gave Braman the job. When former Sixers coach Jim Lynam became coach of the Bullets, he took Braman with him. He also gained a measure of fame when he worked with Shaquille O'Neal on free throw shooting.

The Washington Bullets (now the Wizards) were not the D.C. area's first profession-al basketball team. There were two incarnations of the Washington Capitols. First, the team started by Mike Uline in 1946 and coached by Red Auerbach, that compet-ed in the Basketball Association of America with names like Bones McKinney and Freddie Scolari. That team was absorbed into the NBA, but folded midway through the 1950-51 season. And for one season, 1969-70, we had the Washington Capitols of the American Basketball Association with its red, white, and blue basketball. Everybody called them the Caps, which was stitched onto the front of the green and gold uniforms left over from the franchise's first two years as the Oakland Oaks. Singer Pat Boone had been one of the original owners, but when he and his part-ners suffered huge losses, the team was sold to a group headed by D.C. lawyer Earl Foreman. With no pro basketball team in Washington, Foreman, who had previous-ly been partners with Bullets owner Abe Pollin, figured to make a good go of it. He figured wrong. The Caps played in the Washington Coliseum, which had only 7,000 seats. Despite an excellent roster and a winning team, they averaged less than 3,000 fans a game. With word that Pollin was planning to move the Bullets to Washington, Foreman was encouraged by the other ABA owners to move. He went south and renamed the team the Virginia Squires and played their home games in Norfolk, Roanoke, Hampton Roads, and Richmond. They stayed alive (barely) until folding just before the final NBA-ABA merger in the spring of 1976 because they couldn't come up with a $75,000 league assessment. Money, not players, was the downfall of the franchise. Here are the top names who rolled through during the team's nine-season history, but were cast off for cash reasons.

10. Lavern "Jelly" Tart, Oaks 1967-68. Wasn't a great player, but he had a great name and loved to shoot. He jacked an average of more than 20 shots a game that year, then made his way through five other ABA teams before finishing his career in 1971.

9. Roland "Fatty" Taylor, Caps, Squires 1969-76. At six feet, 180 pounds, he wasn't fat but kept the nickname. Taylor was a rookie during his one D.C. season. He could score a bit (eight points a game) and distribute the ball. Except for the 1974-75 season when he went to Denver, Taylor was a franchise mainstay.

8. Warren Armstrong, Oaks, Caps 1968-70. Was ABA rookie of the year in Oakland, averaging 21.5 points and an impressive 9.7 rebounds a game. Legend has it, even though he was 6-foot-2, Armstrong could jump and touch his forehead on a 10-foot rim. His stats were even slightly better after the team moved to D.C., but he hurt his knee midway through the season. Armstrong wound up in Indiana before the team moved to Virginia, changed his name to Warren Jabali, and was out of basketball by the time he was 28.

7. Willie Wise, Squires 1974-76. Wise's best days were behind him by the time he got to Virginia. The 6-foot-6 swingman was one of the best players in the ABA between 1971 and '74. Wise hung in long enough to play a year with Denver when the team merged into the NBA. He also made the 1977-78 Sonics (the team that lost to the Bullets in the finals), but played only two games and retired.

6. Larry Brown, Oaks, Caps, Squires 1968-71. Yes, that Larry Brown. He was a player once, who probably should have gotten a better look from the NBA. At 6-foot-5 Oscar Robertson was the prototype guard teams were looking for in those days. Brown was only 5-foot-9 and wasn't taken seriously, despite a great career at North Carolina. Four years after he graduated, the ABA finally provided him a chance. Brown was an outstanding point guard during his three stops with the team and knew how to be the quarterback on the floor. He finished his playing career in Denver in 1972 and went on to become one of the game's great coaches—the first to win an NCAA and NBA championship.

5. Swen Nater, Squires 1973 and '76. Spent parts of two seasons with the Squires before joining the Milwaukee Bucks after the merger. Despite being one of the best rebounders in the game, Nater was on the UCLA bench for most of his college career behind a fellow named Bill Walton. During his three years in the ABA, Nater averaged 13 points and 13 rebounds a game. Nater was part of the money crunch that owner Earl Foreman faced and was sold to San Antonio early in his rookie season for $300,000 dollars.

4. Charlie Scott, Squires 1970-72. Scott was a big star coming out of North Carolina and took the bigger bucks to sign with the rival league. In his second year, he led the ABA in scoring at 34.6 points per game. Scott then jumped again, going to Phoenix in the NBA. He played on the Celtics 1975-76 championship team and finished with Denver in 1980 after playing in three NBA All Star games.

3. George Gervin, Squires 1972-74. One of basketball's greatest scorers (he could finger roll), Gervin was the last superstar to be bled from the franchise. In fact, when Foreman sold "The Iceman" to San Antonio for $225,000, ABA Commissioner Mike Storen (father of Hannah Storm) tried to block it in court on the grounds that it wasn't in the best interests of the league. Gervin wound up in the Squires' lap after he was thrown off the team at Eastern Michigan University for fighting.

2. Rick Barry, Oaks, Caps 1968-70. Barry put the ABA on the map by becoming the first NBA star to jump to the upstart league. A three-year, $225,000 contract and a chance to play for his former college coach and then father-in-law, Bruce Hale, lured him in. His former team, the San Francisco Warriors, got a California court to uphold the option clause in Barry's contract, which prevented him from playing for a year. He kept in shape by playing for a local radio station team captained by morning disc jockey Johnny Holliday (yes, that guy). Barry played a year with the Oaks and reluctantly moved with the team to Washington. Injuries limited him to 52 games, but he scored 55 points against Denver in a playoff game. Barry appeared on the cover of *Sports Illustrated* in a Virginia Squires uniform in the summer of 1970, but was traded to the New York Nets for $250,000. Barry wanted out anyway, telling SI he didn't want to go to Virginia because, "I don't want my son coming home saying 'Howdy y'all.'"

1. Julius Erving, Squires 1971-73. This was when the legend of "Dr. J" was born. He took the game to a new level: above the rim. His 31.9 points per game led the ABA in his second year, scoring 58 in a February game against the Nets. "The Doctor" was awesome, but at $125,000 a year, too expensive for the struggling Squires. In the summer of 1973, Erving and Willie Sojourner were traded to New York for George Carter, the rights to Kermit Washington, and $1 million.

Bottom line: In a perfect world, without money problems, the Caps might have stayed in Washington and these 10 players (ok, minus maybe Lavern Tart) could have stayed together to become one of the great teams in basketball history. Instead, Foreman is remembered as the owner who had four of the greatest names in the history of the game—Erving, Barry, Gervin, and Scott—and couldn't afford to keep any of them.

Top 10 Northern Virginia High School Hoopsters
:: Chris Knoche

Note: Playing for the legendary Red Jenkins, Chris Knoche was an All-District basketball player at WT Woodson, graduating in 1976. After a year at Colorado, he transferred to American University where he became Gary Williams' first recruit (Gary likes to say things got better after that, ha ha). Following graduation, he stayed on as an assistant at AU and had a seven-year run as head coach. Knoche is now the color analyst for University of Maryland basketball games on the radio and frequently appears on the *Sports Reporters* on Sportstalk 980. Still a northern Virginia resident, here are his top 10 players from the other side of the Potomac River.

10. The Hummer Brothers, Washington-Lee, 1963, 1966. Ed led W-L to state championships in '62 and '63, when the team went 24-0. John led W-L to a state title in '66. Both were All-Ivy League at Princeton and went on to the pros. Ed was drafted by the Celtics and played in the ABA. John played six seasons in the NBA, mostly for the Buffalo Braves.

9. Skeeter Swift, George Washington, 1965. A flamboyant talent who walked the walk and talked the talk. At 6-foot-3, 235 pounds, he could overpower most opposing guards. He was All-Met as a junior and senior. Swift went on to star at East Tennessee State and played five seasons in the ABA.

8. Hubert Davis, Lake Braddock, 1988. A hard-working guard who became a great shooter. Some thought was reaching too far when he went to North Carolina, but played 137 games for the Tar Heels and set the school record for 3-point field goal percentage (.435). He was the 20th pick of the 1992 draft by the Knicks and played 12 seasons in the NBA.

7. Dave Koesters, West Springfield, 1974. A three-year starter who led his team to three straight regional titles, two state championship game appearances, and a 72-6 record. As a senior, Koesters averaged 23.5 points a game and helped nearly pull off an incredible upset of Moses Malone's Petersburg team in the Virginia State Championship game. They lost 50-48. He's probably the best shooter ever to play at a Virginia public school. Koesters played college basketball at Virginia.

6. Tommy Amaker, WT Woodson, 1983. A four-year starter at point guard for a premier program. He grew from a 5-foot-7 freshman defensive specialist to a 6-foot do-everything playmaker. After four years as a starter at Duke, he was drafted by Seattle. Amaker has been the head coach at Seton Hall, Michigan, and currently Harvard.

5. Scotty Reynolds, Herndon, 2006. Led Herndon to an 88-18 record, three district championships, and a regional title over three years. Reynolds was the Virginia State Player of the Year as a senior, averaging 28.4 points a game. He scored 53 in a win over Norcom. One of the most highly recruited players in the history of the state, he started off at Oklahoma, but transferred to Villanova after a coaching change.

4. Jim O'Brien, JEB Stuart, 1969. Larry Bird before Larry Bird. A multi-skilled 6-foot-7 redhead who could beat you by scoring 40 or by piling up assists and rebounds. After averaging more than 30 points a game as a senior, he became Lefty Driesell's first big recruit. O'Brien played a couple of years in the ABA before knee problems ended his career.

3. Dennis Scott, Flint Hill, 1986. The best private school player and one of the best shooters in area history. Scott would go on to lead Georgia Tech to the Final Four after being named ACC Player of the Year in 1990. Scott was drafted by Orlando with the fourth pick and played 10 years in the NBA.

2. David Robinson, Osborne Park, 1983. The career highlights came after high school, but let's give the area some love for producing one of the all-time greats. Robinson got talked into playing for the first time as a 6-foot-7 senior. He went to the Naval Academy for the academics, not the basketball, but grew six inches and became a star. Robinson rang up 2,669 points and 1,314 rebounds while taking the Midshipmen to the Elite Eight. As a San Antonio Spur, Robinson was a 10-time All Star, a three-time Olympian, a two-time NBA champion and was picked as one the 50 greatest NBA players of all time.

1. Grant Hill, South Lakes, 1990. Pick a stat, any stat: 2,028 points, three district and one regional championship. At Duke he scored 1,900 points and won two NCAA Championships. Hill became a great NBA player, who likely would have been even better without terrible ankle problems. He remains the gold standard for Northern Virginia high school players.

DeMatha 46 – Power Memorial of New York 43, January 30, 1965

Montrose Christian 74 – Oak Hill 72, March 4, 2006

Despite their separation by more than 40 years, each was a game that if you saw it, you'll talk about it for the rest of your life. Old timers can argue with young kids over which game was better. Here is a breakdown of the key arguing points of the two classics.

9. Attendance. The DeMatha game was played at Cole Field House and drew an announced crowd of 12,500 which was close to capacity in those days. The Montrose game filled every seat (about 4,000) at Coolidge High School.

8. Biggest Star. Some actually refer to the DeMatha game as "The Lew Alcindor game." Alcindor—later to be known as Kareem Abdul-Jabbar—was labeled as one of the greatest players of all time from the moment he entered Power Memorial as a freshman in 1961. At 7-foot-2, he was unstoppable and averaged more than 30 points a game. A year earlier as a junior, Alcindor scored 35 points in Power Memorial's 65-62 win over DeMatha. The big star for Montrose was 6-foot-10 Kevin Durant, who had played the year before at Oak Hill. He had the size of a center and the quickness of a guard, and appeared ready to play in the NBA that night. Two years later he would be the second pick of the NBA draft after a required college pit stop at the University of Texas.

7. Other Participants. Sid Catlett is the biggest name other than Alcindor to emerge from the DeMatha game. He and teammate Bob Whitmore went to Notre Dame together after graduating from DeMatha. Both rosters from the Montrose game would soon be spread out through some of the best college basketball programs in America including North Carolina (Tywon Lawson), Duke (Nolan Smith), and Maryland (Grevis Vasquez and Adrian Bowie).

6. Coaches. DeMatha's Morgan Wootten is regarded by many as the greatest high school basketball coach of all time. This win was what made him a household name in basketball circles. Jack Donohue of Power Memorial had great success in his own right, but had his reputation smudged in Alcindor's (by then Kareem Abdul-Jabbar) autobiography *Giant Steps*. Jabbar said he lost respect for his coach when Donohue tried to use the "N" word to motivate him. Montrose was coached by Stu Vetter, who has sent dozens of players to major colleges over the years. Oak Hill's Steve Smith is the least known of the four.

5. Streak Busters. Power Memorial came in to the game with a 71-game winning streak. The loss was the only one of Alcindor's high school career. Oak Hill carried a 56-game win streak into the game and was ranked number one in the country in a *USA Today* newspaper poll.

4. Strategy. Wootten had Catlett use a tennis racquet in practice to simulate Alcindor's huge wingspan. He also told Whitmore, who was giving up nine inches, to try to deny Alcindor the ball. Vetter said he wanted to control the tempo of the game and have Bowie attack the basket.

3. Hype. The DeMatha game was played in the prehistoric pre-ESPN days, so the buildup was different. But national publications like *Time* and *Newsweek* requested credentials. Also, as tickets were being scooped up, word spread that this was going to be the most significant high school basketball game of all time. The Montrose game had great local buzz, but by the time it was played, ESPN had already televised a number of high school games, including several involving LeBron James.

2. How the Games Played Out. Although the DeMatha game was decided by three (before the days of the three-point line) and wasn't decided at the buzzer, it was a classic. DeMatha led 23-22 at the half. In the second half it was tied three times and the lead changed hands four times. Most significant was the job Whitmore did on Alcindor, holding the giant to just 16 points. Catlett led DeMatha with 13 and Bernie Williams had 12. The Montrose game seemed headed for overtime when Bowie had a put back with one second left for his 19th and 20th points of the game. With Durant in first-half foul trouble, Oak Hill went up by as many as 16 and led by 11 going in to the fourth quarter thanks to Lawson, who scored 14 of Oak Hill's 20 in the third quarter. Lawson, who was operating at a different speed than everybody else on the court, finished with 26. Durant was as good as advertised and finished with a game-high 31, while scoring with equal ability inside and out.

1. Epilogue. Neither game was televised, but each will forever be part of the discussion of the great sporting events (and not just high school) in Washington area history. Alcindor went on to UCLA where he won three national titles and three Player of the Year awards, and is regarded as one of the best college players in history. He followed that up with a 22-year NBA career that included a title with the Milwaukee Bucks and five more with the Los Angeles Lakers. He is also regarded as one of the best NBA players of all time. The fact that he wasn't able to dominate that January night is a tribute to the job done by Wootten and his team. Also, some credit goes to Wootten's wife Kathy. An ambulance sat outside Cole Field House just in case she went into labor. She managed to hold off a few days for the birth of their first child Joe, who is now the head coach at Bishop O'Connell. At press time, Durant is the only player from the Montrose game in the NBA and was Rookie of the Year with the Seattle Supersonics. But he will no doubt soon be joined by at least several others who joined him on that March night at Coolidge in a game for the ages. Best game ever? You decide.

Note: John Thompson is one of the most important figures in the history of basketball. He is also a D.C. guy through and through. After playing on what may have been the best high school basketball team in history at Archbishop Carroll, Thompson went to Providence in 1961 and became an All-American. Following a two-year NBA career with the Boston Celtics playing for the great Red Auerbach, Thompson began a 30-year coaching career at St. Anthony in D.C. At the age of 30 he was named head coach at Georgetown University and built a national powerhouse. His teams went to three Final Fours and won a National Title. In 1984, he became the first African American coach to win an NCAA basketball championship. He was also an assistant under Dean Smith on the 1976 Olympic team and head coach of the 1988 team. Thompson resigned at Georgetown in 1999 and was elected to the Hall of Fame later that year. He now hosts the *John Thompson Show* on Sportstalk 980 and is an analyst for Westwood One Radio and TNT television. Unlike when he was growing up in D.C. playing basketball and later scouting talent as a coach, the playground, he says, isn't what it used to be. However, D.C. has a rich hoop history of talent honed on the blacktop. Here is Thompson's list of where many of the greats played. And who knows, maybe where a few future greats are being grown.

11. 20th and Franklin, NE. Near Rhode Island Avenue. Not necessarily a talent hotbed, but a place to play.

10. Sherwood, 9th and H, NE. A number of leagues held their games there.

9. Parkview, Warden St., NW. Austin Carr played there in the 1960s.

8. New York Avenue Playground, NW. Near First Street, not far from Union Station. A number of boys' club league games have been held here.

7. Rosedale, 17th and Gales, NE. A good place to see players from the local colleges play in the summer.

6. Rose Park, 1404 26th Street, NW. In Georgetown near Rock Creek Parkway.

5. Luzon, 16th Street near Walter Reed, NW. Adrian Dantley, one of D.C's greatest players, played here; so did Donald Washington, who went to North Carolina.

4. Chevy Chase Playground, 4101 Livingston Street, NW. A favorite spot for Red Auerbach to scout talent during the summer. Dave Bing played there. There were tournaments played there when I was growing up, but they weren't open to everybody. I remember being driven there to participate and was told I couldn't play because of my skin color. The men who took me there were embarrassed.

3. Kelly Miller, 30th Street, NE. Sunday league games were played there. There was one memorable weekend when Elgin Baylor was getting married and Wilt Chamberlain came in for the wedding and played in pickup games.

2. Turkey Thicket, 1100 Michigan Avenue, NE. Still a hot spot. Gilbert Arenas has been known to play there during the summer.

1. Henry T. Blow, 19th and Benning Road, NE. Was the place where everybody played when I was growing up. I remember the excitement on Friday evenings when you knew you were going to get a full weekend of games.

Since the advent of the college basketball polls, starting with Number One Kentucky's 46-36 win over Number Two Oklahoma A&M in the 1949 NCAA championship game, the top two teams have met (as of press time) only 37 times. Georgetown was involved in three of those games within a three-month period, twice as Number One and once as Number Two. They won all three between December 1984 and March 1985 by an average of 16 points, which makes their loss to Villanova in the NCAA championship game that season seem even more remarkable. Here are the Hoyas' three One-versus-Two wins.

3. December 15, 1984, Capital Centre, Landover, Maryland—(1) Georgetown 77 — (2) DePaul 57. Wrote Bob Ryan, who covered the game for

the *Boston Globe*, "It may simply mean that Georgetown's only legitimate competition at present comes when it scrimmages itself." Ryan explained that DePaul hadn't played that badly; Georgetown just seemed that good. Actually, with 11:06 left, DePaul was down only two, 53-51. It was then that the smothering Hoyas' defense rose to the occasion. DePaul managed no field goals and only six free throws the rest of the way. Patrick Ewing was awesome with 15 points, 15 rebounds, and six blocked shots.

2. February 27, 1985, Madison Square Garden, New York—(2) Georgetown 85 — (1) St. Johns 69. This will always be remembered as the

"sweater game." St. Johns had won 13 straight, including a 66-65 win at Georgetown a month earlier to stop the Hoyas' 29-game win streak, with coach Lou Carnesecca wearing an ugly brown sweater with red and turquoise stripes. Louie admitted it was ugly, but wasn't about to risk changing his luck by handing it over to Goodwill. Georgetown coach John Thompson, to lighten the mood of his team, opened his suit jacket for the pre game handshake to show Carnesecca what he was wearing: a replica of the sweater. The Hoyas laughed and kept on laughing on their way to an easier than expected win. Reggie Williams led Georgetown with 25 points. Patrick Ewing had 20 points and nine rebounds. St. Johns stars Chris Mullin and Walter Berry combined for 37.

1. March 9, 1985, Big East Championship, Madison Square Garden, New York—(1) Georgetown 92 — (2) St. Johns 80. Ewing played less than half

the game because of foul trouble, but backup Ralph Dalton picked up the slack with nine points and eight rebounds. Georgetown was, for the second time in two weeks, dominant. The Hoyas shot 57 percent for the game and out-rebounded the Redmen (that's what they were called before the politically-correct police took over) 36-19. Michael Jackson (the one without the young-boy fetish) was the top scorer with 19. Coach John Thompson helped cut down the nets, but said, "These aren't the strings I want." Incredibly, he didn't get those. After coasting through the NCAA tournament, including an 18-point blowout of St. Johns in the Final Four, Georgetown fell victim to Villanova's perfect game in the final and lost 66-64, ending a chance to claim one of the greatest seasons in college basketball history.

The Top 11 Georgetown Basketball Players

Few teams in the country have put as many stars in the NBA as Georgetown. Particularly when it comes to big men, Georgetown has really cornered the market. There are some good arguments to be made for a few guys not on the list, but here's how we rank them as college players, leaving out what they went on to do as pros.

11. Paul Tagliabue (1959-63). Yeah, maybe it's bad to start a list with an additional pick, but come on, he went on to become the freakin' Commissioner of the NFL! And here's a stat to impress your friends with: Tagliabue's career rebounding average (9.0) ranks ahead of Alonzo Mourning and Dikembe Mutombo (both 8.6) and is only slightly behind Patrick Ewing (9.2).

10. Merlin Wilson (1972-76). Was John Thompson's first big recruit and he did what Thompson loved best: play defense and rebound. Wilson still holds the school record for season (14.1) and career (11.4) rebounding averages. He also averaged 11 points a game and led the Hoyas to only their second- and third-ever appearances in the NCAA tournament in 1975 and '76.

9. John Duren (1976-80). Became Georgetown's first Big East Player of the Year in 1980 and became a first-round pick of the Utah Jazz. Duren averaged 13.5 points a game for his defensive-minded coach and ranks fourth in career assists and 10th in steals. Helped lead Georgetown to NCAA tournament wins over Iona and Maryland in 1980.

8. Craig Shelton (1976-80). Was a big recruiting score for Thompson and lived up to his high school reputation where he earned the nickname, "Big Sky." Shelton teamed with Duren to lead the Hoyas to their first Big East championship in 1980 and was named Most Valuable Player in the tournament. He averaged over 15 points and seven rebounds a game for his career and was selected in the second round of the NBA draft by the Atlanta Hawks.

7. Eric Floyd (1978-82). Carried the nickname "Sleepy" for his droopy eyes, but was anything but sleepy on the court. Floyd ranks third on Georgetown's career scoring average list at 17.7 points a game. He was a two-time All-American and All-Big East First Team as a junior and senior. Floyd started on the team that lost to Michael Jordan's North Carolina team in '82 and was taken in the first round of the NBA draft by New Jersey. He went on to play 13 years in the NBA, appearing in the All Star game for Golden State in 1987.

6. Jeff Green (2004-2007). Was Big East Player of the Year while leading Georgetown to the Final Four in 2007. Green was part of John Thompson III's first Georgetown team and made steady improvement over his three years. He was taken with the fifth pick of the 2007 NBA draft by Seattle after leaving school before his senior year.

5. Dikembe Mutombo (1988–91). Actually came to Georgetown on an academic scholarship and has the ability to speak seven languages. But as a seven-footer, he let his rebounding and shot blocking speak. He ranks third in career blocks at Georgetown behind Patrick Ewing and Alonzo Mourning with 354 in only 96 career games (47 fewer than Ewing). In his final year, Mutombo set a Georgetown record with 389 rebounds, while averaging 12.2 a game. His actual age is sort of a wink-wink situation (maybe he's 50), but he's been playing in the NBA since becoming a first-round selection of the Denver Nuggets in 1991.

4. Reggie Williams (1983–87). Started on Georgetown's National Title team as a freshman in 1984 and went on to have one of the great careers in NCAA history. As a senior he carried a team Thompson dubbed "Reggie and the Miracles" to the Elite Eight before losing to Providence. That season, Williams led the Hoyas in scoring (23.0) and rebounding (8.7), and became the third pick of the NBA draft by the Los Angeles Clippers. Although his pro career was not distinguished, he remains one of the best ever D.C.-area college players ever.

3. Alonzo Mourning (1988–92). John Thompson had no problem giving 'Zo the number 33 that Patrick Ewing wore. There was little doubt that Mourning was going to be the next great big man for the Hoyas when he arrived on campus. Mourning led Georgetown to four-straight appearances in the NCAA tournament and was Big East Player of the Year as a senior. Mourning was the second pick of the NBA draft by Charlotte and has gone on to win an Olympic gold medal and an NBA championship. He is one of Georgetown's top-five all-time scorers and rebounders.

2. Allen Iverson (1994–96). Was the first John Thompson-coached player to leave school early, but it appears he was ready for the pros (ya think?!). Iverson is Georgetown's all-time scoring-average leader at 23.0 points a game and is considered one of the most amazing athletes in the history of basketball. He was so good, that he may be the only player in Thompson's career to always have the green light on the court. Iverson was the number-one pick of the 1996 draft by Philadelphia and was the Most Valuable Player in the NBA in 2001.

1. Patrick Ewing (1981–85). Would have to be on anyone's list of the greatest players in college basketball history. While leading the Hoyas to three appearances in the NCAA championship game, including a title in 1984, Ewing was a three-time first-team All-American and was the Naismith and NABA player of the year in 1985. Ewing was considered to be such a fortune-changer coming out of college that, to this day, rumors persist that the NBA draft lottery was rigged to give the New York Knicks the selection to take him.

The Top 10 Local Small-College Hoops Legends :: Ken Denlinger.

Note: Former *Washington Post* sports columnist Ken Denlinger has always loved to find big-time talent in somewhat obscure places, like the drafty arena on the Army base at Fort Meyer, where schools like American and George Washington used to play home games until they built on–campus gyms of their own. Denlinger and Len Shapiro also are the co-authors of *Athletes For Sale* (1974), one of the first investigations into college basketball recruiting abuses.

10. Brian Magid, George Washington. The designated shooter.

9. Bob Adrion, Catholic. Became CU's all-time leading scorer in 1973 as a *junior*.

8. Gordon Austin, American. Every team needs a classy point guard.

7. Michael Britt, UDC. A slender swingman who also played defense.

6. Carlos Yates, George Mason. This mid-1980s forward had 2,420 points over four years.

5. Russell (Boo) Bowers, American. A late 1970s scoring machine, he was drafted in the third round by Cleveland in 1981.

4. Mike Brown, George Washington. A 6-9 power forward in the early-1980s, he also played 626 NBA games for six teams.

3. Earl Jones, UDC. A 7-footer, he averaged 23.0 points and was a first-round choice by the Lakers in the 1984 draft.

2. Kermit Washington, American. A first-team All-American in 1973, he also had a 3.7 GPA and a decent NBA career, minus one punch directed at Rudy Tomjanovich.

1. David Robinson, Navy. The admirable Admiral and certain Hall of Famer gave Navy basketball its Roger Staubach.

Before they were famous, the following initially unknown working-stiff "littles" began their careers in the Washington media before they eventually became big-timers in their chosen professions a few years down the road.

10. Winston Groom. After serving a tour of duty in Vietnam, his first job was as a police and court reporter for the old *Washington Star*. In 1986, he returned to his native Alabama, and soon produced a work of fiction, *Forrest Gump*, which sold a modest number of copies. In 1994, the book was made into a movie of the same name, starring Tom Hanks in one of his signature and Oscar-winning roles, and Groom's book sold 1.7 million copies over the next year.

9. Maureen Dowd. A native of Washington, D.C., and one of five children of a Washington policeman, Dowd attended Catholic University and joined the *Washington Star* as an editorial assistant in 1974 before moving up to reporter. When the paper folded in 1981, she first joined *Time*, then the *New York Times*, where she was a metropolitan reporter before joining the Washington bureau in 1986. She became a columnist on the op-ed page in 1995 and within four years won a Pulitzer Prize for distinguished commentary.

8. Marty Hurney. He covered the Redskins for the *Washington Times* during the Joe Gibbs era and became friendly with General Manager Bobby Beathard. When Beathard left the organization in 1989 to take over GM duties for the San Diego Chargers, he hired Hurney as his assistant. Hurney eventually became the Chargers' salary cap expert, a job he held for several years with the Carolina Panthers before being named the team's general manager in 1999.

7. Peter Mehlman. A part-time sports reporter for the *Washington Post* while he attended the University of Maryland in the late 1970s, Mehlman spent two years working for Howard Cosell before joining a mostly unknown comedian, Jerry Seinfeld, as a writer on his new television show in 1989. Over the show's nine-year run, Mehlman produced and wrote some of the more famous Seinfeld episodes, including yada-yada among many others.

6. David Remick. He joined the *Washington Post* in 1982 out of Princeton and covered the Washington Bullets and nemesis Jeff Ruland for a year before moving to the Style section, then a six-year stint in the paper's Moscow Bureau. He won a Pulitzer Prize for his book *Lenin's Tomb* on the fall of the Soviet Union, then joined the *New Yorker* as a staff writer in 1992. Six years later, he was named editor, a position he still occupies.

5. Larry King. After serious legal and financial problems that nearly got him sent to jail in the early 1970s, King became the overnight talk show host on the Mutual Radio Network in 1978, operating out of a studio in Crystal City until it went off the air in 1994. King also joined the fledgling CNN in 1987 hosting his own interview show and remains a popular figure on the network.

4. Rock Newman. A former Howard University baseball player, Newman hosted his own Washington radio show on WOL in the 1980s before hooking up with 1988 Olympic boxing champion Riddick Bowe. As Bowe's manager, he guided the fighter to the world heavyweight title and also promoted a number of fight cards after Bowe's career ended when he went to prison for kidnapping his wife in 1999, serving an 18-month sentence.

3. John Feinstein. A Duke graduate who joined the *Washington Post* as an intern in 1977, he joined the paper as a sports and then metro reporter before taking a short leave of absence to write a book on Indiana basketball coach Bob Knight in 1987. *Season on the Brink* became a runaway bestseller and Feinstein soon left the paper to focus on writing books. As of 2008, he had 23 books to his credit, many of them also bestsellers.

2. Tom Wolfe. The former sports editor of his college newspaper at Washington and Lee in Lexington, VA, Wolfe joined the *Washington Post* as a metro reporter in 1959 and stayed for three years, winning a Newspaper Guild award in 1961 for his reporting in Cuba. He left in 1962 for a reporting job with the *New York Herald Tribune* and within two years was one of the leading practitioners of the so-called new journalism. In 1987, his first novel, *Bonfire of the Vanities*, eventually reached No. 1 on the best-seller list.

1. Jackie Kennedy. After graduating from George Washington in 1951 with a degree in French literature, Jacqueline Bouvier took a job with the old *Washington Times-Herald* as the newspaper's "inquiring photographer." She took your picture, asked a question, and both appeared in the paper the next day. One of her early subjects was a young congressman from Massachusetts, and the rest, as they say, is history.

Note: Raised in northern Virginia, and a graduate of Washington-Lee High School where he was the football team's kicker (with a square-toe shoe; that's how long ago it was), "Buck" has become one of the top names in local sports television. He was the sports guy on Channel 5 from 1984 to 1997 and has been the TV play-by-play voice of the Wizards ever since. Here are his top 10 TV moments going back to his days as a student at James Madison University in the mid-70s.

10. "Shotgun." My first year at Channel 5 I was covering a Redskins practice prior to a playoff game against Chicago. I noticed they were working on the "shotgun" formation, which they had never used in a game under coach Joe Gibbs. After practice, I asked Gibbs about it and was glared at. A short time later, I was summoned to speak with the coach, who if he had a shotgun, might have used it on me. He was as angry as I've ever seen him, accusing me of trying to sabotage the team's strategy in front the entire media, including reporters from Chicago. It led to a ban on reporters being able to watch the entire practice.

9. Proofreading Lesson. It was my first on-air job at WHSV-TV in Harrisonburg, Virginia, where I was still attending JMU in 1977. Because of another assignment, I didn't get in to the studio until shortly before my 11 o'clock sportscast. I rushed to the Associated Press wire machine (in those pre-computer days, stories were printed out on long rolls of paper) and ripped off some stories I thought would be worthy of reading on the air based on the headlines. Well, without checking it over, I began reading a Kareem Abdul-Jabbar story. After the opening line about Jabbar signing a new deal, the copy became garbled and I said, "The Lakers, who were defeated in last year's NBA championship game by the LFT teachers. . . ." After glancing at a horrified news anchor, I said, "Oh well, bad copy, AP got me again." When I got home, one of my roommates said, "Hey those LFT teachers were pretty tough last year, went all the way to the NBA finals."

8. The Washington Astros. Nearly 10 years before the Montreal Expos finally moved to Washington to become the Nationals, I had it cold that a deal had been struck for Bill Collins to buy the Houston Astros and move them to D.C. My best friend was Collins' partner and had sworn me to secrecy, but said he'd give it to me before anyone else in the media as soon as he could. If I wasn't around to take the call, the message would be our secret code word, "Magillacutty." I got the message one night and led the Channel 5 newscast with the story. Unfortunately, the other owners didn't approve the deal. But the deal was done, and I was the only one who had it.

7. The fearsome foursome. It may have never happened before and probably will never happen again. In 1988, with all of the local TV stations in San Diego to cover the Redskins in Super Bowl XXII, Channel 5 director Ernie Baur managed to get Glenn Brenner of Channel 9, George Michael of Channel 4, and Frank Herzog of Channel 7 on our show *Redskins Playbook*. The on-air stuff was great; off-air it was better. During one of the breaks, Brenner (the funniest guy in the history of local TV, who died tragically of a brain tumor in 1992) said, "If Harvey Smilovitz (my weekend anchor who was back in Washington) rolled a grenade up here, he could take over the whole market."

6. Bear Bryant's Funeral. I was working at WSB-TV in Atlanta, where college football is a big deal. I was sent with a photographer to Tuscaloosa to cover the service. The burial was up the interstate in Birmingham. We realized with the huge number of cars in the procession, we'd never make it to the gravesite unless we got ahead of the pack. So we cut across the median and made it. We got our shots, hustled to the airport, and made it back to Atlanta in time to lead the Six O'Clock News with the story.

5. "Farns." Everybody should have a Paul Farnsworth in his life. A former producer at Channel 5 and the most persistent guy I've ever met. He once went to a Bruce Springsteen concert at RFK Stadium without a ticket and got in! In 1984, he was recording Olympic coverage on Channel 4 in our master tape room. Somehow he punched the wrong button and put Channel 4 on Channel 5! It only lasted about 30 seconds, but it caused major chaos. Somehow "Farns" didn't lose his job.

4. The Day Glenn Brenner Died. It wasn't just a day that changed local TV sports, it changed local TV completely. Glenn had run the Marine Corp Marathon in October of 1991 and had collapsed at the finish line. It was first thought that he'd suffered a stroke, but it later turned out that the stress of the race had burst a blood vessel that was holding back a massive brain tumor. The day he died, it was almost as if time stood still. The entire city was in mourning. The funeral brought everybody together. I remember running into Joe Gibbs outside the church and embracing. Not long after Brenner's death, the entire TV market, which had been stable for many years, completely changed. Anchors and reporters, who had been at all the stations for years, began to move around. Channel 9, which had been a rock-solid 1 or 2 for years, has never really recovered. Gordon Peterson, who was part of what may have been the best anchor-sportscaster chemistry in history with Brenner, now works at Channel 7. It's not the same, and like the rest of us, he's never been the same.

3. "Playboy!?" After the Redskins lost to the Jets in the final 1991 preseason game to finish with a 1-3 record, I was interviewing Joe Gibbs live in the locker room on Channel 5. I said, "With just two weeks to go before the start of the regular season, I'd be concerned if I were the head coach, especially with everybody saying this is the best squad the Skins have had in a long time." Gibbs looked at me and said, "Who's everybody?" Well, wouldn't you know, the first thing that popped in my head was my most recent, hmm, reading material. "*Playboy* is picking you to go to the Super Bowl," I said. "*Playboy*!?", the born-again coach said, veins popping out of his neck. He then ripped me up and down live on the air. He apologized on air a week later. And at the end of the season when they won the Super Bowl, I got Gibbs on the air to say, "They were right. For the first time, they were right."

2. Dr. Benjamin Ladner—Not! It's halftime of an American University basketball game that I was broadcasting on Home Team Sports. The color commentator and stage manager disappear and I'm sitting there alone with my headset on, waiting for my guest, AU President Dr. Benjamin Ladner. A guy walks up with a big smile on his face. We shake hands and he sits down. I put the headset on him. I come back from a commercial and say, "I'd like to introduce to you the President of American University, Dr. Benjamin Ladner." He shakes his head and mouths the words, "I'm not Benjamin Ladner." After about five seconds, which seems like five hours, the producer takes a wide shot of the arena. This gives me a chance to take his headset off and ask him who he is. He says, "I'm Jason Shrinsky." Well, we were live on the air, and at that moment, Shrinsky had to suffice. I asked him about the AU program and he said, "I think that Steve Yocky is doing a great job as coach." The actual coach at the time was Chris Knocke. I ended the interview, went to break and came back with the actual Benjamin Ladner. The producer doing the game from the truck was an AU graduate and never bothered to say to me, "Hey Buck, that's NOT Benjamin Ladner."

1. The Scoop. After finishing my sportscast on Channel 5's 10 O'Clock News in early March of 1993, I went to Champions in Fairfax. About 12:30 in the morning, my buddy Jim Speros comes up to me and says his dad (who had worked for the Redskins) had told him that Joe Gibbs was going to retire. Now Gibbs was only 52 at the time and was only a year removed from winning a Super Bowl. I told him he was crazy, but you hear something like that you have to check it out. I got up at six (an hour I never see unless I'm still up) and called Redskins general manager Charley Casserly. His wife said he was swimming. Oy vey. I called back at 6:45 and managed to get him. I told him what I'd heard and after a slight pause, he said, "You can say Gibbs is retiring because of health reasons, none of which are life threatening, and that Richie Petitbon will take over as head coach." By telephone in my underwear, I reported the story live on the Channel 5 morning news. It soon became one of the biggest sports days in the history of Washington. The Redskins had hoped to hold the news through the weekend, but after it broke, Gibbs was forced to return from a scheduled speaking engagement in Richmond for a news conference at Redskins Park. When he saw me, his eyes rolled to the back of his head.

Note: Ernie Baur helped invent the modern TV sportscast. Warner Wolf's famed instruction, "Let's go to the videotape," was directed at Ernie as he directed Warner's sportscast. He has spent more than 40 years at local stations as a producer and director. Baur even pre-dates Warner at Channel 9, where he worked from 1967 to '83. He then spent 16 years at Channel 5 before becoming Executive Producer at Comcast SportsNet in 1999. If you want to learn about the history of TV sports in D.C., Ernie is the guy to have a beer with. Even if you don't want to learn the history, Ernie is still a great guy to have a beer with. Here are his top 10 moments over a long and distinguished career.

10. Weekday Specialty Shows. With programs like *NFL Live* and *College Basketball Live* filling out the schedules at ESPN, nobody gives the roundtable discussion show much thought. While at Channel 5 in the early 80s, I put together *Redskins Playbook*, which was the first local sports roundtable show. Bernie Smilovitz hosted it from the newsroom with guests like Sam Huff and a young sportswriter who was interested in being on television named Tony Kornheiser. I had them sit back with loosened ties and shoot the bull about the Skins. At Channel 9, I started the *Warner Wolf Show*, which morphed in to *Redskins Sidelines*, complete with a live studio audience.

9. George Allen's Resignation. *The Washington Post* was on strike at the time, early in 1978. I was then working with Glenn Brenner at Channel 9. A disgruntled striker called Brenner and told him that Redskins owner Edward Bennett Williams had fired Allen and that Williams was having dinner that night with the paper's executive editor Ben Bradlee. We led the newscast that night with the story, but credited the *Post*.

8. The Three-Man Booth. Roone Arledge may have invented it for football when he teamed up "Dandy" Don Meredith with Howard Cosell and play-by-play man Keith Jackson for the first ABC *Monday Night Football* telecast in 1970, but I did it in baseball for Senators games a couple of years earlier. Ray Scott did the play-by-play, Warner Wolf was the analyst, and we tried different ideas for the third spot. Sonny Jurgensen did a game. So did comedian Flip Wilson, who periodically went into his character Geraldine. I thought he was great and laughed at everything he said. Scott didn't, and apparently quite a few in the TV audience didn't either, and it ended an idea that was ahead of its time.

7. Red Hat, Orange Sleeves. How does the referee know when a commercial ends so he can start play? He looks at the guy on the sidelines with the red hat and orange sleeves (or in cold weather, orange gloves). I was that guy at RFK Stadium for more than 10 years, working as a freelancer for CBS and Fox. I wore a headset and the network producer would let me know in my ear when it was time to signal the ref to start play. I also did this for six Super Bowls and various championship games, although I was almost thrown off the field during a Bears-Giants game because the Chicago training staff thought I was tipping plays to the Giants.

6. Televising Redskins Scrimmages. The Dallas Cowboys had done it in the past, but not to the extent of what we pulled off at Channel 5. We put microphones and earpieces on the assistant coaches so we could talk with them from the booth. One of the highlights was seeing Gerald Riggs running out of bounds and into the side of a Toyota truck we were using as a vehicle for our sideline camera. Riggs wasn't hurt, but he did $950 dollars in damage to the truck. Also, public relations director Charlie Dayton once jumped in front of owner Jack Kent Cooke so the elderly owner wouldn't get run over by a running back heading out of bounds. John Madden asked for the tape and put Charlie on the All-Madden Team.

5. Joe Gibbs Resignation. I can thank the nightlife of bachelor Sports Director Steve Buckhantz for breaking this one. "Buck" went out after work (the 10 O'Clock News) in early March of 1993 and ran into Jim Speros, who was working for the Redskins at the time. Speros gave him the story and Buck had to make the decision whether to go to sleep and risk oversleeping the Fox 5 Morning News. He stayed up and broke it before dawn. The Redskins were angry and so was Gibbs, who had to leave Richmond that day (a Friday) and fly to Redskin Park for a news conference. They had wanted to hold it until Monday.

4. Super Bowl MVP John Riggins Almost Oversleeps the Parade. I was at Channel 9, directing live coverage of the parade to celebrate the Super Bowl XVII victory, when I was told that Riggins was on the phone and wanted to talk to me. I was skeptical, but I took the call and sure enough "Riggo" said his watch was still on California time. He explained that when he turned on the TV, he realized he wasn't where he was supposed to be. I told him I could get him to the parade if he'd let our reporter (Ron Sarro) and a cameraman ride along for an exclusive interview. He agreed and a police escort got him there for at least some of the celebration.

3. 1983 Super Bowl Trip with Channel 9. This was the strike year, so the season wound up being compressed. The Redskins beat Dallas for the NFC title on a Saturday and by the following afternoon we were set up at the South Coast Westin in Costa Mesa, California with a team of about 15 people. Reporter Mike Buchanan seemed to have the most fun, questioning people he had never met about their whereabouts and why they didn't call when they entered the lobby after a night out. Somehow the evening at the piano bar that we charged to a rival station never came back to bite us. It was a wild week capped off by the Skins first championship in 40 years.

2. Guy Le Guy (pronounced "gee la gee"). The success of *Redskins Sidelines* convinced us to extend the show past football season and call it *Sidelines*. Glenn Brenner and Sonny Jurgensen were the hosts on a night where we were going to focus on the Washington Capitals. Unfortunately a snowstorm prevented the guest from getting there, but the show had to go on. So Brenner introduced an exclusive interview with a Venezuelan hockey player named Guy Le Guy who was actually legendary anchorman Gordon Peterson. One of his insights was that it was difficult to practice hockey in Venezuela because the ice kept melting. To this day, Peterson says that of all the major news stories he's covered, that show is probably what he'll be remembered for.

1. Let's Go to the Videotape. Warner Wolf didn't really use scripts. He made a few notes on envelopes and pretty much ad-libbed his sportscast. One night I was directing the *11 O'Clock News* while being distracted by some behind-the-scenes issues. Warner led to the highlights of the Milwaukee Bucks–Golden State Warriors game involving a matchup of Kareem Abdul-Jabbar and Nate Thurmond. I didn't hear him give me the lead, and when the tape didn't come up he finally said, "Ernie roll the Jabbar (he pronounced it "jah-BAR") tape." That got my attention. After the show we talked about how we could avoid this happening again, and Warner's famous phrase was invented.

ESPN couldn't get on the air without a whole slew of on-air broadcasters and behind-the-scenes production people who all have Washington area connections. Two of the network's most popular shows, *Around the Horn* and *Pardon the Interruption,* originate from studios in D.C. Two of the town's four network affiliated anchors, Brett Haber at Channel 9 and Dave Feldman at Channel 5, are ESPN anchor/reporter alums and Channel 7's Tim Brant still does occasional college football games for the network. Andy Pollin co-hosted an ESPN Radio weekend show for several years and was Tony Kornheiser's sidekick when the network aired Mr. Tony's radio show. The good news: way over-exposed Chris Berman and boo-yah Stuart Scott came from somewhere else.

10. Joe Theismann. A fixture on *Sunday Night Football* and the first year of *Monday Night Football* on the network until he was pushed out by Ron Jaworski after the 2006 season. Joey T. still shows up very occasionally on the air and writes a column for ESPN.com, but he also got paid the final four years of a five-year deal essentially to do nothing except stew over the demotion.

9. Mike Patrick. The longtime play-by-play man on *Sunday Night Football* also was re-assigned when ESPN won the rights for MNF in 2005. But ESPN put him back on college football and basketball, sports he's always loved anyway, and he remains one of the network's most versatile play-by-play voices, with a little moonlighting on the side for regional cable networks.

8. Sage Steele. She began her broadcasting career with the old Home Team Sports, working as an anchor and reporter for the regional cable network that eventually morphed into Comcast SportsNet. She's now in the regular anchor rotation for ESPN's flagship *SportsCenter* show.

7. Chris McKendry. A Philadelphia native, she was an anchor at Washington's Channel 7 from 1994 to 1996, and left the station to work for ESPN as an anchor in '96. She helped launch ESPNews that year, and now mostly handles extended *SportsCenter* broadcasts on the weekends.

6. Tim Kurkjian. A native of Bethesda and a graduate of Walter Johnson High School and the University of Maryland, Kurkjian began his newspaper career at the old *Washington Star* and worked for newspapers in Dallas and Baltimore before going to *Sports Illustrated*. He left the magazine in 1998 to join ESPN's *Baseball Tonight* show. He's become one of the most respected baseball analysts on television, and appears regularly on *SportsCenter*, also writing for the web site and *ESPN The Magazine*.

5. Pam Ward. Another Maryland graduate, Ward was working as an on-air announcer for WTEM, Washington's only all-sports radio station, when ESPN hired her as a sideline reporter in 1996. She hated the job, convinced her superiors to let her try play-by-play, and has been a pioneer as the first woman to call major college football on television, in addition to a wide variety of other assignments.

4. Scott Van Pelt. He graduated from Sherwood High and the University of Maryland and once tried and failed to walk on to Lefty Driesell's Terrapin team. He served as an anchor and reporter at The Golf Channel until ESPN hired him in 2001. Almost immediately, he became one of the network's most popular *SportsCenter* anchors. He still keeps his hand in golf, as the network's on-site anchor and reporter for the major championships. He also does the best Seve Ballesteros impression on the planet.

3. Rachel Nichols. A former *Washington Post* sportswriter who covered the Capitals for several years, Nichols has become one of ESPN's top on-air general assignment reporters since leaving the newspaper five years ago and also has been assigned to the network's investigative magazine format show, *E:60*.

2. John Walsh. You've probably never heard of him, but Walsh, a former editor in the *Post's* Style section, has been one of the main forces in building ESPN's news operation. He was primarily responsible for hiring print reporters en masse when he first joined the network in 1988 because he wanted to establish journalistic standards into the fledgling news operation. He's also overseen the growth of *ESPN The Magazine* and the web site.

1. Tony Kornheiser and Michael Wilbon. The two great friends and *Washington Post* sports columnists have anchored the juggernaut *Pardon the Interruption* franchise since its inception five years ago, and the show's format even spills over into *SportsCenter* and halftime of *Monday Night Football*, where Kornheiser is one of three men in the booth. Wilbon also shows up for halftime shows, and has become a major presence on ESPN's NBA coverage. We'll just list them as No. 1 and 1A and, dear reader, you can decide on the proper order.

10. Ken Broo. Brought in to replace Warner Wolf at Channel 9 in 1996, he lasted four years before heading to the NBC affiliate in Cincinnati as sports director in 2000, where he still works.

9. Nick Charles. The lead sports anchor at Channel 4 from 1976 to 1979, he left the station to join the fledgling CNN cable network in 1980. He's now the main blow-by-blow voice for boxing on the Showtime cable network.

8. Martin Wyatt. A former running back at the University of Washington, Wyatt worked the weekend sports desk at Channel 4 in the mid-1970s, then left for his native California in 1980, eventually becoming sports anchor at the ABC affiliate in San Francisco. He retired in January, 2007.

7. Scott Clarke. A weekend anchor at Channel 7 in Washington, Clarke left in 1986 to become the weekday sports anchor at the ABC affiliate in New York, where he became one of the city's most popular sportscasters.

6. Frank Herzog. The longtime radio play-by-play voice of the Washington Redskins and an anchor and reporter at Channel 7 and 9 since the early 1970s, Herzog was taken off the Redskins assignment in 2003. He now fills in as a part-time news anchor at WTOP radio and also has done work as a movie extra.

5. Rich Gilgallon. The former Georgetown bartender hosted a popular afternoon drive-time sports show with Kevin Kiley on WTEM from 1992-94 before the bean counters took them off the air. Gilgallon relocated to Palm Springs, California, where he flies solo with an afternoon radio talk show on KPSI. Kiley works out of Dallas and co-hosts a radio talk show with former Cowboy receiver Michael Irvin on an ESPN affiliate.

4. Ken Beatrice. A pioneer in radio sports talk, he had a popular show on WMAL Radio from 1977 to 1995 before moving over to WTEM. He remained on the air until he retired for health reasons after his last broadcast on April 20, 2000.

3. Ron Weber. The Washington Capitals radio voice from 1974 to 1997, he called the action on 1,936 hockey games, never missing a single contest. He was let go after the '97 season and has never done play-by-play again, though he's been a regular in the stands at Verizon Center ever since.

2. Bernie Smilovitz. Born in Brooklyn and raised in Washington, Smilovitz began his career doing sports on WTOP radio before becoming an anchor at Channel 5 in the early 1980s. He left the station in 1986 to join the NBC affiliate in Detroit, and with the exception of a two-year stint at WCBS-TV in New York in the mid-1990s, has been in the Motor City ever since.

1. Warner Wolf. The man who made "let's go to the videotape" his signature expression, he began his broadcasting career handling intercom duties at Washington's Coolidge High School in the 1950s. He was by far the most popular sportscaster in town from 1965 to 1975 on Channel 9 before leaving for a job with the ABC television network. He eventually went back to sports anchoring in New York, with a three-year stint in Washington from 1993 to 1995 as Glenn Brenner's replacement. He was fired from WCBS in New York in 2004 and has mostly done radio work at WABC, also in New York, where his signature expression was altered only slightly to "let's go to the audiotape."

Note: All Tony ever wanted to be was a sportswriter. Right after college he started covering high school sports for *Newsday* and soon moved to the *New York Times*. He eventually became a columnist for the *Washington Post* and thought he would finish his career as an ink-stained wretch. Then along came the 1990s and radio success, followed by unimaginable television success on ESPN with *Pardon the Interruption* and *Monday Night Football*. The Long Island kid who grew up wanting to write about famous people became one in his early 50s. Famous people now consider Tony a famous person. Wow! Tony now says he has no more words to write and would never agree to type out a list (c'mon, he's *Mr.* Tony now), but he did give Andy Pollin his favorite Mr. Tony moments since being touched by fame.

12. "Please just drop by. We'll feed you." This actually started before the television shows. Usually a woman would call saying she was throwing a 40th birthday party for her husband, who I don't know, and who is of course, "a big fan." She asks if I could just come by between eight and 10 o'clock and just say hello. Her husband would really get a kick out of it. Right.

11. "You're so f---ing good." What James Carville said to me at the Palm shortly after, *hello!* He got Bill Clinton elected President of the United States. He was with his wife Mary Matalin and they wanted to meet ME! This was long before I had done any regular television work. He loved my writing and appearance on *The Sports Reporters* on ESPN and despite my fears that he and Mary would soon dump me, we became friends. Mary had me sit in on her television show *Equal Time* when co-host Jane Wallace was away.

10. "Kornheiser? Is that Swedish?" I got hooked on golf in my early 40s. It's still the only thing that really relaxes me. When it came time to join a country club, I wanted one that was close to my house. I joined Columbia, which is mostly Irish-Catholic. The first time I went out in a foursome, Jim Bugg asked me that question. Oy.

9. "That Thing You Do." I love that movie which starred Tom Hanks in the 90s. It's a fictional account of rock band that quickly rose and fell in the 1960s. Hanks plays their manager. I've talked about it many times on the radio over the years and how great I feel every time I hear the title song of the film. I don't know if Hanks has heard me talking about it, or someone told him, but he autographed a CD for me and sent a note saying how much he enjoys "PTI."

8. "So what are the Dodgers doing with their infield?" A question asked to me by Don Rickles, who actually thought I knew. I was at a fundraiser hosted by Larry King, who's been very nice to me over the years. Rickles is his good friend and knew I worked in sports. He came right up to me and started babbling about the Dodgers and their triple A prospects. Before I knew it there were cameras and boom mics all around us. It was bizarre, but I loved it.

7. "I saw you were on and came right over." Said by Regis Philbin to Michael Wilbon and me when we appeared on the *David Letterman Show*. Regis loves "PTI" and has mentioned the show a number of times on his own show *Live*. He loves to talk about Notre Dame. The fact that a big star like Regis came over to see us was very flattering.

6. "Who let this guy in?" Actually I said that at a Jacksonville restaurant and the tape of it appeared on Youtube. I'm glad I didn't curse. I was having dinner with my high school friend Ira and his friend Melvin. Some guy walks in off the street and starts talking to us. The owner quickly sees what's going on and escorts the guy out. How or why this got on Youtube, I'll never know.

5. "He can't get away from me fast enough." What I was thinking when I tried to talk to Larry David at the correspondents dinner in D.C. in 2007. We're both Long Island kids about the same age and know some of the same people. I thought we'd have a lot to talk about. Apparently not. Not long after I started talking he began to back away and had to be thinking, "Why is this guy following me?" I was wearing sunglasses at the time because bright sunshine was streaming into the room where we were. Maybe that was it. I'm told he doesn't like to talk to people wearing sunglasses.

4. "That works, keep doing it." Said to me by former Baltimore Ravens coach Brian Billick when we met on a train going to New York. He came over to me and introduced himself. I told him I'd been calling him "a preening schmo" in print and on the air and wondered if he wanted me to stop. He said no. And as if we were Martin and Lewis in the 50s, he said, "that works, keep doing it." I was really disgusted at the way he lectured the media on how to do its job during the week of his Super Bowl win over the Giants, but I rolled over like a dog and started to like him. Wilbon and I eventually bought dinner with him at a charity event and had a good time when we cashed in.

3. "I'm Ernie Harwell and I really enjoy your work." Ernie Harwell. Ernie Harwell! He said that to me in a stairway at Camden Yards when I was still writing columns. I had never met him before and he couldn't have been more complimentary. This is a guy who is one of the greatest baseball announcers in history. I was thrilled.

2. "Don't worry, they can get more." What I said to Rolling Stones drummer Charlie Watts. I had been invited to watch them perform at FedEx Field by Dan Snyder. The Danny was so pumped up about having dinner with them before the show. He had his wife Tonya take a bunch of pictures. I'm in one of them in the back looking like I have a disembodied head. Anyway, Snyder presents the Stones with a Redskins helmet and Watts asks, "Well what are the players going to wear?"

1. "So, getting tight with the president?" What my son Michael (Michael Phillip Kornheiser; I wanted to call him "Mick" but it never caught on) said to me in a moment of great embarrassment. He was a freshman at Penn at the time. The athletic director, Steve Bilsky, who I've known for years, invited me to watch a basketball game with him. The game was about five minutes old when an attractive blond woman sat down next to us. She was never introduced and I assumed she worked for Bilsky and I started asking condescending questions like, "Have you ever been to a game at the Palestra before?" She was polite and said, "A few." After the game I met up with Michael, who had been watching the game in the student section across the arena. That's when he asked me the question. "President?" I said. It was Amy Guttman, the president of the University. I told Michael I may have cost him the ability to stay in school. I didn't. Michael graduated in 2008.

Honorable mention. This one happened after I left ESPN radio in 2004 and went back to work for WTEM. I loved that the building was five minutes from my house, but the bathroom situation was bad. The men's room had only one stall. I said I wouldn't work there unless the situation was remedied. It was quickly fixed. The signs on the men's and women's room were switched. I don't think the women who worked in the building were thrilled, but most of them were salespeople and my show was number one for men 25-54 in my time slot. What's one stall for a lot more cash?

Note: It's shown throughout the world on ESPN, but "PTI" is produced in D.C. and hosted by legendary *Washington Post* columnists Tony Kornheiser and Michael Wilbon. They took their act of yelling at each other in the *Post* hallways and put it on the worldwide leader in sports. As Tony likes to say, "Who knew it would be such a hit?" He's always quick to credit the people behind the scenes for making the show the success it is. Producer Erik Rydholm, associate producer Matt Kelliher, and director Bonnie Berko have been with "PTI" since its debut in 2001. Here is their list of the top five most-repeated catchphrases on the show.

5. "Your boy." Used to attach a co-host to a noted or notorious person whom they may or may not have supported at some point.

4. "Check the tape." Used in intense arguments when one host believes the other host is contradicting himself without admitting to it. The tape is never actually checked.

3. "Strugg-a-ling." First said/slurred infamously when Joe Namath was incompleting a sideline pass to Suzy Kolber. "I do not care that the Jets are strugg-a-ling. I want to kiss you."

2. "You play to win the game!" Stolen from former Jets coach Herman Edwards, who once explained the purpose of football to a reporter using those words.

1. "Uranus." A never-fail punchline for juvenile humor. Example:

MW: *PTI, but I'm Mike Wilbon. Space news, Tony! A space probe has discovered lightning on Venus!*

TK: *I'm Tony Kornheiser. Really? Before the show I think I heard thunder from Uranus.*

Lenny Hale is a veteran horseman and longtime racing official now based in Middleburg, Virginia. He is currently executive director of the Charles Town Horseman's Benevolent Protection Association and is the former racing secretary for the New York Racing Association and The Maryland Jockey Club.

10. Pleasant Colony. Bred at Buckland Farm in Buckland, VA, Pleasant Colony won the first two legs of the 1981 Triple Crown before finishing third in the Belmont. He retired to stud in Kentucky in 1982, and died at the age of 24 in 2000 at Blue Ridge Farm in Upperville, VA.

9. Seeking the Pearl. Bred at Lazy Lane Farm in Upperville, he won eight of 21 starts, mostly in Japan, but became the first Japanese-trained horse to win a Group One race in Europe with a victory in the 1998 Maurice de Gheest in Deauville, France. He retired in 1999 after winning over $4 million in purses, the all-time money-winner among Virginia breds.

8. Sea Hero. Owned by the late Paul Mellon, the banker and philanthropist and long-time owner and breeder of championship horses, he was bred at Mellon's Rokeby Stables in Upperville. He won the 1993 Kentucky Derby as a 13-to-1 shot, the first Derby victory for Mellon, jockey Jerry Bailey, and trainer Mac Miller, all now members of the Racing Hall of Fame in Saratoga Springs, New York.

7. Genuine Risk. Winner of the 1980 Kentucky Derby and owned by Diana Firestone of Newstead farm in Upperville, she was only the second filly to win the Derby and the first filly in history to finish in the money in all three Triple Crown races that year, earning second in the Preakness and Belmont.

6. Saluter. Born and bred in Nokesville, Virginia, and trained in Butler, Maryland, by Jack Fisher, he was arguably the greatest steeplechase horse of the modern era after winning the Virginia Gold Cup in The Plains, Virginia, an unprecedented six times, the last in 1999, and winning 21 timber races over a brilliant career.

5. Battleship and Mongo. Both horses were bred at the Montpelier, Virginia, estate of Marion duPont Scott. Battleship, a steeplechase horse, became the first American-bred and American-owned horse to win the Grand National Steeplechase in Aintree, England in 1938. Mongo won over $800,000 and was declared the champion grass horse in 1963, including a victory that year in the Washington International at Laurel.

4. Riva Ridge. Owned by Penny Chenery of Meadow Stables in Doswell, Virginia, he won the 1972 Kentucky Derby and Belmont Stakes and earned $1.1 million in a career that included 17 victories in 30 starts, with three seconds and a third.

3. Mill Reef. Also owned and bred by Mellon at Rokeby, he was thought to be more suited to turf than dirt tracks and competed in Europe, winning the Epsom Derby in 1971 and the *Prix de l'arc de Triomphe* in 1972. He was named European Horse of the Year in 1971 and won 12 of his 14 starts, with two second-place finishes.

2. Cigar. A product of Maryland's oldest thoroughbred breeding operations, Country Life Farm in Bel Air, Cigar didn't race as a two-year-old but made up for lost time and became one of the most popular champions in racing history. He also set a record with $9.99 million in earnings over a career that saw him go 19-4-5 in 33 starts, including 16 straight victories, tying the all-time mark first held by Citation, before retiring in 1996. A two-time Horse of the Year, he also won the Breeder's Cup Classic in 1995.

1. Secretariat. Arguably the greatest racehorse in the modern era, he was born at Meadow Farm in Doswell, Virginia, and was also owned by Penny Chenery. In 1973, he became the first horse in 25 years and only the ninth in history to win the Triple Crown, setting track records in all three races that still stand. His 31-length victory in the Belmont, knocking two seconds off the record for 1½ miles, remains the most dominating performance in the history of American racing. Big Red also had a successful career at stud at Claiborne Farm in Paris, Kentucky, where he lived from 1974 until his death in 1989. In 21 starts, he won 16 races, was second in three and third in one.

My Five Greatest Days at the Race Track :: Andrew Beyer

Note: Harvard-educated and backstretch-schooled Andrew Beyer remains a living legend among horse players nationwide. A longtime *Washington Post* columnist and author, he's written passionately about horse racing and "mortal lock" gambling for nearly 40 years. His own self-devised "speed figure" formula is must reading in the *Daily Racing Form* for anyone stepping up to a $2 (or much higher) window at tracks or off-track betting emporiums around the country.

5. Sunday Silence beats Easy Goer in the Breeders' Cup, 1989. Decisive
showdowns don't materialize as often in racing as fans would like, and often they are anticlimactic. But the drama at Gulfstream Park was perfect. Sunday Silence had won the first two legs of the Triple Crown, Easy Goer had trounced him in the Belmont Stakes, and now the 3-year-olds were meeting for the final time. Sunday Silence charged to the lead on the turn; his rival rallied in the stretch as announcer Tom Durkin yelled, "It's Easy Goer with . . . one . . . final . . . surge!" The surge fell short by a stride, and Sunday Silence was the champion.

4. Canonero II wins the Preakness, 1971. The Venezuelan colt Canonero II
had shocked the racing world by rallying from far behind to win the Kentucky Derby. He became a cult hero among Spanish-speaking fans, but he was widely dismissed as a fluke when he came to Pimlico for the Preakness. Most handicappers assumed his stretch-running style would doom him on Pimlico's speed-favoring track. It was an electrifying moment when the gate opened and Canonero II charged to battle for the early lead. He drew away to win the Preakness and set the stage for an unforgettable (though ultimately disappointing) bid to win the Triple Crown.

3. The "bet of the year," 1970. I had started writing a horse racing column for
The Washington Daily News a year earlier, and in December, 1970 I told readers that I had a Christmas present for them. Sun in Action, a cheap horse running at Liberty Bell Race Track was the "bet of the year." I drove with a friend to the Philadelphia track, bet everything in my pocket, and watched as Sun in Action's furious rally fell short by a nose. When the stewards disqualified the winner, Sun in Action paid $43.20 to win, and the page-one banner headline in the next day's *Daily News* read: "Andrew Beyer's Horse Comes In!" The remainder of my life has been an anticlimax.

2. The double triple, 1990. The biggest non-Preakness day in the history of
Maryland racing was April 14, 1990. Nobody had hit the double triple—a wager requiring bettors to pick the 1-2-3 finishers in two different races—for three weeks, and the jackpot bonus had grown to more than $1 million. The atmosphere at the track was frenzied. I was part of that frenzy, making one of the largest bets of my life, and I was one of ten holders of winning tickets that paid $134,682 each—the first six-digit score of my gambling life.

1. Secretariat wins the Belmont Stakes, 1973. Secretariat was already hailed as a superhorse, and expectations were high that he would become the first Triple Crown winner in 25 years. Yet few of us at Belmont Park could have anticipated what we saw that day: the greatest single performance ever by an American thoroughbred. Secretariat's 31-length runaway, in record-smashing time, remains the standard by which all horses are measured.

Note: Liz Clarke has been a sportswriter for *The Washington Post* since 1998 and has covered NASCAR since 1991. She is the author of *One Helluva Ride: How NASCAR Swept the Nation.*

10. Pit Stops. No kidding. In less time than it takes to locate a good station on the car radio, a NASCAR pit crew can change four tires, clean the windshield, re-fill the gas tank, and adjust a racecar's handling—all with cars screeching in and out of the pits around them. It's a manic 14-second ballet in which track position is won and lost.

9. The Infield. It's certainly not for everyone—best described as the sports world's equivalent of Bourbon Street in New Orleans on Mardi Gras. But at NASCAR's biggest tracks, which boast enough room to allow RVs in the infield, it's where stock-car racing's rowdiest fans congregate, camping out the entire weekend to celebrate the sport they love with endless kegs of beer. Shirts optional.

8. Eavesdropping. The NFL brass slapped the New England Patriots with steep penalties for spying on the New York Jets in 2007. In NASCAR, eavesdropping on play-calling is fair game for rivals and fans alike. All you need to listen in on Dale Earnhardt Jr. hashing things out with crew chief Tony Eury Jr. is a radio scanner, headphones and frequency list—available for rent or purchase at every track.

7. Esprit. The most boisterous Cleveland Browns fans congregate in the Dawg Pound. But in NASCAR, every section of the grandstands is packed with passionate fans who wear their loyalties on T-shirts, jackets, coolers, and tattooed into their skin. It's hard not to get swept up in the fervor as NASCAR Nation rises in unison for the National Anthem, then proceeds to bellow and bray at the cars zooming past.

6. The Fantasy That You Could Do It, Too. It's impossible for the typical NBA fan to picture himself dunking over Shaquille O'Neal. But nearly everyone—short or tall, fit or not—drives a car. And it's not too much of a stretch to picture yourself slicing and dicing on the high banks in NASCAR, too. That's the essential myth stock-car racing is built on, after all—that it's a sport in which everyday people battle in everyday cars.

5. Jeff Gordon and Tony Stewart. There's little crossover in the fan bases of these two, who wheel the No. 24 Chevrolet and the No. 20 Toyota, respectively. But as stock-car racers, they share monstrous ability behind the wheel. They're simply head and shoulders above their peers in talent and guile. So take your pick—Gordon or Stewart—and follow his car through a race. You're bound to see a move ordinary drivers can't make.

4. Bristol Motor Speedway. It's the closest thing to the Roman Colosseum in American sports—a cramped, high-banked, half-mile oval in the hills of southeastern Tennessee that's completely encircled by stands that shoot straight to the heavens. More than 160,000 flock here for its two annual NASCAR races. The second race, in August, is staged at night, under the lights, which guarantees that sparks fly and tempers flare.

3. The Start. There's nothing like the unbridled roar of 43 stock-car engines when the green flag flies. The cars are stacked up two abreast, nose to tail, as they hurtle into the first turn. It's so loud you can feel your bones rattle. TV announcers may scream "Boogity! Boogity!" and "Crank up the volume!" all they want, but there's nothing that captures the sensation quite like hearing the deafening din in person.

2. The Daytona 500. It's NASCAR's Super Bowl, and it kicks off the season each February on the circuit's most awe-inspiring track. Daytona International Speedway is 2.5 miles around—so huge that it can be raining in one turn and sunny in another. Carburetor restrictor plates, which prevent cars from exceeding 200 miles per hour, keep the action close and guarantee that even after 499 miles, a gaggle of cars will be inches apart on the last lap.

1. The Fan Comes First. Stock-car racing's king, Richard Petty, retired in 1992. But his edict of treating stock-car racing fans with respect still endures. NASCAR drivers may be millionaires these days, but Petty taught them that fans pay their bills. As a result, drivers are uncommonly accessible to media and, with rare exception, courteous to fans—whether that means signing autographs, posing for pictures, or flashing a smile even at the boo-birds.

Why I Love to Hate NASCAR

Sorry Liz, but I started hating NASCAR the first (and last) time I ever covered a race for the *Post* in 1976, when it took me three weeks to get my hearing back after the checkered flag came down.

17. Unlike thoroughbred racing, the animals are in the stands, not on the track.

16. Everybody says they don't go or watch on TV just to see the crashes. They lie.

15. The mechanics can't cheat anymore because all those engineers in the pits won't let 'em.

14. Too many NASCAR wannabes are practicing their moves on the nation's highways, particularly the Washington beltway.

13. It's even more boring on television than the America's Cup, and that ain't easy.

12. You can't bet on the races.

11. Too many tattoos and pierced tongues populating the bleachers, and they're definitely not drinking Chablis.

10. Joe Gibbs Racing started in 1991, and two years later one of his cars, driven by Dale Jarrett, won the Daytona 500, the equivalent of an NFL expansion team winning the Super Bowl in its second year of existence.

9. It's Supreme Court Justice Clarence Thomas's favorite sport.

8. Drivers only know how to steer left, and hardly any of them are liberal Democrats.

7. One of the cars is actually sponsored by Viagra, and its driver is always up for any race he enters.

6. Whoever heard of a big-time sporting event being held in Martinsville, Virginia?

5. Does the season ever end?

4. Their idea of drafting has nothing to do with finding mobile, agile, or hostile middle linebackers.

3. Why is Ricky Bobby never around when you need him for a little comic relief?

2. No one carries moonshine in the back seat anymore, and the revenuers are nowhere to be seen.

1. Here's what NASCAR really stands for: Non-Athletic Sport Centered Around Rednecks. I rest my case.

During my junior high and high school years, while living in Chevy Chase, Maryland, I woke up every morning to the Johnny Holliday Show ("It's a Holliday every morning") on WWDC 1260 AM. Although I loved listening to Johnny and his bits (he did a great George McGovern), the morning highlight was getting the sports from Tony Roberts, who later became the legendary voice of Notre Dame football and basketball. It was Roberts, as much as anyone, who inspired me to pursue a career in sports radio. Sixteen years at Sportstalk 980 is a nice run, but it won't put me close to those on this list of the giants who have ruled the airwaves in D.C.

10. Doug Tracht "The Greaseman" (1975–2007). Although he was one of the most talented performers in the history of radio, taking you right up to the edge, he went over it in a big way and it cost him his career. Tracht started out on the "Great 98," spinning the hits on 980 AM in the mid-70s. But he wanted to be more than a nighttime DJ and left when the program director told him to stick to his real name and drop "The Greaseman" shtick. Tracht refined the act for about six years in Jacksonville and when Howard Stern was fired at DC101 in 1982, "The Greaseman" returned and held on to Stern's number one ranking. At the top of his game he left for Los Angeles in 1993 to try national syndication, which never worked out. He returned to D.C. to work at WARW in 1997, but lost his job in 1999 after a horrible racial remark. Considered untouchable by major stations, he tried to make a go of it in syndication, but finally threw in the towel at the end of '07.

9. Trumbull and Core (1976–96). A couple of real pros, they made the evening commute a pleasure for 20 years. Smart move by WMAL to pair up veteran Bill Trumbull with young Chris Core, who had joined the station fresh out of college just a couple of years earlier. After Trumbull retired, Core tried to make a go of it first with the late Brooke Stevens and later alone, but it wasn't the same without his smooth partner. Core was fired after 34years at WMAL in March 2008.

8. Don and Mike (1985–2008). Don Geronimo (real name Mike Source) was a boy wonder on local radio, starting out at WINX at the age of 13. He wound up at WAVA in the mid-80s, where he paired up with Mike O'Meara for a morning show in 1985. Six years later, the station was sold and the format was changed to religion. They immediately jumped to WJFK, which was looking for a strong afternoon show with Howard Stern from New York in syndication starting to kick butt in the morning. Within two years, their show was picked up by Westwood One for syndication. They remained strong, but Geronimo, influenced by a number of factors including the tragic death of his wife in a car accident, announced his retirement in spring 2008. The show is now called The Mike O'Meara Show.

7. Ken Beatrice (1977–2000). Ken wasn't the first to host a sportstalk show in Washington. Warner Wolf did one in the late 60s and early 70s at WTOP, and Shelby Whitfield was doing one about the same time at WWDC. But Ken was able to establish himself on WMAL almost immediately after coming here from Boston and was unchallenged for many years. Beatrice was famous for what he made listeners believe was encyclopedic knowledge of sports years before you could just Google anything. His thick New England accent crackled through the airwaves every evening with trademark phrases like, "Yoooure next" and "Gawd love you, you keep these phone lines lit every night." The emergence of WTEM and its all-sports format ended Beatrice's run at WMAL in the mid 90s. He squeezed out a few more years at WTEM before retiring in 2000.

6. Howard Stern (1981–82). Hard to believe that Stern was only on the air at DC 101 for about a year. His impact was immediate and strong as he drove his show to number one. Stern was Washington's first "shock jock" and took the shock thing a bit too far when he called Air Florida on the air shortly after one of their planes crashed into the 14th Street Bridge and asked how much it would cost to buy a ticket from National Airport to the bridge. There is some debate whether he was fired or he quit after that, but his days in D.C. were over. After a stint at WNBC AM in New York, Stern took his show to an FM station with a syndication deal. WJFK picked up the show here, where it remained strong for years until Stern jumped to XM radio in 2005.

5. Jamie Bragg (1957–95). You could make the case that Bragg invented the job of all-news anchor. He had been at WTOP for 11 years when the station became one of the first in the country to go all news. Bragg (born Casper James App) fit the format like a glove. He combined a great voice and great delivery with an easygoing style. He shifted from traffic and weather reports to sports and Wall Street news like a conductor of a symphony. Cancer forced him to retire after 38 years as the best at what he did. Bragg died just a few months later.

4. Johnny Holliday (1968–). Johnny was already a radio legend by the time he came to D.C. to work for WWDC. He had been one of the top rock and roll disc jockeys in the country in Cleveland, New York, and San Francisco. Johnny introduced the Beatles at Candlestick Park for God sakes. Even though his morning show couldn't topple Harden and Weaver, he stayed on the air for 11 years at WWDC, even coming back from a plane crash that could have claimed his life. Ageless (he's now 70) and always full of energy, Johnny jumped right into another love: play-by-play. He's been the voice of the University of Maryland football and basketball for more than a quarter of a century, while continuing his many other interests including dinner theater.

3. The Joy Boys (1955–74). Willard Scott and Ed Walker met at American University in the early 50s and became lifetime friends. Walker, who is blind, has the incredible voice and Scott has the silly sense of humor. Their afternoon show on WRC combined shtick and warmth in a simpler time. Their theme song started like this, "We are the Joy Boys of radio, we chase electrons to and fro." Scott used the show to launch other gigs including becoming the original Ronald McDonald clown and weatherman on Channel 4. WRC dumped the show in 1972, but it was picked up for two years by WWDC. Scott later jumped to the *Today Show* and Walker continued to make radio magic on WMAL, while voicing many commercials. Both remain D.C. treasures.

2. Donnie Simpson (1976–). Donnie arrived from Detroit at the height of the disco craze to work for WRC FM. They called it Disco 93.9, which was later renamed WKYS. The format eventually went the way of leisure suits and platform shoes, but Simpson had staying power. He rode the new urban format to number one for many years before leaving for WPGC-FM in 1993. With a voice from heaven and good looks to go along, Simpson also found success on TV and even did sports casting work on Channel 4 in the early 80s. Simpson continues to be the top dog in the morning with a great vacation schedule and time to get out and play 36 at Robert Trent Jones Country Club on most warm days. It's good to be Donnie Simpson.

1. Tie: Harden and Weaver (1960-92), and Eddie Gallaher (1947-2000).
Too close to call. Only Frank Harden was still alive at press time, but these three men make up a huge chunk of the history of radio in D.C. Harden and Jackson Weaver started their show on WMAL in 1960 and stayed on top of the ratings for most of their 32 years together. Weaver died in 1992, but Harden stayed on with Tim Brandt and others for a number of years after that. Some thought their voice bits were corny, but those Harden and Weaver live commercials rang the WMAL cash register for decades. Gallaher, whose voice sounded like it came out of a syrup bottle, stayed on the air for an unbelievable 53 years. After arriving from Oklahoma, he landed at WTOP in 1947 and stayed until the station went all news in 1968. Gallaher then went to WASH for another long run before finally finishing up at WWDC at the turn of the 21st century. A pro's pro, Gallaher did just about everything during his half century in radio, including Redskins play-by-play in the 50s. There will never be another like him reading a live commercial. It's been said he could make you hungry for linguine at six o'clock in the morning. Gallaher died at the age of 89 in 2003.

Note: Frank Herzog served as the Redskins' radio play-by-play announcer for 25 years, working with Hall of Fame analysts Sonny Jurgensen and Sam Huff, until he was inexplicably replaced by Larry Michael in 2004. Herzog's signature call was "Touchdown, Washington Redskins!" The games just haven't been the same without him.

10. Buffalo vs. Washington, Super Bowl XXVI in Minneapolis. Quarterback Mark Rypien puts the icing on the cake.

"Back he goes, good protection again, going deep. He's got Clark in the end zone, touchdown Washington Redskins!"

(Redskins win, 37-24.)

9. 1991 NFC Championship Game vs. Detroit Lions.

"Andre Ware is back, throws it to the left side . . . picked off at the 33 yard line! Here comes the return by Darrell Green. He's back to the ten, cuts to the five, TOUCHDOWN, Washington Redskins!"

8. Mark Moseley's winning kick in the season finale for the eighth win in the last 11 games in Joe Gibbs first season, 1981.

"Will it be long enough? Will it go through? Yes! The football game is over!"

7. Buffalo vs. Washington, Super Bowl XXVI in Minneapolis.

"Kelly to pass, blitzed up the middle, has to dump it off, PICKED OFF!!! Intercepted at the 25, to the 20, the 15. It's Gouveia to the 5, almost to the end zone, forced out of bounds at the 2."

(That interception began the second half, leading to a Redskins touchdown and a 24-0 lead.)

6. Redskins vs. Denver Broncos, Super Bowl XXII in San Diego. Redskins explode for 35 points on 18 plays in the 2nd quarter.

"Williams with a great fake this time—faked out everybody—he's got Sanders in the clear at the 10! Touchdown, Washington Redskins! We are seeing a virtuoso performance."

5. Minnesota at Redskins, 1987 NFC Championship Game.

"Fourth down and four, one down to the Super Bowl. Joe Gibbs down on one knee where he can see; now down on *both* knees. Wilson takes the snap, lookin' left, throws it into the end zone . . . batted away INCOMPLETE! Redskins are goin' to the Super Bowl! Joe Gibbs looks like he's ready to collapse."

4. New York Giants at Washington, 1982, in the snow. Moseley goes for record 21st straight field goal.

"The 42-yard attempt . . . plenty long enough . . . it's GOOD! Mark Moseley has broken the National Football League record!"

3. Redskins at Chicago, 1987 NFL playoffs, game tied 14–14 in the 3rd quarter.

"Green driven back to midfield on the far side. He's got the ball. Over to the 45, far side 40, a seam to the 35. Vaults a man at the 30, breaks to the near side 25. Watch out! To the 20, near side 10, he's gone . . . TOUCHDOWN, Washington Redskins! Darrell Green returns the punt 50 yards!"

2. Dallas Cowboys at Redskins, 1982 NFC Championship Game. Gary Hogeboom at quarterback for an injured Danny White, late in the game.

"Play-action fake to Dorsett—hid the ball well. Set up the screen. Ball batted in the air, picked off by Darryl Grant . . . TOUCHDOWN, Washington Redskins!"

1. Redskins vs. Dolphins, Super Bowl XVII in Pasadena. Fourth quarter, fourth and one at the Miami 43-yard line.

(Sam Huff: "Here comes the diesel.") "There's the snap, handoff to Riggins, good hole. He's got the first down at the 40—he's GONE! The 35, the 30, the 20—he's gone, he's gone . . . Touchdown Washington Redskins! Holy Cow, what a play. A 43-yard touchdown run on fourth and a foot. John Riggins has given the Redskins the lead in Super Bowl 17. That, gentlemen, may be the nail in the coffin." (Sonny Jurgensen: "No question, it IS the nail in the coffin.")

Bonus Special. Herzog's call on the last seconds of the Washington Bullets clinching victory over Seattle to win the 1978 NBA Championship is his personal favorite among all the sports he's ever handled.

"Unseld grabs the rebound, outlet to Dandridge, he breaks down-court. Warm up the Fat Lady, Warm up the Fat Lady, the Bullets are gonna' win!"

Note: Before you could plug those ear buds into an I-pod, we got our music the old fashioned way—on the radio. Marty grew up in D.C. listening to the great "jocks" who played the hits. They not only knew the music, they knew how to keep it moving with great banter in between the records (yeah they actually cued up songs on albums and 45s). Marty got his foot in the radio door while still in high school and was on the air by 1973. He made his mark while working with some of the best. Now the production director at Sportstalk 980 and still playing those great songs of the 70s on XM radio, here is his list of the greats who crank out those "stax of wax."

10. Mark Kessler. One of the best "on the street" DJs on the planet. Originally from upstate New York, he's made the local rounds at stations like Classic Rock WCXR 105.9, Oldies 100.3, and WARW Arrow 94.7. Mark is one of those guys who loves being on the air and you can hear it through the speakers. He's also the Redskins' stadium announcer at FedEx Field.

9. Jim London. Originally from Pittsburgh, he really peaked with partner Mary Ball in the 1980s. They were such a nice fit, even if you didn't care for country music they were fun to listen to. They started at WPIK 105.9 before moving over to 98.7 WMZQ and commanding huge ratings for many years. Jim later did solo morning shows on Oldies 100 and WGAY 99.5. He also went back to country for a midday show on WMZQ called "America's Music." Jim is retired from radio, at least until somebody tries to pull him back in.

8. Renee Cheney. A great smooth, silky voice that was perfect for classical music. She was heard for many years on WGMS and was legendary for the personal relationship she was able to develop through the speakers with her listeners.

7. Jim Elliot. Another transplanted upstate New Yorker. Elliot helped usher the music from AM to FM in the 1970s. He started out as the overnight guy at the "Great 98" (WRC-AM) and then moved to WPGC, which was simulcasting on AM and FM. Eventually he teamed up with Scott Woodside for the very popular morning show "Elliot and Woodside." Later he became a record representative for Arista in New York.

6. Barry Richards. If you grew up in D.C. in the 70s, you know that he was a household name. Richards was hip, edgy and loved the soul music he played on AM radio. For a while, he was our Dick Clark with a TV dance show on WDCA Channel 20.

5. Cerphe. A pioneer in "underground" album rock. While attending American University, Cerphe got his start at the legendary WHFS (then 102.3 FM) in Bethesda. He wore a ponytail before it was popular, so you knew he was ahead of his time. Cerphe has also been on the air at WWDC-FM, WAVA, and WJFK. He currently does the afternoon shift at The GLOBE 94.7 FM.

4. Loo Katz. A Wheaton kid who got his radio start at WHON in Herndon. Quite a few of us got our start there. He moved on to work as an engineer (when DJs still needed an engineer) at WRC AM 980 and figured out how to do both jobs at once on the weekend. No one had ever done that before. That launched on-air work at WPGC, WAVA, and WRQX. Loo currently commands high ratings at WASH-FM.

3. Bobby Bennett. The "Mighty Burner" ruled the D.C. airwaves in the 1960s and 70s at WOL 1450 AM. He's an expert on soul music and has written books about it. Many of us went to school on soul thanks to Bobby. He's the voice of a number of businesses including Cavalier Men's Store and Ben's Chili Bowl. Bobby is currently program director of the Soul Street Channel on XM.

2. Jack Diamond. A boy wonder, he was "Bruce" Diamond on WINX-AM 1600 while still attending Peary High School in Rockville. He later worked at 1300 AM WEEL ("the Golden Wheel") in Fairfax. After success in San Diego, Jack has been back in his hometown for many years with a strong morning show on WRQX.

1. Donnie Simpson. Gets as much credit as anybody for starting the urban FM revolution. In his younger days, Donnie was both the morning DJ and program director of WKYS, Kiss 93.9 Beautiful Music. Now at WPGC, he continues to dominate the ratings, as he has for more than 30 years.

Note: Johnny Holliday has been on the air in one medium or another for 51 years, including the last 29 years as the radio play-by-play voice of Maryland football and basketball. He's also an accomplished song and dance man, doing his first professional show in 1962 playing the part of Og in a Cleveland production of *Finian's Rainbow*. Over the last 46 years, he's appeared in 25 other musicals, many of them performed before appreciative audiences in dinner theaters all around the Washington area. Here are his ten all-time favorite roles.

10. Oscar in *The Odd Couple.* I never had to dress up, which is sort of what I like to do on weekends. I loved smoking a cigar, since I've never smoked. It was quite a challenge, to say the least.

9. Paul in *Carnival.* Since I love to do voices and impersonations, as Paul the Puppeteer I got to be the talking and singing voice of several puppets, as well as playing the role of Paul, a less than happy member of the Carnival. This was the first show I did after a small plane crash on January 29, 1975, that had me laid up in Sibley Hospital for 29 days and off the radio for two months. I had some doubts as to whether I would be able to do the show, but everything worked out for the best.

8. George in *Same Time Next Year.* Since there are only two members of the cast, George and Doris, you can figure out which role I played. I loved the scene of me playing the piano and the emotional roller coaster my character went through. Probably the most difficult of all the shows, just because there were only two of us on stage all the time.

7. Albert in *Bye Bye Birdie.* Dancing, singing, mugging, all the while thinking I was Dick Van Dyke, then coming home after the show and being reminded I wasn't.

6. Finch in *How to Succeed in Business without Really Trying.* This was the first show I ever saw on Broadway and I said to myself, "I can do that, it's a perfect role for me." I ended up doing this show at four different theaters and loved every one of them.

5. Robert in *Company.* A Sondheim classic and the first of 15 shows I did at Harlequin Dinner Theater. Great cast, wonderful score, and a perfect role to play.

4. Harold Hill in *The Music Man.* There's nothing like performing "Trouble" and "76 Trombones" eight times a week for three months, even though the song "Trouble" seemed as if it lasted about a half hour. Still, it was the least difficult of the numbers for me to perform. "The Sadder but Wiser Girl" was the hardest, thanks to director Buddy Piccolino reminding me every night not to forget the lyrics. The production I was in at Clarice Smith Performing Arts Center at the University of Maryland was incredible, with the entire Maryland marching band coming on stage and filling the aisles during the curtain call. Now that was a sight to see!!

3. Buddy in _Follies_. I will always remember the director Tony Ornstein telling me this would be the most challenging role I'd ever do, and how right she was. Another Sondheim classic, with wonderful music and a magnificent cast of veteran actors and actresses. Some nights we had to laugh when folks would ask, "When does Will Rogers come on?"

2. William in _Me and My Girl_. A hilarious musical comedy and a show that depended on me to set the tone with an energetic opening scene and more up-tempo energy throughout the show. Lots of dancing, and I learned to do the Lambeth Walk. How many of you can do it? I used a cockney accent throughout the show, with lots of pratfalls. It often seemed as if I never left the stage, although following one performance I was heading to my car and stopped to ask a lady if she enjoyed the show. She said she did, and I told her I would tell the cast. Then she asked me if I was in the show!

1. Julian Marsh in _42nd Street_. You could not beat the songs, the choreography, or the scenery. This was just a feel-good show that had members of the audience singing as they left the theater. Julian Marsh was a hard-driving, sometimes unsympathetic director who finally showed a soft side in the final scenes. I played the role at four different theaters and can't wait to do it again.

Washington's first all-sports radio station made its debut on Memorial Day weekend in 1992. It was on the 570 AM frequency and was called Sportsradio 570 WTEM. Patterned after WFAN in New York, which nicknamed itself, "The Fan," WTEM called itself, "The Team." That handle was dropped six years later when the station moved to the 980 AM frequency and became known as Sportstalk 980. Here are eight who worked at the station and have left (either their choice or the station's) for bigger and better things.

8. Mike Ritz (1992-93). Ritz is a Montgomery County native who graduated from Churchill High School, loving golf. He worked in a variety of news and sports jobs in television after graduating from the University of Wisconsin and returned to the D.C. area about the time WTEM started up. Ritz did some fill-in anchor and reporting work in the early days of the station. In 1994, Ritz was the first reporter hired by the Golf Channel where he continues to work today as an anchor and reporter.

7. Andrew Siciliano (1994). He actually never drew a paycheck from WTEM, but was offered several chances to do so. Siciliano (who, by the way, had a Bar Mitzvah; Mom had the say on religion at home) is a Northern Virginia kid who is yet another Syracuse University success story in the sportscasting business. He interned at WTEM in the summer before his junior year and went to the coveted basketball play-by-play job during his senior year as the Orange made it to the national title game before losing to Kentucky. He now hosts the 4-7 pm West-Coast slot on Fox Sports Radio in Los Angeles and makes frequent television appearances. He's become a cult hero among NFL junkies for his work as the host of the Red Zone Channel on Direct TV.

6. Mitch Levy (1992-94). As a sharp and confident 24-year-old, Mitch was hired to produce the station's two big stars—CBS's James Brown and *Washington Post* columnist Tony Kornheiser—as WTEM made its debut. Mitch not only gained their respect and admiration, he absorbed some of the things that made them so successful. He was actually let go in a big budget slash, which turned out to be his big break. Mitch was, by now, ready for his own show. Early in 1995 he joined KJR in Seattle as host of *Mitch in the Mid Day*, and soon was placed in the big moneymaking slot. He has hosted *Mitch in the Morning* for more than 10 years and has two children with his former D.C. girlfriend, who he finally convinced to move West and marry him in 1999.

5. Dan Miller (1992-97). Dan joined WTEM a few months after its start to become the host of the overnight show. He quickly moved to evenings and then to middays with Doc Walker while cutting his teeth in television as a weekend anchor at Channel 5 and Channel 7. Late in '97, Dan's strong TV skills were recognized, and he became the number-one guy at WJBK-TV Fox 2 in Detroit. He continued to freelance in radio, and did a number of national TV NFL games on Fox. In 2005, Dan became the radio voice of the Lions.

4. Andrew Brandt (1994-95). Brandt, a law school graduate who had done work as an agent, was hired to host a weekend show called *The Business of Sports*. No one can remember exactly how or why that ended, but Brandt soon found himself on the other side of the agent business. He served as the Green Bay Packers' capologist for nine years, leaving after the 2007 season.

3. James Brown (1992-94). "JB" was already big time when he joined the station as host of the *James Brown Show*," which aired from noon to 3 pm weekdays. He was with CBS at the time, calling college basketball games and hosting various weekend shows. While he loved doing the radio show, opportunities were pulling him in too many different directions. After a couple of years it became too much and he left. He didn't tell anyone what he was headed for. Fox had just obtained the rights to NFC games and "JB" soon was setting the standard as the host of the highly entertaining pre-game show with Terry Bradshaw, Howie Long and Jimmy Johnson. He left Fox for CBS before the 2006 football season. Not surprisingly, ratings for the CBS pre-game show have gone up and ratings for the Fox pre-game show have gone down.

2. Tony Kornheiser (1992-2006). Tony's star was in print when he signed up for the 10 to noon spot. He told sidekick Andy Pollin, "I'm only going to do this for two weeks and then I'm quitting. Lupica (*New York Daily News* columnist Mike Lupica) told me the radio show will hurt the column." In fact, Tony found he was not only a natural on the radio, but doing the show helped his column. In 1998, the show was picked up by ESPN Radio, where it ran for six years and was carried by WTEM. During that time, he and fellow *Washington Post* columnist Michael Wilbon launched the wildly successful TV show, *Pardon the Interruption*. Tony returned to WTEM in the fall of '04 and stayed until leaving for the *Monday Night Football* booth in the spring of '06.

1. Greg Garcia (1992-93). One of the best broadcast stories ever told. Garcia was fresh out of Frostburg State when he showed up looking for any kind of work he could get. Told that there were openings for board operators, Garcia interviewed and told operations manager Rich Bonn that he had plenty of experience running a board, and was hired. That night, he showed up at the station and asked the board operator on duty to teach him to run a board. He'd never done it before. By luck of the draw, he wound up as the board op on the *Tony Kornheiser Show* and was soon complementing Tony's work with funny sound bites and sly on-air comments. After about six months, Garcia said, "I've got enough money, I'm out of here." He explained he was off to Hollywood to produce television shows. Sure enough, with the same type of chutzpah that landed him a job in radio with zero experience, Garcia got himself in the door. He was soon producing the very successful sitcom, *Yes Dear*, and won an Emmy in 2006 for *My Name is Earl*. Greg Garcia, the kid who wore shorts even in bitter cold weather, is now one of the most successful writer/producer/directors in the TV business and now goes by the name Gregory Thomas Garcia.

Presidents, high-profile politicians, media pundits, and lobbyists usually get star treatment in the Nation's Capital, but we've also produced our fair share of big-time celebs in the entertainment industry who grew up or now live here and/or honed their crafts inside and far outside the beltway.

11. Paul Attanasio. A Harvard graduate and former *Washington Post* movie critic (1983-87), he switched over to the far more profitable other side and became one of Hollywood's most sought-after screenwriters, with movie credits that include *Donnie Brasco*, *Quiz Show*, *Disclosure*, and *The Good German*. He's also executive producer of the hit television series *House*.

10. Lynda Carter. The Amazonian "Wonder Woman" on the hit 1980s television series of the same name, Carter, a Phoenix native, became a Washingtonian when she married attorney Robert Altman in 1984. They've lived in the Montgomery County suburbs ever since.

9. Christopher Meloni. He's been detective Eliott Stabler in *Law & Order: Special Victims Unit* series since 1999 and made a major name for himself on HBO's chilling prison series *Oz*, playing a bisexual psychopath. He was born in Washington, D.C., and attended St. Stephens High School in Northern Virginia.

8. Robert Duvall. He's not a Washington native, but fell in love with the Virginia hunt country, where he purchased a cattle farm once owned by Jack Kent Cooke in The Plains, VA, and has lived there since the mid-1990s when he's not off making movies and television shows, or taking his Argentina-born wife tango dancing in Buenos Aires.

7. Fred Thompson. The former senator and presidential candidate from Tennessee broke into the movie business playing a bit part in *All The Presidents Men* and has appeared in a number of first run movies and prime time television dramas, including his most recent success as a New York district attorney in NBC's hit police drama, *Law & Order: Special Victims Unit*.

6. Robert Prosky. The veteran character actor paid his dues as a longtime regular at Washington's Arena Stage, where he's had over one hundred stage credits, riding that success into a number of roles on the big screen, including *The Natural*, *Mrs. Doubtfire*, and *Hoffa*. He still lives on Capitol Hill.

5. Julia Louis-Dreyfus. Elaine Benes in *Seinfield* and now with her own network sit-com, she grew up in Bethesda and went to The Holton Arms School. One of the writers who helped make her famous on *Seinfeld*, Peter Mehlman, graduated from the University of Maryland and worked as a part-time reporter at *The Washington Post* before meeting up with a young comedian named Jerry Seinfeld.

4. Edward Norton. The grandson of Columbia founder and developer James Rouse, he grew up in the Maryland new town, and graduated from South Lakes High

School in 1987 before becoming a Hollywood leading man, often in rather dark and depressing roles like *Fight Club* and *American History X.*

3. Goldie Hawn. A 1963 graduate of Montgomery Blair High and an American University dropout, she burst into the national consciousness as the ditzy, sock-it-to-me blonde on *Rowan & Martin's Laugh-In*, the breakthrough comedy hour TV show of the 1960s, then became one of the most beloved comedic actresses in the world.

2. Sandra Bullock. A regular Miss Congeniality, she grew up in Arlington and graduated from Washington-Lee High School in 1982, where she made the cheerleading squad and acted in school productions before heading off to East Carolina University, dropping out before her senior year to pursue an acting career in New York.

1. Shirley MacLaine and Warren Beatty. Sister and brother, they both graduated from Washington-Lee High in Arlington. MacLaine says she's had close encounters with aliens, has been re-incarnated several times, and wrote in a memoir that she once made love to Charlemagne on a religious pilgrimage through Spain. But it all started in Northern Virginia for the dancing, singing, acting whirlwind who counted Frank Sinatra and the Rat Pack among her best pals. Her little brother, Warren Beatty, also went from W-L, where he was a star football player, all the way to Beverly Hills, where he's been a heartthrob leading man for decades, even in roles where he played somewhat loveable, larcenous, and lethal gangsters (Clyde Barrow and mobster Bugsy Siegel), offset by his title portrayal in *Dick Tracy* and a randy hairdresser in *Shampoo.*

Washington may be known more for high-powered politics than Hollywood glitz, but there have been many great films made in or about the District. Here are our ten most notable movies.

10. *Being There* (1979). This may have been Peter Sellers' all-time best role, playing Chance the Gardener, who's never spent any time outside the gates of his late employer's mansion but takes a ride in a limousine and suddenly finds himself turning into a Washington insider pundit.

9. *Heartburn* (1983). Nora Ephron's semi-autobiographical novel about her failed second marriage to Watergate heartthrob Carl Bernstein was better in print than on the big screen, despite a big-time cast that included Meryl Streep and Jack Nicholson. If you pay close attention, you might also see future Oscar winner Kevin Spacey in a bit part as a subway thief.

8. *Pelican Brief* (1993). Another book-better-than-movie deal, but John Grisham's novel focusing on the killing of two Supreme Court Justices clearly has some moments and lots of scenes in and around the District. Denzel Washington plays a reporter for the *Washington Herald*, only because *The Washington Post* wouldn't give permission to use the name of the paper, and Julia Roberts is a feisty law student who helps crack the case wide open.

7. *Quiz Show* (1994). Directed by Robert Redford and written by former *Washington Post* movie critic Paul Attanasio, most of the film based on the quiz-show scandals of the 1950s is set in New York. But the congressional-hearing scene looking into The Big Fix is classic Washington drama, complete with preening pols and nervous witnesses testifying under oath.

6. *Advise and Consent* (1962). Based on the Pulitzer Prize winning novel of the same name by Alan Drury, the plot centers on the selection of a politically liberal secretary of state played by Henry Fonda and the machinations involved in getting his nomiation through the United States Senate, complete with a scandal/suicide involving the sexuality of a prominent senator played by Don Murray.

5. *Nixon* (1995). Another of Oliver Stone's historically challenged films, this makes our top ten list solely on two of the all-time brilliant performances—Anthony Hopkins as Nixon and Joan Allen as his wife, Pat. Both were nominated for Oscars but neither won—a travesty. Also loved David Hyde Pierce, who gained fame as prissy shrink Niles Crane in the television sit-com Frazier, playing John Dean.

4. *Charlie Wilson's War* (2007). Based on the true story of an ethically challenged Texas congressman, played by Tom Hanks, who nevertheless conspires with a CIA operative to secretly fund resistance to the Soviet Union's Afghanistan invasion, ultimately leading to the Russians' defeat and, some believe, the end of the Cold War. Philip Seymour Hoffman won an Oscar as best supporting actor for his portrayal of the CIA man, Gust Avrakotos.

3. *Forrest Gump* (1994). Based on the novel by former *Washington Star* reporter Winston Groom, Tom Hanks plays a young man with an IQ of 75 and a knack for somehow always being in the right place at the right time, including a memorable scene at the Reflecting Pool on the Mall as the backdrop for a massive anti-war rally during the Vietnam era. Hanks won an Oscar for his performance, and the movie also won Best Picture among six Oscars that year.

2. *Mr. Smith Goes to Washington* (1939). Frank Capra's ode to the notion of what a difference one man can make remains the quintessential American classic on the machinations of backroom Washington politics and corruption in American government. It also may be Jimmy Stewart's signature role in a film that was nominated for 11 Academy Awards, but only won one—Lewis R. Foster for his original screenplay.

1. *All the Presidents Men* (1974). Arguably the all-time best newspaper movie, Robert Redford and Dustin Hoffman starred as indefatigable reporters Bob Woodward and Carl Bernstein unraveling the Watergate scandal that ultimately led to Richard Nixon's resignation. Jason Robards won a Best Supporting Actor Oscar for his portrayal of *Post* executive editor Ben Bradlee, a man larger in real life than anything Hollywood could ever create on film. *The Post* refused to allow filming in its newsroom, so a $500,000 set was constructed in Hollywood to make it look very much like the real deal, right down to the cluttered desks.

The Best Washington-centric Sports Movies

Note: While Washington has been the backdrop for countless Hollywood movies over the years, not many had sports themes, instead focusing on Capitol Hill, the CIA, and the White House. Here are five sports movies with connections to the Nation's Capital.

5. *Glory Road* (2006). The story of the 1966 Texas Western college basketball team, the first team to start five black players in the NCAA Final Four, played that year at cavernous Cole Field House on the University of Maryland campus in College Park. Josh Lucas plays folksy head coach Don Haskins, with a bravura performance from Jon Voight as crusty Kentucky coach Adolph Rupp.

4. *The Life and Times of Hank Greenburg* (1998). Washington-based film-maker Aviva Kempner spent years meticulously producing this inspiring documentary on Hall of Fame first baseman Hank Greenburg, who fought anti-Semitism throughout his career. Several Washingtonians are interviewed on camera, including former Michigan senator Carl Levin, who idolized Greenberg, and *Washington Post* columnist Shirley Povich, who covered him and considered Greenburg a good friend.

3. *Damn Yankees* (1958). The blockbuster Broadway musical with the devil making a Faustian bargain in exchange for propelling the lowly Washington Senators and their new hero, Joe Hardy, to the pennant, hit the silver screen three years after the curtain went down on the stage version. Hardy was played by Tab Hunter (a Northern Virginia resident for a number of years) in the movie version, with Gwen Virdon as the lovely and seductive Lola, and Ray Walston (pre-*My Favorite Martian*) as the devilish Mr. Applegate.

2. *The Replacements* (2000). Based on the strike-shortened 1987 NFL season when owners hired replacement players for their striking veterans to keep playing games, Gene Hackman stars as the Washington Sentinels head coach, though any resemblance between Hackman and Joe Gibbs is truly coincidental. No, make that impossible.

1. *Remember the Titans* (2001). Denzel Washington stars as Herman Boone, the new and controversial head coach for the 1971 T.C. Williams High School football team that won a state championship in a year when three Alexandria schools were consolidated into one. There's a little more fiction than fact, but it's still an inspiring tale, and the Titans did go 13-0 that year, shutting out nine of their opponents and allowing only 38 total points.

10. Rocky (1976). Yo Adrian, how could you not love the first in a series about a loveable loser of a Philly palooka whose non-Hollywood ending led to standing ovations coast to coast.

9. Caddyshack (1980). The funniest golf movie ever made, maybe the best golf movie ever made. Drop-dead hysterical (and Bill Murray's defining role), at least for those of us in the soft-spiked set.

8. Chariots of Fire (1981). A movie about runners preparing for the 1924 Olympics, with an awesome score and a memorable opening beach scene that was more painting than celluloid shot not far from the 18th hole at St. Andrews, was stirring enough to win the Best Picture Oscar.

7. Eight Men Out (1988). Another period piece, this one telling the story of the 1919 Black Sox scandal. Loved the ball-field scenes, not to mention awesome performances by then mostly unknown John Cusack as third baseman Buck Weaver, who claimed not to fix any games, and David Strathairn as the cheating pitcher, Eddie Cicotte.

6. Bull Durham (1988). Susan Sarandon was a living, breathing wet dream as a Baseball Annie named Annie and Tim Robbins was the brilliant wild and wacky pitcher Nuke LaLoosh. Even Kevin Costner managed to shine as over-the-hill catcher Crash Davis, maybe his best-ever sports role, just ahead of his performances in *Tin Cup* and *Field of Dreams*.

5. Hoosiers (1986). Gene Hackman got the role of Coach Norman Dale when Jack Nicholson turned it down. He was dead solid perfect leading the little Indiana team that could all the way to a state title in a sort of true story, with lots of Hollywood liberties taken.

4. Field of Dreams (1989). If you build it, they will definitely come, and Costner's character, Ray Kinsella, built that ball field in his Iowa cornfield and watched long dead Hall of Famers come to life right before his and our very eyes, including a very young Ray Liotta as Shoeless Joe Jackson and a very old Burt Lancaster as Archie "Moonlight" Graham, a long-forgotten player from the 1920s.

3. Raging Bull (1980). It doesn't get much better than Robert DeNiro as Jake LaMotta directed by Martin Scorcese. It was filmed in black and white, which is exactly how many of LaMotta's brutal fights were aired back in boxing's 1950s heyday.

2. Slap Shot (1977). Paul Newman plays Reggie Dunlop, the aging player-coach of a small-town minor-league hockey team that starts getting much better when he recruits the whack-job Hanson brothers, three guys who love to cheap-shot brawl and high stick maul whenever they can. Former Washington Capitals coach Tom McVie insisted this movie was based on his own life story, only better.

1. The Natural (1984). Bernard Malamud's book was a classic in its own right, but the goose-bump meter goes off the charts in the movie version when aging Roy Hobbs, played by Robert Redford, takes a mighty swing of his bat, "Wonderboy," and knocks the stuffing out of a baseball, shattering the outfield lights in one of the more memorable baseball scenes in Hollywood history. Too bad about that shooting.

If timing is everything, our timing has really sucked with some of the greats of the games. Here are 10 who left too soon or arrived too late.

10. Joe Coleman, Washington Senators 1965–70.
Coleman is the name not often mentioned in the stupid Denny McLain trade before the 1971 season. He was considered a throw-in with Ed Brinkman and rising young star Aurelio Rodriguez for the former 31-game winner McLain. Coleman had been a starting pitcher for six years with the Senators, losing more games than he won, but had two dozen-win seasons and was only 24 when he was dealt. While McLain lost 22 games in his only season in Washington, Coleman went on to win 20 games twice for the Tigers, helping them win a division title in 1972. In 1979, Coleman finished his career on a Pirates team that beat the Orioles in seven games for the World Series, helping again to break the hearts of a number of former Senators fans who became Oriole fans when they lost their team to Texas in '72.

9. Terry Metcalf, Washington Redskins 1981.
Metcalf had been one of the top kick returners in the 70s with the St. Louis Cardinals. He was also an excellent third-down running back. In 1975, Metcalf set a record for all-purpose yards in a 14-game season with 2,462. After three years in Canada, Metcalf was 30 years old and pretty much out of gas by the time he played his last pro season in Washington. Another ex-CFL-er, Mike Nelms, wound up being the Skins kick returner. Metcalf, though, did make one major contribution to the team in his one year in Washington. He showed a young wide receiver the workout regimen necessary to become one of the best. Art Monk listened well, and it served him well.

8. Ben Davidson, Washington Redskins 1962-63.
At 6-foot-8, Davidson had grown up playing basketball. It wasn't until he went to the University of Washington for his last two years of college that he became serious about football. The Giants drafted him in 1961, but traded him to Green Bay in training camp. The Packers won the championship, but as big as Davidson was, he rode the bench and was cut at the end of the season. The Redskins picked him up, but coach Bill McPeak didn't have a great idea how to handle what could have been a quarterback's nightmare. Even though Davidson was 6-foot-8, they told him they wanted him under 268 pounds. When he showed up for training camp in 1964 at 270, the Skins cut him. The Raiders, from the rival AFL, called and "Big Ben" with the handlebar mustache became one of the most feared defensive ends in the game. He was a three-time All Pro and helped the Raiders get to the second Super Bowl. Oh well.

7. Andre Reed, Washington Redskins 2000.
Reed caught 951 passes, 87 for touchdowns, during his 16-year NFL career. Unfortunately for the Redskins, 941 of those passes and 86 of those touchdowns were caught in a Buffalo uniform. Reed was picked up when Michael Westbrook went down with yet another season-ending injury. He was over the hill, but did catch a touchdown pass. That's more than you can say for Brandon Lloyd, who was with the Skins for two years and didn't catch any, walking away with $10 million dollars in guaranteed money.

6. David Akers, Washington Redskins 1998. Akers played one game for the Skins, missing two field goals before being cut. He wound up with the Eagles in 1999 and has been there ever since, making three Pro Bowls. Akers is also the Eagles' all-time leading scorer. Between 1999-2007, while the Redskins employed a dozen different kickers, Akers was the Eagles' one and only.

5. Ben Wallace, Washington Bullets 1996-99. Typical for the Bullets in those days, they were so impatient to get a big rebounder that they didn't know they had one of the best on their roster. Wallace had made the team as a free agent out of Virginia Union and developed slowly, but steadily. In his third year with the team, he averaged over eight rebounds a game. But the Bullets couldn't wait, sending Wallace along with Tim Legler, Terry Davis, and Jeff McInnis to Orlando for Ike Austin. Wallace became a defensive force and rebounder (although not with the Magic; he was in the Grant Hill sign-and-trade deal) in Detroit, and helped them win an NBA championship. Austin, who had been motivated for one year while playing for Pat Riley in Miami, stunk in Washington.

4. Deacon Jones, Washington Redskins 1974. One of the greatest players in the history of the NFL, although not by the time he got here. Jones was the star of the famous "Fearsome Foursome" in Los Angeles with Merlin Olson, Lamar Lundy, and Rosey Grier. He was an awesome pass rusher whose head slap was so devastating that the NFL eventually banned it. After 13 years of punishing quarterbacks, there wasn't much left of ol' Deacon by the time he got here. He's probably best remembered in Washington for kicking the last extra point of a 42-0 win over Chicago, because coach George Allen wanted to give Mark Moseley's leg a rest before the upcoming playoffs.

3. Moses Malone, Washington Bullets 1986-88. We actually missed out on the best of Moses twice. Moses was Lefty Driesell's greatest recruiting catch when he landed the Petersburg, Virginia star in 1974. Unfortunately for Maryland fans, Moses attended exactly one class and signed with the ABA's Utah Stars. Had he played for Maryland, Lefty almost certainly would have gotten to the Final Four. As it was, the team that Moses would have played on as a freshman made the Elite Eight. By the time the Bullets brought Moses to Washington from Philadelphia for Jeff Ruland, he'd spent a dozen years in the pros playing big minutes and going all out at both ends of the floor. He was only 31, but it was clear Moses' best days were behind him. He still averaged more than 20 points and 11 rebounds a game both years here, but he wasn't the force he'd been about five or six years earlier.

2. Harmon Killebrew, Washington Senators 1954-60. It wasn't just Killebrew who left Washington too soon; the whole team went with him. After the 1960 season, the Senators went to Minnesota to become the Twins and were immediately replaced by the expansion Senators. The Twins went to the World Series five years later. The expansion Senators were lousy for most of their 11 years in Washington. Killebrew hit 42 homers for the Senators in 1959, but really became a star in Minnesota. He hit more than 40 homers seven times for the Twins and broke the hearts of Senators fans once again in 1969 when he hit 49 homers and beat Frank Howard by one for the home run title.

1. Red Auerbach, Washington Capitols 1946-49. Red actually lived in Washington from the time he came to George Washington University in 1936 until he died in 2007, but enjoyed his greatest success in Boston. After a stellar playing career at GW, Auerbach became a successful high school coach in D.C. (future baseball commissioner Bowie Kuhn rode his bench at Roosevelt for a few years). Local millionaire Mike Uline noticed his success and hired him to coach his new pro team in the Basketball Association of America. Auerbach's first team finished 49-11, but lost in the finals. After his 1948-49 team lost in the finals to George Mikan's Minneapolis Lakers, the BAA merged with the NBA. Auerbach knew he'd have to upgrade his team to stay competitive. But when Uline didn't buy his ideas, he quit. Auerbach soon wound up in Boston where he won nine of a possible 10 NBA championships with the Celtics between 1956 and 1966. The Capitols soon left town and Washington wouldn't have NBA basketball again for more than 20 years. Almost 30 years after Red went to Boston, Washington won the NBA championship. Thirty years later, we're still waiting for another one.

There's nothing worse than picking up a big-name player who made his mark—and left all his talent—in the previous decade. Here are ten Redskins who got to D.C. on an empty tank of gas, and had nothing left in the tank when they stepped on the field.

10. Boyd Dowler. Steady receiver on the great Lombardi Green Bay teams. Best known for hurting his shoulder early in Super Bowl I, which brought in hungover back-up Max McGee who went on to catch two touchdown passes. Was brought in as a player-coach by George Allen in 1971 after a year of retirement. Dowler caught 26 passes and retired for good.

9. Frank Ryan. Was the quarterback on the great Jim Brown teams in Cleveland including the one that won the championship in 1964. Backed up Sonny Jurgensen in 1969 and '70, playing in only two games, completing two passes on five attempts. Spent his free time working on his Ph.D. in mathematics. He's now Dr. Frank Ryan.

8. Gary Hogeboom. Provided Redskin fans with one of their best memories when, as a Cowboy, he threw the pass that Dexter Manley tipped and Darryl Grant picked off and took into the end zone to send them to Super Bowl XVII. Hogeboom was brought in during the 1990 season after the famed "Body Bag Bowl" in Philadelphia had KO'd all their quarterbacks.

7. Billy "White Shoes" Johnson. Wasn't ready to give up the game after great runs in Houston and Atlanta. Played in only one game for the Skins in 1988, returning his last three NFL punts. There would be no last rubber-legged end zone dance in D.C.

6. Jim Kiick. Teamed with Larry Csonka in the famed "Butch and Sundance" backfield of the early 70s in Miami. Was active for one game as a Redskin in 1977, but didn't carry the ball.

5. Jim Hart. After a remarkable 18-year run in St. Louis, Hart had started his new career as a TV reporter when he ran into former Cardinals assistant coach Joe Gibbs as he prepared his team for Super Bowl XVIII in Tampa. Gibbs asked him if he'd like to keep playing. Hart said, "Sure." It was Joe Theismann's last healthy year, 1984. Hart played in two games, throwing seven passes.

4. Jim Tyrer. Was considered the best offensive tackle of his era during a 13-year run with the Kansas City Chiefs, and blocked for Len Dawson in the Chiefs' historic Super Bowl IV win over Minnesota. Showed up in Washington to play for the Father Flanagan of veterans, George Allen, in 1974. Tyrer started one game and finally gave up. Six years later, he murdered his wife and killed himself.

3. Leonard Marshall. Most famous for knocking out Joe Montana in the NFC title game to send the Giants to Super Bowl XXV. Was on the field during the 1994 season, but without Lawrence Taylor playing behind him, it was as if he wasn't there.

2. Deacon Jones. May have been the best defensive end ever to play the game. He may have totaled more sacks than all-time leader Bruce Smith, but sack totals weren't kept until eight years after the leader of the "Fearsome Foursome" retired. George Allen rewarded him for the great years he gave him with the Rams and signed up the 36-year-old for the 1974 season. In his last regular season game, with Mark Moseley wanting to rest his leg for the playoffs, Jones kicked the 42nd point in a 42-0 win over Chicago. It was the only kick of his career.

1. Matt Millen. Unlike his run as president of the Detroit Lions, Millen knew how to pick winners to play for. After being on two Super Bowl winners with the Raiders, he moved to the 49ers and collected a third ring there. Wanting to finish his playing career close to home in Pennsylvania, Millen spent the 1991 season in Washington and collected his fourth ring from a third different team and promptly retired. Now that's the way to go out.

Despite sophisticated scouting methods there are some who just go overlooked, or through circumstance emerge with talent that even the sharpest scouts couldn't see. Here are 10 athletes who went far beyond what anybody could have expected when they joined area teams.

10. Mike Oliphant, RB Redskins 1988. It's not what Oliphant did as a Redskin as much as what he did FOR the Redskins. In fact after his one season in burgundy and gold, it looked like general manager Bobby Beathard had reached too high on this third-round pick. Oliphant played at Division III, University of Puget Sound, the kind of place where Beathard was famous for finding hidden gems. But Oliphant looked just average as a kick returner. Somehow, working his last draft for the Skins in 1989, Beathard managed to get the Browns to give him Earnest Byner for Oliphant. All Byner did was run for a thousand yards twice and help the Redskins to three playoff appearances and a Super Bowl championship. Oliphant was out the NFL within two years.

9. Darrell Green, CB Redskins 1983-2002. How can a first-round draft pick be on a list of the overlooked? Well, Green was the last player taken in the '83 draft coming out of Texas A&I. He had tremendous speed, but his program size, 5-foot-10 (yeah sure) probably scared some people off. In his first game in the NFL, size didn't seem to matter much as he ran down Tony Dorsett from behind. He went on to one of the great careers in Redskins history and was elected to the Hall of Fame in 2008.

8. Steve Francis, G University of Maryland 1998-99. There was definitely some buzz over Francis when he came to College Park, but few had seen him play. Allegheny Community College had been his second stop after a high school career that included a few stops. It didn't take long before Coach Gary Williams realized what he had, telling an assistant in the first game of the season that he expected to have Francis for only a year. That's what he got. After being named All-American, Francis opted for the NBA draft and was the second player taken.

7. Earl Jones, C University of the District of Columbia 1980-84. Jones was seven feet tall, but quite skinny. Still, seven feet is seven feet and credit UDC coach Wil Jones (no relation) for uncovering this West Virginia area gem. Jones led the Firebirds to the Division II national title. The Lakers, with a nearly 40-year-old Kareem Abdul-Jabbar, took Jones with their first-round pick in '84. Jones wound up playing only two games for the Lakers and a dozen more with the Bucks before being shown the door. However, for a brief period of time in the 80s, he put UDC on the basketball map.

6. Yinka Dare, C George Washington University 1992-94. Mike Jarvis, who had coached Patrick Ewing in high school in Boston, was able to quickly build a strong team at GW by recruiting internationally. He found Dare in Nigeria before the start of his second year and the payoff was instant. With Dare averaging double digits in points and rebounds, the Colonials authored a Cinderella story in 1993, not only getting to the NCAA tournament for the first time in 32 years, but advancing to the Sweet 16. After a second trip to the NCAA's the following year, the seven-footer thought he was ready for the NBA. Unfortunately for the New Jersey Nets, they thought he was too, and took him with the 14th pick. Dare turned out to be an NBA bust and tragically died of a heart attack at the age of 32 in 2004. But he put George Washington on the basketball map, where they have stayed for more than 15 years.

5. Kermit Washington, F American University 1969-73. The world knows him best as the guy who punched Rudy Tomjanovich in the face, but it doesn't represent who he is and what he was as a college player. Washington drew little interest coming out of Coolidge High School and had few options other than the scholarship Tom Young offered. While at AU, Kermit worked his butt off on the court and in the classroom, becoming an academic All-American. As a senior, he averaged more than 20 points and 20 rebounds a game. He clearly could have played anywhere in the country and was well on his way to proving worthy of being the Lakers' first-round pick when the unfortunate incident with Rudy T occurred in 1977.

4. Jess Atkinson, K University of Maryland 1981-84. Atkinson went to Maryland, hoping to "walk on" the soccer team. He lasted one day and was cut. Bored, he wandered over to the football field and decided to give the funny-shaped ball a try. Coach Bobby Ross liked what he saw. By the time he graduated, Atkinson had been All ACC and a two-time honorable mention All-American. He held the Maryland scoring record for 20 years before it was broken by Nick Novak. Atkinson was good enough to kick for four NFL teams and even picked up a Super Bowl ring with the Redskins. He's gone on to a successful television career.

3. Joe Smith, C University of Maryland 1993-95. The top high school center coming out of Virginia in '94 was Joey Beard of South Lakes, who turned out to be a bust at Duke. Smith drew little attention coming out of Norfolk and signed with Maryland because UVA didn't seem all that interested. Mistake. Smith became an instant starter at Maryland and became the consensus pick as Player of the Year in '95. He also joined David Thompson and Ralph Sampson as the only sophomores to win ACC Player of the Year. It would have been nice to see him play another year at Maryland, but he was the number-one pick of the NBA draft by Golden State in '95.

2. Herb Mul-Key, RB Redskins 1972–74. Mul-Key literally did come out of nowhere, as in no college. He was discovered at an all-comers open tryout at Georgetown University on a Saturday morning in the early spring of '72. After driving in from Buffalo, he'd slept in his car outside the football field gates. In his second year, lining up to return a kick in St. Louis, CBS announcer Jack Whitaker, reading his name from a roster said, "There's Herb Mul-Key from none (he pronounced it no-knee) college." A producer, in his ear, straightened out the legendary announcer. "Oh, that's none." Despite the short career, Mul-Key did play in a Super Bowl for the Skins and led the NFC in returns in 1973 when he made the Pro Bowl.

1. David Robinson, C Naval Academy 1983–87. Robinson didn't play basketball until his senior year of high school at Osbourne Park in Manassas. And that was only because the coach talked him in to it. He was 6-foot-7, big enough but not a giant. After being All District, several colleges expressed interest but he chose the Naval Academy to study math. Talk about a late bloomer, Robinson grew six inches in Annapolis and went on to one of the great careers in college basketball history. As a junior, he put a bunch of future sailors and pilots on his back and took the Middies to the Elite Eight in the NCAA tournament. He was the number-one pick of the NBA draft by San Antonio, which happily waited two years for his service commitment to expire. Robinson helped the Spurs win two NBA championships as every college coach in America kicked himself for not taking a chance on the Admiral.

The NFL calls them "preseason games," but let's be honest, they're exhibition games. The results don't count. But the games are still televised and you have to pay full price to get in. More importantly, it's the best way for the coaches to evaluate players, and sometimes legends are made in August. Here are 10 Redskins who stood out in the summer swelter.

10. Jeff George: 2000. Ah the summer of Dannyworld. Despite warnings from others about George being a locker room cancer, Dan Snyder had to have the well-traveled former number-one pick of the draft with the big arm. Signing him as a free agent, Snyder paid George more money than his starter Brad Johnson, who was coming off a Pro Bowl season. Snyder also came up with the brilliant idea of charging admission for fans to watch training camp. George and Johnson would warm up next to each other, and watching George loft those beautiful spirals was a sight to see. He did little to distinguish himself in either preseason or regular season games, but oh what a thrill it was to pay your ten bucks and watch the QB with the million dollar arm and ten cent head throw long.

9. Mark Stock: 1993. One of the classic feel-good stories of summer. Stock was a 5-foot-11 27-year-old free agent out of VMI who made the team through sheer grit and determination. With some big plays on special teams, Stock impressed the coaches enough to make the roster and wound up playing three games that season.

8. James Thrash: 1997. A Philadelphia Eagles castoff who got himself noticed by returning a kickoff for a touchdown in his first preseason game in burgundy and gold. Thrash became a do-everything guy on special teams and proved valuable as a third receiver. He went back to Philadelphia in 2001 for three years and returned to Washington when Joe Gibbs came back in 2004. Gibbs called him, "a real Redskin."

7. Herb Mul-Key: 1972. A great George Allen find. Mul-Key was signed after an open tryout camp at Georgetown University. He'd never played college football, but impressed Allen with his speed. Mul-Key was impressive enough in his first training camp to make the practice squad, which was then known as the "taxi squad." Later that season he filled in for an injured Larry Brown against Dallas and gained 60 yards. Mul-Key also had some big kick returns in the playoffs.

6. Bob Brunet: 1970-77. For a guy who totaled only 406 yards and three career touchdowns, Brunet managed to carve out a nice, long career. After making the team as a seventh-round pick in 1968, he quit football during the 1969 preseason because he couldn't deal with Vince Lombardi. Brunet returned in 1970 and made his mark as the preseason workhorse. In those days they played six preseason games. Since there was no point in getting star Larry Brown banged up in meaningless games, Brunet carried the load and then took his place on special teams once the real season started. It's possible that Brunet has more preseason carries than any back in Redskin history. Although who would bother to keep track of such things?

5. Matt Elliot: 1992. Elliot is the last true "Mr. Irrelevant." He was the last draft pick of the last NFL draft that went 12 rounds (it's now seven rounds). Although he was a starter at center at Michigan, Elliot was considered undersized for the NFL. But with famed Hog Jeff Bostic and versatile Raleigh McKenzie on the roster, Elliot made the team and stuck around for a couple of years before becoming the starting center of the expansion Carolina Panthers.

4. Joe Jacoby: 1981. One of the great stories in Redskins history. Despite great size, 6-foot-7 and nearly 300 pounds, Jacoby went undrafted out of Louisville. After being signed as a free agent, new coach Joe Gibbs assumed "Jake" was a defensive lineman and began telling him what defensive coordinator Richie Petitbon would be expecting of him. Shy and nervous, Jacoby couldn't muster the courage to tell Gibbs he actually played on the offensive line. When Gibbs found out, he wanted to cut him because they had too many linemen in camp, including first-round pick Mark May. Fortunately, Gibbs changed his mind. Jacoby was not only good enough to make the team, he started ahead of May at left tackle and stayed there for most of the next 13 years.

3. Brian Mitchell: 1990. Mitchell had played quarterback at Southwest Louisiana, but had shown his great speed at the NFL combine. The Redskins drafted him in the sixth round of the 1990 draft and figured they'd look at him at a variety of positions. His first preseason game was played in Chapel Hill, North Carolina, against Atlanta in what was an attempt to drum up support for an expansion team for the area, which they eventually got with the Carolina Panthers four years later. "B Mitch," who had never returned a kick in a game, took the opening kickoff and returned it 92 yards for a touchdown. He went on to become the most productive kick returner in NFL history.

2. Ifeanyi Ohalete: 2004. Ohalete had worn number 26 for the three previous seasons with the Redskins when Clinton Portis joined the team as a free agent. Portis had worn number 26 in Denver and wanted to wear it in Washington. Ohalete agreed to give it up for $40 thousand. Portis made a $20 thousand down payment, but when Ohalete was cut late in training camp, he refused to pay the other half of the deal. Portis maintained he shouldn't have to pay because Ohalete was no longer with the team. The dispute wound up in the court docket before finally they agreed to settle for $18 thousand of the remaining $20 grand. Thirty eight grand to give up a number he was going to have to give up anyway. That's heroic.

1. Babe Laufenberg: 1985 and 86. Laufenberg hung around the NFL for eight years while playing in only 16 regular season games. Drafted out of Indiana in 1983, he stuck on the roster as a third string quarterback. With his job on the line during the '85 preseason, he came off the bench in the 4th quarter against New England and threw a 75-yard touchdown pass to Gary Clark and a 25-yard TD pass to Clint Didier with four seconds left to pull out a one-point win. He was cut. Back on the roster in '86, Laufenberg did it again, pulling out an overtime victory over Pittsburgh in the second preseason game. Despite a "save the Babe" campaign, he was cut again for the last time. He finally wound up getting some playing time in San Diego and Dallas and even backed up Troy Aikman in Dallas for a couple of years. He makes his living as a TV sportscaster and Cowboys radio analyst these days. It's the ultimate "up yours" to the team that cut him twice.

10. Jay Schroeder (1984-88). It is important to remember Schroeder for his beginning in Washington, rather than his ending. In his second year with only a few college starts under his belt (Schroeder left UCLA after his sophomore year to give baseball a try in the Blue Jays organization), the blond bomber came in after Joe Theismann broke his leg against the Giants in 1985. Schroeder not only won that one, but started the last five games, winning four of them and nearly getting the Redskins into the playoffs. The following season, he set team records for attempts (541) and yards (4,109) and took the Skins to the NFC title game. Although he was benched in '87 for Doug Williams, Al Davis saw enough promise in Schroeder to give up All-Pro tackle Jim Lachey in return in a trade with the Raiders.

9. Norm Snead (1961-63). Snead had the misfortune of playing on some really awful Redskin teams, including the last all-white NFL team in '61. Still, he threw 22 touchdown passes in '62 and made the Pro Bowl a year later. After the '63 season, Snead was dealt for Sonny Jurgensen, who appears much further down this list.

8. Brad Johnson (1999-20). After taking over as owner of the Redskins in May, 1999, Dan Snyder wondered whether he could reverse the trade of Johnson from Minnesota made months earlier. The question set the tone for Johnson's stay in Washington as Snyder signed strong-arm, weak-head Jeff George a year later and paid him more money than Johnson, who was coming off one of the best years in team history. Johnson threw for 24 touchdowns and over four thousand yards, finishing with a passer rating of 90.0! Despite taking the Redskins to the NFC East title and a playoff win, Johnson was never appreciated and left to take Tampa Bay to a Super Bowl Championship.

7. Doug Williams (1986-89). After the USFL folded, Williams took the only offer he got and reunited with Joe Gibbs who was his position coach with Tampa Bay as a rookie in 1978. Williams sat for a year behind Jay Schroeder, but beat him out at the end of the '87 season. Williams not only made history by becoming the first African-American quarterback to start and win a Super Bowl, he threw four touchdown passes in one quarter and was named the game's MVP.

6. Billy Kilmer (1971-78). His passes wobbled, but ol' "Furnace Face" was a winner. Kilmer replaced injured Redskins legend Sonny Jurgensen at the start of the '71 season and put the team on the sports map with a 5-0 start. He followed that with Washington's first trip to the playoffs in a quarter century. In '72, Kilmer again stepped in for an injured Jurgy and took the Redskins to their first Super Bowl. Plus, he tipped the Toddle House counter guy a hundred bucks after a night of one too many.

5. Eddie LeBaron (1952-53, 55-59). Only 5-7, 165 pounds, LeBaron could never physically fill the shoes of Sammy Baugh, but he made up for it in other ways. Like a great basketball guard, LeBaron was a great ball-handler who seemed to make magic on the field. His teams weren't very good, but LeBaron went to four Pro Bowls as a Redskin and one more as a Cowboy in 1962.

4. Mark Rypien (1986-93). The only sixth-round pick to win a Super Bowl MVP until Tom Brady started making it a habit. "Ryp" didn't become a full-time starter until 1990, but had one of the great years in NFL history in 1991. His passer rating was 97.9 as he threw for 28 touchdowns and only 11 interceptions while leading the NFC with more than 3,500 yards through the air.

3. Joe Theismann (1974-85). Joey T also bided his time, sitting behind Sonny and Billy until he finally became the number one guy in '78. He was so bored, he volunteered to return punts in '74 and actually led the team in that category. Theismann became the first Redskins quarterback to win a Super Bowl and holds team records in completions and yards gained over a career.

2. Sonny Jurgensen (1964-74). Even though he never won a playoff game, Sonny remains one of the most beloved figures in team history. Nobody threw a more beautiful pass than Sonny, and his 31 touchdown passes in 1967 remains a team record. His work as analyst over a quarter of a century in the booth has only helped to enhance his legacy.

1. Sammy Baugh (1937-51). Slingin' Sammy was considered the best player in NFL history when he retired, and it's possible to argue that he is still that. In 1943 he led the league in passing, punting, and interceptions caught (11 in only 10 games!). Baugh was one of the original inductees into the Pro Football Hall of Fame class in 1963, and his number 33 is the only one that's officially retired by the team.

The 10 Worst Redskin Quarterbacks

If scouting quarterback talent was easy, Tom Brady wouldn't have been a sixth-round pick and Joe Montana wouldn't have lasted until the third round. Here is more proof of that with a list that includes two Heisman Trophy winners and a former number-one pick of the NFL draft.

10. Al Dorow (1954-56). Started 13 games in his three years in Washington. Dorow wound up on the Pro Bowl roster in '56, but managed to put the ball in the other team's hands too many times. Dorow threw 16 touchdown passes and 26 interceptions as a Redskin.

9. Bob Holly (1982-83). The bad thing about Holly, who was drafted in the 11th round out of Princeton, was that he couldn't play. The good thing was, he didn't have to. Joe Theismann remained remarkably durable during Holly's two years as a Redskin. He has a nice shiny Super Bowl ring to show all of his friends.

8. Rudy Bukich (1957-58). Bukich managed to hang around the NFL for 15 years, mostly with the Bears. He was a backup on their 1963 championship team and started in Chicago for a couple of years in the mid-60s when the best thing he did was hand off to Gayle Sayers. As a younger man though, Bukich was not very good, throwing one touchdown pass and four interceptions as a Redskin.

7. Dick Shiner (1964-66). A local product from the University of Maryland, Shiner hung in the NFL for 11 years, including three years as Sonny Jurgensen's backup. When he had to play, Shiner failed to shine in Washington. He completed only 39 percent of his passes.

6. Jeff George (2000-01). George had one of the great arms ever seen on a quarterback. Unfortunately he didn't have the head to match. Just like Indianapolis and Atlanta, it ended badly for George in D.C. In his last NFL start, George led the Skins to a pathetic eight first downs and 137 total yards in a 37-0 Monday night loss in Green Bay in the second game of the 2001 season. A day later he told the media that leadership is overrated and was released.

5. Rich Gannon (1993). You're right. He did lead the Raiders to the Super Bowl, but in Washington Gannon was so awful that he spent the following year out of football. One of three different starters that 4-12 season, Gannon threw only four touchdown passes and seven interceptions.

4. Tim Hasselbeck (2003-04). Started the last six games of the 2003 season after Patrick Ramsey went down for the year with a foot injury. Considering he wasn't signed until mid-season when Steve Spurrier had enough of Rob Johnson, Hasselbeck could have been worse. He did win two of the six games. However, what can't be forgotten is the Blutarsky-like passer rating of 0.0 in a 27-0 home loss to Dallas. He completed only six of 26 passes for 56 yards with four interceptions. Yeecch!

3. Danny Wuerffel (2002). After helping Steve Spurrier to his greatest glory in 1996, when he won the Heisman and Florida won the National Title, the Ol' Ball Coach couldn't get it into his head that Wuerffel just wasn't an NFL quarterback. Finally, owner Dan Snyder yanked the cord on Wuerffel, cutting him before the '03 season.

2. Gary Beban (1968-69). The Redskins traded a first-round draft pick to get the 1967 Heisman winner from the Rams. Beban finished his NFL career with exactly one pass attempt, which fell incomplete.

1. Heath Shuler (1994-96). One of the biggest busts in NFL history. Shuler was the third pick of the 1994 draft and missed half of his first training camp in a holdout dispute. He never seemed to recover. In his final season in Washington, Shuler came in for one play and was booed by the home crowd at RFK Stadium. Shuler was supposed to hand off on a reverse, but fumbled. A fitting end.

Every team in the NFL has its list of favorite players who have never been enshrined in Canton, but the Redskins seem to have had more than their fair share. At least the travesty of having only two in the Hall from the three-ring Joe Gibbs era (Gibbs and John Riggins) was corrected in 2008 when Art Monk and Darrell Green received their belated invitations—though a couple more are worthy. This list is in no particular order, because they're all deserving.

Chris Hanburger. From 1966 through 1976, this undersized 218-pound linebacker and 18th-round pick from North Carolina made nine Pro Bowl teams, more than any defensive player in Redskins history. Hanburger, who was never very media friendly, also has never been among the top 15 candidates discussed at the Hall's annual selection meeting the day before the Super Bowl. He's now eligible as a senior candidate.

Pat Fisher. A 17th-round choice from Nebraska in 1961, he played cornerback in the NFL for 17 years and was one of the first to employ and perfect the bump-and-run tactic of knocking receivers off their stride both at the line of scrimmage and down the field, the latter no longer allowed in the NFL. He was listed as being 5-foot-9 and 170 pounds, both generous numbers, and played with unbridled ferocity and little regard for his own safety. Also eligible as a senior candidate.

Larry Brown. An eighth-round pick out of Kansas State in the 1968 draft, Brown became one of the most feared running backs in the NFL under George Allen and was the league MVP in the 1972 season, when he also led the NFL in rushing. Allen tried to give him the ball as often as possible, and Brown's body eventually succumbed to the pounding. He retired because of knee injuries in 1976 after seven seasons in the league, six of them as the team's leading rusher.

Len Hauss. He was taken in the ninth round of the 1964 draft from the University of Georgia and still holds the team record for most consecutive games started, with 192, as well as most consecutive games played, with 196. He was undersized for a center, weighing about 250 pounds, but was the leader of the team's offensive line for most of his career and went to the Pro Bowl six straight times starting in 1967. Now eligible as a senior candidate.

Russ Grimm. A 280-pound guard, he was taken in the third round of the 1981 draft and quickly became one of Joe Bugel's Boss Hogs on a famous offensive line that dominated defenses throughout the first Joe Gibbs era. He was a fearsome blocker, particularly on sweeps, and also plowed in front of Hall of Famer John Riggins to open countless gaping holes.

Joe Jacoby. He came to the Redskins as an undrafted free agent who actually played on the defensive line at Louisville. Discovered originally by assistant general manager Charley Casserly, Jacoby was converted to an offensive tackle and was a massive 300-pound presence on the Hogs, and also an effective run blocker and pass protector.

Brian Mitchell. He'll become eligible for possible induction in 2009; we include him here in anticipation that he probably won't make it on the first ballot "because he was a kick returner." He was the 130th player taken in the 1990 college draft from Southwestern Louisiana, where he played quarterback. When he retired as a member of the N.Y. Giants in 2004, he was the leading all-purpose yardage producer in NFL history, seeing action as a punt and kickoff returner as well as running back.

Note: Brian Mitchell spent 14 years in the NFL with the Redskins, Eagles, and Giants. At press time he held the all-time record for kick returns for touchdowns with 13 in the regular season and one in the playoffs. He currently co-hosts the *John Thompson Show* on Sportstalk 980 in Washington, D.C. Here's how Mitchell ranks his returns.

14. 84-yard punt return versus the Giants at RFK Stadium, 11-1-92. I
put this one at the bottom of the list because it not only came in a loss, but was the only touchdown in a blowout loss. It was a Sunday night game in the rain and the Skins lost 24-7.

13. 59-yard punt return at Philadelphia, 10-8-95. Eagles coach Ray
Rhodes, who later was the Redskins defensive coordinator, kept telling his special teams to kick the ball away from me. I picked up a short punt off of a bounce on the run and cut up the sideline for a score. We lost the game 37-34 in overtime on a field goal from Gary Anderson, but the game helped me get to the Pro Bowl and I wound up on the cover of the Redskins media guide the next season.

12. 63-yard punt return at Arizona, 12-7-97. The Skins had gone winless in
our last three games and needed this one to get back in the playoff race. My touchdown was the first score of the game and helped ignite us to victory. We lost the following week though at New York, and missed the playoffs at 8-7-1.

11. 66-yard punt return at Cincinnati, 9-22-91. We had scored 45, 33, and
34 points in our first three games. This score got us over the hump in a game that was going back and forth. We won 34-27 to go 4-0.

10. 78-yard punt return at Los Angeles, 12-24-94. This was the last game
the Rams played on the West Coast. There were probably only about 20 thousand people in the Big A to see it. We had came in with a 2-13 record and really wanted to win. It was also special because the Rams' special teams coach was Wayne Sevier, who was my first coach. We won 24-21.

9. 97-yard kickoff return at Pittsburgh, 9-7-97. This was my eighth year in
the league, but it was my first kickoff return for a score. It was the opening kickoff of the second half and it gave us a 10-7 lead. I stepped out of bounds, but it wasn't called and since the NFL didn't have instant replay that year, it couldn't be changed. It didn't matter because Jerome Bettis scored on a one-yard run in the fourth quarter and the Steelers won 14-13. The next year a football card showed me returning the ball with one foot out of bounds.

8. 94-yard kickoff return at Arizona, 11-5-01. This was my second year with
the Eagles and I told my teammates before the game that I always had big games in Arizona. During the return I broke kicker Martin Gramatica's nose.

7. 76-yard punt return at San Francisco, 11-26-02. This was the last return
of my career, but it was big because it allowed me to pass Eric Metcalf for number one on the all-time list. Metcalf had been signed by the Redskins the previous season and

had scored on an 89-yard return.

6. 72-yard punt return at New Orleans, 9-25-00. It was my first game back in my hometown since joining the Eagles. This actually should have been a two-return game, but a 94-yard kickoff was called back because of a clip. About five minutes later I returned this punt for my first score as an Eagle.

5. 89-yard kickoff return at Veterans Stadium versus Atlanta, 10-2-00. It was a Sunday night game, so I knew the Redskins were watching. When they released me the previous summer, they'd said I'd lost a step. After this return they claimed I was released because I was a bad influence on the younger players.

4. 74-yard punt return at New Orleans, 9-11-94. This was my first game back in my hometown. It must have been the fuel. The night before the game my mom brought fried turkey to the team hotel for me and my teammates. We won 38-24 to go 1-1, but we finished the season 3-13.

3. 101-yard kickoff return at Jack Kent Cooke Stadium versus San Diego 12-6-98. This was my only return at the new stadium. I broke free with a stiff arm against Jimmy Spencer, who I didn't like. After starting the season 0-7, we were starting to roll. We won 24-20, our second of four straight wins.

2. 100-yard kickoff return at Tampa, 1-15-00. This was my only postseason return and it came at a great time. It was the opening kickoff of the second half and it put us up 13-0. I thought the game was over. It wasn't. We lost 14-13 in what was my last game as a Redskin.

1. 69-yard punt return at RFK Stadium versus Detroit, 9-1-91. It was the opening game of my first year as the full-time kick returner. During the week I got a DUI (which was later thrown out). Coach Joe Gibbs said I had better play well. We won 45-0, our first win of the last Redskins Super Bowl season.

Good Breeding: Fathers, Sons, and Daughters

It's been "all in the family" for scads of Washington sports figures over the years. Here are some of the more noteworthy family ties. And by the way, just to set the record straight, Abe Pollin is not Andy Pollin's father, though they are very distant cousins.

10. Abe Pollin and Wes Unseld. Okay, so they're not related by blood, but they might as well be. They've been closer than close ever since Pollin's Baltimore Bullets team used a No. 1 pick on Unseld in the 1968 NBA draft, with Unseld occupying virtually every position in the organization over the years, from player to head coach to general manager. The tie continues into a third generation, with Wes's son, Wes Unseld Jr., serving as an assistant coach and advance scout.

9. Peter O'Malley and Susan O'Malley. Peter O'Malley was a widely regarded and politically well-connected Prince George's County attorney and one of Abe Pollin's closest advisers for many years. His daughter Susan joined the organization in 1986 and within five years rose to the rank of team president, the first woman in NBA history to hold such a lofty title.

8. Lindsay Czarniak and Chet Czarniak. The Channel 4 sportscaster and budding NBC star isn't the only media-savvy member of her family. Her father Chet is a longtime reporter and editor at *USA Today* and USA Today.com. Lindsay shares the anchor desk at Channel 4 with Dan Hellie after legendary sportscaster George Michael retired in 2006, and NBC executives plan to use her more often in NFL, Olympic, and NASCAR coverage

7. Lefty Driesell and Chuck Driesell. Lefty Driesell had a grand run as head coach at the University of Maryland from 1969 to 1985, including four years of coaching his son Chuck, a talented point guard. Chuckie, as he was always known, was an assistant under his father at James Madison, and in 2006, he returned to his alma mater as an assistant coach and recruiter under Gary Williams.

6. Joe Gibbs and Coy Gibbs. One of the main reasons Joe Gibbs cited when he returned for a second stint as head coach of the Redskins in 2004 was the opportunity to give one of his two sons, Coy, a taste of coaching in the NFL. Coy played linebacker at Stanford and thought he wanted to coach pro football, but after two years, he decided to return to the family NASCAR business back in Charlotte.

5. Morgan Wootten and Joe Wootten. The legendary DeMatha basketball coach, the first high school coach ever inducted into the Basketball Hall of Fame, was at death's door in 1996 suffering from major kidney problems. His son Joe, also a fine prep basketball coach in his own right, donated a kidney to save his father's life and extend his coaching career, which lasted from 1956 until he finally retired in 2002.

4. George Allen, Bruce Allen, and Jennifer Allen. When then Redskins head coach George Allen flew off late in the 1977 season to California to negotiate a contract to coach the Los Angeles Rams the following year, he told reporters he was missing a Saturday practice to visit his punter son Bruce's college game at the University of Richmond. Bruce is the only one of Allen's three sons to stay in the football business, working as a player before moving into front office positions with the Oakland Raiders and now the Tampa Bay Buccaneers, where he's the general manager. Jennifer Allen, the youngest of four children and the only daughter in the family, wrote a poignant memoir, *Fifth Quarter*, about growing up in an alpha-male-dominated football family headed by her father. She now lives in Southern California and works as a writer, reporter, and producer for the NFL Network.

3. Calvin Hill and Grant Hill. Running back Calvin Hill was the Dallas Cowboys' No. 1 draft choice out of Yale in 1969 and was the NFL's rookie of the year. He and his wife Janet, a suitemate of Hillary Rodham Clinton at Wellesley, saw their only child Grant blossom into one of the nation's top prep playuers at South Lakes High School in Reston. Grant was an All-American at Duke and played on the Blue Devils national championship teams in 1991 and '92 before becoming the first overall pick in the '94 NBA draft. After playing on the gold-medal-winning U.S. team in the Atlanta Olympics, he's had an injury-plagued professional career, playing for Detroit, Orlando, and Phoenix.

2. John Thompson Jr. and John Thompson III. At 6-foot-10 and the wrong side of 300 pounds, John Thompson Jr. was the biggest man on Georgetown's campus for 27 years as a pioneering and wildly successful head coach. His son, John III, a fine high school player at Gonzaga, chose to play college basketball at Princeton and coached the Tigers for four seasons, winning the Ivy league title his first season. Georgetown hired him in 2004, and in 2007 he took the Hoyas to the Final Four. There's also another famous father-son connection on his team—Patrick Ewing Jr., the son of the All-American center and longtime NBA star, was a starting forward on that Final Four team.

1. Jack Kent Cooke and John Kent Cooke. Jack Kent Cooke bought a 25-percent interest in the Redskins in 1961 and became majority owner in 1974. He hired Joe Gibbs in 1981 and watched his team win three Super Bowl titles from 1981 through the '92 season. When he died in 1997, the trustees of his estate sold the team to a group headed by Daniel Snyder, who outbid Cooke's son, John Kent Cooke, to purchase the team and the stadium for $700 million, a record price at the time. The father did not leave the team to his son, preferring to use the bulk of the club's sale price to fund a foundation that offers scholarships to worthy graduate students. John Kent Cooke reportedly inherited $50 million and now lives on an estate in Middleburg, Virginia, where he has invested millions in his Boxwood vineyard and winery and now lives the relatively simple life of a small-town country squire.

Note: Al Pollin was born in 1928 and grew up in Washington, D.C., graduating from Central High School in 1946. His son Andy Pollin was born in 1958 and grew up in Chevy Chase, Maryland, graduating from Bethesda Chevy Chase High School in 1976. His son Jeremy Pollin was born in 1991 and grew up in Rockville, Maryland, and will graduate from Woottton High School in 2009. At press time, Jeremy was 17. Here are the favorite teenage local sports memories of three generations of Pollin men.

Favorite Baseball Team:

Al: The original Washington Senators who played at Griffith Stadium. I remember taking the streetcar with my younger sister to see a twi-night doubleheader against the Yankees in 1941 or '42. Bill Zuber threw a 1-0 shutout in the second game. What I remember best was the ticket prices, $1.10 for grandstand, $1.20 for reserved grandstand and 55 cents for the bleachers. We had grandstand tickets. I was only about 13 and didn't know the difference, so we just sat down in what turned out to be reserved seats. In the second game, the people who had those seats showed up and the usher had to kick us out. A number of people sitting behind us thought it was mean and unfair to kick a couple of kids out and let the usher know it. It turned out not to be a big deal. Griffith Stadium wasn't exactly selling out in those days.

Andy: The expansion Senators who played at D.C. Stadium, which was renamed RFK Stadium after the death of Robert Kennedy in 1968. My dad took me to my first game when I was not quite eight in 1966. It was a beautiful Saturday afternoon in the spring and I believe they were playing the Red Sox. My experience was very much like the one Billy Crystal describes in the movie *City Slickers* when he went to his first Yankee game with his dad. Like Crystal, the only television set we had was black and white and I had never seen grass that green. We sat in reserved grandstand (Dad had learned the difference by then) and I remember a man with one arm who yelled at the top of his lungs for the entire game. My dad tried to teach me how to keep score, but I don't remember being very interested. The game, though, was a wonderful experience. The Senators left town for good after the 1971 season when I was 13. I waited 34 years to have a favorite baseball team again. I never adopted the Baltimore Orioles. Not until the Expos moved to Washington in 2005 and became the Nationals, did I feel like I had a team again.

Jeremy: The Chicago Cubs. That's what happens when you grow up in a city that doesn't have a baseball team. We had WGN on our cable system and I used to come home from school and from camp and watch their games. I watched every pitch of Kerry Wood's 20-strikeout game against Houston. When I heard that Harry Carey died, I cried. For my ninth birthday in 2000, my dad took me to Chicago to see a Friday afternoon game at Wrigley Field. He arranged for me to meet Steve Stone and Chip Carey, who were doing the games on WGN at the time. Ironically the game was against the Expos. Sammy Sosa hit a bases-clearing triple and the Cubs won. We took the El to the game and went out for deep dish pizza after the game. The first regular season Nats game we went to was, of course, against the Cubs. I wore a Cubs hat and my dad wore his Nationals hat. The game didn't start until 10 p.m. because of thunderstorms and unfortunately the Nats won. In the last year the Nats played at RFK Stadium, I went to a game with my dad, my grandfather, my cousin and my uncle. It was against the Orioles, who won a close game.

Favorite Baseball Player:

Al: George Washington Case. He was an outfielder who had actually been a track star, but in those days you couldn't make money in track so he played baseball. Case played for the Senators from 1937 to '45. He led the majors in steals five straight years from 1939 to '43. He had 61 steals in '43.

Andy: Frank Howard. A giant of a man in those days at 6-foot-7 and nearly 300 pounds. Howard had played basketball at Ohio State and was a platoon player with the Dodgers when they won the World Series in 1959. Traded to the Senators in 1964 for Claude Osteen, Howard became an immediate fan favorite with his monster home runs. You may have seen the upper deck white seats when the Nats still played at RFK. That's where Howard's shots went. I remember going to opening day in 1968. It must have been about 35 degrees with the wind blowing and Howard was playing in short sleeves and toweling himself off between innings. He was from Green Bay and loved the cold.

Jeremy: Sammy Sosa. I was seven when Sosa and Mark McGwire went at it for the home run title. I was really rooting for Sosa to get it and really got mad when McGwire tied Roger Maris's record. When we went to Chicago, I bought a Sosa refrigerator magnet which is still on the fridge at home.

Favorite Football Team:

Al: The Washington Redskins who played at Griffith Stadium. I don't remember going to my first game until I started driving. My dad wasn't a sports fan, so he wasn't going to take me. Plus during the depression, our family owned a corner store. It was open seven days a week so somebody had to be there at all times. The first game I remember was in 1945 when I went with some high school friends. It was an exhibition game against the Detroit Lions. I did listen to their games on the radio. Harry Wismer did the play-by-play. I remember he never used the word "lateral"—instead he would say, "and Sammy Baugh throws a backward pass." Baugh was my favorite player. He threw bullet passes. I don't know whether the story is true, but I heard he once threw a pass at an opponent's head and knocked him out.

Andy: The Washington Redskins who played at RFK Stadium. My dad took me to my first game in 1968. It was the last game of the year against the Detroit Lions and both teams were going nowhere. The temperature was in the teens, but I insisted on staying until the final gun, even though the Redskins were comfortably ahead. Tickets were tough to get in those days and I wasn't sure when we would go back. I wound up with the flu the next day. We managed to go to one game a year and watched the road games on TV. The NFL didn't allow teams to televise home games until 1973 when I was in the 10th grade. Before that we listened to Steve Gilmartin do the home games on WMAL. On Monday nights Gilmartin would go on Channel 20 and show the coaches film of the game. That was the only way to see it if you weren't at the stadium. The NFC championship game was televised on New Year's Eve 1972, even though it was at RFK. Watching the Skins beat Dallas was incredible. Watching them lose to Miami in the Super Bowl two weeks later was heartbreaking.

Jeremy: No team. I don't have a favorite football team. I watch the Redskins games, but I'm not emotionally invested. The Redskins are not a good organization. I'm told I was at a Super Bowl party in New Jersey when the Skins won, but I was only six months old and don't remember it. I do like Clinton Portis; he's a G (that means gangster, a good thing in teenage boy talk).

Favorite NBA Team:

Al: There was no NBA when I was growing up. In the late 40s we had a team coached by Red Auerbach that played at the old Uline Arena. I think I went to one game. They were called the Capitols and the player I remember was Freddy Scholari.

Andy: The Baltimore/Washington Bullets. My dad took me to my first game at the old Baltimore Civic Center in 1968. It was against the Celtics in what was the second game of a doubleheader. The Harlem Globetrotters played in the first game. I don't remember much about the game other than the ring of smoke that filled the arena by the third quarter. In those days you could smoke in your seat. A few years later we went to one of those classic playoff games against the Knicks. Believe it or not, we just drove up the day of the game and bought tickets at the window. Also about that time, the Bullets started playing some home games at Cole Field House. We went to several of those, including one against Wilt Chamberlain and the Lakers. By the time the Bullets moved to the Capital Centre in 1973, I could drive there with my friends. We could buy student tickets for four dollars and sneak down to the lower level. I also remember watching the 20 or so games a year that Channel 20 televised with Jim Karvelas doing the play-by-play with future agent Jerry Kapstein, who was then a George Washington Law School student.

Jeremy: The Washington Wizards. My dad and my mom have taken me to games at the Verizon Center. You can take the metro so my mom doesn't have to worry about parking and driving in D.C. Gilbert Arenas is my favorite player. We went to a playoff game in 2005 against Chicago, which the Wizards won. I'm told I saw the Bullets play at the U.S. Air Arena, but I don't remember it.

Favorite College Basketball Team:

Al: I don't remember going to a game until I was in college at George Washington. College basketball just wasn't big in the D.C. area in those days.

Andy: University of Maryland. I first started watching their games shortly after Lefty Driesell arrived in 1969. Billy Packer and Tom Thacker used to do the ACC Game of the Week on the Mizzlou Network. I think Channel 7 carried the games. My dad took me to my first game in 1972. I think it was the first game John Lucas played at Maryland. On Super Bowl Sunday 1973, hours before the Redskins lost to the Dolphins, I went with a friend and his dad to see Maryland play NC State with David Thompson at Cole Field House. It turned out to be a double-heartbreak day. Thompson took an alley-oop pass from Monte Towe in the final seconds and dropped it in for the game winner. In those days you weren't allowed to dunk. NC State finished unbeaten that season, but was banned from the NCAA tournament for illegally recruiting Thompson. It turned out to be worth it. A year later they beat Maryland in an overtime classic in the ACC tournament final and went on to beat UCLA in the NCAA semifinals on their way to a championship. With only 24 teams in the NCAA tournament in those days, what may have been the best Maryland team ever was left out.

Jeremy: University of Maryland. Maryland games are a big deal in our house. My mom went there when Buck Williams and Albert King played in College Park. There's so much tension that sometimes we all watch the games on separate TVs. I have been to a number of games both at Cole Field House and Comcast Center. Most of my favorite sports moments revolve around Maryland basketball. My favorite all time player is Steve Blake because he knew how to run a team and hit big shots. My favorite play was when Blake stole the ball from Jay Williams at mid court and scored a layup at the other end in the closing seconds of the first half of a win over Duke. Later that year Maryland won the NCAA championship, which is my favorite sports memory. The best game I ever went to was when Maryland upset Duke in overtime in 2005. Comcast Center went nuts. Nothing is better than being at a Maryland game when they win. My sister goes to Wisconsin, which has a great basketball team, but she says Maryland basketball is a bigger deal.

Favorite Hockey Team:

Al: Hockey? That was a game played in Canada when I was growing up.

Andy: The Caps. We didn't get a team until my junior year in high school. And what we got was the worst team in hockey history. It was fun to go to the games in the early days, but we knew there wasn't much chance of winning. The Caps did have a Jewish goalie, Bernie Wolfe. That was cool.

Jeremy: The Caps. I went to the first game the Caps ever played at the Verizon (then MCI) Center. It went to overtime and the Caps won. Peter Bondra is my favorite all-time player. He was the best player when they were good.

How We Listened and Watched:

Al: Mostly radio. My father bought one of the first televisions available in Washington in 1948, but I was already out of high school. The Senators games were broadcast by Arch McDonald and Russ Hodges (before he joined the Giants and made his famous, "The Giants Win the Pennant!!!" call when Bobby Thomson hit the homer to beat the Dodgers). You could always tell the score by the sound of McDonald's voice. When they were up, he was up. When they were down, he was down.

Andy: Network and UHF TV. I didn't get cable TV until I was out of college. The Redskins and Senators games were on Channel 9. First Channel 5 and then Channel 20 did the Bullets, and some Maryland basketball games were on Channel 7. Channel 4 didn't have much in the way of local sports, but Super Bowl VII was on NBC. Before the Senators left, I listened to them on WWDC with Shelby Whitfield and Ron Menchine. Tony Roberts did their last year after Bob Short fired Whitfield at the end of the 1970 season.

Jeremy: You name it. It's a rare game that isn't televised. If I miss anything, there are plenty of highlight shows on Comcast and ESPN. And I can always find it on the internet. I started watching SportsCenter in the morning before school when I was in the first grade and still start my morning the same way.

Some guys just get under our skin. Here are the top ten non-NFLers who rub us the wrong way—some for being too damn good, and the rest for being just plain bad.

10. Joe Paterno. How do you hate the grand old man of college football, the beloved JoePa? Easy answer if you're a Maryland football fan, as in Penn State's 35-1-1 record in its last 37 meetings against the Terrapins.

9. Phil Ford. The great North Carolina point guard from 1975-78, he ran Dean Smith's stall-ball Four Corners offense to perfection, allowing Carolina to protect leads, ice games, and infuriate opposing fans from Tobacco Road to College Park, and anywhere else he happened to play.

8. Mike Krzyzewski. His Duke teams are so good and his teams have been so successful against Maryland for so many years. But he's just so smug sitting there surrounded by all those All-Americans, many of whom couldn't get into Duke without basketball as their extra-curricular credential. Let's see how good he'd be at Navy. Then again, Coach K was pretty good at Army. Aaah, we still don't like him.

7. Bill Walton. A big-time pill with the media, and often the fans, wherever he played in the NBA, Walton was the classic athlete who learned how to say hello as a broadcaster when it was time to say goodbye as a petulant player. Now you can't shut him up, save for the mute button.

6. Kwame Brown. The first high school student ever to be taken with the first overall pick in the NBA draft, he had four stormy seasons in Washington before being shipped to the Lakers in 2005. His last season in Washington, he feuded with coach Eddie Jordan, with his teammates, and with the fans. He missed a practice during the 2005 playoffs with an alleged stomach ailment, only to be seen chowing down at a Chinese restaurant that night, causing the team to suspend him, and then trade him. Good riddance.

5. Chris Webber. We actually rejoiced when the Wizards traded Tom Gugliotta and three No. 1 draft choices to Golden State to re unite the second-year power forward with Michigan college teammate Juwan Howard in 1995. But Webber quickly wore out his welcome, the crowning blow coming when he was arrested for speeding, resisting arrest, assault, and driving while under the influence of marijuana while driving to a practice at the MCI Center in 1998. He was traded to Sacramento, and what looked to be a budding championship contender evaporated into more mediocrity. Washington fans have booed Webber whenever he returned with the Kings, 76ers, or Pistons.

4. LeBron James. An incandescent talent, we'll never forgive the Cleveland Cavaliers superstar for whispering sweet somethings—perhaps as in "choke you dog, you're gonna miss"—into Gilbert Arenas's ear as he stepped to the free throw line in Game Six of a playoff series in 2006. Arenas missed, the Cavs won, and we've despised not-so-sweet baby James ever since.

3. Jim Boeheim. Has a Syracuse player ever committed a foul without the longtime, seemingly long-suffering head coach of the Orangemen whining about a rotten call? Has a Syracuse player ever taken a shot when he hasn't moaned that his man was hacked in the act? Why does he look like a Maalox-deprived guy with a perpetual ulcer? Waaa, Waaa, Waaa. Who says there's no crying in basketball? At Syracuse, it's a way of life.

2. Jaromir Jagr. He was fabulous in Pittsburgh before he got here, he was terrific in New York when he left here. So what happened with the Washington Capitals? Why was he such a dog here who alienated his coaches, his teammates, and fans who should have adored him, but wound up jeering his every move, then and still? No Czech mate here in the Nation's Capital, where he'll always be despised.

1. Michael Vick. Ryhmes with sick. When he comes back to football, as he almost surely will when he gets out of jail for unspeakable animal cruelty, fans almost certainly will dog him for the rest of his playing life. What a shame.

Everybody has to love somebody some time, but everybody who's ever followed the Washington Redskins also has plenty of NFL villains to hate most of the time—many of them, you may notice, of the Dallas Cowboys persuasion.

10. Clint Longley. His name forever will live in infamy for that 50-yard touchdown pass thrown to Drew Pearson with 28 seconds remaining to beat the Redskins, 24-23, and prevent them from clinching a playoff berth in 1974. Longley, a rookie from Abilene Christian also known as "The Mad Bomber" was playing in his first NFL game in relief of injured Roger Staubach.

9. Conrad Dobler. An offensive lineman with the then St. Louis Cardinals, he was considered the dirtiest player in the NFL back in the 1970s, and his leg-whipping tripping technique was particularly loathsome to the Redskins. No wonder the guy needed two knee replacements thirty years later.

8. Jerry Glanville. The loud-mouthed Atlanta Falcons coach known for always leaving a couple of tickets at the will-call window for Elvis Presley before home games always did a lot of trash talking before, during, and after games. One year, after getting drilled by Joe Gibbs' Redskins, he upset Coach Joe by dashing to the locker room after the final gun, purposely avoiding a post-game handshake.

7. Allie Sherman. This actually was one man's hatred. Sam Huff despised his former head coach with the N.Y. Giants for trading him to the Redskins in 1964, and he got his revenge in a game against the Giants two years later. The Redskins were leading the Giants, 69-41, at RFK Stadium toward the end of the 1966 season and were in scoring position late in the fourth quarter. Taking a knee would have been the appropriate finish, but Huff convinced head coach Otto Graham to send out the kicking team and boot a rub-it-in field goal for a 72-41 win.

6. Thomas "Hollywood" Henderson. The Cowboys' gifted linebacker back in the 1970s also was a formidable trash talker who usually backed up his words with plenty of big-play deeds, many of them against the Redskins of that era. He was a tackling terror who could rush the passer and cover backs and wide receivers downfield, at least until he started sniffing that white stuff that prematurely ended his career, and none too soon for Washington fans.

5. Bill Belichick. A native son of Annapolis, the New England Patriots head coach nevertheless infuriated Redskins fans, not to mention head coach Joe Gibbs, with a roll-it-up 52-7 victory during the 2007 season. The Patriots could have and should have taken a knee in the fourth quarter but continued to throw and score with the game well in hand. Still, the Spygate cheater at least got his in the end when the Giants shattered his team's bid for a perfect 19-0 season with a 17-14 victory in Super Bowl XLII.

4. Tom Landry. The Cowboys' longtime Hall of Fame coach just looked so damned smug standing there on the opposite sidelines in his signature hat, nattily dressed in pressed slacks and tie and sportscoat. George Allen took verbal shots at him every chance he got, and Redskins fans drank the Kool-Aid, even if Landry happened to be one of the classiest coaches in NFL history.

3. Jimmy Johnson. He was one of the least classy coaches in NFL history, and a Redskins nemesis during an era when the Cowboys won three Super Bowls in the 1990s, two of them on his watch. Washington fans also knew that Johnson had coached popular Redskins defensive end Dexter Manley in college at Oklahoma State, and we always wondered how Manley could stay academically eligible for three years, and not be able to read, when he was drafted by the Redskins in 1981. Don't ask Jimmy. Maybe he was too busy getting that hair to look just right to really care.

2. Deion Sanders. We despised "Prime Time" when he played shut down corner in Dallas, even if he never hit anyone, but we truly loathed him following a singularly unproductive season when he joined the Redskins as a high-priced free agent in 2000 with a $56 million contract that included an $8 million signing bonus. Sanders was a part-time player for the Redskins that season, and was gone the following year after pocketing more than $10 million of Dan Snyder's money. What a shame for two guys who definitely deserved each other.

1. Michael Irvin. The Dallas Cowboys wide receiver called himself "The Playmaker" and made plenty of them against the Redskins back in his prime, infuriating fans with his kneel down and look-toward-the-heavens touchdown celebrations in the Washington end zone. But we hated him even more after he stopped playing because somehow he got into the Pro Football Hall of Fame a year ahead of beloved Washington receiver Art Monk, who had more catches, total yards, and touchdown catches than the yappy Cowboy, but had to wait much longer for his own ticket to Canton.

As you know (or don't know, or don't care), I have been on the sports staff of the *Washington Post* since 1969. Over the years I've been a reporter, editor and columnist, the author of five books, and an adjunct professor in the journalism department of my alma mater, the University of Wisconsin, where I once wrote some of the worst columns in student newspaper history under the headline (ugh): "Splinters from the Bench." If there's one thing I do know, it's good sports journalism. Here are my Top Ten sportswriters from the D.C. area.

10. Morris Siegel. The late *Washington Star* and *Washington Times* columnist was a stitch in person who kept press box denizens laughing for decades with his *bon mots*, one-liners and often-repeated stories. Mo had terrific sources, but if he had written the way he talked, he might have been much higher up on the list.

9. Kenneth Denlinger. A deep thinker with a great passion for college sports, particularly basketball, his thoughtfully understated *Washington Post* columns were always balanced, fair, and meticulously reported, and were aimed at the thinking man/woman reader.

8. William Gildea. One of the most graceful and versatile writers in the *Post's* sports section over the last 40 years, his true forte was the long feature profile, but his columns on soccer and hockey—two sports most other *Post* columnists have generally avoided over the years—were always elegantly written with a purposeful point of view.

7. Sally Jenkins. A brilliant wordsmith, the daughter of the great author and sportswriter Dan Jenkins is a singular talent in her own right. She often takes contrary positions to the general conventional thinking, making her even more of a must read in the *Post*, even if she's not in the paper as much as she ought to be.

6. Tom Callahan. Though most of his early career was spent writing columns in San Diego and Cincinnati, he came to the *Washington Star* in its last days and lifted the entire sports section with his thoughtful and sharply opinionated pieces, which also appeared for several years in the *Post's* Sunday sports pages.

5. Thomas Boswell. Arguably the most literate baseball writer of his generation, Boswell on baseball and professional golf in the *Post* has been must reading for Washingtonians since the 1970s, and now that we have a baseball team to call our own, this native of the District of Columbia may never put down his computer.

4. Michael Wilbon. One of the most passionate writers in the country, Wilbon came up through the *Post* ranks as a summer intern and beat reporter covering Maryland, Georgetown, the Redskins, and the NBA. He's both thoughtful and fearless on issues of race, and because of his beat reporting background and high profile TV work, he may have the best NFL and NBA sports Rolodex in town. Somehow, he also still finds the time to tap out two or three columns a week despite a full broadcasting schedule with ABC and ESPN.

3. Tony Kornheiser. Until the lure of radio and television broadcasting took him away from the keyboard, Mr. Tony wrote the country's most humorous sports column in his newspaper prime, but also could be deadly serious and wickedly opinionated when he had to be, skewering "preening schmoes" who never even knew they were bleeding once he got through with them. His Sunday columns in the Style section of *The Post* were laugh-out-loud must reading, as well.

2. Dave Kindred. Arguably one of the most versatile sportswriters on the planet, Kindred had a grand run as *The Post's* lead sports columnist in the 1970s and early 80s before moving on to *The National*, America's short-lived national sports daily, followed by stints at the *Atlanta Constitution* and *The Sporting News*. Equally adept writing long features, magazine stories, columns, or books—all exhaustively reported and lovingly crafted—many of his colleagues around the country regard him as best in breed over the last 30 years.

1. Shirley Povich. The legendary and late longtime *Washington Post* sports editor and columnist was a fabulous fixture in the daily and *Sunday Post* for 75 years before his death in 1996, as contemporary in his 90s as he was in his earlier years when his presence in the paper was about the only thing that kept the *Post* alive. A dapper, often elegant dresser, he could make his readers laugh, cry or—if you were bigoted Redskins team owner George Preston Marshall—wish you were never born. He also trained countless young sportswriters over the years in how to write, how to report, and most of all, how to go about their business in the classiest manner possible.

Not That Guy: Redskins Draft Choices that Create Confusion

When you look over old Redskin draft lists, you may find a few names that cause you to do a double take. Here are five.

5. Tom Petty. Taken in the 30th round out of Virginia Tech in 1955. Since he went so low, it was no heartbreaker when he didn't make the team.

4. Dick Weber. A guard from Syracuse who went in the 13th round of the 1943 draft. We don't know if he was capable of picking up the 7-10 split, but he probably passed some of those cold winter nights in upstate New York rolling the big balls

3. Bob Cummings. The Redskins loved that Bob, but not that much. The center from Vanderbilt went in the 29th round of the 1945 draft. He was gone before the season started.

2. Bob Mathias. Actually it was that guy. The famed decathlon winner played football at Stanford. In 1951 against USC, he returned a Frank Gifford kickoff 91 yards for a touchdown. The Skins were pretty sure he wouldn't play pro football, but used a 30th round pick on him anyway in 1953.

1. Quinn Buckner. Actually it was that guy again. Buckner had played safety as a freshman at Indiana. George Allen took a shot in the 14th round in 1976. Buckner had just finished leading the Hoosiers to a National Championship and was a basketball All-American. Not that he had much interest in football, but the NFL voided the pick anyway.

Shirley Povich's 10 Greatest Newspaper Leads
:: George Solomon

Note: George Solomon, the longtime former sports editor of the *Washington Post*, helped compile and edit *All Those Mornings...At The Post*, a compendium of the greatest sports columns written by legendary *Post* sports columnist Shirley Povich, who plied his craft in the Nation's Capital for nearly 75 years and died in 1998 at the age of 92 the day after his final column appeared in *The Post*. Solomon, who produced the book in 2005 with Povich's children, Maury, David and Lynn, selected his ten favorite Povich column leads.

10. September 23, 1971, The Washington Senators Leave Town, Again:

"They won't hear it in Washington next spring when the cry throughout the rest of the land is the joyful sound of 'Play Ball,' the command that remobilizes a million dreams of pennant, however fanciful. After 71 years, the vacuum and the stillness. The Washington Senators are no more."

9. October 4, 1951, Bobby Thomson's Shot Heard 'Round the World:

"New York—And so it came down to the absolute last pitch of the 157-game season before it was decided that the Giants, not the Dodgers, would be in the World Series against the Yankees.

"Hollywood's most imaginative writers on an opium jag could not have scripted a more improbable windup of the season that started in April and had its finish today in the triumph of Bobby Thomson and the Giants.

"Into that last blur of white that came plateward out of the pitching fist of Brooklyn's Ralph Branca was compressed the destiny of the two clubs that had battled for six months to get to today's decision. Before Thomson swung, it was the Dodgers winning the pennant. A split second later, the Dodgers were dead, and the Giants had it."

8. March 9, 1971, Ali vs. Frazier: "New York—In round 11 he wouldn't go down. There was a definite sag to his knees, and there was hurt on Muhammad Ali's face, but he wouldn't go down from that murderous left hook to his jaw. His pride was propping him up and it was his defiance against Joe Frazier in this moment of his trouble and he lasted the round out.

"But in the first minute of round 15, there was no time for Muhammad Ali to summon his pride to avert a knockdown because he was already on the flat of his back, deposited there by another of Frazier's thunderbolt lefts. He was up at the count of three, but he had to take the mandatory count of eight, and now he knew he was a beaten fighter for the first time in his professional life."

7. September 7, 1972, Avery Brundage and the Olympic Massacre:

"Munich—This was the most cheerless day in Olympic history which has a natal year of 776 B.C. It began with Beethoven's funeral march. It was concluded with Avery Brundage seizing on the scene to get in more plugs for his cherished Olympics in a tasteless pep talk to his captive audience of 80,000 heavy hearts in the big Munich Olympic Stadium.

"In exactly 27 words at the start of his speech, Brundage brushed off the mass murder of 11 Israeli Olympic athletes and team officials by Arab terrorists Tuesday. This was the tragedy that fetched the thousands of mourners to today's memorial services. Oh there were the standard amenities by Brundage. He did say that 'every civilized person recoils in horror at the barbarous criminal intrusion of the terorists.' And he said with evident sincerity that 'we mourn our Israeli friends.'

"Well so much for that. Time now in Brundage's speech, which could be measured in ugly contrast with the humble searches for guilt by the dignitaries who preceded him in the program, to make a quick switch to the Rhodesia mess and also the high importance of continuing the Olympic Games that Brundage has fathered for the last 20 years as International Olympic Committee president."

6. April 8, 1987, Sugar Ray Leonard Upsets Marvin Hagler: "Las Vegas— So they said it couldn't be done. So they said he was unrealistic and a giddy fool for even thinking comeback from a ring rust of nearly five years. And that he could get half-killed and even half-blinded against this brutish battler who for 11 years had been destroying natural middleweights.

"So what chance did they give Sugar Ray Leonard, a puffed up welterweight with a once damaged retina, against Marvelous Marvin Hagler, the monster nobody had licked in more than a decade? And without even a tuneup. More arrogance. The odds were 6 to 1 when the match was made, meaning Leonard's chances were rated miniscule at best. And when they closed at 3 to 1, it was still tantamount to saying Leonard had only a fat chance.

"And so the new middleweight champion of the world is Sugar Ray Leonard. Monday night, he battered Hagler good, made him look like a chump, left the champion chasing a will-o'-the-wisp who had a strong will to fight back when necessary, and when it was desirable to get out of trouble he out-punched the puncher. And never was Hagler or any other champion ever hit with so many right-hand leads, a no-no in all of boxing's textbooks. Leonard was audacious."

5. September 8, 1995, Cal Ripken Outlasts Lou Gehrig: "Baltimore—Four hundred twenty five miles from Baltimore, in Boston's Fenway Park, there erupted on Wednesday night a noisy, five-minute ovation for Cal Ripken. The scoreboard there had just flashed the news: Lou Gehrig's consecutive-games record was history. Long Live Cal Ripken, and the new number is 2,131."

4. September 24, 1927, The Long Count Tunney-Dempsey Heavyweight Fight: "New York—Out of the maze of doubt of the cross-fire that has questioned his supremacy, the shadows that would becloud his claim, Gene Tunney today stands against the pugilistic horizon in bold relief, the heavyweight champion of the world, and worthy of the crown that has been worn by past masters. By right of might Gene Tunney proved himself a champion in every sense that the word implies, proved inconclusively, convincingly, and the scoffers were shown."

3. January 6, 1982, The Death of Red Smith: "Red Smith died at noon yesterday, and there has to be a sorrow in the land. He won't write those columns any more, and Red Smith fans are more than saddened, they're deprived. There has been a withdrawal of one of the steady joys of reading the artist at his work. Red wouldn't agree, but he was like that in his persistent modesty. He preferred to call himself a working stiff.

"Those, of all persuasions, who had an appreciation of the written word were attracted to him and his facility for using the language. He raised the sports-writing trade to a literacy and elegance it had not known before. Red wouldn't agree to that either, but only the most ungrateful of sportswriters would fail to genuflect to the one-time redhead gone white-haired on the job. He also gave their business class."

2. October 31, 1960, Jim Brown Integrates the Redskins Goal Line: "For 18 minutes the Redskins were enjoying equal rights with the Cleveland Browns yesterday, in the sense that there was no score in the contest. Then it suddenly became unequal in favor of the Browns, who brought along Jim Brown, their rugged colored fullback from Syracuse.

"From 25 yards out, Brown was served the football by Milt Plum on a pitch-out and he integrated the Redskins goal line with more than deliberate speed, perhaps exceeding the famous Supreme Court decree. Brown fled the 25 yards like a man in an uncommon hurry and the Redskins goal line, at least, became interracial."

1. October 9, 1956, Don Larsen's Perfect Game: "The million-to-one shot came in. Hell froze over. A month of Sundays hit the calendar. Don Larsen today pitched a no-hit, no-run, no-man-reach-first-base game in a World Series.

"On the mound at Yankee Stadium, the same guy who was knocked out in two innings by the Dodgers on Friday came up today with one for the record books, posting it there in solo grandeur as the only Perfect Game in World Series history.

"With it, the Yankee right-hander shattered the Dodgers, 2-0, and beat Sal Maglie, while taking 64,519 suspense-limp fans into his act."

This just in! On any given day and at any time, a story may break that will be remembered and talked about forever. Here are the biggest-breaking stories in our estimation to hit over the last two-score years.

10. A Very Good Year. That would be 1969, when three of the nation's biggest coaching names came to work for local teams (okay, call this entry three stories in one). Vince Lombardi was named head coach of the Washington Redskins, Ted Williams became manager of the Washington Senators, and Lefty Driesell took over the Maryland basketball program. Lombardi died from colon cancer in 1970, Williams was out when the Senators moved to Texas after the 1971 season, and Driesell was fired in 1986 in the wake of the death of his star player, Len Bias, from a cocaine overdose.

9. MJ Joins the Wiz. On January 19, 2000, Michael Jordan was named president of basketball operations and made a part owner of the Washington Wizards, with mostly mixed results. He also decided to come out of retirement and played two more seasons before team owner Abe Pollin fired him from the front office on May 7, 2007, mainly because he felt Jordan wasn't working very hard at his front office job.

8. Capital Centre Opens. The Washington Bullets beat the Seattle Supersonics in the first basketball game ever played in Abe Pollin's new beltway arena on December 2, 1973. The 18,000-seat venue was the home of the Bullets/Wizards, Washington Capitals, and Georgetown basketball team for more than 25 years, but gave way to Pollin's new downtown-Washington MCI Center in 1997. The building was imploded on December 15, 2002, and the real estate converted into The Boulevard at The Capital Centre, a town-center-style development.

7. Joe T. Breaks a Leg. On November 18, 1985, Redskins quarterback Joe Theismann was sacked by N.Y. Giants linebacker Lawrence Taylor, on what would be the final play of his NFL career, during a Monday Night Football game. Theismann suffered a compound fracture of the tibia and fibula in one of the most gruesome plays in league history. If you ever get a chance to see the replay, don't.

6. Joe Gibbs Retires. After a 12-year run that included three victories in four Super Bowl appearances, Gibbs retired as the Redskins head coach in 1993, stunning his players, team owner Jack Kent Cooke, and disconsolate fans. Gibbs, later diagnosed as a diabetic, cited concerns about his health and a desire to spend more time with his family as his main reasons for walking away as the most succesful head coach in Redskins history.

5. Joe Gibbs Returns. On January 7, 2004, Gibbs, voted into the Hall of Fame in 1996, announced that he was returning to the Redskins as the team president and head coach, lured out of retirement by team owner Daniel Snyder with a five-year, $30 million contract that gave him total autonomy over football operations. His first year, the Redskins went 6-10, but the team had two playoff appearances in the next three seasons.

4. John Thompson Retires. On January 8, 1999, in a profanity-laced news conference, Thompson announced he was retiring after 27 years as the Georgetown basketball coach, citing problems stemming from divorce proceedings with his wife, Gwen. Thompson's teams won 71 percent of their games and made 24 postseason appearances, including 20 in the NCAA tournament. In 1984, he became the first African American coach to win the NCAA title when his team defeated Houston in the championship game.

3. The Death of Jack Kent Cooke. On April 6, 1997, the Washington Redskins owner died from cardiac arrest at the age of 84, touching off a bitter struggle to gain control of the football team. Cooke's son, John Kent Cooke, led an under-financed group trying to purchase the club from his father's estate, but in the end, NFL owners approved the sale to Daniel Snyder, who purchased the team and Jack Kent Cooke Stadium for $700 million in 1999.

2. Bye-Bye Baseball. In 1971, citing poor attendance and a bonanza television and radio contract offered by officials in Arlington, Texas, Minnesota businessman Robert Short moved the Washington Senators out of RFK Stadium and into a new ballpark in the Dallas suburbs. Within two years, Short had sold the team to Texas interests, but Washington remained without baseball until. . . .

1. Baseball Comes Back. After numerous near misses in trying to lure a team back to the Nation's Capital, baseball returned to RFK Stadium for the 2005 season when baseball owners approved the move of the Montreal Expos. A year later, Ted Lerner, a longtime Washingtonian and wealthy developer, purchased the team, and in the spring of 2008, the Washington Nationals moved into a new $600 million stadium in southeast Washington.

Note: Phil Hochberg is a prominent Washington, D.C., attorney who may have done more public address announcing than anyone in area history. He did the Senators from 1962–68 and the Redskins from 1962 to 2000. He's also done games for George Washington and Maryland, and presidential inaugural parades since 1973. Here are his top 10 moments behind the microphone.

10. 1999 Women's World Cup. Nigeria, led by Chiejine, Okosieme, Nwadike, and Eberechi Opara, plays Denmark. Fortunately, I only have to introduce the Nigerians once. And for three years doing the Maryland press box PA, I stumble every time I go to announce Eric Obagu, to the point where I try to avoid announcing him.

9. The "Fugitive" Comes to Town. In 1966, I'm given a PA page for "Dr. Richard Kimble" to report to the Personal Service Room. A few moments later I'm given another page, this one for "Lt. Philip Gerard." How was I to know that they were characters on ABC's *The Fugitive* and Lt. Gerard had been chasing Dr. Kimble for years? I spend my time watching baseball, not television. Twenty five years later, at a Redskins game, I'm given a page for a name that just cannot be real; after all, I should know, because I've been doing this kind of work for so many years. I refuse to make the announcement, only to find out three weeks later that it's the name of a prominent Washington lawyer.

8. Gerald Riggs, Hero and Goat. Riggs gains a Redskins record 221 yards rushing against the Eagles on September 17, 1989, then coughs up the ball with seconds left in the game and linebacker Al Harris brings it back 77 yards to set up the winning touchdown. Redskins blow an 11 point fourth-quarter lead. I'm so angry that I don't want to announce anything at the end of the game; I just want to get the hell out of the stadium.

7. Nats Close Out RFK. Charlie Brotman (my predecessor with the Senators) and I got to do part of the lineups for the final Major League game at RFK, September 23, 2007.

6. Introducing Ryan Kuehl as a Starter for the Redskins in 1997. Little Ry-Ry, the kid who grew up next door to us, my son Jeff's best friend, starting for the Redskins. He goes on to play 12 years in the NFL.

5. Redskins Beat a Truly Nameless Detroit Lions Team in a January 2000 Playoff Game. Five weeks earlier, the Redskins had lost in the Pontiac Silverdome in a game where the Lions ratcheted up the sound, causing multiple Washington off-side penalties. We'll show them; I'm instructed not to mention the name of a single Detroit player in doing the playoff game PA Detroit still manages to play the game.

4. Introducing New Single-Season Home Run King Roger Maris in His First At-Bat at D.C. Stadium in 1962. "Batting third, the right fielder, number nine . . . ROG-ER MARIS." And having Bob Addie, the dean of Washington baseball writers, chew me out for overdoing it, a lesson too publicly learned at the time, but remembered for the next 45 years.

3. Darell Green Saves the Day—January 17, 1988. Number 28, who a week earlier had returned a punt in Chicago—a return etched in Redskin memories forever—to set up a Redskins victory, knocks down a last-second Vikings pass to send the Redskins to the 1988 Super Bowl. And my family ends up having dinner that night with Jack Kent Cooke.

2. Announcing the 1962 All-Star Game. Here I am, 21 years old, announcing the mid-season classic. Only I make a mistake in having the rosters re-typed and Yankee catcher Elston Howard is left standing in the dugout, unintroduced.

1. Introducing Joe DiMaggio at the 1982 Cracker Jack Old Timers Game. Literally chills down the spine in introducing "Baseball's Greatest Living Player, The Yankee Clipper, number 5, Joe DiMaggio." I tell DiMaggio the following year what a thrill it had been to introduce him and, in return, get a blank stare.

Besides writing for the *Washington Post* forever, I've also written biographies of Sam Huff (*Tough Stuff*, 1985) and John Thompson (*Big Man on Campus*, 1991), and collaborated with former *Post* columnist Ken Denlinger on an investigation of college recruiting (*Athletes for Sale*, 1974). In addition to these titles, here are my all-time favorite sports books written by authors with Washington connections. Many of them have multiple titles to their credit, but for this list I allowed only one per customer.

15. Bill Gilbert, *A Coach for All Seasons*. A biography of DeMatha basketball coach Morgan Wootten by one of Washington's most prolific authors.

14. Mark Maske, *War Without Death*. A compelling insider's journey through the 2006 season in the NFC East by the *Post's* veteran Redskins and NFL reporter.

13. Andy Beyer, *Picking Winners: A Handicapper's Guide*. America's best-known horse-racing handicapper tells you how to do it, or *bettor* yet, how not to do it.

12. John Ed Bradley, *The Best There Ever Was*. A fictional look at a southern football coach's last hurrah from an all-conference LSU center turned author and sportswriter who modeled the protagonist after his own college coach.

11. Christine Brennan, *Best Seat in the House*. A poignant memoir of her late father and his impact on her life and career as a pioneering sports journalist, the first female beat writer ever to cover the Washington Redskins and now a *USA Today* columnist.

10. George Solomon, *All Those Mornings . . . at the* Post. A collection of the late, great Shirley Povich's columns over 75 years along with loving recollections of one of America's greatest sportswriters compiled by Solomon, the *Post's* longtime former sports editor.

9. Thomas Boswell, *How Life Imitates the World Series*. A charming collection of essays, columns, and feature stories by the *Post's* cerebral baseball writer and columnist.

8. Ken Denlinger, *For the Glory*. A meticulously reported opus following a freshman recruiting class through five years of Joe Paterno and Penn State football, the alma mater of the former *Post* columnist.

7. Jane Leavey, *Sandy Koufax: A Lefty's Legacy*. A loving biographical look at the enigmatic Hall of Fame Brooklyn Dodger pitcher, one of her childhood heroes who sort of cooperated with the former *Post* sportswriter on the book.

6. Bill Nack, *Big Red of Meadow Stable*. The beautifully written saga of one of the greatest thoroughbred champions (that would be Secretariat) in racing history, by the longtime *Sports Illustrated* writer.

5. Bill Gildea, *When the Colts Belonged to Baltimore*. With his typical exquisite touch, the former *Post* columnist blends memories of his childhood growing up in Baltimore of the 1950s with delightful profiles of many of his favorite players.

4. Tom Callahan, *Johnny U: The Life and Times of John Unitas*. The author, a former columnist at the *Post* and *Washington Star*, tells us not only who Unitas was and where he came from, but why he mattered, often with priceless anecdotes, old and new.

3. Dave Kindred, *Sound and Fury*. The intersecting paths of Muhammad Ali and his friend and foil, Howard Cosell, by one of America's greatest sports columnist, who knew them both so well.

2. David Maraniss, *When Pride Still Mattered*. The life and legend of Vince Lombardi, warts and all, by a Pulitzer Prize-winning journalist and longtime *Post* writer and editor.

1. John Feinstein, *A Season on the Brink*. The prolific author and former *Post* sportswriter launched his book-writing career with this fascinating inside look at Bob Knight and his Indiana basketball program. It became the best-selling sports book of all time.

Note: Dan Steinberg is among the most skilled and incredibly prolific newspaper sports bloggers in the country. His must-read D.C. Sports Blog appears virtually every day on Washingtonpost.com, and often is excerpted on page two of the *Post's* sports section.

10. D.C. Optimist (http://dcoptimist.blogspot.com/). Likely has a pretty limited readership, since virtually every post is written in an ironic, tongue-in-cheek, over-the-top-with-optimism style. But these guys can write, and they're funny, and they manage to link to all the big news for a variety of teams. With the relative lack of sports blogs focusing on all D.C. teams across sports, this is well worth a daily peek.

9. Oleanders and Morning Glories (http://mvn.com/mlb-nationals/). There are any number of additional Washington Nationals blogs that could go in this spot, including Ball-Wonk, Just a Nats Fan, Nats 320, and Nationals Enquirer. OMG is updated frequently, with thought-provoking arguments and a healthy amount of media criticism, making it a valuable part of what's called the Natosphere.

8. Hogs Haven (http://hogshaven.com/). Likely the best among a pretty scant number of Redskins blogs, considering the team's popularity. Mixes links—many to other blogs—with opinions and analysis. Really surprising, though, how few Washington Redskins blogs there are that are updated consistently and comprehensively.

7. Off Wing Opinion (http://www.ericmcerlain.com/offwingopinion/) and Japers Rink (http://japersrink.blogspot.com/). Two venerable Washington Capitals bloggers who have moved onward and upward, writing for various national publications about the wider NHL. Both were instrumental in the Caps becoming one of the most blogged-about teams in the country, and both have a talent for finding relevant news from a variety of sources and packaging that news with cogent commentary.

6. Bullets Forever (http://bulletsforever.com/). Stats-and-links-heavy Wizards site, both comprehensively compiled. If a writer for the *Billings Montana Weekly Advocate* mentions something about backup guard Roger Mason Jr., you'll find the link here.

5. Mister Irrelevant (http://www.misterirrelevant.com/). By rights should probably be higher, but since I have a business relationship with one of them I'll try to overcompensate. Jamie and Chris Mottram have quickly become the first bloggers of blogging, with Jamie supervising Yahoo! Sports's blogging efforts and Chris doing likewise for the *Sporting News*. They stay true to their D.C. roots with their personal blog, which concentrates on the absurdities of D.C. teams and their fans. Boasts great visuals, and great video clips.

4. On Frozen Blog (http://www.onfrozenblog.com/). One of the best hockey blogs in the U.S. succeeds by getting very different writing styles from its several different hosts. Not exactly independent, as they've accepted paid trips from Ted Leonsis, and their constant carping about the mainstream media is both tiresome and unnecessary, but any follower of the Capitals (and their minor-league affiliates) would do well to monitor this site.

**3. Gilbert Arenas's Blog
(http://my.nba.com/forum.jspa?forumID=400032200&start=0).**
Widely acknowledged as one of the best athlete blogs—if not celebrity blogs—in the world. His epic, wide-ranging posts—which are actually dictated to an NBA.com staffer—will range from his basketball game to his teammates' antics to his relationship troubles to the games he plays with his daughter. What sets it apart is his insistence on using his blog to break news—for example, about his health—and in recognizing the sort of inside information that interests fans (like his paintball fight with several teammates this fall).

2. Capitol Punishment (http://dcbb.blogspot.com/). Mixing a love of the Nationals with an unending supply of criticism and cynicism, Chris Needham's Nats blog provides links to hard news stories, commentary, and analysis. His daily reading list ("What to read today") also is an invaluable guide to stories across Major League Baseball and D.C. Also wickedly funny.

1. Wizznutzz (http://wizznutzz.com/). Not for everyone, but certainly the most unique team-centric sports blog in the country, most famous for coining the "Agent Zero" nickname for Gilbert Arenas that eventually became ubiquitous in the mainstream media. Ninety percent of what they write is pure fiction, and yet the site simply makes it more fun to follow Washington's pro basketball team. Their NBA t-shirt collection is also far more interesting than anything you'll find in the NBA Store.

Note: Charlie Brotman has been promoting sports in the Nation's Capital for more than 50 years as the town's preeminent and much beloved sports public relations man. He began his career working for the old Washington Senators in 1956, doing PR as well as serving as the stadium public address announcer, a gig that also led to handling the PA for presidential inaugural parades because Dwight Eisenhower liked the way he once introduced him at a Senators game. Brotman started his own public relations firm, Brotman and Associates, in 1969. These are some of the teams and sporting events (many of which no longer exist) he helped, or maybe hindered, over the years, with his considerable public relations skills. Brotman turned 80 in January, 2008, and continues to thrive, and promote, as a partner in Brotman, Winter, Fried Communications based in Falls Church, VA.

Basketball

Washington Tapers. They were a top AAU club team in Philadelphia, but moved to Washington in 1960 to join the American Basketball League. Uline Arena, which later became the Washington Coliseum, was their home for a season, until the club moved to New York after a year.

Washington Capitals. Maryland entrepreneur Earl Foreman bought the Oakland Oaks franchise in the old American Basketball Association and moved the club to Washington in 1969. Rick Barry and Larry Brown were the stars on a team that played its home games at the old Washington Coliseum, where they drew sparse crowds, the main reason Foreman moved them to the Tidewater region as the Virginia Squires after one season.

Hockey

Washington Lions/Washington Presidents. They played in the old Eastern Hockey League from 1957 to 1960, and won the league title in the 1957-58 season before the team folded, due to lack of interest.

Washington Capitals. The team has its own in-house public relations operation, but Brotman has been involved in a number of special projects over the years. The franchise owned by Ted Leonsis is still alive and well, but perhaps the "Brotman Curse" is the main reason the Caps have never won a Stanley Cup.

Pro Football

Washington Federals. Owned by Washington attorney Berl Bernhard, who once compared his club to a team of trained gerbils, the Feds played for two years in the old USFL, averaging fewer than 8,000 fans a game at RFK Stadium. The team was dreadful, losing 13 of its first 14 games the first year in 1983, and 10 of the first 11 games in 1984 before the franchise was sold and moved to Orlando.

Soccer

Washington Whips. A bunch of wealthy American sports franchise owners, including Jack Kent Cooke, imported a number of European teams to play in the United Soccer Association. The Whips, otherwise known as the Aberdeen (Scotland) Football Club, also were owned by Earl Foreman, but the league morphed into the North American Soccer League, and the club changed ownership several times playing as the Washington Darts and Washington Diplomats before the league folded in 1984.

Professional Golf

Kemper Open, FBR Open, Booz Allen Classic, AT&T National. Brotman has always handled the publicity for Washington's annual PGA Tour event, which first came to Congressional Country Club in 1980. The event has been immensely popular, even if it did start changing title sponsors in 2003. Brotman remains involved in publicizing the AT&T event at Congressional, Tiger Woods' signature tournament, as well as the Prince George's County Open, an event on the Nationwide Tour.

Chrysler Cup. In 1986, the international team competition was played at the TPC at Avenel, which had just opened for business. U.S. Captain Arnold Palmer made back-to-back holes-in-one at the third hole, the first in a Tuesday practice round, the second in a pro-am event the next day. A plaque near the third tee commemorates the achievement, but the Cup has never come back to the Nation's Capital.

Mazda LPGA Championship. Bethesda Country Club hosted one of the LPGA's four major championships from 1990 to 1993 until auto sales went kaput and Mazda pulled out of its sponsorship. The tournament moved to Wilmington, DE, where McDonalds became the title sponsor.

Presidents Cup. Played at the Robert Trent Jones Golf Club in Gainesville, VA, the Ryder Cup-like competition was staged off the shores of Lake Manassas in 1994, 1996, 2000, and 2005, until the PGA Tour decided to take the event on the road, moving it to San Francisco in 2009. Brotman was not retained.

Tennis

Washington Star Tennis Championships, Colgate Tennis Championships, Volvo Tennis Championships, Avon Tennis Classic, Virginia Slims Championship. Brotman did the PR and usually the PA for all of those events, none of them around any more, though the old Washington Star tournament keeps going every summer in the District, under a wide variety of corporate sponsors.

Auto Racing

Cadillac Grand Prix. A three-day car-racing festival staged around the streets near RFK Stadium was held in July, 2002. It never returned.

Note: In one stunning move, Tony Perkins proved that money can't buy happiness and that you CAN go home again. Tony walked away from the fame and fortune of *Good Morning America* after a successful six-year run (1999–2005) and returned to his beloved hometown of Washington, D.C. He even reclaimed his old job on the *Fox Morning News* on Channel 5. A graduate of Mount Vernon High School and American University ('81), Tony started out doing stand-up comedy. He later took that to radio, where he worked with Donnie Simpson, and later to local TV. His sense of humor and easygoing style ticketed him for network TV, but it included a move to New York City. You could take Tony out of D.C., but you couldn't take D.C. out of Tony. He's back where he wants to be and is planning a return to the stand-up stage. Only his own humility keeps him from including his name on this list.

10. Jeff Penn. Unknown to the public at large, he's the one who booked the hottest comedians in the country into Garvin's Comedy Club. In the 70s and 80s, it was Washington's premiere comedy club. Although he is not a natural performer, and has never claimed to be, most comics will tell you he is just naturally one of the funniest people. Jeff has advised and counseled many D.C. comics, and has quietly written great lines for most of us, and helped shape our acts. (Thanks Jeff!)

9. Tom Shales. The longtime TV critic for the *Washington Post* has become one of the most respected (and feared!) writers about television ever. When he likes it, he's eloquent in his praise (Johnny Carson, *All in the Family*, etc.). But he is at his most entertaining when he dislikes (Kathie Lee Gifford). He can rip without somehow seeming cruel, largely because his is so witty and urbane, but also because he is usually right!

8. Sam Jones, a/k/a "Sam I Am" and "Huggy Low Down." He was already provoking riotous laughter from club audiences for years as "Sam I Am" when, in 1999, he assumed the persona of "Huggy Low Down," a gossipy and eventually equal-opportunity-basher of all personalities in need of a beat-down. Originally a character written by Chris Paul and voiced by Sam on Donnie Simpson's radio show, "Huggy" became an enormously popular radio star in his own right. Sam could book himself into a club as "Sam I Am" one weekend and "Huggy Low Down" the next. Ingenious!

7. Bob Somerby. Bob hails from Baltimore, but is a D.C. regular. His sharp observational humor about topics intellectual, political and mundane is as on target as Jerry Seinfeld's ever was. Bob has literally read passages from a philosophy book on stage and made it hysterical. For years he ended his act by pulling out a succession of boxes of breakfast cereal, commenting on their claims, ingredients and art work. Since seeing it, I haven't looked at a box of Raisin Bran the same. Bob's college roommates at Harvard were Al Gore and Tommy Lee Jones.

6. Brett Leake. Orginally from Richmond, Brett has been adopted by D.C. A victim of muscular dystrophy, Brett gets around in a motorized wheelchair, but that's beside the point. He is, simply, the smartest and most clever comedian to grace a Washington stage. His act has a heart with a lesson. And although he deals directly with MD in his act, it is not what his act is about. Brett has appeared on the *Tonight Show with Jay Leno* several times, but deserves to be much more famous than he is.

5 and 4. Don Geronimo and Mike O'Meara. The "Radio Gods" dominated afternoon radio for many years at WJFK-FM, after first teaming up as the "Morning Zoo" at WAVA-FM. Don's mercurial persona and willingness to expose his entire life on the air, warts and all, and Mike's amazing talent for impersonating the rich and famous made for outrageously entertaining radio. Newsman Buzz Burbank could be just as funny. They abused their callers, who loved it and kept calling back for more. Don retired after 35 years of radio (23 with Mike) in 2008, three years after the tragic death of his beloved wife and show regular Freda. It was a sad day for radio listeners.

3 and 2. Donnie Simpson and Chris Paul. The morning team at 95.5 WPGC. Donnie doesn't consider himself funny, but he is honestly one of the funniest people I have ever met. Through his close relationships with comedians like me (I was his producer and sidekick for many years at WKYS), and Chris Paul, he has developed the stellar timing of a top comic. Paul is simply the funniest comedian to ever come out of Washington. He does not even think like other comics: as a comedian, he is brilliant.

1. Glenn Brenner. Washington's premiere TV sports anchor from the late 70s to the early 90s, he was the funniest D.C. TV personality ever. Even if you didn't care about sports, you watched him because he was so entertaining. His close relationship with co-anchor Gordon Peterson really came through. And his ability to make sometimes icy co-anchor Maureen Bunyan laugh was priceless. His untimely death from a brain tumor in 1992 rocked Washington, and in many ways WUSA's *Eyewitness News* never recovered from it.

Ten Great Places to Go Fishing around Washington
:: Angus Phillips

Note: Angus Phillips has been writing about the outdoors—as in fishing, hunting, and paddling, among many other pursuits—for *The Washington Post* for more than 25 years. A native of Long Island who now lives in Annapolis, this prolific and often passionate wordsmith is the dean of the nation's newspaper outdoors writers, as well as a longtime chronicler of the America's Cup sailing competition.

10. The middle Chesapeake Bay around Chesapeake Beach in May. Big striped bass (rockfish) are heading back to sea after spawning up the major tributaries. It's common to catch trophy rock over 30 pounds. Charter boats are available at Rod 'n' Reel in Chesapeake Beach and Harrison's Chesapeake House in Tilghman Island, to name two places.

9. Ocean City in high summer, fishing offshore for tuna. Charter boats are expensive, for sure, but yellowfin tuna and dolphin (dorado) are abundant, and you may get lucky and hook a white or blue marlin.

8. Rapidan River. Tiny wild brook trout lurk behind boulders and deadfalls in this scenic, freestone river in Shenandoah National Park. The colorful little fish are wary, but as long as you don't spook them on approach, they'll snap up just about any dry fly that lands nearby.

7. South-Central Pennsylvania limestone streams. These rich trout streams— Big Spring, Boiling Spring, the Letort and Falling Spring to name four—are fed by underground springs and maintain constant temperature all winter, so trout are hungry and willing, winter and summer. Be forewarned, these are educated fish that have seen hundreds of flies. They're not easy to fool.

6. Tidal Potomac around Wilson Bridge in April and May. Largemouth bass spawn in the spring, heading to shallow water along the banks where they freely attack anglers' lures. The 41st President, George H.W. Bush, took off work one day to catch bass around Belle Haven Marina during his term. If it's good enough for the President. . . .

5. Potomac/Shenandoah around Harpers Ferry. The two major rivers meet in a scenic stretch of rocky whitewater that harbors smallmouth bass, rock bass and bluegills. It's ideal for wading shallow areas in summer and fall or exploring by small inflatable raft or canoe. Fish with flies or light spinning gear.

4. Allens Fresh off the lower Potomac for yellow perch in March. These delectable fish rush up the Wicomico River and its tributaries, as well as scores of other small creeks around Washington and on the Eastern Shore, to spawn in early spring. It's a rite of the season to chase after them, and particularly good fun for youngsters.

3. Chesapeake Bay Bridge-Tunnel at Norfolk in November and December. This is a winter congregating ground for big striped bass. The fish feed on rushing tides, staying close to the pilings of the 14-mile span that connects Norfolk to the southern tip of the Eastern Shore. Look for flocks of seabirds diving on bait being chased to the surface by feeding fish.

2. Chesapeake Bay Bridge near Annapolis. From October to December, bluefish, rockfish and perch school around the bridge pilings and feed to fatten for winter. Look for flocks of seagulls diving on bait being driven to the surface by feeding fish, or toss jigs and bucktails close to bridge pilings.

1. Fletcher's Landing in the spring. From March to May, there's no better place to fish than around the 150-year-old boathouse below Chain Bridge on the Potomac. Spawning fish run upriver and are brought to a halt at Brookmont Dam. Perch, rockfish, herring and hickory, and white shad are thick as fleas on a dog's back when the run peaks. Tackle and rental rowboats are available at the boathouse. Fletcher's in the spring is one of the prettiest places in Washington, on par with the cherry blossoms at the Tidal Basin.

Note: It is only fitting that our best burger list is provided by a man who broke in to the sports radio business through food. Scott was working as a waiter at the Cheesecake Factory when WTEM went on the air in 1992. After the restaurant would close up for the night, he would take the leftover cheesecake and bring it to the guys working the overnight shift. After a few months, a job opened up at the station and a career was launched. Scott is now assistant program director at WTEM and part of the morning crew on the nationally syndicated "The First Team on Fox with Steve Czaban." He is also legendary for his burger appetite. In the mid '90s, Scott won a bet with fellow host Al Koken by downing three (3!) Wendy's triples. His health-minded wife was so disgusted she said she would have preferred that he cheated on her. Here are Scott's favorite spots for downing those greasy delights.

Scott Says: I'm not a betting man, but I'd be willing to wager you've had better burgers in dives than you've had at a sunshine-engulfed beach. There really is something about heinously tiled floors or questionable drop ceilings that make a grill's foods taste that much better. I want to know two things before I dive in at a dive: Can I get a legit Cherry Coke or at least a Vanilla Coke (if not, I'll survive)? And will they cook the burger to order? If the answer is, "The patty is done, just dress it up," I'll take a pass, thanks. You can't go wrong with the following.

5. Five Guys (various locations).
Call it primal, call it perfect. There's just something to be said for a double-bacon-cheeseburger wrapped in foil with grilled onions and tomatoes. Their stability in taste and presentation from one branch to another is something to be truly applauded. Great buns, too. Because the branches are almost everywhere, you can always find a burger quickly. The hot dogs are fantastic, as well.

4. Kemble Park Tavern, 5125 MacArthur Blvd, NW.
A newcomer that's slightly upscale. This is no dive, which sort of pokes holes in my floor-and-ceiling theory. My visit was more about the onion rolls, Vermont cheddar, and perfectly tasty burger which needed little help from the tomato or onion. Very sharp bar to grab a beer with that burger.

3. Urban Burger, 5566 Norbeck Rd., Rockville, MD.
Run by Urban Bar-B-Q geniuses David and Lee. With a line of adoring fans out the door, it's hard not to notice this place is loved. Who is to argue? Order the meat cooked to your liking and choose from about a half-dozen toppings. For another buck you can really go all out. Suggestions include the "Blue Bayou," featuring a kick of bourbon sauce, thick cut bacon and blue cheese. My burger was medium rare and very juicy. The buns are dynamite.

2. Ollie's Trolley, 432 11th St., NW (plus a few other locations).
Dive? That's an understatement. Awful formica, a menu board straight from the 60s, blaring Ella Fitzgerald through the speakers; you might call it scary. I call it charmingly unpretentious. The burger was old school with Ollie's sauce (tangy and sweet), cheese, lettuce, tomato and onion. They'll cook it to order. Many "counter" places won't mess with undercooked beef. Great fries seasoned with the Ollie's mix of a hundred (at least it seemed that way) spices. They had a kick and went great with the burger.

1. Lindy's Bon Appetit, 2040 I St., NW. Something a little different, but heaven on a bun. Without this place as a distraction, I may have studied hard enough as a George Washington University student to become a doctor (then again, what doctor would eat three Wendy's triples?). Two oblong patties are served on a long, soft roll. Then you can choose from 26 different toppings with fantastic local nicknames. I like the steak sauce, grilled onion and mushroom combo. If school is in session, be prepared to wait, but it's worth it. The secret is their consistency. The flavor hasn't changed in the two-decades-plus that I've been going to the Bon (pronounced bone).

Honorable mention:

Clyde's (various locations). Love the applewood-smoked bacon. Kid friendly.

Hard Times Café (various locations). Known for their chili, but they bring it between the buns.

Sweetwater Tavern (several Virginia locations). You can get a great burger in the Commonwealth. Hickory BBQ and the cheddar are solid calls.

Childe Harold (off Dupont Circle). I miss you. The black and blue burger had the perfect amount of Cajun blackening punch with the perfect balance of blue.

Note: Jim Hage writes about all things running for the *Washington Post* and knows what he's talking about, if only because he's probably logged more training miles in the area than any athlete on the planet, or at least somewhere close to the beltway. He won the Marine Corps Marathon in 1988 and 1989, and finished eighth in the U.S. Olympic Team marathon trials in 1992.

10. Glover Archibald Trail. Getting to the trailhead is a little tricky: just after the first mile of the C&O Canal in Georgetown, head left down some steps, through a tunnel and then up more steep steps. Or ask anyone who looks sweaty and very dirty near the canal terminus, as they're likely just coming off the trail. It's hilly, rooty and tough. Most runs that start on the trail wind through Rock Creek Park before looping back. Definitely an off-road experience. Bonus off-road running: Theodore Roosevelt Island—flatter, closer to downtown and easier to find on a map.

9. Massachusetts Avenue. Starting from the urban eclecticism of Dupont Circle in Northwest, head north along the avenue of the embassies, past the vice president's house halfway up the long hill at Observatory Circle, and then to the top at the National Cathedral, situated on the highest ground in the District. Ease your way back downtown by traveling east a few blocks to Connecticut Avenue, where either a Metro ride or a few more miles on foot will shoot you straight back to Dupont Circle and a well-earned refreshment of your choice.

8. National Arboretum. Worth a visit, even if you're not running. During the Civil War, Union soldiers camped on the arboretum grounds, which today encompass nearly 500 beautifully preserved acres and 9.5 miles of paved roads. A highlight for runners and slower visitors alike are the National Capitol Columns, which mysteriously and ethereally rise out of the undulating landscape.

7. Beltsville (MD) Agricultural Research Center. If business or pleasure takes you to this close-in suburb, make time for a run through at least some of the 6,700 acres. BARC—just 30 minutes from the White House—is crisscrossed by a network of two-lane farm roads (with very little farm traffic), which makes simple tracing routes long and short.

6. Mount Vernon. It's nearly 10 miles along the Potomac River from Old Town Alexandria to George Washington's home, a scenic drive along the parkway or better, a rolling run along the parallel bike path. In April, the road is closed for the G.W. Parkway Classic 10 Miler, one of the most beautiful runs in the country.

5. Beach Drive. Rock Creek Park without the dirt. Many of the primary roads feature parallel bike paths, and the less-traveled roads more than grudgingly accommodate runners. It's scenic, hilly and generally five degrees cooler than the rest of the city on hot summer days. Pick up Beach Drive near the Kennedy Center and run toward the National Zoo. For your most interesting run of the year, digress into the zoo before turning back. Beach Drive continues out of the city and into Montgomery County in the Maryland suburbs for some 30 miles.

4. Rock Creek Park. When he lived in the White House, President Theodore Roosevelt bushwacked regularly through the surprisingly hilly park. These days, you're more likely to see D.C. Mayor Adrian Fenty traipsing over hill and dale, along with hundreds of his closest friends. The dirt and horse trails provide endless variety in a thickly wooded setting.

3. C&O Canal. A bucolic run—in Washington? The towpath provides an ideal surface on a shaded route along the scenic Potomac River. Need to get in a long run? Really long? The canal extends uninterrupted for 187 miles from Georgetown to Cumberland, MD. Wildlife sightings, including deer, foxes, blue heron and bald eagles, are not uncommon, especially just a little farther up the canal from the city toward Carderock and Great Falls, MD.

2. Potomac River Run. Uninterrupted treks on bike paths along the river are one of the great pleasures of running in D.C. Distance can be adjusted from the Memorial Bridge, one of the loveliest in the country, for a short four-mile loop to the 14th Street Bridge, or longer loops that include stunning vistas from Key Bridge with an optional jaunt through trendy Georgetown for distances up to 10 miles.

1. The Mall. Visitors come from all over the world to visit Washington, but nobody sees the Mall better or more intimately than a runner. It's about two miles from the Lincoln Memorial to the Capitol, and in that short distance runners can take in terrific views of the White House, the Washington Monument, the World War II Memorial and the Jefferson Memorial on pedestrian-friendly and joint-forgiving broad gravel walkways. Extend the route slightly up Capitol Hill past the majestic Supreme Court building and the Library of Congress. You'll never lack for company during a lunchtime jaunt, as even jaded government workers rarely tire of the sights and form a virtual parade of runners along the Mall. Nor will you lack for inspiration running the Mall at night, when the monuments are floodlighted.

The Five Best Naval Academy Pro Athletes

Annapolis is supposed to produce officers and gentlemen, the future admirals of America, but occasionally the Academy on the shores of the Severn River sends a fine athlete—indeed, even a Hall of Fame athlete—to pro football or basketball, despite the post-graduate military commitment they all have to fulfill (with very few exceptions).

5. Phil McConkey. A wide receiver and special teams whiz, McConkey spent four years as a naval officer before signing as a free agent with the N.Y. Giants in 1980. He played for four teams over a six-year NFL career, but will always be remembered for his spectacular performance in Super Bowl XXI, the Giants 39-20 victory over the Denver Broncos in 1986. His 25-yard punt return set up a Giants field goal, a 44-yard reception carried to the Denver one set up a touchdown, and he scored on a six-yard reception when he caught a ball that bounced off teammate Mark Bavaro's hands in the end zone.

4. Joe Bellino. The Massachusetts native went to Navy thinking baseball might be his best sport. Instead, in a spectacular senior season, he was the consummate all-purpose football star, playing running back, returning punts and kickoffs, and even averaging 47.1 yards as the punter. In 1960, he rushed for 834 yards, caught 15 passes, and threw for two touchdowns, leading the Mids to the Orange Bowl (where they lost to Missouri) and winning the Heisman Trophy. Bellino spent the next four years in the Navy, then joined the Boston Patriots in the old American Football League, playing for three seasons.

3. Napolean McCallum. Navy's career leader in rushing, McCallum was a versatile running back and return man and a two-time All-American. He played part-time for the Oakland Raiders in 1986 while also serving in the Navy, and when his commitment ended, he joined the Raiders full time in 1990. He played another four years, mostly as a reserve back and return man, though he did score three touchdowns in a wild-card playoff victory over Denver in 1993. His professional career ended prematurely with a severe knee injury in a *Monday Night Football* game against the San Francisco 49ers to open the 1994 season.

2. David Robinson. The son of a Navy man himself, Robinson was a 6-foot-7 forward when he left Osbourn Park High School in Woodbridge, VA, in 1983 but stretched out to 7-foot-1 when he left the Naval Academy four years later as the most decorated basketball player in school history. Robinson served two years of his military commitment but was allowed to leave the Navy early because his height precluded him from many tasks, including flying or serving on tight-quartered ships and submarines. He was the No. 1 overall choice in the 1987 draft by the San Antonio Spurs, who had to wait two years before he could play. It was worth it. Robinson, also known as "The Admiral," helped the Spurs win NBA titles in 1999 and 2003 in his final season as a pro. A ten-time NBA All Star and the 1995 league MVP, he played on the first U.S. Dream Team in the 1992 Olympics and in 1996 was named one of the top 50 NBA players in history.

1. Roger Staubach. He pushed into Navy's starting lineup early in his sophomore year and as a junior led the Midshipmen to a 9-1 record and won the Heisman Trophy, the last player from a military academy to win that honor. Staubach was selected in the tenth round of the 1964 draft by the Dallas Cowboys, but didn't join the team until the 1969 season, when he was a 27-year-old rookie after serving five years in the Navy, including a stint as a supply officer in Vietnam. Staubach won the starting quarterback position over Craig Morton in the 1971 season and led the Cowboys to a Super Bowl VI victory over the Miami Dolphins that year, earning MVP honors in the title game. A six-time Pro Bowl selection, he was known as "Roger the Dodger" for his uncanny ability to scramble away from trouble and "Captain Comeback" because he directed 23 comeback wins in the fourth quarter over his 11-year career, 17 of them in the final two minutes. Staubach retired in 1979 after one-too-many concussions, and was inducted into the Pro Football Hall of Fame in 1986, a player Tom Landry once described as "possibly the best combination of a passer, an athlete, and a leader to ever play in the NFL."

Washington has traditionally been a hotbed for tennis and has played host to a high-end professional tournament at the Rock Creek Tennis Stadium in the District since 1969. Here are the area's ten greatest players and contributors.

10. Jim Delaney. A Washington native, Delaney was among the most decorated collegiate players in the country in the early 1970s. He was a four-time All-American at Stanford University from 1972-75, winning the NCAA doubles title in 1973 with partner Alex Mayer and again in 1974 with John Whitlinger.

9. Allie Ritzenberg. Born in Washington, Ritzenberg was a star tennis player at the old Central High School (now Cardoza) in the District of Columbia. He won a number of local and regional events but after World War II, he decided against playing professional tennis because there wasn't much money to be made. Instead, he became a teaching professional at Woodmont Country Club and eventually ran the St. Albans Tennis Club for 43 years, where he taught the game to many members of the Washington power elite, including lessons with First Lady Jacqueline Kennedy. In recent years, he's been the No. 1 ranked player in the U.S. in the 85-and-over division of the U.S. Tennis Association.

8. Joni Hannah. The director of tennis at Westwood Country Club in Vienna, VA, Hannah has been a national age-group champion both in singles and doubles. In 2002, she won the U.S. Tennis Association's 40-year-old doubles division, and a year later, she was the singles and doubles winner in the same division. She's also regarded as one of the area's top teaching professionals.

7. Margaret Russo. She came to the Washington area in 1970 after earning status as a top-ten 18-and-under player in her native Australia. In 1973, she and her husband Gene Russo, also an accomplished Aussie junior, played the professional circuit in Europe before settling in the Washington area in the mid-1970s. Over the next 30 years, she won more than 100 tournaments in singles and doubles in the Mid-Atlantic section of the U.S. Tennis Association as well as 25 national titles in a number of senior divisions. She died from brain cancer in 2005 at the age of 56 as one of the most decorated players in the country, and both she and her husband, her longtime partner in mixed-double competition, have been inducted into the Mid-Atlantic Tennis Hall of Fame.

6. Paul Goldstein. A native of Washington, D.C., he won the national 16-and-under singles championship, then won the 18-and-under title in consecutive years in 1993-94, a feat that had not been accomplished in 45 years. He attended Stanford University on a tennis scholarship and was an All-American all four years before turning professional in 1998. He still plays the pro circuit and is active in the Association of Tennis Professionals.

5. Dan Goldie. He grew up playing tennis in McLean, VA, and was a three-time All-American at Stanford. He won the NCAA singles title in 1986 and helped Stanford win two NCAA team championships. He turned professional in 1987 and played the tennis circuit for six years, rising as high as No. 27 in the world in 1989, the same year he beat Jimmy Connors in the second round at Wimbledon on his way to a quarterfinal appearance, where he lost to Ivan Lendl.

4. Fred McNair IV. His father and grandfather both were nationally ranked amateurs and Washington native McNair become one of the world's greatest doubles players as a professional. In 1976, he and partner Sherwood Stewart rose to No. 1 in the world doubles rankings, the same year they also won the French Open doubles title. McNair was a member of the winning 1978 U.S. Davis Cup team and he and his father later teamed to win six father-son USTA national titles.

3. Donald Dell. At Yale, the Bethesda native was a three-time All-American from 1958 to 1960, and he made it to the finals of the NCAA singles championship in 1959 before losing to Whitney Reed of San Jose State. Dell was a member of the U.S. Davis Cup team in 1961 and 1963, and captained the team in 1968 and 1969. He reached the quarterfinals of the U.S. National Championships at Forest Hills in 1961. A member of the College Tennis Hall of Fame, he also was a co-founder of the Association of Tennis Professionals and founded his own sports management firm, Washington-based Pro-Serv. One of the most powerful forces in the sport over the last 35 years, he also founded Washington's longtime summer professional tournament, now known as the Legg Mason Classic, in 1969.

2. Harold Solomon. He learned the game as a youngster growing up in Silver Spring, MD, and was the second-ranked player in the country in the boys 12, 14, and 16-year-old divisions, also winning the boys 18-and-under national clay court championship before attending Rice University in Houston, where he was an All-American player in 1972 before turning professional that year. In 1980, he reached the No. 5 ranking in the world, and eventually won 22 singles titles as a professional, most of them on clay, where he was known as a human backboard who wore out his opponents in marathon matches. He played on four American Davis Cup teams from 1972-74 and 1978, reached the finals of the 1976 French Open, and the semifinals of the U.S. Open in 1976.

1. Pauline Betz Addie. Born in Dayton, Ohio, she grew up in Los Angeles honing her skills on public courts and rising to No. 8 in the world in 1939. Over a long and distinguished amateur career, she won five Grand Slam singles titles, including her only appearance at Wimbledon in 1946, when she didn't lose a set on the way to the title. She was forced to turn professional in 1947 merely because she and several other prominent players were exploring the possibility of starting a professional tour. She won the U.S. National Championships at Forest Hills from 1943-44 and again in 1946. In 1949, she married Washington sportswriter Bob Addie and moved to the Maryland suburbs, where she raised five children and became one of the area's top tennis teachers, opening the Cabin John Tennis Center in 1972. Tennis historian Jerome Scheuer once called her "the fastest woman on foot ever to play the game."

10. Michael Weiss. A native of Fairfax, Virginia, he was a three-time national champion figure skater who made two appearances in the Winter Olympics, finishing seventh in 1998 and 2002.

9. Davey Hearn and Jon Lugbill. Hearn, from Bethesda, Maryland, and Lugbill, from Washington, D.C., both were considered among the world's greatest whitewater canoe and kayak slalom racers. Neither man ever won an Olympic medal—Lugbill was fourth in the 1992 Games in Barcelona—but both competed in the Olympics and both were multiple world champions.

8. Joe Fargis. In 1984, the native of Vienna, Virginia, became only the second American to win an individual gold medal in equestrian, riding Touch of Class to victory. He also won a team gold as a member of the U.S. squad, and won silver in team competition in 1988.

7. David and Karen O'Connor. A husband and wife team from The Plains, Virginia, they became the first married couple ever to win an Olympic team medal at the 1996 Games when the U.S. took home the silver in the Equestrian Three Day Event. David won the individual Three Day Event gold medal in the 2000 Olympics, and both were on the bronze medal winning U.S. team.

6. Allen Johnson. A native of Washington, Johnson won the 110 meter high hurdles at the Atlanta Olympics in 1996 and was a four-time gold medalist in the same event in the track and field world championships.

5. Dominique Dawes. A gymnast from Silver Spring, Maryland, in 1992 she was a member of the bronze medal U.S. Olympic team. Four years later, she earned a team gold medal and also won individual bronze for her floor exercise routine, becoming the first African-American gymnast ever to win an individual gymnastics medal in the Olympics.

4. Tom Dolan. Despite suffering from exercise-induced asthma, Dolan, from Arlington, Virginia, won swimming gold in the 400 meter individual medley in 1996 and came back in 2000 to take gold in the same event plus a silver in the 200 individual medley. He held the world record in the 400 IM for eight years, longer than any swimmer in history.

3. Sugar Ray Leonard. The native of Palmer Park, Maryland won a boxing gold medal in the light welterweight division of the 1976 Montreal Olympics, and his championship fight was the 145th victory of his illustrious amateur career. Leonard announced his retirement from the ring after the Games ended, but a lack of endorsements and mounting bills at home forced him to turn professional, where he earned multiple world titles and became one of the greatest and most popular champions in boxing history.

2. Mia Hamm. Born in Alabama, she moved to Northern Virginia as a teenager and attended Lake Braddock High School, where she became one of the best young soccer players in the country. A brilliant striker with a nose for the goal, she was on the gold medal U.S. Olympic women's soccer teams in 1996 and 2004 and won a silver in 2000, as well as being the most talented member of the U.S. women's World Cup championship team in 1999. She has more goals in international competition than any woman in the history of the game.

1. Melissa Belote. At the age of 15, the Springfield, Virginia, athlete won three gold medals at the 1972 Munich Olympics—the 100 and 200 meter backstroke and the medley relay. Considered one of the greatest backstrokers in Olympic history, she set a world record in the 200, and the relay team, with Belote swimming the first leg, also set a world record in the event.

Ten Greatest Washington Soccer Moments :: Steve Goff

Note: Steve Goff has covered professional soccer for *The Washington Post* since 1992, including four men's and three women's World Cup competitions.

10. College Success. Virginia won five NCAA titles in six years between 1989 and '94; Maryland claimed the 2005 championship; Howard took home two crowns in the 70s (but had to give one back because of ineligible players); and American reached the 1985 finals. George Mason won the '85 women's title.

9. The Early Years. The Washington Whips (1967-68), owned by then Los Angeles sports impresario Jack Kent Cooke, and Washington Darts (1970-71) played before small crowds, but paved the way for the Diplomats' birth in 1974.

8. Washington Freedom. Superstar Mia Hamm led the local entry in the Women's United Soccer Association for three years before the league ran out of money.

7. 1996 Olympics. Early-round matches were played outside of Atlanta, including men-women doubleheaders at Washington's RFK Stadium, which included the Ghana men's team's 3-2 upset of Italy and the U.S. men's 1-1 tie with Portugal before a sell-out crowd.

6. 1980 Soccer Bowl. An RFK sellout of 56,000-plus and a national TV audience watched Giorgio Chanaglia, Franz Beckenbauer, and the New York Cosmos defeat the Fort Lauderdale Strikers 3-0 in the North American Soccer League (NASL) title game.

5. World Cup Qualifiers. Between 1996 and 2004, the U.S. national team's road to the World Cup stopped at RFK five times and included three crowds of more than 50,000.

4. MLS Cups. RFK Stadium hosted Major League Soccer's premier game three times, drawing an average of more than 45,000 spectators, and, despite heavy rain in 1997, was sold out for United's 2-1 victory over Colorado.

3. The Diplomats' Rise. Led by Dutch superstar Johan Cruyff and other foreign-born players, the Diplomats made their mark in the NASL and introduced the sport to a new generation of Washington soccer fans in the 1970s and early 80s.

2. D.C. United's Launch. A dozen years after the NASL's demise, top-level pro soccer returns to an ethnically diversifying city and provides MLS with both a strong fan foundation and its first dynasty.

1. 1994 World Cup. The biggest event in the globe's most popular sport arrives at RFK Stadium for four first-round matches and a round-of-16 game, rekindling interest in international soccer in the Nation's Capital.

10. John Harkes. The U.S. national team veteran and industrious midfielder left behind a successful English Premier League career to become the handsome face of a new franchise.

9. Raul Diaz Arce. A Salvadoran forward and crowd favorite scored 38 goals the first two years of MLS, and after being traded for salary cap reasons, returned in a smaller role.

8. Ryan Nelsen. A New Zealander who provided a bruising presence in central defense and, after helping United win the 2004 title, moved to Blackburn in England's Premier League.

7. Richie Williams. Despite his small stature, this former University of Virginia (UVA) star was a terror in the defensive midfield who badgered opposing playmakers into mistakes and supplied the ball to United's attack.

6. Jeff Agoos. A versatile defender from UVA offered a powerful left foot and wise decision-making as United established itself as an early power in MLS.

5. Ben Olsen. The club's heart and soul on the field and its most eloquent speaker off it, the former UVA star filled various midfield roles and overcame serious ankle injuries to guide United back to prominence.

4. Eddie Pope. The stoic central defender anchored United's back line in the early years by dominating the aerial game, anticipating opposing maneuvers and igniting the attack with finesse and ball distribution.

3. Christian Gomez. The Argentine midfielder arrived late in 2004 and, with a blend of dangerous passes and a lethal scoring touch, sparked United to the best regular-season record twice and one championship while winning the 2006 MVP.

2. Marco Etcheverry. This Bolivian was a creative force in the middle of the pitch whose exquisite passing, bending free kicks and fiery determination guided United to three titles in four years and earned him the MVP award.

1. Jaime Moreno. The Bolivian forward joined United midway through the 1996 inaugural season to become perhaps MLS's most creative attacker and its all-time leading scorer through the league's first dozen years.

The Washington area can hardly be considered the cradle of coaches, but we've had our share of big names, and a few smaller ones, who honed their skills on local teams before moving on up to bigger and better jobs.

10. Tom Davis. He served as coach of the University of Maryland freshman basketball team in 1969 while earning his doctorate in education. Dr. Tom took over as head coach at Lafayette in 1972 and eventually held head coaching jobs at Boston College, Stanford, Iowa, and Drake, retiring after the 2007 season with 598 victories, 16 seasons with at least 20 wins, and 18 postseason appearances.

9. Gary Williams. A 1968 Maryland graduate and the Terps' point guard/captain his senior season, Williams got his first coaching job as a graduate assistant to freshman coach Tom Davis in 1969 and also worked for Davis as an assistant coach at Lafayette in 1972. His first head coaching job was at American in 1978, followed by stints at Boston College, Ohio State, and Maryland since 1989.

8. Tom Young. Captain of the 1958 Maryland basketball team that won the school's first Atlantic Coast Conference Championship, Young became head coach at Washington's Catholic University the season after he graduated, launching a career that included head coaching jobs at American, Rutgers, and Old Dominion. At Rutgers, he coached current Wizards head coach Eddie Jordan on a 1976 team that made The Final Four. Young worked for Jordan as a Wizards assistant for three seasons until he retired in 2007.

7. Bear Bryant. Before he coached "The Junction Boys" as head coach at Texas A&M in the 1950s, and before he became a legendary Hall of Fame head coach at Alabama, Paul "Bear" Bryant's first head coaching job was at the University of Maryland, where his first and only team in 1945 finished 6-2-1. Bryant became involved in a power struggle with school president Curley Byrd, a former Terrapins head coach himself, and Bryant resigned after his only season in College Park, taking over the University of Kentucky team.

6. Bill Belichick. He grew up in Annapolis, the son of Navy assistant coach/scout Steve Belichick, who became his first coaching mentor. Young Billy was a constant presence at Navy football practices as a youngster, and often helped his father break down film from opposing teams, an invaluable education for a future Hall of Fame coach and three-time Super Bowl champion.

5. Morgan Wootten. The all-time winningest high school basketball coach, Maryland graduate Wootten was hired in 1953 as an assistant coach at St. John's High School in Washington by his mentor, eventual longtime rival Joe Gallagher. Wootten spent three years at St. John's before leaving for DeMatha in 1956, remaining at the Hyattsville school until he retired in 2002. He is the only high school coach inducted into the Basketball Hall of Fame (2000) in Springfield, MA.

4. Ralph Friedgen. Maryland's current head football coach played offensive line for the Terrapins, and his first coaching job was as a graduate assistant in the Terrapins program in 1971. After assistant coaching stints at The Citadel, William and Mary, and Murray State, he returned to College Park as the Terrapins offensive coordinator under head coach Bobby Ross in 1982. The Fridge followed Ross to assistant's jobs with Georgia Tech and the San Diego Chargers before taking his first head coaching position at Maryland in 2000.

3. Jack Pardee. One of Bryant's "Junction Boys" at Texas A&M, Pardee had a distinguished career as an NFL linebacker, and came to the Washington Redskins from the Los Angeles Rams in a 1971 trade engineered by George Allen. Pardee retired as a player after the 1972 season, but served as an assistant linebackers coach for the Redskins in 1973 before moving up as head coach of the Chicago Bears in 1976. He also was head coach of the Redskins (1978-81), University of Houston (1987-89), and Houston Oilers (1990-94).

2. John Thompson. A graduate of Washington's Archbishop Carroll High School, Thompson gave up pro basketball after two seasons backing up Bill Russell with the Boston Celtics and returned home to coach St. Anthony's High School in 1966. He turned the school into a national power, and was hired to coach Georgetown's basketball team in 1973. He stayed for 27 years, becoming the first African American to win an NCAA basketball championship and the first to coach a U.S. Olympic basketball team.

1. Red Auerbach. The legendary head coach, general manager, and team president of the Boston Celtics played his college basketball at George Washington. He coached the high school teams at St. Albans and Roosevelt in Washington, and after three years of service in the Navy during World War II, he was hired to coach the Washington Capitols of the old Basketball Association of America, which merged into the NBA four years later. His first Capitols team finished 49-11, the precursor to the greatest coaching career in NBA history. He coached nine Celtics NBA title teams, was GM for seven other championships, and was the maestro of one of the greatest dynasties in the history of American sports.

Never mind the 34–year baseball-less gap we suffered through (1972–2005), when we've had a major league team here, it's generally been lousy. Thus, only one manager makes this list. But D.C. has a rich pro football and college basketball history. Here are the top 10 who have called the shots.

10. Vince Lombardi. Yes, of course he's at or near the top of every list of all-time coaches. But, you have to remember, cancer claimed Lombardi after only one year on the job as coach of the Redskins. His legacy is in Green Bay. Still, his 1969 record of 7-5-2 was the first winning season for the organization in 14 years. You wonder what might have happened had he lived. Upon seeing Sonny Jurgensen in training camp, Lombardi remarked to an assistant that if he had the redhead in Green Bay, the NFL would have declared the Packers a monopoly. Jurgensen laments never playing in a Super Bowl, but feels like he made a good trade getting to play for Lombardi.

9. Red Auerbach. Another one who would have to be near the top of the list, but his nine NBA championships were won in Boston. A native New Yorker, Auerbach came to Washington to play basketball at George Washington. After graduation, he coached high school, including teams at Roosevelt that included a benchwarmer named Bowie Kuhn. Auerbach also coached early Washington pro teams known as the Capitols, but never won a title. Our loss was Boston's gain as Auerbach went on to unprecedented success as a coach and general manager with the Celtics. Yet he remained a Washington resident until his death in 2006.

8. Bucky Harris. The one baseball guy on the list. Harris was called the "Boy Wonder" when he was the regular second baseman and manager at the age of 27, when the Senators won their last World Series in 1924. He won another pennant in 1925 and left after the 1928 season. Harris returned as a manager only from 1935-42 and again from 1950-54. He died in Bethesda in 1977 at the age of 81.

7. George Allen. His Redskin teams never won the Super Bowl, but he won and he won right away. Allen's picture and saying, "The future is now," appeared on the cover of *Newsweek* when his "Over the Hill" gang got off to a 5-0 start in his first season in 1971. That team got into the playoffs for the first time in a quarter-century and he followed it up with a Super Bowl appearance the following year. Although he never won a playoff game after that, every one of his seven Redskin teams had winning records. Allen was inducted in to the Hall of Fame in 2002.

6. Ray Flaherty. He came to Washington from Boston when the football team relocated in 1937, and won two championships over the next six years. Two years after the worst butt-whipping in NFL history, 73-0 by the Bears in 1940, Flaherty's Skins beat Chicago for his second title. He left right after that to fight in World War II. Flaherty was inducted in to the Hall of Fame in 1976.

5. Lefty Driesell. The record shows that Lefty never made a Final Four and was forced to resign at Maryland after the tragic death of Len Bias in 1986. But that's only part of the story. Lefty made college basketball matter in the Washington area when he came to College Park in 1969. A master showman, he put seats on the floor at Cole Field House, invented midnight madness, and created roundball excitement that no one in the area had ever seen. Lefty recruited some of the best talent in the history of college basketball and said he would make Maryland the "UCLA of the East." It never quite happened, but he won 348 games at Maryland, including an ACC championship.

4. Gary Williams. Like the scrapper he was as a player at Maryland in the late 60s, Williams takes his best shots from the critics and keeps on winning. He pulled the probation-ravaged program off the floor in the early 1990s and took the Terps to their first Final Four in 2001. Then he turned around and won the National Championship in 2002. He has won more games than any coach in Maryland history and will someday wind up in the Basketball Hall of Fame.

3. Morgan Wootten. He is more than just in the argument for greatest high school basketball coach of all time. Consider this quote from UCLA legend John Wooden: "I know of no finer coach at any level-high school, college or pro. I stand in awe of him." Wootten coached at DeMatha from 1956 to 2002, winning nearly 1,300 games. He sent numerous players to the NBA, including Adrian Dantley, Kenny Carr, Hawkeye Whitney, and Danny Ferry. His 1965 team pulled off one of the most historic high school wins of all time when they stopped Lew Alcindor and Power Memorial's 71-game winning streak. Wootten became the first high school coach to be inducted in the Basketball Hall of Fame in 2000.

2. John Thompson. A basketball trailblazer. A great high school and college player who spent two years playing for Red Auerbach with the Boston Celtics, Thompson took what he learned and built a powerhouse program in his hometown at Georgetown University. Thompson was one of the first black coaches at a predominately white college when he got the job at Georgetown in 1972. Seven years later, his team became one of the original members of the basketball-only Big East Conference. With Patrick Ewing, his teams played in three national championship games between 1982 and '85, winning the National Championship in 1984. He was inducted into the Hall of Fame in 1999.

1. Joe Gibbs. When he returned to coach the Redskins in 2004 after an 11-year absence, his wife warned him that he risked ruining his legacy. But even a four-year record of 30-36 with his two worst seasons (6-10 and 5-11) couldn't do that. The first go-round from 1981 to 1992 was football Camelot. After an 0-5 start in his first year, Gibbs changed his offensive philosophy and made a run at the playoffs, finishing 8-8. The next 10 years brought five appearances in the NFC championship game, four Super Bowl appearances and three titles. He was inducted into the Hall of Fame in 1996.

Note: John Feinstein has been paying close attention to college basketball ever since he matriculated at Duke in the mid-1970s. The prolific best-selling author of 23 books, he began his career as an intern at *The Washington Post* and still writes regularly for the newspaper and its web site, in addition to doing color commentary on radio broadcasts of Navy football and countless appearances on national radio and television shows. During the basketball season, he's just as likely to turn up courtside at an AU-GW game as he is at The Final Four, and he's even learned not to cheer too loudly for his beloved Blue Devils whenever he's watching Duke in action from press row.

10. Jack Kvancz. He actually had Catholic headed in the right direction in the early 1980s as a Division I program before some dolt president pulled the rug out and sent Catholic back to Division III. In 1980, Catholic beat St. Joseph's in triple overtime. Why was that such a big deal? That St. Joe's team went on to beat No. 1 seed DePaul in the NCAA Tournament that year and reached the Elite Eight. Jack beat them on the night John Lennon was killed.

9. Jimmy Patsos. You have to love anyone who can survive 12 years as an assistant to Gary Williams at Maryland. He was fired exactly 4,386 times during that period. He's since taken over at Loyola in Baltimore and the Hounds have gone from 1-27 the year before he arrived to 18 wins in 2007 and a shot at the NCAA Tournament in 2008. What's more, when his team travels to the New York area, Jimmy does things like take the players to the stock exchange. For a hoops coach, that's way outside the box.

8. Jeff Jones. He took over a dying American University program in 2000 and made the Eagles competitive again. He never takes himself seriously and usually has a pretty good perspective on wins and losses. After losing a game at Colgate a couple years back on a half-court shot at the buzzer, he said, "We didn't work on defending that shot enough in practice. I guess that's on me."

7. Don DeVoe. He took Navy to three NCAA Tournaments in the 90s without David Robinson. DeVoe had Bob Knight-intensity (he once worked for him at Army) but also had a dry sense of humor. One night when a kid named Jeremy Toten tried and missed an open three, DeVoe screamed at him for taking the shot. "Coach, I was open," Toten said. "Jeremy," DeVoe answered, "there's a REASON why you were open."

6. Paul Evans. He came to Navy in 1980 and was told you can't run at Navy—by me, among others. He ran anyway and all he did was produce a final-eight team and three straight NCAA Tournament bids. You can say he had David Robinson, but in Robinson's freshman year—when Navy won 24 games—David was still 6-foot-7 and averaged six points a game. The guy could really coach.

5. Ed Tapscott. He replaced Gary Williams at American, a tough act to follow, and succeeded. He's probably the most cerebral coach we've had in the Washington area (he has a law degree) and he always had a slightly different view of the world. When John Thompson stopped playing AU after the Eagles beat Georgetown in 1982, Eddie shrugged and said, "I guess he figures he'll NEVER beat me."

4. Karl Hobbs. First, he rebuilt George Washington hoops when it was down in the dumps in 2001 and made The Smith Center a fun place again. Second, his on-court histrionics are worth the price of admission. Once, when he was jumping and whirling and screaming and pointing during a game, Red Auerbach turned to my son Danny and said, "is coaching really THAT hard?"

3. Jim Larranaga. He would make the list for George Mason's 2006 Final Four run alone. It's the single most amazing feat in the history of local college hoops—maybe in the history of the town. Beyond that though, he ENJOYED every moment of it, didn't change at all when it was over, and let everyone else enjoy the ride along with him and his team.

2. Gary Williams. He put Maryland back on the map after the Bob Wade disaster in the late 80s. A true Jekyll-Hyde, he's as warm and funny away from the court as he is crazed on it. My favorite Gary moment during a game: He screamed at the ACC supervisor of officials during an ACC Tournament that he KNEW one of the officials on the game—who Gary thought was awful—would NEVER be assigned to a f———Duke game. The supervisor, Fred Barakat, immediately shot back, "Gary, this IS a f——— Duke game." Maryland was playing Duke.

1. Lefty Driesell. He's No 1 not just because he put big-time college hoops on the map at Maryland when he arrived in 1969 but because he had the best, self-deprecating sense of humor of any coach I ever covered. Once, when I pointed out to him that he had set up his defense on a final play to guard a player who had FOULED OUT he just shook his head and said, "Well, I guess that shows how dumb I am." He could never hold a grudge, no matter how angry he might get at you.

10. Babe McCarthy, George Washington Basketball 1966-67 (6-18).
Babe takes an important spot in the history of college basketball. As coach at
Mississippi State in 1963, he literally snuck his team out of town to play Loyola of
Chicago in the NCAA tournament. The administration did not want their white players
to participate in a game with black players, but McCarthy saw the value in the risk of
defying his bosses and played the game anyway. He wasn't fired at GW. The team he
took over had won only three games the season before. Babe's heart was in the south
and he left to become the first coach of the ABA's New Orleans Buccaneers and later
became the upstart league's first coach to win 200 games.

9. Leonard Hamilton, Wizards 2000-2001 (19-63). Team president Michael
Jordan had decided to hire a college coach. Having never coached, Jordan somehow
believed he could mold an NBA coach who had no pro experience exactly the way he
wanted. Hamilton, who had been successful at the University of Miami, was hypnotized
by Jordan and actually agreed to buy his own way out of Miami. The season was a disaster, with Hamilton at one point needing to get security to remove belligerent Tyrone
Nesby from his bench. After the last game of the season, Hamilton was talking to the
media about his plans for the following season when he was suddenly called to a meeting. At the meeting Jordan fired Hamilton and said his hand-picked guy just wasn't
ready for the job.

8. Richie Petitbon, Redskins 1993 (4-12). With Joe Gibbs' surprise retirement
in March of 1993, there was no time to search for a replacement. But Petitbon was the
logical choice. His work as a defensive coordinator was a major factor in the Redskins'
four trips to the Super Bowl under Gibbs. After three straight trips to the playoffs,
including a Super Bowl championship, nobody snickered when Richie promised it
would be, "business as usual," with the change of head coaches. It wasn't. After a 41-
7 loss at home to the Giants, he declared, "I think we're at rock bottom." Not yet. There
were 11 games left to play and the Redskins lost eight of them. Richie was fired two
days after the season ended.

7. Jimmy Anderson, Caps 1974-75 (4-45-5). Anderson was the real-life version of Paul Newman's Reggie Dunlop character in the movie *Slap Shot*. He had
played 23 years of hockey, all in the minors, except a seven-game cup of coffee with
the Los Angeles Kings at the age of 37. With a couple of coaching years under his belt
(in the minors of course), he seemed like a decent choice to coach the expansion Caps
since most of their players belonged in the minors anyway. But even expansion teams
have only so much patience. With only four wins in 54 games, Anderson was put out
of his misery. Red Sullivan finished the year.

6. Gar Heard, Wizards 1999-2000 (14-30). On the same day the Lakers hired Phil Jackson at a salary of more than six million a year, Heard was hired by the Wizards at a salary just under a million. Owner Abe Pollin claimed money was no object in the hire and then uttered the immortal words about the interview that led to his new coach's hire, "Gar Heard blew me away." At midseason, Michael Jordan was hired as team president and said in his introductory press conference, "I'm going to be at practice. If Gar doesn't like it, that's too bad. I'm his boss." About three weeks later, Jordan blew Gar Heard away.

5. Lou Saban, Maryland Football 1966 (4-6). Later in his career, Saban would practically put the patent on one-and-done. And it was usually his choice after a successful year. Saban actually came to College Park after winning back-to-back AFL championships with the Buffalo Bills. He claimed he was fed up with the pros and his heart was in college coaching. It was. For one year. In 1967, Saban was back in the AFL coaching the Denver Broncos.

4. Bear Bryant, Maryland Football 1945 (6-2-1). Realize that Bryant had replaced Clarence Spears, whose team had managed an 8-6 win over VMI in the last game of the season to finish 1-7-1. They had averaged five points a game! So you'd think Bryant, even though he was years away from reaching God-like status at Alabama, would have gotten anything he wanted after one of the best seasons in school history. Apparently not. Historians say he lost a power struggle with former football coach Curley Byrd, who was by then the school's president. Bryant left for Kentucky the next year. Fifteen years later, he benefited from Maryland's decision not to admit a Pennsylvania high school quarterback who they said didn't have the grades to get in. The Bear managed to get him in at Alabama instead. His name was Joe Namath.

3. John Whelchel, Redskins 1949 (3-3-1). Dan Snyder may be impatient, but it seems that George Preston Marshall was worse. Figuring his team lacked discipline, he fired former star tackle Turk Edwards after a 7-5 finish in 1948. Better things were expected of retired Admiral Whelchel, who had been head coach at Navy going 5-4 and 8-1 with wins each year over Army in 1942 and '43 before going off to more important duty in World War II. But when Whelchel dropped to 2-3-1 after a tie with the underdog New York Bulldogs, he knew he was on his way out. Down at halftime against Pittsburgh the following week, Whelchel told his players this was going to be his last game and that they should go out and win it for him. They did, 27-14 and Whelchel was carried off the field by his players. The next day he was booted and replaced by assistant coach Herman Ball, who won only one of his last five, but returned the following season.

2. Marty Schottenheimer, Redskins 2001 (8-8). This was Snyder's first head coaching hire. Terry Robiskie finished the 2000 season on an interim basis. Marty had said on ESPN only weeks before being hired that he could never work for an owner like Snyder. A five-year, 20 million dollar contract and complete control of the team changed his mind. It was bad out of the gate. The Skins scored only 32 points in the first five games to start 0-5. But then things turned around. They got to 5-5 and finished a respectable 8-8. Not good enough for Snyder, who decided he'd given Marty too much control. Steve Spurrier replaced Marty a week after the season ended.

1. Dutch Bergman, Redskins 1943 (6-3-1). The record may not seem all that impressive, but it includes a trip to the NFL championship game. Bergman replaced Ray Flaherty, who won his second NFL title in 1942 and then went off to fight World War II. The Skins didn't seem to miss a beat, starting the '43 season 6-0-1. But they lost at home to the Steagles (a wartime combo of the Steelers and Eagles) and then lost back-to-back games to the Giants, which forced a playoff game at New York. In what was their third straight game against the Giants, the Redskins finally got it right and won 28-0. But it apparently wasn't enough. After losing the NFL title game at Chicago 41-21 the day after Christmas, Bergman was fired after only one year. Dudley DeGroot, who replaced him, lasted two years, but was fired after also losing the NFL championship game.

"In a hierarchally structured administration, people tend to be promoted to their level of incompetence."

—Dr. Laurence J. Peter, *The Peter Principle*

For every Joe Gibbs (who had never been a head coach at any level and went on to win three Super Bowls) and John Thompson (who had never coached in a college game before taking over at Georgetown and building a basketball dynasty), there are many who have been promoted and failed. Here are the top 10 who hit their head on the ceiling when they were promoted to the top job.

10. Charley Casserly (Redskins GM 1989-98). We know you're going to say, "He was the Redskins general manager when they won the Super Bowl." Yes he was. But realize that Casserly was the beneficiary of being in a fortunate situation. The story of Casserly's rise through the organization after being hired as an unpaid intern by George Allen in 1976, is well told. He was assistant general manager for many years before being hired to replace Bobby Beathard before the 1989 season. Beathard though, had made a couple of shrewd moves to stock the cupboard for the new guy before leaving. He traded Mike Oliphant to Cleveland for Earnest Byner, and had drafted Mark Schlereth in the 10th round of the '89 draft. Credit Casserly for some excellent Plan B free agent signings, but his record at the top of the draft isn't very good. The holy trinity of Redskin busts—Desmond Howard, Heath Shuler, and Michael Westbrook—all occurred during his watch. Casserly was fired just before the start of the 1999 season. He got another shot with the expansion Houston Texans, but lost that job before the start of the 2006 season. Casserly was excellent in helping Beathard build champions, but never really cut it as the top guy.

9. Norv Turner (Redskins head coach 1994-2000). Another case of, "Hey, wait a minute." Yes, we know Norv led San Diego to the AFC title game after the 2007 season. But it's remarkable that he got the chance to do it, considering what a bust he was as a head coach with the Redskins and Raiders. The hiring of Turner before the 1994 season was considered to be a coup for Redskins owner Jack Kent Cooke. Turner was coming off back-to-back Super Bowl championships as offensive coordinator in Dallas. But after two expected rebuilding seasons, 3-13 in '94 and 6-10 in '95, the Redskins began to get just close enough to fail. After a 7-1 start in '96, they somehow managed to miss the playoffs at 9-7 and in '97, typified by Gus Frerotte knocking himself out of a game by head-butting a stadium wall in a 7-7 tie with the Giants, they missed again at 8-7-1. He should have been fired after an 0-7 start in 98, but managed to hang on for almost two full years. He did win the division in '99, but his overall Redskins record was 49-59-1 with a 1-1 playoff mark. Take away the '07 season and you have an excellent offensive coordinator who is a mostly failed head coach.

8. Wes Unseld (Bullets head coach 1987-94, GM 1995-2002). One of the greatest players in the history of the NBA who, as a coach and a general manager, was a great . . . player. In 14 years as a player, Unseld never used an agent and worked out a new contract every season by shaking the hand of owner Abe Pollin. That loyalty was rewarded with a lifetime job in the Bullets organization after he retired as a player in 1981. Early in the 1987-88 season, Unseld replaced Kevin Loughery as head coach and got the Bullets into the playoffs, where they took Detroit the distance before losing the series in five. That proved to be the high point of his coaching career. Unseld was forced out after the 1993-94 season with an overall record of 202-345. Not long after that, he replaced the man who pushed him out as coach: John Nash. As general manager, Unseld did put together one playoff team, but otherwise was a failure. His two major moves involved trading young and big for old and small—not a good formula. Rasheed Wallace and Chris Webber enjoyed success elsewhere, while the Bullets/Wizards bottomed out with Rod Strickland and Mitch Richmond. Unseld, the greatest player in the history of the franchise, met the Peter Principle twice.

7. Dan Henning (Falcons head coach 1983-86, Chargers head coach 1989-91). A tough, cigarette-smoking New Yorker who is revered by the offensive players who have worked with him. Although Joe Gibbs called the plays, Henning was his eye in the sky in the press box for the first and third Super Bowl championships. After the first one, Henning became head coach of the Falcons and failed. He returned to the Redskins and, after the third one, Henning became head coach of the Chargers and failed. However, he's been mostly successful as an offensive coordinator and was hired for that job in Miami by Bill Parcells to help rebuild the 1-15 Dolphins after the 2007 season.

6. Matt Millen (Lions GM 2001-?). He could walk the walk and talk the talk, but he has been a spectacular failure in his latest job. The former Penn State linebacker won two Super Bowl rings with the Raiders and another one with the 49ers, before collecting a fourth as a member of the Redskins in his final NFL season in 1991. A great talker, Millen eased right in to the broadcast booth with CBS and Fox and was well on his way to becoming the heir-apparent to John Madden as the best analyst in the business. But despite his broadcast success, Millen said he missed the competition. He said he felt somewhat empty leaving a game because he hadn't won or lost, and wanted a job as a general manager. Millen got it and soon wasn't wanting for losses anymore. As the beneficiary of some of the greatest patience in sports history, the Lions have stayed with Millen despite a seven-season record of 31-81 with no playoff appearances. Millen himself calls it, "beyond awful." Unless he reverses a very long trend, Millen will go down in history as being as bad as a GM as he was good as a player and broadcaster.

5. Mark Duffner (Maryland head football coach 1992-96). He had a spectacular record as head coach at Holy Cross. In six years, his Crusaders went 60-5-1 with an 11-0 record in his final year. Duffner was full of enthusiasm and seemingly the right choice to revive the Maryland football program when he was hired to replace Joe Krivak, who had gone 2-9 in 1991. However, not enough consideration was given to the fact that Holy Cross had given scholarships while most of the teams they competed against didn't. Duffner ran a run-and-shoot offense, which could produce lots of points like it did in a season-ending 53-23 win over Clemson in '92. But when those passes went the other way, it could get ugly like it did with a 70-7 loss to Penn State at home in '93. He produced one winning season, 1995, when they won their first four but lost five of their last seven to finish 6-5. In five seasons at Maryland, Duffner went 20-35 with no bowl appearances. He's managed to stay in the NFL since then, where he seems better suited as an assistant.

4. Roy Lester (Maryland head football coach 1969-71). A legendary high school football coach in Maryland. Several of his teams at Richard Montgomery, which included future NFL star Mike Curtis, were considered the best in the state in the days before Maryland had playoffs. Lester seemed like a fresh new idea when he was hired before the 1969 season. Maryland had been through three coaches in the previous four seasons. Bob Ward had gone 0-9 in '67 and 2-8 in '68. Lester improved that mark by a game in '69, but was fired after back-to-back 2-9 seasons in '70 and '71. His first two years, Lester lost the Penn State game 48-0 and 34-0. He hung 27 on the Nittany Lions in '71, but lost 63-27. Lester went back to coaching high school and won a state championship at Magruder in 1984. The younger kids seemed to suit his talents better.

3. Craig Esherick (Georgetown head basketball coach 1999-2004). After a four-year playing career that ended in 1978, and three years in law school, Esherick wanted to get back in the game. Head coach John Thompson hired him as an assistant in 1982. Several of Esherick's recruits played on the 1984 championship team and the one that went back to the title game in '85. When Thompson abruptly resigned early in 1999 with a 7-6 record on the season, he tapped his 17-year assistant to take his place. Esherick managed a 15-15 finish and a spot in the NIT. Two years later he led the Hoyas to a 25-8 record before losing to Maryland in the Sweet 16 of the NCAA tournament. But his fortunes soon declined and Georgetown finished the 2003-04 season by losing their last nine to finish 13-15. With only one NCAA tournament appearance in five-plus years on the job, Esherick was fired and replaced by John Thompson III. In his third season, Thompson took Georgetown to the Final Four, proving the program seems to do its best with a Thompson in charge, not an Esherick.

2. Bob Wade (Maryland head basketball coach 1986–89). Wade was a reactionary hire in the wake of the tragic death of Len Bias in 1986. Wade had incredible success as a high school coach at Dunbar in Baltimore, going 341-25 in 10 years. He sent a number of players to big-time college programs and the NBA, like Reggie Williams, Muggsy Bogues, and the late Reggie Lewis. But the fact that Wade had no college experience should have been a bigger consideration when Maryland chancellor John Slaughter decided to replace Lefty Driesell in an attempt to calm the basketball program after Bias' death. Wade not only led the program to the bottom, finishing 9-20 in his last year, he helped put the program under severe probation restrictions. After the NCAA determined that Wade had lied to them, Maryland was banned from television for two years and couldn't appear in the ACC tournament. It took new coach Gary Williams four years to dig out of the probation hole, before taking Maryland to the Sweet 16 in 1994. In the end, Wade would have been better off staying at the high school level or trying to work his way up as assistant before becoming a head coach in college.

1. Richie Petitbon (Redskins head coach 1993). If they ever put defensive coordinators in the Pro Football Hall of Fame, Richie would have to be among the first considered. Every time Joe Gibbs looks at one of his three Super Bowl rings, he can thank Petitbon for the job he did with the defense. Gibbs was smart enough to leave him alone, and it was rare that Petitbon didn't make some kind of halftime adjustment to help secure the win. The best example was the Super Bowl XVII win over Miami when David Woodley and Don Strock failed to complete a Dolphin pass in the second half. There was no one who thought Petitbon wasn't the right choice to replace Gibbs when he stepped down in March of '93, citing health reasons. But Richie was left with an aging roster and a terrible first free-agent class put together by Charley Casserly (Al Noga for God sakes!) that soon hit, as he put it, "rock bottom." "The Bone" suffered through some of the worst losses in Redskins history, including 41-7 to the Giants and 3-0 to the Jets, both at home. He was fired days after his 4-12 season ended and never coached again. It's tough to judge him on just one season, but his head coaching experience was a far cry from his success running just the defense.

Obviously Joe Gibbs' first go-round as head coach of the Redskins (1981–92) was more successful than his second stint (2004–07). Gibbs won four NFC championships and three Super Bowls, cementing a spot in the Pro Football Hall of Fame before stepping down after the 1992 season. His four-year comeback resulted in an overall losing record (31-36) and just one playoff win. But beyond the wins and losses, here are the reasons it was just better the first time around.

10. Weight. Gibbs' weight would fluctuate, but tended to go up during the season because he liked to munch on chocolate during those famed late-night strategy sessions with his coaching staff. Diabetes forced Gibbs to control his diet the second time around. Like Rosanne Barr, Gibbs proved to be much better fat.

9. Glasses. Maybe Gibbs could actually see better with those aviator specs he wore in the 80s. Yes the eyewear styles changed, but the smaller glasses may have caused him to miss some of the minute details that never passed him by during the glory years.

8. Giggling. Gibbs wasn't much for jokes the first time around. The first thing many fans noticed in his early press conferences the second time around was an Arnold Horshack guffaw that followed lines that he found funny. Nobody was giggling over records of 6-10 and 5-11.

7. 7-11 Coffee. On rare nights he went home to sleep during the week, Gibbs would stop at 7-11 to pick up his morning coffee on his way in to the office. In his second stint it was Starbucks coffee. He could certainly afford the more upscale brand, but maybe there was something in those 7-11 grounds.

6. Film. In the 80s when Gibbs would tell the media, "I need to look at the film," he actually did. NFL Films once featured the coach rolling the projector back and forth. Perhaps he never really adjusted to watching game video on a computer screen.

5. Sons. Gibbs has two sons who both played college football and followed him into the racing business. They were kids during the first stint, too young to be married. The second time around, JD and Coy were married with children. The "grandbabies," as Gibbs called them, may have prevented him from devoting his complete concentration to coaching.

4. NASCAR. Gibbs got into the racing business late in his first stint. Less than a month before he called it quits the first time, his team won the Daytona 500. Although he claimed that JD was in complete charge of Joe Gibbs Racing while he was coaching the Redskins in stint number two, it's hard to believe some of his focus wasn't on racing.

3. RFK Stadium. When the old 55-thousand-seat bandbox shook, it was a home field unlike any other in the NFL. Fedex Field holds nearly twice as many, but the old magic was just never there in the second stint.

2. Free Agency. Gibbs had his "core guys" in the first go-round who stayed, in a number of cases, all 12 years of his run. Few had a choice. In fact two of the Hogs, Jeff Bostic and Joe Jacoby, started all 12 years and Russ Grimm played 11 of those years. The second time around, while Gibbs loved buying free agents, he lost several players he had called "core guys."

1. Just Head Coach. Gibbs's title the second time around was Head Coach and Team President. The second part of that title may have been his undoing. General managers Bobby Beathard and Charley Casserly gave him players to win with the first time. Team President Gibbs proved to be not so good at that the second time.

Tale of the Tape: Coach Z versus Chief Zee

On February 10, 2008, Jim Zorn was introduced as the 27th head coach of the Washington Redskins. Somewhere along the line he has been, or will be called, "Coach Z." Redskins fan Zema Williams, known as "Chief Zee," has been wearing a buckskin outfit and a full headdress with feathers to Redskins games since 1978. Zee has been recognized as the team's unofficial mascot and was honored by the Pro Football Hall of Fame in 2000 as the Redskins' number one fan. With apologies to Nick Bakay, who did wonderful work at ESPN with match ups by the "tale of the tape," here is ours.

Chief Zee. Has lived in Washington, D.C. for a large portion of his life.

Coach Z. Has lived in Washington State for a large portion of his life.

Advantage: Chief Zee

Chief Zee. On February 8, 2008, he was given no chance by the media to become head coach of the Redskins.

Coach Z. On February 8, 2008, he was given no chance by the media to become head coach of the Redskins.

Advantage: Push

Chief Zee. Has proudly rooted for the burgundy and gold for more than 30 years.

Coach Z. Announced at his introductory news conference that his family had started wearing the colors of the Redskins, "maroon, black, and yellow."

Advantage: Chief Zee. He knows the Redskins colors are burgundy and gold.

Chief Zee. Has appeared in an Eastern Motors Auto commercial.

Coach Z. Could have strolled down Connecticut Avenue prior to February 10, 2008, without being recognized.

Advantage: Chief Zee

Chief Zee. Has never been considered to be a candidate to become head coach of the Redskins, and has never spent a night in Dan Snyder's guest house.

Coach Z. Because he was originally brought in from Seattle to become a coordinator, not a head coach, he has never spent a night in Dan Snyder's guest house.

Advantage: Push

Chief Zee. Lives on social security.

Coach Z. Signed a five-year, $15 million contract.

Advantage: Coach Z

Chief Zee. Was once beat up in Philadelphia.

Coach Z. Was beat up in print by Sally Jenkins of the *Washington Post*.

Advantage: Push

Chief Zee. Hates the Dallas Cowboys because . . . well, because they're the Dallas Cowboys.

Coach Z. Hates the Dallas Cowboys because they cut him as an undrafted rookie in 1975. They had some fellow named Staubach. It turned out to be a huge favor as he became the starting quarterback of the expansion Seattle Seahawks.

Advantage: Chief Zee

Chief Zee. Has been in the stands for Super Bowl wins.

Coach Z . Has never been a part of a Super Bowl winner as a player or coach.

Advantage: Chief Zee

Chief Zee. Is not really a Chief or an Indian.

Coach Z. Is, believe it or not, actually the head coach of the Redskins.

Advantage: Coach Z

Scoreboard: Chief Zee, 5 – Coach Z, 2

Quiet, please, as we introduce the ten best golfers ever to hail from the District.

10. Kim Williams. A native of Bethesda, Williams joined the LPGA Tour in 1987 after a highly successful amateur career. She finished second in the 1984 U.S. Amateur championship and also played on the 1986 Curtis Cup team. She may be best known for being struck in the neck by a stray bullet while she was walking into a drug store in Youngstown, Ohio, in 1994. She survived the incident and returned to play the tour the next season.

9. Martin West III. A longtime member of Columbia Country Club, West, a Washington businessman, has been among the more decorated national amateur players. He's played in two U.S. Opens and made the cut in the '76 event, been a member of two American Walker Cup teams (1973 and 1979), and played in three Masters tournaments and 19 U.S. Amateur events.

8. Kris Tschetter. Born in Detroit and raised in South Dakota, Tschetter moved to the Washington area in the early 1990s. She played college golf at Texas Christian University in Fort Worth, Texas, and befriended the great Ben Hogan, who helped her work on her game and played a number of practice rounds with her at the same Fort Worth club used by the TCU women's team. Tschetter joined the LPGA Tour in 1988 and had one career victory, though she finished second to champion Annika Sorenstam in the 1996 U.S. Open at Pine Needles in Southern Pines, N.C. She's also married to a teaching professional, Kirk Lucas, who works with several players on the PGA and LPGA tours.

7. Olin Browne. A graduate of St. Albans High School in Washington, Browne didn't start playing golf until he was a 19-year-old college student at Occidental in California. He joined the tour in 1992 and has won four events, with a career-best $2.1 million in earnings in 2005, when he was the leader after the first two rounds of the U.S. Open at Pinehurst No. 2 before fading to a tie for 23rd. He also shot a stunning 59 at Woodmont Country Club in Rockville to qualify for the Open that same year.

6. Bobby Brownell. Considered one of the finest amateur golfers in the Washington area, Brownell won the Washington junior championship as a high school student in 1934, then went on to become an 11-time champion of the Washington Amateur championship. He also was a five-time Middle Atlantic Amateur champion and played in a number of major national amateur events, including the U.S. Amateur. Once an FBI agent, he eventually went into the insurance business and was a long-time member of Burning Tree Country Club, where he played or practiced virtually every day until his death in 2006 at the age of 86.

5. Deane Beman. Born in Washington in 1938, Beman won two U.S. Amateur titles and the British Amateur and worked in the insurance business before turning professional in the 1960s, winning four times on the PGA Tour. He also was named commissioner of the PGA Tour in 1974, and over his visionary 20-year tenure, players saw a dramatic rise in purses, events and other benefits. He also came up with the concept of The Players Championship, now one of the most prestigious events on the tour schedule, often called the fifth major.

4. Lee Elder. He was born in Dallas and taught himself how to play as a caddie on Texas municipal courses. One of the finest players on the United Golf Association, a national tour for African-American golfers, by the late 1960s Elder took up residence in the Washington area and at one point helped run the District's public golf courses. He also became the first African-American golfer to play in the Masters, qualifying for the 1975 event, the same season he won three of his four PGA Tour tournaments. A member of the 1979 Ryder Cup team, Elder also had a fine career playing on the Champions Tour, winning eight tournaments on the senior circuit.

3. Fred Funk. A native of Prince George's County, he played golf for the University of Maryland and also coached the school's golf team from 1982-88. Though he dominated tournament play in the Middle Atlantic section of the PGA, Funk did not join the PGA Tour full-time until 1989 when he was 32, but quickly made up for lost time as one of the tour's more consistent money winners. He's won eight times on the regular tour, including the prestigious 2005 Players Championship, and in 2007 won an event on both the regular tour and the Champions Tour. He's a short hitter, but annually leads the tour statistic for fairway accuracy.

2. Fred McLeod. A wee Scotsman who stood all of 5 feet 4, he came to the U.S. as a teenager and settled in the Washington area. McLeod won the 1908 U.S. Open and to this day remains the shortest Open champion in the history of the tournament. He became the first golf professional at Columbia Country Club in Chevy Chase in 1912 and was the head pro at the club until 1967. McLeod also won the 1938 PGA Seniors Championship and served as an honorary starter for 15 Masters.

1. Lew Worsham. One of four boys reared in Cabin John, Maryland, Worsham won four titles on the PGA Tour, including his greatest victory, beating Sam Snead in a playoff at the 1947 U.S. Open at the St. Louis Country Club for a first-place check of $2,000. He also had six top-ten finishes in major championships, but never played in the British Open or PGA. In 1953, he led the PGA Tour's money list, earning $34,000. His little brother Bubby, who roomed with Arnold Palmer at Wake Forest University, may well have been the best player in the family but was killed in a car accident in 1950 at the age of 22.

5. East Potomac, Langston, and Rock Creek Park, Washington, D.C.

There are only three golf courses within the District of Columbia, all public facilities. East Potomac near the Tidal Basin has an 18-hole course with Potomac River views and two nine-hole tracks; it first opened in 1935. Rock Creek off 16th Street in Northwest Washington has a 4,800-yard course where only mountain goats need apply in the caddy shack. It's tight and it's hilly and bunches of fun. When Langston, less than a mile from RFK Stadium, was built in 1939 it was the only course African American golfers could play in the District. Lee Elder called the place home for many years and it's now listed on the National Historic Register. The priciest greens fee at any of the courses is $32 on the weekend, not including cart.

4. Northwest Park, Silver Spring, Maryland.

It's the longest public course in Montgomery County at 7,200 yards from the tops. The course, filled with fully mature trees and wide, welcoming fairways, was designed by well-known local architect Ed Ault, and there is also a shorter nine-hole track on the property. Greens fees range from $15 to $40.

3. University of Maryland Golf Club, College Park, Maryland.

Fred Funk once manned the pro shop and coached the Terrapins golf team until he found fame and fortune on the PGA Tour. The hilly, mature course measures 6,700 yards from the tips, and greens fees range from $32 to $62, depending on the season.

2. Stonewall Golf Club, Gainesville, Virginia.

Built next door to the Robert Trent Jones Golf Club and designed by Tom Jackson, the back nine has some of the more stunning holes of any venue in the area, including lovely views of Lake Manassas. Lots of new homes on the property, but some holes remain pretty and pristine. Greens fees range from $90 to $119.

1. Westfield Golf Club, Fairfax, Virginia.

Fred Couples, who won his first event on the PGA Tour in Washington, also designed his first golf course in the area. Westfield is as challenging and as well-maintained a public course as you'll ever find, with gorgeous tree-lined fairways, yawning greens and just enough water to make it very interesting. It's 6,900 yards from the tips, with greens fees from $89 to $109.

We take our golf very seriously in the Washington area, with several hundred courses within a 90-minute drive of the Capitol building. We picked five of the more exclusive clubs in the area, and no, we did not include Burning Tree in Bethesda among them, even if it has been a longtime golfing playground for presidents, politicians and even Bryant Gumbel. Nevertheless, they do not allow women members, and any club that discriminates on the basis of race, religion or gender has no business being on anyone's list of swankiest Washington golf clubs. Silly boys.

5. The Members Club at Four Streams, Beallsville, Maryland. A relatively new course in the far-out Maryland suburbs, this is a golf purist's paradise, with an exquisitely manicured 7,100-yard course designed by major championship winner Nick Price. No pool, no tennis. Just all golf all the time. Initiation: $45,000. Monthly dues: $625.

4. Columbia Country Club, Chevy Chase, Maryland. The club formed in 1898 and the 6,600-yard golf course, designed by Walter Travis, a prominent player of that era, opened in 1911. Columbia was the site for the 1921 U.S. Open won by Englishman James Barnes. The runner-up, Scotsman Fred McLeod, wound up as Columbia's club professional for many years and is buried on the property. Initiation: $80,000. Monthly dues: $445.

3. The Chevy Chase Club, Chevy Chase, Maryland. Just down Connecticut Avenue from Columbia, the club was organized in 1892. The 6,800-yard course was designed by renowned golf architect Donald Ross, and if your shirt isn't tucked in on the first tee, someone in the pro shop will tell you to do so or leave the premises. Initiation: $85,000. Monthly dues: $525.

2. Congressional Country Club, Bethesda, Maryland. Six former presidents have been members of the club located off River Road. There are two 18-hole courses—the 6,800-yard Gold and the 7,250-yard Blue, a Golf Digest Top 100 track redesigned by Rees Jones in preparation for the 1997 U.S. Open won by Ernie Els. The club hosted the 1964 Open (won by Ken Venturi) and the 1976 PGA Championship (won by Dave Stockton) and is the site for Washington's regular PGA Tour stop, the AT&T National hosted by Tiger Woods. Initiation fee: $100,000. Monthly dues: $420.

1. Robert Trent Jones Golf Club, Gainesville, Virginia. Opened in 1991, the 7,300-yard course and a golf-and-only-golf club about 35 miles from Washington was designed by the world famous architect whose name it bears. The venue, also annually ranked as a Top 100 course, has been the site for four Presidents Cup competitions, in 1994, 1996, 2000 and 2005, all won by the U.S. The bad news? For years, a junkyard occupied the property right next door. Initiation: $140,000. Monthly dues: $1,000.

Major Championships of Golf in the Washington Area

1921 U.S. Open at Columbia Country Club in Chevy Chase. James M. Barnes wins, shooting nine-over par 289, beating runners-up Fred McLeod and Walter Hagen, both at 18-over 298.

1964 U.S. Open at Congressional Country Club in Bethesda. Ken Venturi wins, shooting four-under 276, beating runner-up Tommy Jacobs at two-over 282.

1976 PGA Championship at Congressional. Dave Stockton wins, shooting one-over 281, beating runners-up Raymond Floyd and Don January, both at two-over 282.

1997 U.S. Open at Congressional. Ernie Els shoots four-under 276, beating runner-up Colin Montgomerie at three-under 277.

2011. The U.S. Open is scheduled at Congressional.

Tiger Woods, the No. 1 golfer in the world, has played professionally since 1996, but had only made four appearances in Washington-area tournaments through 2007 and never played in the area's longtime regular PGA Tour tournament—the Kemper Open, and later the Booz Allen Classic—at the TPC at Avenel in Potomac, MD. Woods is now expected to be a Washington-area summer fixture as the host of his own annual tournament, the AT&T National hosted by Tiger Woods at Congressional Country Club, at least through 2009. Tiger's Washington-area starts:

1997. The U.S. Open at Congressional in Bethesda, where he tied for 19th place.

2000. The Presidents Cup at Robert Trent Jones Golf Club in Ganiesville, Va., where he posted a 3-2 match record in a 21½ to 10½ U.S. victory over the International team.

2005. The Presidents Cup at Robert Trent Jones Golf Club, where he posted a 2-2-1 match record in an 18½ to 15½ U.S. victory over the International team.

2007. The AT&T National at Congressional, where he tied for sixth place.

The Top 10 Injuries That Impacted Washington Sports History

Injuries are a part of the game, particularly football. However there are some which can't be overcome and leave you wondering how history might have been different had they not occurred.

10. Nick Johnson: Broken Leg 2006. Just when it looked like Johnson was ready to put his long history of injuries behind him, the Nationals first baseman broke his right femur in an outfield collision in a late-September game against the Mets in New York. The injury forced GM Jim Bowden to look elsewhere for first base help. He signed Tigers castoff Dmitri Young, who went on to hit .320, made the All Star team and was named Comeback Player of the Year in 2007. It earned Young a two-year contract extension worth 10 million dollars.

9. Jim "Yazoo" Smith: Broken Neck 1968. After being drafted in the first round of the 1968 draft, Smith (who was nicknamed "Yazoo" because he was from Yazoo, Oregon) turned in a solid rookie year for the Redskins, but was hurt in the last game of the season. Although the injury wasn't paralyzing, he never played football again. It apparently scared the Redskins away from the first round of the draft. Over the next 21 years, they used their own first rounder only twice. Once for Art Monk in 1980 and once for Darrell Green in 1983. True, both became Hall of Famers, but you have to think they missed a few others during those years.

8. Joe Theismann: Broken Leg 1985. If you're ghoulish and didn't see it when it happened, you can check it out thanks to sickos who posted the leg-breaking play on YouTube. The injury ended Theismann's career (of course it did!). Thing is, you have to wonder if the injury saved coach Joe Gibbs from making a move he probably needed to make. Theismann was 36 when it happened and appeared to be a shell of his former Pro-Bowl self when he got hurt. Jay Schroeder not only won the game that night against the Giants, but won four of the last five as the Redskins just missed the playoffs at 10-6.

7. Dwight Eisenhower: Broken Leg 1912. Ike was, according to written accounts, a very good football player at Army and competed that season against Jim Thorpe and the Carlisle Indians. Besides his Army commitment, there was no NFL for Eisenhower to go to. But is it possible the ending of his football career made him change his focus away from sports and more towards things like becoming a five-star general and President of the United States? Could President Eisenhower have wound up as Coach Eisenhower instead?

6. Chris Kelley: Three Torn ACLs 2000-02. Kelley may have been the best football player in the history of Montgomery County, quarterbacking Seneca Valley to three Maryland State titles and a 39-0 record. He first tore his left ACL in a summer all-star game and redshirted his freshman year at the University of Maryland. He tore the same ACL just before his first year of eligibility, but managed to play in two games in 2001. Just when it looked like he'd turned the corner and was ready to live up to his great promise, Kelley tore his right ACL in a 2002 spring game. Amazingly he rehabbed in time for fall practice, but didn't have the same zip and was beaten out by Scott McBrien. Kelley switched to safety for his last two years and started as a fifth-year senior. His request for a sixth year of eligibility was turned down by the NCAA. After being cut by the Ravens late in training camp in 2005, Kelley's football career ended. Without the ACLs, who knows.

5. Chris Webber: Dislocated Shoulder 1995. After being named Rookie of the Year at Golden State at the end of the 1993-94 season, Webber let it be known he was unhappy with coach Don Nelson. That forced a trade to the Bullets early in the '94-95 season where he reunited with former Fab Five Michigan teammate Juwan Howard. Ironically in his first game back at Golden State, Webber dislocated his shoulder. He managed to finish the season without surgery. Despite being advised by a number of doctors to have the shoulder operated on in the off season, Webber finally found a physician who said he could do without it. He couldn't. Fifteen games in to the '95-96 season, the shoulder went out again and he was through for the year. That allowed Howard to (no pun intended) shoulder the load and he nearly took the Bullets to the playoffs. Now a free agent, Howard commanded enormous dollars. Following a lowball offer from the Bullets followed by a short stay in Miami, Howard wound up back in Washington after a commissioner's ruling for a contract that called for more than a hundred million dollars. It proved to be an albatross. He wasn't that good and it took years to unload Howard. Without Webber's injury, he might have wound up being paid for what he is, a complimentary player.

4. John "Hot Plate" Williams: Knee Injury 1989. He actually didn't pick up the "Hot Plate" nickname until he returned from the injury. It appeared he'd rehabbed at Burger King. Drafted with the 12th pick of the 1986 draft, Bullets' GM Bob Ferry declared that they'd just taken the next Magic Johnson. Not quite, but Williams was tracking to be an excellent player. He averaged 14 points and seven rebounds a game during the '88-89 season. But after returning from the injury, Williams played only 33 more games for the Bullets and eventually ate his way out of the NBA. Since the team had been built around him, it changed the Bullets' fortunes for many years.

3. Charley Taylor: Broken Ankle 1971. The Redskins were the talk of the NFL at the start of the '71 season. Their 5-0 start put them on the cover of *Newsweek* with George Allen's famous saying, "The future is now." But in the sixth game of the year at Kansas City, Taylor's ankle snapped while being tackled in the end zone by future Hall of Famer Emmitt Thomas. The Redskins not only lost that game, but went 1-2-1 over the next four without their own future Hall of Famer. The offense just wasn't the same. They did get into the playoffs at 10-4, but lost in the first round at San Francisco. The Skins made it to the Super Bowl the following season with Taylor back, but several players have said the '71 team with Taylor was actually a better team

2. Sonny Jurgensen: Torn Achilles 1972. Even though he was 38, Sonny had it going early in the season with two things he'd been missing most of his career; a running game and a defense. Larry Brown would go on to win the rushing title and George Allen's "Over the Hill Gang" defense was among the best in football. Off a win over Dallas, the Skins were 5-1 and beating the Giants at Yankee Stadium when Sonny stepped in a hole and tore his Achilles, finishing his season. Billy Kilmer was good enough to roll up an 11-3 record, two playoff wins and a trip to the Super Bowl, but he wasn't good enough to overcome Miami's "No Name" defense shutting down his running game in Super Bowl VII. With Sonny's arm, who knows. We might still be waiting for an undefeated team.

1. Tim Strachan: Broken Neck 1993. Although Tim is an amazing story of triumph over tragedy, we'll always wonder what he might have become as a football player. Strachan was heading into his senior year at DeMatha High School and was rated among the top quarterbacks in the country with names like Peyton Manning and Donovan McNabb. After a game of beach volleyball, he dove into the surf and broke his neck. Although he was left a quadriplegic, both Maryland and Penn State said they would honor the full scholarship offers he'd been given. Tim accepted the Maryland offer and graduated on time while working as an assistant coach with the football team. He went on to become an accomplished radio analyst for the team and graduate from Georgetown Law School. He is now married with a young son.

10. Ernie Davis. The former Syracuse University running back and 1961 Heisman Trophy winner was the Redskins number-one draft choice in 1962, the first overall pick. He also would have been the first African-American player on the team until team owner George Preston Marshall traded him to the Cleveland Browns for Bobby Mitchell, who became Washington's first black player and eventually made the Pro Football Hall of Fame. Davis was diagnosed with leukemia before the now defunct college All-Star game in 1962 and never played a down in the NFL, dying at age 23 on May 18, 1963.

9. George Allen. The former Redskins coach revitalized professional football in the Nation's Capital and was best known for his defensive genius, his quirky sayings— "The future is now"; "losing is like death"—and his penchant for keeping old veterans and trading away rookie draft choices. He took the team, known as The Over The Hill Gang, to its first Super Bowl, a 14-7 loss to Miami after the 1972 season, and was fired following the 1977 season. After a three-week stint as head coach of the Rams in 1978, he was fired there, too, and never coached again in the NFL. He died at the age of 72 on December 31, 1990 from ventricular fibrillation after collapsing in his California home. He had been doused with a Gatorade victory bath following a season-ending win by his Long Beach State team in the last game of the season and caught a chill that worsened over the next few weeks and ultimately led to his death.

8. Marvin "Bubby" Worsham. One of the most promising young golfers ever to play in the Washington area, he was killed at age 22 in a car accident on October 22, 1950 while a senior at Wake Forest University. Worsham roomed with fellow Wake golfer Arnold Palmer, who was so distraught over his friend's death that he temporarily gave up golf and joined the Coast Guard. An annual local junior golf tournament, the Bubby Worsham Memorial, has been held in his honor since 1951.

7. Pete Wysocki. A Redskins linebacker and special teams standout, Wysocki died at age 53 after a long battle with non-Hodgkins lymphoma on June 14, 2003. Wysocki came to the Redskins from the Canadian Football League and quickly became one of the more popular players in the locker room, mostly because of his rapier wit and classic imitations of his teammates, coaches and Hollywood celebrities. After his retirement, he became a successful commercial real estate salesman who kept his competitive juices flowing racing motorcycles until a few weeks before his death.

6. Harold McLinton. Another Redskins linebacker in the George Allen era, McLinton was known as "Tank" to his teammates because of his muscular build and 240-pound frame. He manned the middle linebacker spot and played from 1969 through 1978. He was killed at the age of 33 on October 31, 1980, when he was hit by a car as he stood on the side of Interstate 295 in the District. One of his children, Kevin McLinton, went on to become a starting point guard for the University of Maryland basketball team.

5. Jerry Smith. Known as the "Peach from Long Beach," the former Redskins tight end died at age 43 from complications of AIDS on October 15, 1986. Smith played for the Redskins from 1965 to 1977 and was considered one of the finest pass-catching tight ends in the game. He was believed to be the first NFL player to die from AIDS, and while he never publicly discussed his homosexuality, his friend and former teammate, Dave Kopay, who had come out of the closet years earlier, confirmed Smith had been one of the NFL's gay players.

4. Vince Lombardi. The Hall of Fame coach of the Green Bay Packers stunned the football world when he left that organization to coach the woebegone Redskins in 1969. Washington finished 8-8 in his first and only season, but Lombardi was diagnosed with colon cancer the following summer, succumbing on September 3, 1970, after several weeks at Georgetown University Hospital. Doctors said Lombardi, who died at age 57, likely would have lived years longer if he hadn't always refused routine colonoscopy procedures to detect the disease.

3. Glenn Brenner. One of the most popular sportscasters in Washington history, Brenner was diagnosed with a terminal brain tumor shortly after he had competed in the 1991 Marine Corps Marathon and died at age 44 on January 14, 1992. He had joined Channel 9, the Washington CBS affiliate, in 1977 and battled George Michael, on the NBC owned station, for ratings supremacy in the market for most of his 14 years on the air. He was best known for his offbeat interviews, self-deprecating humor and hysterically funny sportscasts, including a popular "Weenie of the Week" feature.

2. Sean Taylor. The Washington Redskins Pro Bowl safety from the University of Miami was enjoying the best season of his four-year career when he was shot and killed during a robbery attempt at his Miami-area home on December 3, 2007. Taylor, a fierce hitter considered the most gifted athlete on the team, was rehabilitating a knee injury he suffered three weeks earlier and was expected to return to the field late in the 2007 season. Intruders broke into his house and he was shot in the groin area and died from massive bleeding when the bullet ripped his femoral artery. He was 24.

1. Len Bias. The University of Maryland All-American basketball player died at age 23 from a cocaine overdose on June 19, 1986, only two days after the Boston Celtics had made him their No. 1 choice and the second-overall pick in the 1986 college draft. Many NBA observers, including then team president Red Auerbach, who made the pick, felt Bias's death set the team's fortunes back for years and Celtics star Larry Bird called it "the cruelest thing I've ever heard." His controversial death also resulted in a major overhaul of the Maryland athletic department, including the eventual dismissal of longtime head coach Lefty Driesell.

For fans a championship season is unforgettable, even though coaches will tell you that the losses stay with you longer than the wins. Here are 10 seasons which, for the men who coached them, were unforgettable. For the fans, very forgettable.

10. 1998 Redskins, 6-10. While the record may not seem historically bad, the way the season unfolded was. General manager Charley Casserly had beefed up the defense before the season by signing NFL defensive MVP Dana Stubblefield as a free agent and dealing for the number-one pick of the 1993 draft, Dan "Big Daddy" Wilkinson. Casserly pretty much guaranteed a spot in the playoffs with the moves, but the season started badly and got worse. Coach Norv Turner benched starting quarterback Gus Frerote in the season-opening loss at New York (Giants) and during a 41-7 loss at Minnesota to drop the Skins to 0-7; Darrell Green was seen crying on the bench. Somehow they managed to win six of their last nine and Turner saved his job, mainly because owner John Kent Cooke was distracted while unsuccessfully trying to hang on to the team.

9. 1988-89 Maryland Basketball, 9-20. This was mercifully the last year of the Bob Wade era. Wade, who had no college coaching experience, was hired in the wake of the death of Len Bias and the ouster of Lefty Driesell and proved to be in over his head. The team was a reasonable 6-5 heading into ACC play, which proved to be a disaster. They won only one conference game, 98-87 over Clemson at Cole Field House. Incredibly, after losing their two regular-season games to North Carolina State by margins of 23 and 17, they clobbered the Wolfpack 71-49 in the opening round of the ACC tournament. That would be Wade's last hurrah. He was fired after a 30-point loss to North Carolina in round two.

8. 2003 Redskins, 5-11. In a bizarre five-minute news conference the day after the season ended, Steve Spurrier said, "Well we wound up 5-11, not the best, but not the worst." Two days later Spurrier phoned in his resignation from the golf course. Truthfully he'd lost interest in coaching in the NFL long before that, possibly when owner/general manager Dan Snyder cut his beloved former Gator, Danny Wuerffel, before the season started. The season had actually started with great promise. After wins over the Jets and Falcons, they lost in overtime to the Giants and then beat the Patriots to go 3-1. New England wouldn't lose again until the following season. The Redskins, however, would go 2-12 the rest of the way. The final win, 20-7 over the Giants at the Meadowlands, was highlighted by Bruce Smith breaking Reggie White's sack record by bringing down "The Bachelor" Jessie Palmer.

7. 1963 Senators, 56-106. The season opened with 43,000 in the stands at two-year old D.C. Stadium and President Kennedy throwing out the first ball. That's about as good as it got. The Orioles won the game 3-1 and Senators starter Don Rudolph absorbed the first of his 19 losses that season. Tom Cheney wound up with the best record on the staff at 8-9. Not only did the Senators finish in dead last, the headline on the team's yearbook the following season read, "Off the Floor In 64."

6. 1994 Redskins, 3-13. It wasn't pretty to watch, but it was a season you could have braced for. Rookie coach Norv Turner still had a sparkling reputation from his days as offensive coordinator in Dallas and the rebuilding year figured to be part of the short-term pain for the long-term gain. Norv's new team proved to be no match for his old team, losing by scores of 34-7 and 31-7, but the Cowboys were two-time defending champs. The worst part of the season was the story of bust-to-be Heath Shuler being written. Shuler, the third pick of the draft, threw six interceptions in an overtime loss to Arizona. The following week he was replaced by seventh-rounder Gus Frerote, who wound up as NFC offensive player of the week after a stunning 41-27 upset of the Colts in Indianapolis.

5. 2000-01 Wizards, 19-63. This was Michael Jordan's first full season as president of the Wizards. His grand plan was to hire a college coach with no NBA experience and mold him into his vision of what an NBA coach should be. After insulting St. John's coach Mike Jarvis with a lowball offer, Jordan managed to get Leonard Hamilton to buy his way out of the University of Miami. Hamilton proved to be in over his head with troublesome veterans like Rod Strickland and Tyrone Nesby (who once had to be removed from the Wizards bench by MCI Center security guards). When he did bother to show up and watch this mess, Jordan was apparently sickened enough to decide to suit up the following season. He fired Hamilton less than an hour after the final game of the season, pulled on his long shorts again and tabbed his old Bulls coach Doug Collins for the 2001-2002 season.

4. 1971-72 Georgetown Basketball, 3-23. With no Big East or big television money on the line, pressure to win basketball games in those days was relatively low. Still, even Georgetown had its limit with sixth-year coach John Magee. Two years earlier, he'd taken the Hoyas to the National Invitational Tournament and lost a one-point game to Pete Maravich and LSU. But that seemed like ancient history when this team lost the second game of the season at home to St. John's by 40. They even lost a home game to Assumption. Magee was fired at the end of the season and new coach John Thompson was told, "It would be nice if we could make the NIT every once in a while." He did, with a National Title and a few Final Fours thrown in.

3. 1961 Redskins, 1-12-1. If ever a record was deserved, this was it. This was the last all-white team in NFL history. Owner George Preston Marshall had refused to add a black player to the roster for fear it would hurt his ratings on the television network he'd strung together for his games in the south. They were shut out three times, including a 53-0 debacle at Yankee Stadium to the Giants. The only team they didn't lose to was second-year expansion team Dallas. The Skins started 0-9 before a 28-28 tie at Dallas and took an 0-12-1 mark into the season finale against the Cowboys at D.C. Stadium. Tackle Fran O'Brien said when they walked off the field with a 34-24 win, "It felt like we had won the Super Bowl."

2. 1988-89 George Washington Basketball, 1-27. After three years on the job at GW, coach John Kuester's record was a very mediocre 35-50 heading into the 1988-89 season. If you wondered why he was still there to start the season, you had to be amazed that he was still employed at the end of the season. Without a midseason win over Massachusetts, this would have been an 0-for. The Colonials were reasonably competitive in most games, which is probably why they decided to give Kuester another year. But despite his best year—14-17 with a win over St. Bonaventure in the Atlantic 10 Tournament—Kuester was fired at the end of the season and replaced by Mike Jarvis.

1. 1974-75 Capitals, 8-67-5. We were just happy to have a hockey team so the record was somewhat irrelevant, but these guys were historically bad. Outside of Yvon Labre, this was an expansion collection of has-beens and never-weres. Labre was the first Capital to have his number retired—more than anything, for enduring this kind of embarrassment. They went through three coaches, Jimmy Anderson (4-45-5), Red Sullivan (2-16) and Milt Schmidt (2-6). After losing games on the road with scores like 12-1 at Boston and Pittsburgh and 10-0 at Montreal, Schmidt led them to their only road victory of the year, 5-3 at the California Golden Seals on March 28. After the game one of the players wrote in magic marker on a trash can, "Stanley Cup," and the players paraded it around the locker room.

Often when looking back you might say to yourself, "Yeah I can see how that happened." But at the time, it knocked your socks off. Here are 11 that had us saying at the time, "Oh my God!"

10. Redskins Hire Jim Zorn as Head Coach, February 9, 2008. Redskins owner Dan Snyder had taken more than a month to make his fifth head coaching move in eight years. True, the second retirement of Joe Gibbs had caught him off guard, but no one had expected the search to take this long. Several of the candidates who had been through Snyder's lengthy interview process had suggested Zorn be their offensive coordinator, even though he'd never risen above the level of quarterbacks coach in the NFL. Still, Snyder made the unusual move of hiring Zorn as OC while still conducting his head coaching search. Zorn started work at Redskins Park, even though he didn't know who he'd be working for. After the Super Bowl, once Giants' offensive coordinator Steve Spagnolo turned down the job, it was assumed that former Giants' head coach Jim Fassel would be named within days. But early on a Saturday evening, the Skins confirmed that Zorn would be their head coach. Snyder, who had made previous splashes with Marty Schotteheimer, Steve Spurrier and the return of the great Joe Gibbs, really snuck this one under the radar.

9. Raiders 38 – Redskins 9 SBXVIII, January 22, 1984. This game was going to be the final crowning of one of the great teams of all time. With a Super Bowl win over Miami the year before followed by a record-setting offensive year (561 points), the Redskins would take their place with the Packers and Steelers as the only teams to win back-to-back Super Bowls. Wrote Thomas Boswell in the *Washington Post* the morning of the game, "Add it all up and what you have is a two-touchdown or more victory by the Redskins. Their mastery of the Raiders will be even more convincing than their defeat of the Dolphins a year ago. The general perception that the Redskins and Raiders are evenly matched is a delusion. The Redskins are one of the better teams in NFL history; the Raiders are not." Maybe not. The Raiders' 29-point margin of victory was, to that point, the largest in Super Bowl history.

8. Unversity of Maryland's 2001 Football Team. In the 10 seasons before the hiring of Ralph Friedgen, Maryland had just one winning season (6-5 in 1995) and no bowl appearances. The hope was that Friedgen could build up the recruiting base and somehow get the Terps to a bowl in a year or two. There were few expectations for his first year on the job. Well, after giving up a touchdown on the first defensive play of the season to North Carolina, Maryland went on to win the game 23-7 and didn't lose until nearly two months later. They finished the regular season 10-1, losing only at Florida State, and captured their first ACC championship in 16 years. The title carried an automatic spot in a BCS Bowl. And despite being overmatched by faster Florida in the Orange Bowl, Friedgen was named National Coach of the Year and overnight a football program to be proud of was born.

7. Redskins Hire Marty Schottenheimer as Head Coach, January 3, 2001. Marty had spent two seasons on TV as an analyst for ESPN, where he had made it quite clear he wasn't interested in the Redskins job. He said, "I could never work for an owner like Dan Snyder." So when he in fact decided to do so, it caught many of us off guard. After one dinner with Snyder, Marty was convinced that "Dan just wants to win." And Snyder helped convince him with a five-year contract worth more than 20 million dollars with complete control. Snyder wanted to win, but not with Marty in complete control. A week after his first season ended, Marty was fired.

6. Allen Iverson Is This Good, Summer 1994. Iverson's name had been in the news. He had been jailed during his senior year of high school in Hampton, Virginia, after being arrested in a bowling alley melee. After four months in prison, he was released by Governor Douglas Wilder and his record was expunged. Still, despite eye-opening football and basketball talent, he was considered a risky recruit. John Thompson took him at Georgetown after Iverson's mother came to him and said, "Please save my son." The first glimpse of AI came during a Kenner League summer game at McDonough gym. There were no television cameras to record it, but people who saw it could not believe their eyes. Word spread on the sports talk shows that this was an unbelievable talent. Which is something the rest of the country soon found out.

5. Senators Hire Ted Williams as Manager, February 21, 1969. Bob Short, who was sort of the Dan Snyder of his day, bought the Senators for $9 million late in 1968. He immediately fired general manager George Selkirk and manager Jim Lemon. When first approached by Short about becoming manager, Williams, who had been retired as a player for nearly 10 years, said he was happy fishing. Apparently not happy enough to not take the bait Short dropped in the water. Williams signed a five-year deal that included the title Vice President with an option to purchase a share of the team and move to the front office if he didn't like managing. Having a living legend in charge of one of the worst teams in baseball changed our outlook. Short's slogan for the 1969 season was, "A Whole New Ballgame."

4. Redskins Hire Vince Lombardi as Head Coach, February 7, 1969. Not only did it happen two weeks before Ted Williams was hired by the Senators, Lombardi had been there, done that with coaching. After winning his second-straight Super Bowl and fifth championship in seven years with the Packers, Lombardi had retired a year earlier to concentrate on being Green Bay's general manager. Although Lombardi missed the sidelines, it took Skins owner Edward Bennett Williams offering a piece of the team to make it happen. After stumbling through a dozen non-winning seasons, the greatest coach in the history of the game was coming to Washington. Wow!

3. Joe Gibbs Retires as Head Coach of the Redskins, March 5, 1993.

See the following #3.

3. Joe Gibbs Is Re-hired as Head Coach of the Redskins, January 8, 2004.
It's hard to break the tie of where each of these events ranks on the stun meter. Gibbs was only 52 when he retired and with four Super Bowl appearances and three championships. He had reached the lofty Don Shula level where he could have stayed forever. It also stunned us because it happened almost two months after the season had ended. The re-hiring caused just as much of a stir because, after 11 years out of the game, we thought he had reached the point of no return. With only one playoff appearance in the years he'd been gone, it was if the Messiah had returned.

2. George Mason Advances to the Final Four, March 2006.
This was a George Mason team that many college basketball experts said didn't belong in the NCAA tournament in the first place. They had lost in the first round of the Colonial Athletic Association tournament. The CAA is considered a one-bid league and if there was one team from the conference that deserved an at-large bid, some thought, it was Hofstra. But Mason got in and refused to leave. They upset three of the previous six nationalchampions—Michigan State, North Carolina, and Connecticut—on their way to reaching the unthinkable. Even though they were clobbered by eventual champion Florida in the Final Four, it was an unforgettable ride for the first mid-major to get that far.

1. Len Bias Dies, June 19, 1986.
Just two days after being chosen as the second pick of the NBA draft by the Boston Celtics, Bias dropped dead in a University of Maryland dorm room. It was unthinkable that one of the strongest and best athletes in the country could die at the age of 22. We didn't know until weeks later that Bias had died of a cocaine overdose. The effects of his death are still felt today and changed the fortunes of the entire Maryland athletic program for many years to come.

Note: Carol Maloney has been with Comcast SportsNet since 2001 as an anchor and reporter. Yes she's very attractive. No she's not available. Carol is happily married with two young sons and is quite an athlete herself. She was a varsity basketball player at Drake University and still plays in the Catholic nursery school mom's league. A couple of years ago Carol tore her Achilles executing a tomahawk dunk (well maybe it was just a regular dunk). Anyway, despite nearly 30 years of women reporters working in locker rooms, Neanderthal athlete attitudes apparently haven't changed. Carol has compiled a list of lines that she's heard and heard about from her female colleagues.

8. "What's your story?" It's subtle, yet direct. Women know what the athlete really wants to know, but it's easy to back off if early indications point to rejection. It's like the line, "Do you want to dance?" "No? I mean, you look fat in those pants."

7. "I want to make love to you." One of my personal favorites. It gets right to the point. A number of my female reporting friends have heard this one directly. Sidney Ponson (former Orioles pitcher) is the only one we know of in this area to say it in the middle of the interview. Never mind that the lights were on, the camera was rolling and the photographer was right there. Now that's classy.

6. "Let's make babies." Another direct shot. My tall (6 ft.) Comcast colleague Keli Johnson has heard this one. I haven't heard this one directly. Maybe they're looking for height in this odd proposed reproductive game.

5. "I'll do a post-game interview with you, but only while we shower together." Whether it's a four RBI night or 0-for-four, no matter. Media-shy Marty Cordova (former Oriole) knew what the answer would be. Hence, no interviews. But we are all impressed with his commitment to hygiene.

4. "Can I at least have a fake number?" One of the many opening lines by Caps center Brooks Laich. He says he always gets a laugh. But I imagine sweet, genuine Brooks has no trouble meeting women, especially after he takes his shirt off.

3. "You can do better." A pick-up line list isn't complete without this gem. But learn from one athlete's misfortune. Make sure the woman in question ISN'T out with her brother that night.

2. "I'm 7-feet and I'm proportional. Think about it!" This basketball player's bold statement was never confirmed by friends or relatives (thank goodness).

1. "Come hither." It's a complete strikeout on women reporters, but not the gorgeous ladies known to hang outside locker rooms. I guess that's why they call them "play-ahs!"

The Top 10 Ways Sports Have Changed for Women
:: Christine Brennan

Note: Nearly 30 years after graduating from Northwestern, Christine Brennan has seen major changes in the role of women in the sports world, and she has helped to affect some of those changes. When Brennan was named to cover the top sports beat for the *Washington Post*—the Redskins in 1984—coach Joe Gibbs wrote a letter to the NFL asking that women not be allowed in the locker room. The request was denied. It was another wall knocked down, with many more falling in the following years. As a reporter for the *Post*, commentator for ABC News, ESPN and NPR, and columnist for *USA Today*, Brennan has covered most of the major stories in sports with particular focus on the Olympics. From the perspective of one of the top women in the business, here are the top 10 changes she's seen for women in her field—on the field and off the field.

10. It's a Girl. Dads used to wince. Now they go out and buy a baseball mitt. Those same fathers become the biggest advocates for Title IX (the law requiring gender equity in school-sports funding), which has changed the playing fields of America and allowed the other half of our population to learn about teamwork, sportsmanship, winning and losing at a young age.

9. No Football, But a Full Rose Bowl. The Rose Bowl is filled to capacity not for a college football game, but for a women's soccer match. I can't believe I just wrote that sentence. The 1999 Women's World Cup becomes a sensation in Washington, Pasadena, and everywhere else that the U.S. women's national soccer team plays. When Brandi Chastain whips off her shirt in celebration after the winning penalty kick, she and her teammates make the cover of *Time*, *Newsweek*, *People* and *Sports Illustrated*. No story ever has made those four covers in the same week.

8. Language. This has changed slowly. Newspapers and other media outlets begin using the adjective "men's" because women are playing too: men's and women's basketball, men's and women's lacrosse, men's and women's soccer, etc. Coverage of girl's high school sports rightly explodes; for prep athletes, the adjectives are "boys" and "girls."

7. "Can Boys Be Sportswriters, Too?" A question actually asked to a sportswriter mom. Boys wear Mia Hamm jerseys. Male golf fans flock to watch one-time teen sensation Michelle Wie hit the ball 300 yards.

6. Figure Skating's Rise and Fall. It now has miniscule ratings, but it was once the most popular sport on TV for women and girls. Bring back Tonya Harding.

5. Professional Women's Teams in D.C. The WNBA's Mystics and the WUSA's (now WPS's) Freedom. They don't draw huge crowds, but they give girl athletes a chance to see female role models playing a professional sport.

4. It's Not So Lonely Out Here. Once upon a time, I was the first woman to cover the Redskins. Now, women are covering all of D.C.'s teams, including the Redskins, for TV, radio and print. And equal access to locker rooms, once a huge issue, has been resolved for decades.

3. TV Choices. ESPN and other networks cover women's sports, from basketball to softball, golf to tennis. You can be channel surfing on a weekend and run across 3-4 women's games or events. That wasn't happening 25 years ago—then again, there were only 3-4 channels 25 years ago.

2. Her Name is Sam. Tiger Woods's first child is a girl. Perhaps she will be the first female member of Augusta National.

1. The Boss Is a Woman. Susan O'Malley ran the Bullets/Wizards for years, Sheila Johnson owns the Mystics, Debbie Yow runs the very successful University of Maryland athletic department as Athletic Director.

My Favorite Stats :: Chuck "Stats" Sapienza

Note: A longtime D.C.-area radio producer, he's sometimes called "Statsienza." Now the producer of the *John Thompson Show* on Sportstalk 980, Chuck has made a name for himself by providing the station staff weekly stats nuggets. Here are his top 10 favorite Washington sports stats.

10. The Redskins, Caps, and Wizards/Bullets collectively have never each won a playoff series (or in the Redskins case, a playoff game) in the same season.

9. Washington has not had a first-place baseball team at the end of a season since 1933.

8. Since 1943, the Redskins, Caps, Senators/Nationals, and Bullets/Wizards have collectively won four championships in 172 total seasons. D.C. United has won four championships in their first 13 years of existence.

7. In his first go-round as head coach of the Redskins, Joe Gibbs was famous for putting away games with leads by pounding the ball and killing the clock. In his last 23 losses, Gibbs had the lead in 19 of them. He lost the ability to close.

6. The Bullets' four first-round picks from 1983 to '86 were Jeff Malone, Mel Turpin, Kenny Green, and John "Hot Plate" Williams. Only Jeff Malone was a big contributor, but they passed over Clyde Drexler to get him. For the other three, they passed on John Stockton, Karl Malone, and Scott Skiles.

5. Over the course of six seasons, Maryland, northern Virginia, and D.C. sent teams to the Final Four: Maryland (2002), George Mason (2006), and Georgetown (2007).

4. John Thompson Jr. (Georgetown 1982, '84, and '85) and John Thompson III (Georgetown 2007) are the only father-son combination to coach teams to a Final Four.

3. Darrell Green and Art Monk became Hall of Famers exactly 25 years after the last time Redskin teammates went to Canton together. Sonny Jurgensen and Bobby Mitchell made it in 1983.

2. Wilt Chamberlain's 100-point game against the Knicks in 1962 broke the NBA record for most points in a game by 29. The old record was held by former Spingarn High School star Elgin Baylor. Playing for the Lakers on November 15, 1960, he scored 71, also against the Knicks.

1. In 1913, Walter Johnson not only went 36-7 with a 1.14 ERA and led the American League with 29 complete games, he also went 346 innings without committing an error. Johnson also had more strikeouts than hits allowed (243-232) and won the pitching triple crown. The Big Train also hit two homers, tying him for third on the Senators.

The Top 10 Who Wore the Top 10 Numbers

Single-digit numbers have become popular in basketball in recent years and have always been popular in baseball (see Babe Ruth #3). Keeping in mind that baseball players didn't start wearing numbers until 1929 and that Washington didn't have a baseball team between 1972 and 2005, here are the top players in all sports who wore numbers one through 10.

#10. Earl Monroe and Bobby Dandridge (tie). Ok, we're starting with a copout. We're supposed to pick one guy for each number, but hear us out on this one. Monroe, who had his number retired by the Wizards during the 2007-2008 season, was foolishly traded to the Knicks before the team moved to Washington for the 1973-74 season. That move certainly stunted their development. Dandridge, although he arrived here late in his career, proved to be the missing piece of the puzzle and helped the Bullets win their only title in 1978.

#9. Sonny. Any argument? We didn't think so.

#8. Alexander Ovechkin. Yeah we know he's only played a few years, but this kid looks like the real deal. He is both the present and future of the Washington Capitals. And what the heck, Paul Casanova was the only other logical choice, a .225 lifetime hitter for the old Senators.

#7. Joe Theismann. The only player ever to wear that number for the Redskins and although he's not likely headed to Canton, is likely the last Redskin to wear it. In 2002 new coach Steve Spurrier tried to hand number seven to his boy Danny Wuerffel. Major public outcry. Woeful Wuerffel took 17.

#6. Mike Epstein and Mike Riordan (tie). Maybe our ethnicity got in the way on this one (Pollin and Shapiro). In a less politically correct time, Epstein was called "Super Jew" when he played first base for the Senators in the late 60s. He hit 30 home runs in 1969 and 20 more in 1970. Riordan came to the Baltimore Bullets with Dave Stallworth in the terribly lopsided deal for Earl Monroe. He wasn't a great athlete, but had great smarts. Thanks to being on the receiving end of Wes Unseld's tremendous outlet passes, Riordan averaged more than 15 points a game on the Bullets team that made it to the finals in 1975.

#5. Rod Langway. One of three numbers ever retired by the Capitals. Langway was the first truly great player in franchise history and helped take them to their first postseason appearance in 1983. One of the best defensemen ever to play the game, Langway won the Norris Trophy in '83 and '84. He was inducted into the Hockey Hall of Fame in 2002.

#4. Moses Malone. Yes he was past his prime by the time he became a Bullet in 1986, but Moses was still a workhorse who gave you a great effort every night. He averaged more than 22 points and 11 rebounds during his two years in Washington and made the All-Star team both years. And if they gave an award for shvitzing (sweating), Moses would have won that too. Those Bullet teams also had Gus Williams. Five years earlier we might have been talking dynasty with those two.

#3. Mark Moseley. The only kicker ever to win the NFL's MVP award. He made 23 consecutive field goals during the 1982 season. The photo of Moseley hugging his holder, Joe Theismann, after a game-winner in the snow against the Giants to clinch a playoff spot is one for the ages.

#2. Ken McMullen. An excellent third baseman who was a throw-in from the Dodgers in the deal to bring in Frank Howard for Claude Osteen. McMullen hit .272 in 1969, which enabled the Senators to deal him for Aurelio Rodriguez the following season. Rodriguez would have been one of the building blocks of an up and coming young team, except that stooge Bob Short sent him to Detroit with Ed Brinkman and Joe Coleman for over the hill Denny McLain and hastened the team's departure to Texas. Oy!

#1. Kevin Porter. Actually wore number 10 when he led the NBA in assists with 650 during the 1974-75 season with the Washington Bullets. However Porter was unfairly blamed for the Bullets being swept by Golden State in the 1975 finals. He was then shipped to Detroit for the over the hill Dave Bing. After some terrific years in Detroit, Porter returned to finish his career in Washington (which is when he wore number 1) and again led the NBA in assists during the 1980-81 season.

Yes, many of the best football players were off fighting World War II that year, but the greatest player in Redskins history still deserves plenty of credit for what may be the most complete season in NFL history. Baugh led the league in passing, punting, and interceptions. Here are the top ten numbers from that season. .

10. 10 games. Baseball got credit for staying afloat during the war with encouragement from President Roosevelt, but the NFL with fewer resources did almost as well by playing close to a full schedule.

9. 3 straight losses to end the regular season. And yet, the Skins made the playoffs. After a 21-7 win over the Bears, their record was 6-0-1 with the only blemish a 14-14 tie with the Steagles (the Eagles and Steelers combined team). They then proceeded to lose at home to the Steagles and dropped back-to-back games to the Giants at Yankee Stadium and Griffith Stadium. That forced a return to Yankee Stadium for a playoff which they won 28-0 before losing the championship game in Chicago 41-21.

8. 55.6 completion percentage. Nothing to write home about these days, but good enough to lead the league in '43. Baugh also was number one in attempts (239) and completions (133).

7. 45.9 yards per punt. Yes, some of those were quick kicks on third down, but one of them managed to go 81 yards.

6. 23 touchdown passes. Remember this was accomplished in only 10 games, on bad fields, and from only 239 attempts. So do the math: that's roughly one touchdown pass for every 10 attempts.

5. 11 interceptions. That's not how many Baugh threw; that's how many *he picked off*. He not only knew where to throw them but, while playing D, knew where to be when the other guy threw them.

4. 4 touchdown passes, 4 interceptions, a recovered fumble, and an 81-yard punt. Not season totals; this was one game! It happened November 14th in a 42-20 win over Detroit.

3. 78.0 quarterback rating. A middle-of-the-pack number these days, but good enough to lead the league in '43.

2. 6 touchdown passes in one game. Baugh set an NFL record in a 48-10 win over the Brooklyn Dodgers on Halloween.

1. 33. Not just famous on the Rolling Rock bottle, Baugh's jersey number is the only one officially retired by the Redskins.

Our 10 Favorite Amazing Walter Johnson Numbers

Walter Johnson may be the most underrated baseball star of all time, though many baseball experts regard him as the greatest right-handed pitcher of all time. His misfortune was pitching for mostly bad teams during his Washington Senators career from 1907-1927. Incredibly "The Big Train" wasn't named on ESPN's "Sportscentury" list of the top 50 athletes of the 20th century. And that list included a horse, Secretariat, that Tony Kornheiser had the chutzpah to vote number eight. Shirley Povich must have rolled over in his grave. Anyway, here are the top 10 knock-your-socks-off numbers from the pitcher good enough to have a high school named after him.

10. 21 years with the same team. A number of pitchers have gone that long or longer, but even in the days before free agency, pitchers changed teams. Johnson stayed and never complained even though he appeared in the postseason only twice, 1924 and '25, late in his career.

9. .235 career batting average. Johnson retired 46 years before the American League adopted the designated hitter rule, but he wouldn't have needed it. In an era when home runs were scarce, Johnson hit 24 for his career. Amazingly, at the age of 37 he hit .433. Six of his 42 hits that year were doubles.

8. 417 wins. The Hall of Fame standard is 300. Johnson sprinted past that number on teams that didn't win very many games.

7. 99 miles an hour. Scouts didn't have radar guns in those days, but we'll take the word of Shirley Povich who covered baseball for the *Washington Post* from 1923 to 1998 and said Johnson threw harder than anyone he ever saw.

6. .388 walks-to-strikeouts ratio. Johnson struck out 3,509 batters and walked only 1,363 over his career. Compare that to Nolan Ryan, who struck out 5,714 and walked 2,795 over his 27-year career for a ratio of .489.

5. 25 losses with a 2.22 ERA. In 1909, Johnson lost nearly twice as many as he won (13-25), but obviously from his earned run averaged, pitched well enough to win many more.

4. 36-7 in 1913. You could make the case that this was the greatest season ever for a starting pitcher. Eleven of those wins were by shutout. Johnson struck out 243 and walked only 38 (38!). His ERA was 1.14.

3. 369.2 innings, 0 home runs allowed, in 1916. Granted it was what's considered the dead-ball era, but talk about a record that will never be broken.

2. The original five selected for the opening of the Hall of Fame in Cooperstown in 1936 was made up of Johnson, Babe Ruth, Ty Cobb, Honus Wagner, and Christy Mathewson.

1. 110 career shutouts. Amazingly, 110 times, once the Senators put a run on the board, Johnson could say, "I'm good."

My All-Time Favorite Washington Senators
:: Thomas Boswell

Note: Thomas Boswell, a native of Washington, D.C. is one of the most decorated and literate baseball writers in the country. He grew up in Northeast Washington and spent many spring, summer, and fall days watching the old Washington Senators at Griffith Stadium, and then RFK. An Amherst graduate who played high school baseball at St. Stephens in Northern Virginia, he joined *The Washington Post* in 1969 and now is one of the paper's most popular sports columnists.

10. Dick Hyde. The Nats were always looking for "trick" pitchers that nobody else wanted. Submariners like Hyde and Ted Abernathy, or knuckleballers like Tom Chaney (who once struck out 21 men in a 15-inning game.) Hyde was the best of them—thin, slight, thick glasses and a 1.75 ERA in '58. The Nats always cornered the market on three-legged mules—lefthanded curveballers who had no fastball; ex-patriot Cubans who carried six-shooters with real bullets on road trips.

9. Camilo Pascual. The best right-handed curveball in baseball until Bert Blyleven came along. A genuine "ace" stuck on an awful team. You just counted his strikeouts because you knew the team would undermine him and lose half the time anyway. On Opening Day, he once struck out 15 Red Sox and won, but also gave up a legendary 500-foot home run to Ted Williams over the 438-foot sign on the high green wall in dead centerfield at Griffith Stadium where nobody thought anybody would ever hit a ball. It landed in a tree in somebody's backyard. At least that's the way I remember it. But I was a kid and it all existed at a semi-mythological level.

8. Bernie Allen. Stylish lefthanded-hitting second baseman—No. 7—who hit two line-drive outs in every game he ever played. Made great contact, but "hit 'em where they were." Typical cursed Nat, he'd been a quarterback at Purdue. "Watch," I'd tell whoever was with me at the game, "he's going to hit a nice line drive in the right-centerfield gap, but it will be caught on the run." And he would. World's best .239 career hitter—a perfect Senator.

7. Jim French. The Nats back-up catcher for seven years and a fan favorite. A poor man's Clint Courtney—and that is really poor. He was a five negative tool player: couldn't hit (career .196), hit for power (four homers), field, run, or throw. But he could hustle. Had a crew cut, ran around like crazy, got people cheering (out of pity), and made the greatest/worst catch of a foul pop—that he had already misjudged—that anybody ever saw. He produced a semi-famous photo—diving flat out backwards. Everybody remembers Jim French.

6. Jose Valdivielso and Zoilo (Zorro) Versalles. Both played shortstop for the Senators in '59 and '60. Only true native-born Washingtonians can spell both names. Versalles went to Minnesota and became the American League MVP in '65 and played in the World Series. By then, the "new" Nats were just as bad as the old Nats who had gone on to be great as the Twins.

5. Paul Casanova. To this day, the greatest throwing catcher I have ever seen. Better from his knees than most today are on their feet. Stood 6-foot-4 and, once in a while, hit a 420-foot line-drive home run. But, in six years as Nats catcher, he hit .225. Fans loved him. Like many Nats, he could do one thing well and nothing else at all. Dick Bosman said that "Cazzie" didn't call a very good game. "You'd look in for the sign and you could tell that Cazzie was thinking. You could see the wood burning."

4. Dick Bosman. A genuinely good pitcher for the last three Senators teams, going 42-33, including the '69 ERA title (2.19). Pitched a no-hitter, but not for Washington. Later, when he was a pitching coach, he became a friend and I learned the secret of his greatness. He cheated. He hid a tube of grease inside his glove with a tiny hole in the pocket. When he wanted to "load up," he just caught the throw from the catcher in the pocket, not the web, and "squirt," he had a perfect spitball. When someone yelled, "Boz," we'd both turn around.

3. Ted Williams. As manager in '69 he inspired the only winning Washington baseball team of my lifetime—86-76. Eventually the magic wore off, Teddy Ballgame got on the pitchers' nerves, and everybody left for Texas after '71. But for one season, Washington was in heaven. We had as slick-fielding an infield as anybody, with Ken McMullen at third base (87 RBI), great-glove-no-bat Eddie Brinkman at shortstop, Allen at second, Mike Epstein (30 homers) at first, and Casanova behind the plate. Frank Howard worshipped Williams, followed him around like a puppy and hit 48 homers. I later got to know Williams, but in '68 I was still in college and he was just a larger-than-life figure. Actually, a little too large. Williams was vain about his good looks and wore his Senators warmup jacket over his uniform even in the middle of the summer so fans wouldn't see how big his stomach had gotten.

2. Frank Howard. Drove me crazy as a player. Home run or nothing. Struck out a lot. Poor fielder. Hustled to (over) compensate. But his titanic home runs were our only real dignity in the expansion Senators period after the original Nats went to Minneapolis and became the Twins. After he retired, he became a minor league manager and I went to Spokane, Washington, to interview him for a few days. He treated me just the way he treated his players—as if we were all his long lost sons. Goofy, good-hearted guy. Took his players to a bar and said to them, "How are you going to wheel that lumber tomorrow if you don't pound that Budweiser tonight?" I always thought that might be The Secret of Life, or maybe what the Dalai Lama says when you finally get to the top of the mountain.

1. Roy (Squirrel) Sievers. My No. 1 sports hero. Got his '56 baseball card in one of the first packs I ever bought. The next year, when I was nine, he won the American League home run title just for me with 42, beating Ted Williams and Mickey Mantle. Modest man, perfect hero for a child. When they gave him a "night," he cried when then Vice President Richard Nixon introduced him. One night I went to Hechts department store with my mom to get his autograph. I got lost, and found the right place 15 minutes after Sievers was supposed to have left. Sievers had stayed until they found me. (Of course, my mom was pretty good looking.) I kept the two photos he autographed for years. Kept one in a drawer in perfect condition. Put the other on the wall and threw darts at it when he struck out on the radio. In the movie *Damn Yankees* you can see him twice. They used old movie clips of Sievers—No. 2—hitting home runs in Griffith Stadium and said it was "Joe Hardy." I always said of him, "The most beautiful right-handed batting stroke since Rogers Hornsby." Laid bat off, short, quick, smooth, effortless swing. Yes, I have a copy of the movie as well as all 16 of his Topps cards. Did a "Where Are They Now?" story on him when I was at the *Post*. Just as nice a guy as everybody said. He asked, "How's Bob Addie?"

The expansion Senators replaced the original Washington Senators who left for Minnesota after the 1960 season. Like their ancestors, the "fake" Senators (as old timers still refer to them), also left town. However, during their 11-year run (1961–1971) before leaving for Texas, they collected players who were better known for other things in other places.

10. Tom Brown (1963). Was the Opening-Day starting first baseman as President Kennedy threw out the first ball. That's as good as it got for the former two-sport star from the University of Maryland. After hitting .147 in '63, Brown gave up the game to give football a try. That worked out much better. Brown was a starting safety on Green Bay's first two Super Bowl teams. His interception of Dallas's Don Meredith in the 1966 NFL championship game sent the Packers to Super Bowl I.

9. Minnie Minoso (1963). An excellent player who is better known for playing in five decades as part of another Bill Veeck publicity stunt. After hitting .229 for the Senators, Minoso seemingly finished his career with the White Sox in 1964. That was until Veeck talked him into a comeback at age 50 for a few at-bats in 1976 and at a few more at age 54 in 1980. It made Minoso the only player to appear in the 40s, 50s, 60s, 70s and 80s.

8. Jim Piersall (1962-63). Best known as the subject of the biopic *Fear Strikes Out* starring Anthony Perkins as Piersall and the pre-"don't leave home without it" Karl Malden as his overbearing father. Piersall managed to hit for the expansion cycle in '63 playing for the Senators, Mets and Angels.

7. Lenny Randle (1971). Played in 75 games as a 22-year-old second baseman in his only season in Washington before leaving with the team for Texas. Randle had some solid seasons with the Rangers, but was pushed aside in spring training in 1977 for Bump Wills (the son of Washingtonian base-stealer supreme Maury Wills). When Randle didn't feel like he was getting enough love from manager Frank Luchessi, he punched his boss in the face. Needless to say, Randle was soon sent to Seattle.

6. John Roseboro (1970). Became the Dodgers' catcher after Roy Campanella's paralyzing car accident in 1957. "Rosie's" big moment in baseball history came on August 22, 1965. Giants ace Juan Marichal was at the plate and felt that Roseboro was firing his throws back to Sandy Koufax a little close to his head. A confrontation ensued with Marichal bopping Roseboro in the head with his bat. Roseboro received some stitches; Marichal got off with an eight-game suspension.

5. Zoilo Versalles (1969). Was the American League MVP in 1965 as the short-stop helped the Twins get to the World Series. Although his batting average of .273 that year didn't set any records, Versalles goes down in baseball history as the first Latin player to win the MVP.

4. Dallas Green (1965). Made his mark as manager of the Phillies, winning the World Series in 1980, but had a few decent years as a pitcher. Green appeared in six games for the Senators, but didn't figure in any decisions.

3. Don Zimmer (1963–65). A baseball lifer who finished his playing career in Washington. Even with that plate in his head, "Zim" was a solid third baseman in '64, hitting .246 with a dozen homers. He was much better at that than trading punches with Pedro Martinez.

2. Bill "Moose" Skowron (1964). Only played 73 games for the Senators, but did so after an almost equally brief stop with the Dodgers in 1963. However, he stayed in Los Angeles long enough to appear in an episode of *Mister Ed*. It was the one where Ed slides his hoof across the plate in time to beat the throw. "Moose" had his best years as a first baseman on the great Yankee teams of the late 50s and early 60s.

1. Curt Flood (1971). One of the most important figures in sports history. Flood challenged baseball's reserve clause after being traded by the St. Louis Cardinals to the Philadelphia Phillies. Although he lost, the case went all the way to the United States Supreme Court and paved the way for free agency in all professional sports. Out of baseball for over a year and needing money in 1971, Flood was lured back into the game by Senators owner Bob Short. Flood's stay turned out to be short. With only seven hits in 35 at-bats, Flood quit for good after only 13 games.

Note: Tim grew up in a baseball-loving family in Bethesda with two older brothers who played baseball at Catholic University. Tim was himself an outstanding basketball and baseball player at (naturally) Walter Johnson High School, where he also wrote for the school newspaper, *The Pitch*. After graduating from the University of Maryland, he worked at the *Washington Star* until it folded in 1981. Tim then began a long career covering baseball in Dallas and Baltimore before landing at *Sports Illustrated*. He made the move to ESPN in 1997, where he has become one of the most respected and knowledgeable baseball reporters in the business. Tim is a baseball historian and a Hall of Fame voter. His recent book, *Is This a Great Game or What?*, demonstrates his love of baseball. Here is the Gaithersburg resident's list of the top 10 area natives who made it to the major leagues.

10. Clay Kirby P (Padres 1969-73, Reds 1974-75, Expos 1976). Born in Washington, D.C. and raised in northern Virginia, Kirby managed to win 75 major league games despite playing for some pretty awful teams in the early years of the expansion Padres. He died in Arlington in 1991.

9. Sonny Jackson SS/OF (Colt 45's/Astros 1963-67, Braves 1968-74). Signed with the Colt 45's after graduating from Blair High School in 1963. In 1966, Jackson finished second in the Rookie of the Year voting when he hit .292 and stole 49 bases for the Astros. He retired with a .251 lifetime batting average.

8. Johnny Klippstein P (8 teams including the 1961 Senators). Born in Washington, D.C. in 1927, he appeared in 42 games for the expansion Senators, wining two and losing two. The righthander won 101 games over an 18-year career.

7. Gordy Coleman 1B (Indians 1959, Reds 1960-67). Born in Rockville in 1934 when the city streets were dirt roads. Coleman was big for his day at 6-foot-2, 218 pounds. He had a .273 career batting average and had seasons of 26 and 28 homers. Coleman was elected to the Reds Hall of Fame.

6. Steve Barber P (Several teams over 15 years including the Orioles for seven). Born in Takoma Park in 1938, Barber pitched for Blair High School before signing with Baltimore. He won 121 major league games, including 20 in 1963. He was on the starting staff of the 1966 World Champion Orioles.

5. Paul Hines OF (20 years with various teams. Finished with the Senators in 1891). Was born in northern Virginia in 1855 and died in Hyattsville in 1935. Hines had a career batting average of .301.

4. Lu Blue 1B (13 years with the Tigers, Browns, White Sox, and Dodgers). Blue was born in D.C. in 1897 and died in Alexandria in 1958. Over his major league career from 1921 to 1933, he hit .287 with 1,696 hits.

3. Doc White P (Athletics 1901-02, White Sox 1903-13). Born in Washington, D.C., White attended Georgetown University before signing with the Philadelphia Athletics. He won 27 games for the 1907 White Sox and finished his career with 187 wins and a 2.39 ERA. White died in Silver Spring just short of his 90th birthday in 1969.

2. Don Money 3B (Phillies 1968-72, Brewers 1973-83). Money grew up in Anacostia and LaPlata. He was a great fielder who had the misfortune of playing in the shadow of arguably the greatest in Brooks Robinson. In fact, one of Money's nicknames was "Brooks." In 1972, he set a major league record with 257 straight errorless chances at third with a fielding percentage of .989 and only five errors all season. But at the end of the year Money was part of a seven-player deal with Milwaukee to make way in Philadelphia for another pretty good third baseman named Mike Schmidt. Money was a solid hitter with a .261 lifetime average and 176 homers.

1. Maury Wills SS (Dodgers 1959-66, Pirates 1967-68, Expos 1969, Dodgers 1970-72). Was a great high school quarterback and baseball player at Cardozo. Wills signed with the Dodgers out of high school, but didn't make it to the major leagues until the age of 26. When he did, he changed the game with his speed. In 1962, Wills became the first player in history to steal 100 bases in a season when swiped 104. He also hit .299 and was named Most Valuable Player. Wills played 14 years in the majors and was on World Series winners in 1959, '63 and '65. A number of baseball experts have wondered why he's not in the Hall of Fame.

Why We Hate FedEx Field

The Redskins' new stadium opened for business on September 14, 1997, with a 19-13 overtime victory over the Arizona Cardinals. The venue was privately financed by then owner Jack Kent Cooke and completed in only 17 months on a 200-acre site in Prince George's County. With 91,704 seats, it's the largest venue in the NFL by more than 11,000 seats, and also includes 243 luxury suites. Still, the place has never been a fan favorite, for many of the following reasons.

10. The press box started out at midfield, but owner Daniel Snyder decided to expand his owner's box and construct more lucrative luxury suites in that area, and shifted the box to the end zone.

9. There's far too much tailgate drinking in the parking lots before and after games, and it's not uncommon to see drunk fans staggering around the premises trying to find their cars.

8. Tom Cruise and his wife, Katie Holmes, are occasional guests in the owner's box.

7. Unlike cozy RFK Stadium, where the decibel level was earsplitting because noise reverberated around a more intimate, enclosed building, FedEx is far more wide open, and a lot more hush-hush because sound seems to travel up, up and away.

6. The cheerleading public address announcer is virtually incomprehensible, and the pre-game music piped in on the sound system bombards the senses to the extreme.

5. Snyder has never had the good sense to invite former team president John Kent Cooke to the owner's box, even if Cooke's father, the late Jack Kent Cooke, built the stadium.

4. The Washington Redskins' home field is not in Washington, D.C., it's in Maryland.

3. The prices are outrageous. Forget about tickets now averaging over $100 a seat. How about $30 parking, $10 beers, $7 sodas and $5 hot dogs?

2. The traffic is maddening. Getting there from downtown Washington, normally a 30-minute drive, you better leave home at 9 a.m. for a 1 p.m. start. And leaving the place after a game can take as long as two hours to crawl two miles back to the beltway, with not much help from local police and some of the rudest parking lot attendants on the face of the earth.

1. It's now called FedEx Field, after a Forbes 500 company based in Tennessee that paid millions for the naming rights. It started off simply and properly as Jack Kent Cooke Stadium and also was known in the early days as The Big Jack. Sadly, not any more.

Why We Love FedEx Field

1. Can't think of a single reason.

In the free-agent era, the number of great players who stay with one team their entire career continues to dwindle. Even superstars often go somewhere else to squeeze in a couple more years (see Michael Jordan). Here are nine (we couldn't even get 10) who started and finished here.

9. Olaf Kolzig (1989–?). We assume he'll finish in Washington. Olie the Goalie has been a mainstay on a team that's often changed players, coaches, arenas, even uniforms. Kolzig made his Caps debut at the age of 19, but didn't become the number one goalie until seven years later when, not coincidently, the Caps made it to their only Stanley Cup final. Kolzig won the Vezina Trophy in 2000.

8. Joe Jacoby (1981–93). One of the great stories in Redskins history. Jacoby went undrafted out of Louisville despite size that was considered massive at the time (6-foot-7, 300 lbs). He flew so far under the radar that coach Joe Gibbs assumed he was a defensive lineman and then wanted to cut him because he thought he had too many offensive linemen in training camp. "Jake" soon changed Gibbs's mind, and he went on to play in four Pro Bowls while playing left tackle, right tackle, and guard during his 13 years as a member of the Hogs.

7. Russ Grimm (1981–91). Spent most of his years next to Jacoby on the left side clearing the way for the likes of John Riggins and Earnest Byner. Was one of the best linemen of his day, making four Pro Bowls. Grimm went directly from playing to coaching, remaining on the Skins' staff through 2000.

6. John Thompson (1972–99). Yes he played in Boston, but he is Washington through and through. He was a star high school player at Archbishop Carroll and after two years with the Celtics, had great success as a coach at St. Anthony's. Thompson took over a struggling then-mid-major program at Georgetown and built it into a national powerhouse. Thompson won 596 games while going to 20 NCCA tournaments, winning the National Title in 1984. He's in the Basketball Hall of Fame as a coach.

5. Charley Taylor (1964–77). Retired as the NFL's all-time leading receiver with 649 catches. Elected to the Hall of Fame in 1984. Was drafted as a running back coming out of Arizona State, which is why he was so effective gaining yards after a catch.

4. Darrell Green (1983–2002). Played an amazing 20 years at cornerback and in fact set an NFL record for most years with one team in one city (Jackie Slater played in 20 different seasons with the Rams, but the last one was in St. Louis). Made an instant name for himself by running down Hall of Famer Tony Dorsett from behind in his first NFL game. Early in his career, Green won the NFL's fastest man competition and hadn't seemed to slow down much when he finally retired at the age of 42.

3. Wes Unseld (1968–81). True he started his career in Baltimore, but stayed with the Bullets franchise for more than 35 years as player, broadcaster, coach, and general manager. Unseld pulled off a rare double in 1969, winning both Rookie of the Year and MVP. He was named one of the NBA's 50 greatest players in 1997.

2. Sammy Baugh (1937–51). Baugh was the greatest pro football player of his generation and helped transform the NFL into a passing league. As quarterback, he led the Redskins to two championships and was in the first Hall of Fame class in 1963.

1. Walter Johnson (1907–27). You could make the case that the "Big Train" is the greatest pitcher of all time. Playing for mostly second-rate teams, Johnson won 417 games, an unbelievable 110 by shutout. The only World Series championship ever won by a Washington team was closed out by Johnson in relief. He was part of baseball's first Hall of Fame class.

Our Philadelphia-based editor wondered whether we could come up with a hundred great athletes from the metropolitan area. That was far from the problem. We left out some awfully good ones, including arguably the greatest basketball player ever in Michael Jordan. Yes he was "Floor Jordan" instead of "Air Jordan" by the time he played for the Wizards, but he did play two full seasons in Washington. Jordan just never felt like he was one of ours and proved it by peeling out of town in a Mercedes with Illinois plates.

And selection criteria was based more on feel than anything. We're two middle-aged guys who have spent most of our lives watching and covering D.C.-area sports. We never saw Walter Johnson or Sammy Baugh play, but we know guys who did (including the legendary Shirley Povich, who covered both) and convinced us they're number one and two. Some on this list only played high school ball here like Elgin Baylor, Adrian Dantley, Maury Wills and Willie Wood, but they feel like ours.

You'll also notice multiple names for some of the entries, which actually makes this list longer than 100 names. In some cases, like Tom McMillen and Len Elmore, it's hard to remember one without the other. And although Napolean McCallum and Joe Bellino played in different eras at Navy, their careers were similar. It would have been a shame to leave one out.

Several careers are still being written and it may seem laughable to see Gilbert Arenas at 48 or Alexander Ovechkin at 71 in a few years. You can decide where they go. And if you think Henie Manush at 31 is a joke, look up his stats.

Of all the lists in this book, the top 100 may be the most fun to debate. Have at it.

100. Dave Butz. He cost George Allen two first-round and one second-round picks when he was obtained from St. Louis in 1975 as one of the first 300-pound defensive tackles, a trade that paid off many years later when he became one of the league's best run-stoppers under Jack Pardee and Joe Gibbs. He played on two Super Bowl championship teams before retiring in 1988.

99. Ken Harvey. He came to the Redskins in 1994 after six seasons with the Cardinals and played four more productive seasons at outside linebacker, making four Pro Bowl teams over his career.

98. Cornelius Greene. He played quarterback at Dunbar High School, and the man known as "Flamboyant" and later simply "Flam" became the first African-American to start at quarterback for Ohio State.

97. Sleepy Floyd. A brilliant shooter and playmaker at Georgetown, he was the 13th overall player taken in the 1982 NBA draft and played 13 seasons in the NBA. He still holds the league record for most points scored in a quarter (29) and a half (39) in a playoff game, accomplishing those feats for the Houston Rockets in Game 4 of the 1987 Western Conference semifinals against the Los Angeles Lakers.

96. Alan Webb. A world-class distance runner and graduate of South Lakes High in Reston, Webb ran a sub-four-minute mile when he posted a 3:59.86 at a meet in New York.

95. Donald Dell. A Bethesda native and Yale graduate, he was a two-time Davis Cup player and two-time Davis Cup captain who earned a law degree at the University of Virginia and became one of the nation's leading sports agents in the 1970s. He founded Washington's annual summer professional tennis event at Rock Creek Park.

94. Jeff Bostic. One of the original Redskins Hogs, the Clemson graduate was the cerebral and somewhat undersized (255 pounds) starting center on three Washington Super Bowl championship teams.

93. Mike Gartner. The fourth overall choice in the 1979 NHL entry draft, Gartner played ten productive seasons for the Washington Capitals and 19 years in the NHL for five different franchises. He holds the NHL record with 15 consecutive seasons with 30 or more goals.

92. Bobby Dandridge. A sharp-shooting small forward, he became the missing link for the Washington Bullets when he was traded to the club in 1977, the final piece in the franchise's only NBA championship in 1978.

91. Karen and David O'Connor. This husband and wife team from The Plains, Virginia are among the finest three-day event equestrians in the world. David won an individual gold medal in the 2000 Olympics, and both were on the bronze-medal winning American three-day team.

90. Dikembe Mutombo. A native of Zaire, he still holds the Georgetown record for 12 blocked shots in a single game. A man who speaks English, French, Spanish, Portugese and five African languages, he's also a four-time NBA defensive player of the year and eight-time All-Star.

89. Brian Mitchell. When he retired in 2003, the former college quarterback at Southwestern Louisiana had posted more all-purpose yards than any player in NFL history, many of them gained with the Washington Redskins after joining the team in 1990 as a fifth-round draft choice.

88. Charles Mann and Dexter Manley. The Redskins' bookend defensive ends for Joe Gibbs in the 1980s, their pass-rush prowess put much heat on opposing quarterbacks and helped anchor one of the league's most formidable defenses in the 1980s.

87. Allen Johnson. A District native, he won the 110-meter high hurdles at the 1996 Atlanta Olympics and is a four-time champion in the same event at the track and field world championships.

86. Brig Owens. He wanted to play quarterback, his position at the University of Cincinnati, in the pros at a time when there were no black quarterbacks in the NFL. He switched to safety and became a longtime starter and widely respected team leader for George Allen's Redskins teams. Started law school while still an active player and practices in Washington, including player representation.

85. James Brown. Long before he ever set foot in a broadcast booth, J.B. was a big-time high school basketball star at DeMatha, followed by a brilliant all-Ivy playing career at Harvard, followed by superstardom as one of the most versatile sportscasters in the business at CBS and Fox.

84. Sidney Lowe and Derek Wittenberg. All-Metropolitan stars at De Matha High School in the late 1970s, they also stayed together as college teammates at North Carolina State and were key members of the school's 1983 national championship team coached by Jim Valvano.

83. Bernard King. Albert King's older brother, Bernard starred at Tennessee and became one of the NBA's all-time great scorers, playing five seasons with the Bullets from 1987-91 and ending his career in 1993 after a brief, injury-plagued comeback with the N.J. Nets.

82. Buck Williams and Albert King. They were basketball teammates at the University of Maryland and both were selected in the first round of the 1981 draft, Williams as the third overall pick and King as the tenth overall choice. Williams played 17 years and became one of the league's most prolific rebounders. King played for nine seasons and ended his career as a member of the 1989 Washington Bullets.

81. Tara Heiss. Considered by many as the greatest point guard in U.S. women's basketball history, she starred at the University of Maryland in the late 1970s and started for the 1980 U.S. women's Olympic team. She was voted one of the top 50 all-time athletes in ACC history.

80. Melissa Belote and Tom Dolan. Belote, from Springfield, Virginia, won three gold medals in the 1972 Munich Olympics and remains one of the greatest backstroke swimmers in Olympic history. Dolan, from Arlington, Virginia, won gold medals in individual medley events at the 1996 and 2000 Olympics.

79. Joe Bellino and Napolean McCallum. The two greatest running backs in Navy football history. Bellino won the Heisman Trophy in 1960, and McCallum was a two-time consensus All-American in 1985 and '86 and still holds Navy's all-time career rushing yardage record, with 4,179.

78. Austin Carr. A Washington native and graduate of old Mackin High School, Carr went on to become the leading scorer in Notre Dame basketball history and was named College Player of the Year in 1971. He played for ten years in the NBA after being the first-round draft choice of the Cleveland Cavaliers in 1971.

77. Billy Kilmer and Diron Talbert. The quarterback and defensive tackle came to Washington via trade in 1971 and became major difference makers on their respective sides of the ball as well as two of the dominant team leaders of the George Allen era.

76. Eddie LeBaron. The "Little General" played quarterback for the Redskins from 1952 to 1958 and was a brilliant ball handler and deft passer, despite his size. At 5 feet 7, he remains the shortest quarterback ever to start a Pro Bowl.

75. Monte Coleman. A former 11th-round draft pick, he played linebacker for the Redskins for a record 16 seasons, and was a key member of three Super Bowl championship teams under Joe Gibbs.

74. Jonathan Ogden. A native of the District and the son of a former Howard football player, he graduated from St. Albans High School and was drafted out of UCLA in the first round of the 1996 draft, the fourth overall selection. He's been to 11 Pro Bowls as the starting tackle for the Baltimore Ravens and is considered a virtual lock to make the Hall of Fame.

73. Jake Scott. As a youngster he lived in Arlington and attended Bullis Prep, developing into a five-time Pro Bowl safety for the Miami Dolphins and the MVP of the 1972 Super Bowl. He finished out his career with the Redskins in 1978-79.

72. Bucky Harris. A skilled shortstop with a .276 career batting average, the so-called "Boy Wonder" was the player-manager of the 1924 Washington Senators team that won the World Series, then took the American League pennant the following year. He was elected to the Hall of Fame in 1975.

71. Alexander Ovechkin. When he's done, the Russian hockey star almost certainly will hold every Washington Capitals scoring record. A former No. 1 pick in the NHL entry draft, he made his Washington debut on October 5, 2005, scored two goals in his first game and was named NHL Rookie of the Year.

70. Sam Huff. After making his name as a fearsome middle linebacker with the great N.Y. Giants teams of the 1950s and early 60s, Huff came to the Redskins in a controversial 1964 trade and played here until 1969, when he ended his Hall of Fame career as a player-coach under Vince Lombardi.

69. Boomer Esiason. A Long Island native, he came to the University of Maryland in 1980 and became one of the most successful quarterbacks in Terrapins history, setting 17 school records. A second-round choice of the Cincinnati Bengals (38th pick overall), he played in four Pro Bowls and was the league's MVP in 1982.

68. Davey Hearn and Jon Lugbill. Hearn, from Bethesda, and Lugbill, from the District, were both Olympians and multiple world champions in whitewater canoe and kayaking, dominating their sport in the 1980s and early 1990s.

67. Phil Chenier. The longtime Washington Wizards TV analyst was a silky smooth guard with a deft shooting touch. A three-time NBA All Star, he was a major force on the Washington Bullets 1978 world championship team, playing for the franchise from 1971-79.

66. Mark Moseley. The only NFL kicker ever to be named league MVP in a strike-shortened 1982 season, he was the last of the great straight-on kickers and still holds the Redskins all-time scoring record with 1,207 points.

65. Sean Taylor. A former first-round draft choice, the Redskins' fierce hitting safety was making a huge name for himself around the NFL until he was shot and killed midway through the 2007 season in a bungled burglary attempt at his home in the Miami suburbs.

64. Joe Fargis. A native of Vienna, Virginia, he won individual and team gold medals in equestrian show-jumping competition at the 1984 Olympics in Los Angeles and is still a highly ranked national rider.

63. Jeff Ruland and Rick Mahorn. The bruising twin towers for the Washington Bullets in the early 1980s, they were known as McFilthy and McNasty around the league for their physical style of play.

62. Danny Ferry. A high school All-American at DeMatha, a college All-American at Duke, a serviceable pro forward with a sweet outside touch, he's also been a perceptive general manager for the Cleveland Cavaliers.

61. Gary Clark. A mercurial and highly productive Redskins wide receiver in the Joe Gibbs era, he always wanted the ball, and almost always caught it, often going deep. He finished with 699 career receptions and 65 touchdown catches and was a four-time Pro Bowler.

60. Jerry Smith. The "Peach from Long Beach" played tight end for the Redskins as if he were a wide receiver and became one of Sonny Jurgensen's and Billy Kilmer's all-time favorite targets.

59. LaMont Jordan. A graduate of Suitland High, he remains the leading rusher in University of Maryland history and has been a productive though injury-plagued running back with the N.Y. Jets and Oakland Raiders.

58. Willie Wood. A fixture at free safety in the Green Bay Packers secondary during the Vince Lombardi glory years, Woods was a native Washingtonian and attended Wilson High. He was named to eight Pro Bowl teams and inducted into the Pro Football Hall of Fame in 1989.

57. Frank Howard. "Hondo" blasted baseballs to the far reaches of ball parks all around the major leagues and was among the most popular players in the history of the Washington Senators.

56. Maury Wills. Born in Washington in 1932, he was a skilled shortstop for the Los Angeles Dodgers and one of the most feared base stealers in Major League history, leading the majors in stolen bases for six straight years and earning National League MVP honors in 1962.

55. Mike Curtis. A graduate of Richard Montgomery High in Rockville, Mad Dog became a maniacal Pro Bowl linebacker for the old Baltimore Colts, and finished his 13-year NFL career with the Redskins in 1978.

54. Early Wynn. Signed at 17 by the Washington Senators, he pitched 23 years in the Major League, winning 300 games and posting five 20-win seasons. He was inducted into the Baseball Hall of Fame in 1972.

53. Olaf Kolzig. A constant and consistently grand presence in goal for the Washington Capitals, Olie the Goalie was drafted by the franchise in 1989 and has been with the organization ever since, becoming one of the most popular players in club history.

52. Kermit Washington. The greatest basketball player in American University history, a solid 10-year NBA player who landed one punch that changed his life forever, not to mention the man he hit, Rudy Tomjanovich, in a 1977 NBA game.

51. Craig Shelton and John Duren. Big Sky and Bay Bay, both All-Mets at Dunbar High School in the District, were the first two really big-time recruits for John Thompson's Georgetown basketball program when they arrived in 1976.

50. John Thompson, Tom Hoover, George Leftwich, Monk Molloy and John "Sleepy" Austin. The starting five for most of Archbishop Carroll's run of 59 straight wins between 1958 and 1960. Thompson went on to become a coaching legend at Georgetown, and Molloy played at and became president of Notre Dame.

49. Harold Solomon. Unless you want to count Pete Sampras, who was born in D.C. but moved to California when he was seven, Solomon is the area's best-ever tennis player. He won 22 singles titles over his career and made the French Open final in 1976 and the U.S. Open semifinals in '76 and '77.

48. Gilbert Arenas. His legacy is still being written, but since his arrival in D.C. as a free agent in 2003, the Wizards have been a consistent playoff team. Prior to his arrival, they had made the playoffs only once in 16 years. He combines great scoring ability with a true joy of playing the game. He's also very generous, throwing his jersey into the crowd after every game, and is one of the most popular athletes in the history of D.C. sports.

47. Dominique Dawes. Raised in Silver Spring, she became a three-time Olympic gymnast, winning a gold medal as part of the '96 team in Atlanta. It was the first time a black woman of any nationality had won a gold medal in gymnastics.

46. Renaldo "Skeets" Nehemiah. Almost certainly would have won a gold medal in the high hurdles had the United States not boycotted the 1980 Olympics. "Skeets" won three NCAA titles at the University of Maryland and was the first to ever run the hurdles in less than 13 seconds. Post-Olympics there was no money to be made in track, so he turned to football and caught 43 passes over three seasons with the 49ers, winning a Super Bowl ring in 1984.

45. Gene Shue. An All-American at the University of Maryland in 1953 and '54, he was the third pick of the NBA draft by the Philadelphia Warriors. Shue played 10 years in the league, mostly with the Pistons. He coached for many years in the NBA, taking both the Baltimore Bullets and Philadelphia 76ers to the finals.

44. Adrian Dantley. One of the greatest basketball players in the storied history of DeMatha High School, he rejected an all-out recruiting blitz by Lefty Driesell at Maryland and signed with Notre Dame. After an All-American junior year and an Olympic gold medal in 1976, he turned pro and became one of the NBA's best scorers. Dantley never won a ring, but averaged 24.3 points a game over a 15-year career and averaged over 30 a game for Utah between 1980 and '84.

43. Bobby Foster. He was from New Mexico, but made Washington his home while becoming one of the best light-heavyweights of all time. He successfully defended his title 14 times between 1969 and '73. His career record was 56-8-1.

42. Riddick Bowe. Won a silver medal at the 1988 Olympics, losing to Lennox Lewis in the heavyweight championship match. Bowe hooked up with Rock Newman after turning pro and became one of the dominant heavyweights of the first half of the 1990s. He won a unanimous 11-round decision over Evander Holyfield for the title in 1992. Holyfield won the rematch in a fight most famous for the nut who parachuted into the ring during the fight.

41. Goose Goslin. Started and finished his 18-year career with the Senators between 1921 and '38. A Washington baseball team has never played a postseason game without Goslin in the outfield. His .344 average led the Senators to their only World Series championship in 1924. After being traded in 1930, he returned in 1933, hitting .297 for the Senators' last pennant-winning team. Goslin was elected to the Hall of Fame in 1968.

40. Alonzo Mourning. Was one of the greatest big men in a long line of great big men at Georgetown. "Zo" was an All-American as a senior in 1992 and was the second pick of the NBA draft by Charlotte behind Shaquille O'Neal. In 2006 they teamed up in Miami to win an NBA championship.

39. Juan Dixon. Weighing just 164 pounds, some thought Maryland coach Gary Williams was crazy to give this guy a scholarship. But Dixon already knew plenty about beating the odds. Both of his parents had died of AIDS from intravenous drug use. Dixon's drive helped make him one of the greatest players in Maryland history. He became the first NCAA player to get 2000 points, 300 steals and 200 3-pointers during his career which ended with the school's first NCAA basketball championship in 2002. He was the 17th pick of the NBA draft by the Wizards.

38. Mark Rypien and Doug Williams. Two of the three quarterbacks who won Super Bowls for the Redskins. Both speak to the brilliance of coach Joe Gibbs. Rypien was a sixth-round draft pick who developed into a smart trigger man for an awesome offense. He was the MVP of Super Bowl XXVI. Williams' career was rescued by Gibbs after the fall of the USFL in 1985. He became the first black quarterback to start a Super Bowl and the first to win one, throwing a record four touchdown passes in the second quarter of Super Bowl XXII on his way to being named MVP.

37. Fred Funk. A story of perseverance and belief in one's self. Funk was not a country club kid while growing up in Takoma Park. He played on the University of Maryland golf team, graduating in 1980. He turned pro a year later, but didn't become a member of the PGA tour until 1989. In between he helped pay the bills by coaching the Maryland golf team. With eight PGA tour victories, he remains competitive in his 50s.

36. Lee Elder. Made his mark in golf history by becoming the first African American to compete in the Masters in 1975. Elder qualified by winning the Monsanto Open, the first of his three PGA tour victories.

35. Cliff Battles, Wayne Milner and Turk Edwards. These names probably don't mean anything to the *SportsCenter* generation, but all three are in the Pro Football Hall of Fame. Battles and Edwards were original members of the organization when it started in Boston as the Braves in 1932. Milner was taken in the eighth round of the NFL's first draft in 1936. All three came here in 1937 and helped the Redskins win the NFL championship that year.

34. Tom McMillen and Len Elmore. The two players most responsible for putting college basketball on the map in the area. McMillen was the first high school player to appear on the cover of *Sports Illustrated* in 1970. He originally signed with North Carolina, but Lefty Driesell managed to talk his mother out of sending her boy to Chapel Hill. Elmore was a star at famed Power Memorial in New York. Together they achieved great success on and off the court at Maryland. McMillen was a Rhodes Scholar before a lengthy NBA career and a congressman after it. Elmore graduated from Harvard Law School after a decade in the NBA.

33. Dave Bing. A high school All-American at Spingarn in 1962, he became an All-American at Syracuse and a seven-time NBA All Star with the Pistons and Bullets. Bing was named one of the NBA's 50 Greatest Players in 1997 and has become a business leader in Detroit.

32. Johan Cryuff. If you were one of the few in the stands at RFK Stadium for Washington Diplomats (the Dips) games in 1980 and '81, you saw one of the greatest soccer players in history. Unfortunately there weren't enough of you; the Dips didn't last. But in 1999, Cryuff was named European Player of the Century and the second best player in the world behind a fellow by the name of Pele.

31. Henie Manush. Yes of course it's hard not to giggle when you say his name, but Henie was a great hitter for the Senators between 1930 and '35. He batted .336 for their pennant-winner in 1933 and had an even better year in 1934. While batting .349, Manush put together a 33-game hitting streak and racked up 221 hits for the season, 17 of them triples. He was elected to the Hall of Fame in 1964.

30. Len Hauss. Hopefully will get consideration for the Hall of Fame from the veterans committee one day. Hauss made six straight Pro Bowls at center between 1967 and '72. Never missed a game during his 14-year career, meaning Sonny Jurgensen never pressed his hands against another pair of, ummm, cheeks.

29. Pat Fischer. Inch for inch, may have been the toughest Redskin ever. At 5-foot-9, 170 pounds, Fischer played 17 years in the NFL. A 17th-round draft pick by St. Louis out of Nebraska, the Cardinals figured Fischer was used up when they let him sign with Washington in 1968. He went on to play 10 more years and was one of the key performers on the great George Allen defenses of the 70s. Is best remembered for giving up nearly a foot to Eagles' wide receiver Harold Carmichael and controlling him by taking him out at the knees.

28. Chris Hanburger. Nine Pro Bowls and this man can't get a sniff of the Hall of Fame. Go figure. An 18th-round draft pick out of North Carolina in 1965, Hanburger spent 14 years at linebacker, despite weighing only about 215. He had a nose for the football, once taking the ball out of Ron Johnson's hands at Yankee Stadium and taking it the other way for a score in a key win over the Giants in 1972.

27. Joe Smith. Was as faceless as his name would suggest when he arrived at Maryland in 1993. He became a third-team All-American as a freshman and followed it up by becoming the consensus National Collegiate Player of the Year as a sophomore. Maryland made the Sweet 16 both years. They might have won a national title had he stayed another year, but who could blame Smith for leaving when he became the number-one pick of the NBA draft in 1995.

26. John Lucas. An All-American in both basketball and tennis. Lucas was part of the first freshman-eligible class at Maryland in 1972 and started at point guard for four years, earning All-American honors the last three. After averaging 18.3 points a game over his career, Lucas was the number-one pick of the 1976 NBA draft by Houston. Drug problems as a pro kept him from reaching his potential, but Lucas still managed to get in 14 years with a number of teams including the Bullets.

25. Alan Iverson. Like Smith, he played only two years of college basketball in the area, but left his mark as one of the all-time greats at Georgetown. He was so good that even his coach, who liked to control everything, let him go. "AI" was a consensus All-American in 1996 while averaging 25 points a game. After leading the Hoyas to the Elite Eight, he turned pro and became the number-one pick of the NBA draft by Philadelphia in 1996.

24. Russ Grimm and Joe Jacoby. The left side of the Redskins' offensive line during the glory years. Each gets Hall of Fame consideration every year, but unjustly remain out. Each was a four-time Pro Bowler, three-time Super Bowl winner and the best players on one of the most famous offensive lines in history, the "Hogs." Each has achieved great post-playing success, too—Grimm as a coach and Jacoby as a car dealer.

23. Mia Hamm. Certainly the most famous, if not the best, women's soccer player of all time. After a great career at Lake Braddock High School, she went on to lead North Carolina to four NCAA championships and was Player of the Year three times. She later captained the U.S. women's national team and played with the Washington Freedom from 2001 to 2003.

22. Grant Hill. The son of a great athlete, Calvin Hill, Grant went to Duke after a great basketball career at South Lakes High School in Reston. Was part of great teams with Christian Laettner and Bobby Hurley that won back-to-back NCAA championships in 1991 and '92. As a testament to his own greatness, Hill put the '94 team on his back and took it to the NCAA title game before losing to Arkansas. Injuries have hindered his NBA career, but when healthy has been one of the best players in the game.

21. Rod Langway. Barring injury, Alexander Ovechkin will likely become the best Capital of all time, but he may never have the impact that Langway had. The Caps had never made the playoffs prior to Langway's arrival from Montreal in 1982 and they never missed them in the 11 years he played in Washington. The helmet-less tough guy anchored the Caps defense, winning the Norris Trophy his first two years in D.C. His number 5 has been retired by the organization and he was elected to the Hockey Hall of Fame in 2002.

20. Joe Theismann. While other Redskin quarterbacks may have given as much behind center, no one gave more in front of the microphone. His eagerness to yak when the red light went on, almost led first-year coach Joe Gibbs to trade Joey T when the Skins started off 0-5 in 1981. Good thing he didn't. Theismann led the Redskins to their first Super Bowl title after the '82 season and was Associated Press NFC MVP in 1983.

19. David Robinson. Just a great story. Was finally talked into playing basketball for the first time as a senior at Osbourn Park High School in Manassas, not because he was necessarily good, but because he was tall (6-foot-7). Robinson played well enough to draw interest from the Naval Academy, where his interest was math, not hoops. At the Naval Academy he grew six inches and the rest is history. Navy made the Elite Eight in Robinson's junior year and, even though he owed two years of service, the San Antonio Spurs were more than willing to wait. They took him with the number-one pick of the 1987 draft and he helped them win two NBA championships.

18. Len Bias. By far the worst sports tragedy in the history of the area. One of the greatest basketball players in ACC history during his four years at Maryland, Bias was an All-American as a junior and senior. At 6-foot-8, he was an unbelievable combination of size, strength and quickness, leading Digger Phelps to hauntingly describe him as, "Jordan with size." Bias was made the number-two pick of the 1986 draft by the Boston Celtics and died two days later of a cocaine overdose.

17. Roger Staubach. Seeing this name at this spot on this list may turn the stomach of Redskin fans, but he was something else during his quarterbacking years at Navy. It's one thing for Army to have great teams during World War II, it's another for Navy to make a run at the National Title in 1963. But Staubach was that good as a junior when he won the Heisman Trophy and took Navy to the Cotton Bowl against Texas. The Longhorns won the game, but Staubach cemented his place in college football history.

16. Larry Brown. He left it all on the field every Sunday. Drafted in the eighth round out of Kansas State in 1969, coach Vince Lombardi liked how he ran, but noticed he was a bit slow off the snap count. A hearing aid in his helmet solved the problem and Brown went on to become the Redskins second-leading rusher of all time. Playing mostly in George Allen's predictable offense, Brown sacrificed his body to lead the league in rushing in 1972 and was named the NFC's MVP. If you watched him play, it's hard to imagine respecting anyone's effort any more.

15. Patrick Ewing. One of the greatest college basketball players in history. Period. Ewing took Georgetown to the national championship game three times, winning a title as a junior in 1984. He was the 1985 Player of the Year, when he was named a consensus All-American for the third straight year. Ewing was considered such a franchise-changer when he finished college, that there are those who believe to this day that the '85 draft lottery was rigged to give the Knicks the number-one pick.

14. Elvin Hayes. "EEEEE." Not the best loved by his teammates off the floor, but a tireless worker on it. Rarely missed a game during his 15-year career while averaging 21 points and 12.5 rebounds a game. Hayes was the first pick of the 1968 NBA draft ahead of Wes Unseld. Four years later they teamed up in Baltimore and came to Washington with the team a year after that. "E" and Wes were the centerpieces of three Bullets teams that made the finals, including the one that won it in 1978.

13. Bobby Mitchell. Wasn't just a Washington sports pioneer, Mitchell is one of the greatest players in Redskins history. Owner George Preston Marshall finally caved in to Congressional pressure (they weren't going to let the Redskins play at D.C. Stadium, located on federal land) and made Mitchell the team's first black player in 1962. Coach Otto Graham switched Mitchell from halfback to flanker and he became a favorite target of Sonny Jurgensen. He was inducted in the Pro Football Hall of Fame in 1983.

12. Art Monk. Broke records for most career catches and most consecutive games with at least one catch, but had to wait seven years to be selected for the Hall of Fame in 2008. Part of the problem was Monk's quiet personality; he didn't like to sell himself. But teammates say he was one of the most important players on the Redskins' three Super Bowl championship teams. The "Fun Bunch" (a group high-five in the end zone) was invented as a tribute to Monk, who was hurt late in the 1982 season and couldn't play in the first Super Bowl championship.

11. Charley Taylor. Retired as the NFL's all-time leading receiver after the 1977 season. His number 42 tips you off that he came to the Skins as a running back out of Arizona State in 1964, but turned out to be better suited as a receiver. Taylor led the NFL twice in receptions. He caught 72 passes in 1966, 12 for touchdowns, which ties a team record. Taylor was inducted into the Hall of Fame in 1984.

10. Randy White. If he played an offensive position as well as he played defensive end for Maryland in the early 70s, you'd hear Randy White's name mentioned along with names like Herschel Walker and Roger Staubach. Opponents always ran to the opposite side of the field he was on, and he still made the tackle. White was the number-one pick of the NFL draft by Dallas in 1975 and is a member of both the College Football and Pro Football Halls of Fame.

9. Sonny Jurgensen. His television and radio work puts him higher on the list of D.C. sports icons, but since he wore number 9 this is a good spot for his quarterbacking. "Jurgy" was one of the best pure passers in NFL history, and with the running game he had for most of his days with the Skins, he pretty much had to purely pass. He never appeared in a playoff win for Washington, but provided many thrills over the years, spraying beautiful spirals all over RFK Stadium. In a 14-game season in 1967, Jurgensen threw 32 touchdown passes and had the NFL's first-, second- and fourth-leading receivers in Charley Taylor, Jerry Smith and Bobby Mitchell.

8. Ken Houston. Possibly the best safety in NFL history. The signature play of his career was tackling Walt Garrison at the one-yard line to preserve a 14-7 Monday Night Football win over Dallas at RFK in 1973. However, Houston was also great in the open field, intercepting 49 passes and recovering 21 fumbles. In 1971 with the Oilers, he returned four interceptions for touchdowns and scored another TD on a fumble return. Some fans are still pissed that coach Jack Pardee wouldn't put Houston in the game for his last RFK appearance in 1980. He was inducted into the Hall of Fame in 1986.

7. Elgin Baylor. Called by Hall of Fame coach John Thompson, "The best high school basketball player in D.C. history." After starring at Spingarn in the mid 1950s, Baylor went on to play at the College of Idaho and the University of Seattle. Drafted by the Minneapolis Lakers in 1958, Baylor became an instant star, changing the way the game was played. A pre-Julius Erving high flyer, Baylor averaged more than 30 points a game between 1960 and '63. He was an 11-time NBA All Star and may be the best basketball player never to win a championship.

6. John Riggins. One of the true characters in the history of the NFL. "Riggo" came to Washington in 1976 during a trial year of free agency, which lasted only a year. He already had a "flake" reputation from the Jets for shaving a Mohawk into his head. After back-to-back thousand-yard seasons in 1978 and '79, Riggins retired in a contract dispute. But after a year out, he was talked into returning by new coach Joe Gibbs. The famed "I'm bored, I'm broke and I'm back" news conference is part of Redskins lore. His shedding of cornerback Don McNeal on his way to the winning touchdown in Super Bowl XVII has been named the greatest play in Redskins history. Riggins was inducted into the Hall of Fame in 1992 and asked NFL Commissioner Paul Tagliabue, who he barely knew, to be his presenter.

5. Sugar Ray Leonard. The Palmer Park native burst onto the national scene by winning the light welterweight gold medal at the 1976 Olympics. He announced soon afterward that he wouldn't be turning pro and would attend the University of Maryland to become an example. But his Olympic gold didn't turn into endorsement gold and he soon found himself fighting for dough. Sugar Ray then spent the next two decades retiring and un-retiring while winning numerous titles at various weight classes. His fights with Roberto Duran, Thomas Hearns and Marvin Hagler are among the most legendary in boxing history.

4. Wes Unseld. We're talking about the athlete only. Wes won't make any halls of fame for his coaching or work as a general manager, but he's the best player in the history of the Bullets/Wizards franchise. One of only two players, along with Willis Reed, to be named both Rookie of the Year and MVP in the same season. An incredible rebounder at only 6-foot-7, Unseld averaged 14 boards a game during his 13-year career. He was the heart and soul of four teams that made the NBA finals and locked up the 1978 championship at the free throw line, even though he was only a 63-percent free-throw shooter for his career. Unseld was named to the Basketball Hall of Fame in 1987 and was picked as one of the league's 50 Best Players 10 years later.

3. Darrell Green. Every team in the NFL had a chance to draft him, before the Redskins selected Green with the last pick of the first round of the 1983 draft. At a position where most start to fade after five years, he lasted 20 years at cornerback, shattering longevity records for the position and games played with one team. Speed was his game and if he hadn't dropped his amateur status by playing pro football, he could have been in the 1984 Olympics in track. He says that Carl Lewis was the only U.S. sprinter who was faster. Was named on the first ballot to the Pro Football Hall of Fame in 2008.

2. Sammy Baugh. When his 16-year NFL career ended in 1951, he was considered the best player in the history of pro football. As a rookie in 1937, "Slingin Sammy" led the Redskins to the NFL championship and won a second title in 1942. He was unmatched as a passer during his prime, which was only part of what he did for the team. In 1943, he led the league in passing, punting and interceptions. He was named to the NFL's 75th Anniversary Team in 1994 after being inducted as one of the original members of the Pro Football Hall of Fame in 1963.

1. Walter Johnson. Since there are very few still alive who saw the "Big Train" pitch, we'll have to let the numbers do the talking: 417 wins, 110 by shutout, 3,509 strikeouts and only 1,363 walks; a .388 ratio. It's hard to argue that he wasn't the greatest right-handed pitcher of all time, and you wonder how staggering the numbers may have been had he pitched for good teams. In a career that spanned from 1907 to 1927, Johnson appeared in only two World Series and actually helped the Senators win their only championship as a reliever in 1924. Johnson was an original inductee of the Baseball Hall of Fame in Cooperstown in 1936 with only one other pitcher, Christy Mathewson, a lefty. The rest of the class was Ty Cobb, Honus Wagner and Babe Ruth.